A THOUSAND YEARS OF THE
ENGLISH PARISH

THE AUTHOR Anthea Jones read Modern History at Oxford and later obtained a doctorate at the University of Kent. In 1991 she retired from a position as Head of History and Director of Studies at Cheltenham Ladies College to devote more time to writing and research, including five years of journeys throughout England for this book. *Tewkesbury* was published in 1987 and *The Cotswolds* in 1994.

A Thousand Years of the

English Parish

Medieval Patterns & Modern Interpretations

Anthea Jones
Photographs by Glyn Jones

CASSELLPAPERBACKS

First published in the United Kingdom in 2000 by
The Windrush Press
High Street, Moreton-in-Marsh
Gloucestershire GL56 0LL
Telephone: 01608 652012
Fax: 01608 652125
Email: windrush@windrushpress.com
www.windrushpress.com

Reprinted 2000, 2001

This paperback edition first published in 2002 by
Cassell Paperbacks, Cassell & Co
Wellington House, 125 Strand
London, WC2R 0BB

Distributed in the United States of America by
Sterling Publishing Co., Inc.
387 Park Avenue South,
New York, NY 10016-8810

A CIP catalogue record for this book is available
from the British Library

ISBN 1-84188-182-1

Designed and Typeset by Miranda Harvey
Printed and bound by Bath Press, Bath

CONTENTS

PART 2: THE PARSON'S PLACE

ILLUSTRATIONS

ACKNOWLEDGEMENTS

It is a pleasure to thank the people who have helped in the course of preparing this book. During visits to many places to understand the story of the parish, helpful information and discussion have often been made available on doorsteps, in parsonage houses, whether past or present, and in churches and churchyards. Many are specially mentioned, but to all a sincere thank you.

For special encouragement and help I would like to thank: Dr R.J.W.Evans, Regius Professor of Modern History, Oxford University, also Mr P.Bell and Mr D.S.Clark, surveyors to Canterbury Diocese, Canon G.Betteridge, Revd P.J.Brownbridge, Mr Geoffrey Hutchinson, Property Secretary to Manchester Diocese, Revd I.L.Johnson, Lady Anne Kerr, Very Revd John H.Lang, former Dean of Lichfield, Prebendary Francis Palmer, Dr Anthony Russell, the Rt Revd the Bishop of Dorchester, the late Revd J.Hurst, Canon W.Hurdman, Mr and Mrs G.D. Trower, the Rt Revd Frank Weston, Bishop of Knaresborough, formerly Archdeacon of Oxford, and the Very Revd J.Methuen, Dean of Ripon.

Information was kindly supplied by Mr T.Ashworth of Salford Local History Library, Mr Tony Carr of Shropshire Records and Research Centre, Mr M.E.Corbett of Central Library of Calderdale, Ms Sylvia Kent of Gloucester Diocesan Office, Mrs Sarah Holmes of Carlisle Diocesan Registry, David Owen, Professor C. Harris of Manchester Metropolitan University Library, Ms A.Rowe of Cumbria Record Office, Kendal, Mr Richard Talbot, Mr D.Taylor of Manchester Central Library, John Wallace.

There are at least thirteen thousand potential illustrations; it is inevitable that even those photographs which have been obtained cannot all be used. Gratitude is expressed here to all who generously allowed the photographer and writer to walk round their house and garden, and who shared their knowledge. Alistair Baird and Barrie Roberts, the talented pair at The Darkroom Professional Photographic Services at Cheltenham, have also contributed a great deal, continuing a long-term association which has been much appreciated.

Grateful acknowledgement for permission to use a photograph is made to: Mr & Mrs M.C.Adams, Dr B.Allen, archivist of Jesus College, Oxford, Lord and Lady Archer, Mrs Sue Bagnall, Mr & Mrs A.R.Barraclough, the Brontë Society, Mr & Mrs G.Collins, Mr P.Condon, Mr & Mrs D.Corr, Mr & Mrs I.R.Cunningham, the Dean and Chapter of Salisbury Cathedral, English Heritage, Mrs A.Everitt, Mr & Mrs G.Faux, Major & Mrs R.Ferguson, Mr & Mrs R.Fleming, Mr M.Ford, Mr & Mrs T.Fraser, the Headmaster of The King's School, Canterbury, Mr T.P.Moore-Bridger, Headmaster of King Edward VI School, Stratford upon Avon, Revd.P.Hullah, Headmaster of Chetham's School of Music, Mr P.Keene, the National Trust, Mr & Mrs N.Rainey, Mr & Mrs W.Scoles, Mrs C.Shapiro, Mr & Mrs M.Todhunter, Major and Mrs Charles

Trevelyan. The following incumbents are gratefully acknowledged: Canon B.Abell, Revd G.Austen, Revd J.Boston, Revd J.Bradshaw, Canon J.P.Brown, Canon P.Bryan, Revd G.G.B.Canning, Revd W.Cole, Revd M.Dent, Revd P.Foster, Revd F.R.Higgins, Revd M.A.Houston, Revd R.Johnson, Revd T.Knapp, Revd C.N.R.Mansell, Canon C.Morris, Revd D.Muston, Revd Dr P.Newing, Revd F.Parr, Revd A.Priddis, Revd P.Ratcliff, Revd A.J.Rees, Revd P.Rivett, Revd D.Rowley, Canon E.Ruddock, Revd D.Searle, Revd D.Shaw, Revd M.Shepherd, Revd P.Slater, Revd G.Sterry, Canon D.Stiff, Very Revd David A.C.Stranack, Revd R.Thomson, Canon J.C.Tomlinson, Revd A.J.Watkins.

I wish to thank Victoria Huxley and Miranda Harvey for their enthusiasm, pleasant cooperation and effort in the production of this book.

The whole project has been encouraged and shared in by my husband, Glyn Jones, to whom, with a former alumnus of Jesus College, Oxford, Reginald Jones, I dedicate this book.

Preface

'Parish' is a very familiar notion. It seems firmly rooted in English tradition. We all think we know something about it. A parish is a locality: maybe too local, given the associations of the parish pump. It is a structure: a unit of administration, managed these days by a parish council. Most importantly, it is a religious entity: a community focused, however residually now for many, on a parish church. Yet few people could say much more about it. Few, for example, could explain the difference – though we feel there must be one – between a rector and a vicar. Fewer still, perhaps, realise that the parish has been the bedrock of European society as a whole, with its close parallels over much of the Continent.

In this book Anthea Jones brings alive in a new way the long, complex and above all colourful story of the English parish. She does so, first of all, by literally opening our eyes, with a novel and telling approach of marrying illustrations closely to her text, as the starting-point for successive stages of her exploration. Her technique is to move from individual case to broader configurations, ranging across the centuries and across the country, even if there are naturally a few favourite regions – like the Cotswolds and Cumbria – to which she often returns.

Every parish contains at least one church; and churches as buildings must stand centre-stage in a study like this, their fabric the embodiment of the parish past. But Anthea Jones has not written another architectural survey; nor –though she has valuable things to say about it – is she primarily concerned with organisational matters. This is pre-eminently a book about parish people, especially about the clergy: their background and culture, their style of life, their relation to the flock in their charge. Here we have one of the richest themes in English social history, illuminated – as a splendid chapter here shows – by some of our finest novelists, often drawing on their own experience.

The parish system has proved remarkably enduring. Its foundations indeed, as the title suggests, stretch back roughly ten centuries, to the later Anglo-Saxon period which also witnessed the consolidation of an English state. Parochial boundaries, in particular, were jealously defended over the years. Having long been rooted in the countryside and in patterns of rural experience, the system gained its second wind in a largely urban setting after the industrial revolution – and it is another strength of this book to address the ecclesiastical townscape as well.

Yet there have been times of dramatic flux too: as with the coming of the Normans; or in the age of the Reformation and dissolution of the monasteries; or during the great nineteenth-century reorganisation in its several phases. Never has the future of the parish appeared more uncertain than at the dawn of its second millenium. An unparalleled transformation is being wrought in our own time, with ecclesiastical bureaucracy and redundant churches, team ministries and women priests, rectories sold off and pension funds established, secularisation of the parish's civil functions and lay involvement in many of its formerly clerical ones too.

Thus Anthea Jones's subject is richly topical, as the last chapter confirms, and she has opinions to contribute. Yet hers is first and foremost a sterling work of history. That is why I, as a professional historian, am particularly gratified to be associated with it. Having ventured no further myself in this direction than compiling a short guide to my own local parish church, I can recognise the store of learning here, over a range of highly intricate issues, as well as the artistry whereby it is so lightly worn. As a work both authoritative and accessible I commend it to the wide readership it deserves.

Robert Evans
Oxford, March 2000

INTRODUCTION

For many centuries, the parish provided an unchanging framework to everyday life: people belonged to a parish. Their houses, farms, fields and cottages were located within a parish; they had their exits and their entrances recorded in the church, and the arrival of each season and the passage of each year was marked by the festivals of the church. The boundaries of the parish, which perhaps they walked round each Rogationtide, were also the boundaries of their farming world, with pasture, meadow, arable fields and wood all comprised within them. People went to school in the church, they looked after the roads of the parish, they maintained the church, the central focus of the parish, and they also maintained the parson. For the poor, help was drawn from the parish. Parish ties were tightened from the mid-sixteenth century and loosened three hundred years later by many changes in social conditions. Horizons were extended, and the functions which had been placed on parish organisation were transferred elsewhere; the parish lost its importance in everyone's daily life. The changes have been described as 'secularisation'. An immense effort was made to alter and reform the Church of England, to make it relevant, establish a presence where there was none, save it by making it efficient. There were new parishes, new parsonage houses, new centralised administration.

The word parish implied two things: spiritual care of a group of people, and a territory with definite boundaries. The territorial pattern of English parishes emerged gradually and was substantially in place by the end of the twelfth century. It had roots in agricultural practices probably ancient when Augustine landed on the coast of Kent in 597, and it was shaped by Anglo-Saxon thegns and Norman lords of the manor, and by bishops and archbishops. A parish was the result of tensions between organisation and piety, hierarchy and community. The tensions persist, but a renewal of the idea of the parish is important for the church and for society, with its special contribution to a sense of identity and community.

LEFT: Barnack, Cambridgeshire - St John the Baptist's church tower may be a thousand years old: good building stone was quarried at Barnack by the ninth century, and long and short quoins and vertical strips or pilasters indicate Anglo-Saxon workmanship; pilasters were not just decorative but had a structural function in rubble walls, imitating a timber-frame. The bells have been restored to ring in the Millennium.

Parish vocabulary

The universal language of the Christian church was Latin, a legacy of the Roman empire. The Bible was studied in Latin, statements of faith in the Creeds were formulated in Latin, prayers and services conducted in Latin, saints' lives written in Latin, and bishops' decisions and even property transactions recorded in Latin. Latin made communication with those speaking different languages possible. Churchmen needed to pass on knowledge of the language and naturally were teachers. The words for the basic elements of the church's organisation had been absorbed into Latin from Greek, and then passed into Anglo-Saxon. Bishop derived from the word for an overseer; diocese from an administrative district; cathedral from the bishop's throne, his seat or 'see', placed in a particular church, from which the diocese was named; priest or presbyter from an elder; monastery from solitary, so describing the community of men or women who devoted their lives to the service of God away from the world.

Words changed their precise meaning over the centuries, but gradually a specialised and precise vocabulary was developed by medieval church lawyers as they defined rules or canons governing the parish. The word parish itself derived from the Greek word for the households within an area, *parochia*, and at first described the territory for which a bishop was responsible. Later, as bishops delegated the duty of spiritual care to others, parish came to decribe a smaller area under the control of a rector, the governor or head priest of a parish church. The bundle of rights supporting the rector was called the 'rectory'; it probably included a house and 'glebe', *gleba* meaning soil or earth, fees for services paid by parishioners and 'tithe', Anglo-Saxon for 'tenth'. Tithe was a primitive tax paid to the rector in kind: every tenth sheaf of wheat, for example, a tenth of the hay crop, of wool, and of other produce of the land. If a rector were not willing to serve the parish in person, he could arrange a legal substitute, a vice or *vicarius*, to whom he gave up a part, often rather small, of the rectory revenues. Parishes where this arrangement had been made were termed vicarages and had a vicarage house. They therefore had both rector and vicar, and sometimes there was both a rectory and a vicarage house. The distinction implied a difference in status and usually in income; in general, rectors were wealthier than vicars, having all the tithes of the parish, though there were innumerable variations in the particular arrangements. Income also depended on the wealth and size of the parish. There could be poor rectors and, though less common, wealthy vicars.

The fundamental concern within each parish was the cure of souls, *cura* meaning care, baptism above all in importance. A curate had the cure of souls without being either a rector or a vicar, and was paid a stipend. He might stand in during a vacancy or serve a parish in place of a rector or vicar who had another living elsewhere; much later he might assist a resident rector or vicar in his duties. Sometimes a perpetual curacy was established instead of a vicarage; a perpetual curate might collect some offerings from parishioners and some part of the dues paid for marriages and burials.

Rectors, vicars and perpetual curates, once appointed, could not be removed from their positions; they had a benefice, *beneficium*, property doing good to the holder for his lifetime. 'Living' was the alternative Anglo-Saxon term. Village farmers had livings - lifetime tenancies of fields and farmhouses - but they had to pay a sum of money to the lord of the manor in recognition of their subservient status, or even carry out practical work tasks for him, like reaping his corn or carting his hay; they were not freeholders. The parson was free of these tasks and so church livings were freeholds.

Within a parish there could be one or several subordinate churches termed chapels. Chapel and chaplain had a curious origin, and reveal the influence of the Franks on the western Christian church: the *capella*, or cape, of St Martin of Tours who died in 397, was preserved by early Frankish kings in a special sanctuary. From this the word chapel came to describe an area with an altar within a church, or within a separate building. A curate or chaplain might serve a chapel. The distinction between church and chapel was of some importance particularly in the north of England, where chapels within large parishes were numerous. Centuries later, 'chapel' was appropriated by Dissenting congregations.

A rector was the embodiment or *persona* of the parish church, which was a legal corporation, but 'parson' has become a convenient term for either rector or vicar, and 'parsonage house' for his residence. Minister, Latin for servant, described anyone who served either church or chapel; after the Reformation it avoided the connotations of 'priest', associated with Mass. Incumbent was another general term for one drawing income from a parish, from *incumbere*, to lie or lean upon; he pressed on or encumbered the living, a peculiarly English

North Leigh, Oxfordshire - the former vicarage house appears rightly positioned next to St Mary's church, which has a Saxon tower. The main income of the living was taken in 1279 by Hailes abbey in Gloucestershire, which provided the vicar with an existing rectory house, a little land, and parishioners' offerings. This house was built about 1726. In 1811 the vicar said it was 'too small for occupation' and it was enlarged; in 1981 it was sold because too big.

usage. During the nineteenth century parliament provided mechanisms for assigning 'districts' to churches, and for creating new parishes. The traditional status of rector and vicar was preserved and new district ministers were legally perpetual curates. Incumbent acquired a tone of lesser status. Anthony Trollope, who was a keen observer of clerical nuance, wrote in *Clergymen of the Church of England* in 1866 that incumbent

> carries with itself none of that acknowledged right to respect which is attached to other clerical titles ... Every parish person in the kingdom is no doubt an incumbent, but in ordinary parlance we hardly apply the name to the country rector or to the vicar blessed with a pleasant parsonage. The incumbent, as we generally recognise him, is a clergyman who has obtained a town district.

There were exceptions: the act of parliament in 1850 dividing Manchester created 101 rectories in the old parish. But even in 1943, it was considered appropriate to specify in a Measure relating to new parishes that their ministers should be perpetual curates. In 1968, all perpetual curates were renamed vicars. In the later twentieth century, a new category of unbeneficed 'priest-in-charge' has been introduced. With the frequent combination of two or more livings, the same man can be the successor to a rector in one, to a vicar in another, and be a priest-in-charge of a third. For his parishioners, his proper title can be in doubt. At the same time, some vicars have been restyled 'rector' where they are at the head of a team ministry, and the other team clergy are 'vicars'. The Church of England maintains the distinction, albeit increasingly blurred, between rector and vicar.

COUNTING PARISHES

In 1288 Pope Nicholas IV gave Edward I the right for six years to collect the taxes normally paid to the pope, to encourage him to a crusade against the Turkish infidels. The king immediately instigated a nationwide survey of the incomes of churches, cathedrals and monasteries, which was completed in Canterbury province in 1291 and in York the following year. This document was preserved, to be published by the Record Commission in 1802 under the title *Taxatio Ecclesiastica Angliae et Walliae auctoritate P.Nicholai IV. Circa AD 1291*. It is the first countrywide list of parish churches, and shows that there were at least 8000 in England and Wales. A second, fuller enquiry into ecclesiastical incomes was made under the direction of Henry VIII in 1535; the *Valor Ecclesiasticus*, published by the Record Commission between 1810 and 1834, listed 8838 parish churches, a small increase since 1291. Inevitably there were some omissions – monasteries particularly did not always itemise all the churches which they controlled, and there were at all dates ambiguities of status: 'church' was used in a legal sense to indicate control of a parish but some chapels were occasionally included. Thomas Wilson, in his essay 'The state of England AD1600', suggested a figure of 9725 parish churches, some 900 more than the *Valor*. His figure is close to Gregory King's rounded estimate of 10,000 clergy holding glebelands about 1688. Both included Wales with England.[1]

In the first national census in 1801 three questions concerning church registers were directed to the 'Rector, Vicar, Curate or other officiating Minister in each parish, township or place'. There were 10,157 returns from England and 835 from Wales. John Rickman, who wrote reports on the first four censuses, considered that 279 were missing, making a total of 11,271 parish registers. This figure included some chapel registers. In his 'Preliminary Observations' on the 1821 census, Rickman said: 'the Question What is a Parish? has often occurred, and has been found not easily determinable'. He emphasised 'various degrees of the dependence of Chapels on their Mother Churches'. A chapel could not be regarded as parochial simply because it had the right of baptism and burial, 'inasmuch as almost every Chapel of Ease would thereby constitute a separate Parish'. He decided

> that where the Curate is appointed and removable by the Incumbent of the Mother Church, and more certainly where Church-Rates still continue to be paid towards the Repair of such Church, the Chapelry is not Parochial. On the other hand, a perpetual Curacy has not been struck out of the List of Parishes merely because the Curate is appointed by the Incumbent of the Mother Church, his permanent Tenure ... seeming to alter the case materially.

Rickman had accepted that a benefice indicated a parish, and concluded that 'the doubtful cases are not many; and for any general purpose the number of Parishes and Parochial Chapelries in England and Wales may safely be taken at 10,693'. His final figure does not indicate any considerable expansion of parishes since 1535.

Returns relating to 10,540 benefices were published in 1835 in the Report of the Royal Commisson to inquire into the Ecclesiastical Revenues of England and Wales.[2] Only a few returns were missing. The church, too, counted benefices rather than legal parishes, which obviated awkward questions of definition. In nearly five and a half centuries since the Pope Nicholas taxation there had been no large changes, but the provision of churches in new and growing centres of population had already begun and by the end of the century 3750 districts had been carved out of old parishes. Before the First World War there were 14,400 benefices, probably the highest number ever, but the population of England and Wales had quadrupled since 1801.

After 1945, parishes were very often combined in united benefices, or grouped in team ministries. The *Church of England Yearbook* for 1994 showed that the number of benefices had dropped to 8770 although there were 16,364 churches and 13,083 parishes still forming the local structure of the English church; these figures no longer included the dioceses in Wales, because the Welsh church had been disestablished after the First World War. The number of parishes in the medieval period and of benefices in 1994 are very similar, a little under 9000. This may seem surprising. In the late twentieth century, however, more parishes are urban, and many circumstances of the parsons' work are wholly changed.

NORTH AND SOUTH

The maps drawn to accompany the *Valor Ecclesiasticus* demonstrate a striking and important contrast between the parish structure in the north and in the south of the country. North of a line from the Humber to the middle reaches of the Severn, parish names are thinly scattered; to the south, and particularly in the south-east, the map is dense with names. Of the 8071 rectories and vicarages in the *Valor*, only one eighth was north of this line. It has been calculated from the *Valor* that in East Anglia the average parish was three square miles, in Kent and most of the South between four and six square miles, and in Devon and Cornwall nearly eight square miles; but in the North average parish size varied from nine square miles over much of Yorkshire, through sixteen square miles in Cheshire, twenty-four in Cumberland and Westmorland, and thirty-five in Lancashire, to seventy in the western half of Northumberland.[3] It might be expected that the northern pattern corresponded with the Province of York, at that time containing only three dioceses, York itself, Durham and Carlisle, but this was not the case; Lancashire, Cheshire, Derbyshire, Staffordshire and part of Shropshire, in fact most of Lichfield diocese, shared the northern pattern.

The early nineteenth-century censuses confirm this fundamental division of the country. In his observations on the 1821 census, Rickman noted that '(generally speaking) parishes in the north average at seven or eight times the area of those in the southern counties'. The 1831 census contained parish areas, published after much accurate information had been collected in connection with assessing local taxes, and prior to the widespread adjustments to parish boundaries which began later in the decade.[4] There were large parishes in the south, like Tonbridge in Kent, twenty-three square miles, or Ramsey in Huntingdonshire, twenty-eight square miles, but they were exceptional. In the North, examples of large parishes include Prestbury in Cheshire, which was just under a hundred square miles; Kendal and St. Bees in Cumbria, over a hundred square miles; Halifax in Yorkshire, 118 square miles; Whalley in Lancashire, 170 square miles; and most strikingly, Simonburn in Northumberland, which stretched thirty-three miles from Hadrian's Wall north of Hexham to Liddesdale in Scotland; it covered almost all the North Tyne valley, 249 square miles - a quite exceptional district to be served by one rector and one parish church.

Northern parishes were large because moor and mountain were included within their bounds, but the censuses also show two other distinguishing features. The first is that they contained numerous separate adminstrative areas or townships. In 1821 there were more than 5000 returns from townships and 'places' in addition to those from parishes, most relating to northern townships. In the South, a majority of parishes were small enough to be single administrative units, but in the North single township parishes were relatively unusual except in the East Riding of Yorkshire; in Cumbria they were a 'small proportion'; in Northumberland, seven out of sixty-two were single township parishes, in Durham ten out of sixty-five and in Lancashire nine out of fifty-six. The Lancashire parish of Whalley in 1831 contained forty-eight sub-divisions including the borough of Clitheroe; Kendal parish contained twenty-seven;

LEFT: *Huish Episcopi, Somerset - St Mary's church tower, on the cliff above the Somerset levels, stands out with glowing grey and yellow stone and intricate carving. Huish belonged to the bishop of Wells before 1066, although Episcopi was added to the name in the eighteenth century. Less than half a mile away, at Langport, King Alfred built a defended town to resist the Danes and the church, now closed, has a similar Somerset-style tower.*

Prestbury thirty-two and one district formerly regarded as in the parish but extra-parochial by 1831; Halifax twenty-three of which two had become separate townships only in the immediate past; Simonburn nineteen; and St Bees, which included the western Lake District mountains, twelve. 'The divisions of the landscape of northern England into townships was so much a part of life that most writers took it for granted and seldom described it, even though the system continued until the late nineteenth century'.

The second feature of northern parishes is that they commonly contained a number of Church of England chapels subordinate to the parish church, quite distinct from the increasing numbers of Nonconformist chapels. Often they were an ancient part of the Church of England's organisation. Kendal had fifteen chapelries in 1831, Prestbury twelve, Whalley eleven, Bakewell nine. The census designation 'Chapelry' instead of township is particularly problematical; it was used when a township chapel was deemed parochial, but there was no provision for indicating other townships in its district. Many chapelries were not documented. For example, five were noted in Halifax, but there were altogether ten medieval chapels in the parish and six or seven later ones. Comment on Whalley in 1831 illustrates the complexities of northern parishes, and displays John Rickman's unrivalled knowledge acquired in organising the census since 1801. Whalley was mainly in Lancashire, but also included land in the West Riding of Yorkshire and in Cheshire. One township, Whitewell in Bowland Forest in Yorkshire, extended by 2890 acres into Whalley parish and its chapel, which was not noted, was subordinate to Whalley church. Willington in Cheshire was also regarded as in Whalley; the census note said 'it seems as if Willington is to be in Whalley Parish, for no better reason than it formerly belonged to Whalley Abbey; for Parochial Rates inhabitants resort to St Oswald's, Chester; but they pay part of the Great Tithes to the Rector of Wene, and part to the Rector of Tarvin'. Was Willington really within any parish? The censuses gradually built up a clearer view of the numerous anomalies in the parochial structure, and naturally led to calls for reform.

Townships and parishes

Parish boundaries were founded on an older territorial structure of townships, but their fundamental importance both in the North and in the South has been obscured by the dominance of the parish in record-keeping from the mid-sixteenth century. Townships were the divisions of the countryside by which the resources of arable fields, meadows, pastures, woods and rough grazing land were shared between communities.[5] A township had its distinguishing name and defined area; it survived as a land unit even when there were no inhabitants. Although many had ancient boundaries, there were also changes and new townships were created by dividing old ones, resulting sometimes in scattered pieces of land forming a new unit. Because of a township's rights and responsibilities, inhabitants needed to know where the boundaries lay; 'Consequently a great deal of time and effort was expended in defining them - banks, ditches, hedges, walls, large cut stones, gates - all testify to this abiding need to know their precise course within the valuable, intensively cultivated land. An alteration could be to the detriment of the inhabitants and could result in action - legal or illegal'. Two places called Threapland in Cumbria are indications of argument: the Anglo-Saxon word *threap* meant dispute, and cases of disputed boundaries encountered by nineteenth-century Ordnance Surveyors were often of long-standing.[6]

Township and parish coincided in much of the South and in fertile, arable areas of the North, and there was one central and compact settlement, although enclosure and tithe maps of the eighteenth and nineteenth centuries can reveal unsuspected townships in apparently simple parishes. But many parishes contained more than one township. A parish was often known by the name of the township in which the church was located. For example the church in Shipton under Wychwood in Oxfordshire served the township of that name and five other townships; groups of six townships frequently occur. Alternatively, the parish was known by the name of the church itself; the white church of the parish of Whitkirk in Yorkshire was located in Colton township and there were five or six other townships in the parish and the ash, or perhaps east, church of Ashchurch in Tewkesbury, Gloucestershire, was in Newton township and again served five other townships. Stoke on Trent church was in Penkhull township, and altogether there were twelve vills and fifteen townships in this Staffordshire parish; 'Stoke' was a word for an administrative centre.

The Latin word for township was *villa*, anglicised as 'vill', which did not have the restricted modern sense of a Roman farmstead or house but had a specialised administrative meaning.[7] By the tenth century it was assumed that all men belonged to a vill and that each vill had a reeve who was responsible for collecting tax or 'geld'. In practice, a vill for collecting tax did not always correspond with one simple agricultural township; there might be several vills within one township, or one vill might include several townships; the same place-name could describe a larger or smaller area in different contexts. A vill might also include one or more hamlets, sometimes many more; the distinction between township and hamlet was based on the level of independence - a hamlet had its defined area of land but was not independent in all respects. Northowram in Halifax parish contained at least forty-one individually named medieval hamlets and farmsteads, and on this basis Halifax parish might have covered 900 separate small settlements.

The Domesday survey in 1086 was organised on the basis of vills. An account written in Ely abbey said that 'The King's barons inquired by the oath of the sheriff of the shire and of all the barons and of their Frenchmen and of the whole hundred, the priest, reeve and six villagers of every vill.' Nearly all the 13,400 or so place-names can be identified with medieval and nineteenth century townships. But many townships were not named: their taxes were collected within a larger vill which was also a manor. The name of the *mansio*, or manor house was the first piece of information obtained from each vill's witnesses. A manor was a free estate whose lord had some control over the tenants of land within it, and a responsibility for paying geld; from it, concepts of land ownership have developed. Manors varied greatly in size and there could be several small manors in one vill. Cooperation between lords of the manor and other landholders was often necessary to create parishes.

Vills continued to be the basis of administration for centuries. The obligation to maintain roads, causeways and bridges was confirmed in Magna Carta in 1215. The evidence of landholding in the Hundred Rolls (1255 and 1274) was collected by vill. In the thirteenth century responsibility for maintaining law and order was placed on the vill, absorbing an older organisation in which ten men were bound together to keep the peace in their area; in later Anglo-Saxon England, every male over twelve years old and legally free had to be in a tithing. In a large vill, tithings continued to be independent units with their own constable, and were known as constablewicks in the north, and boroughs in Kent. Each vill registered men for military service: the *Nomina Villarum* was a list of vills in 1316 responsible for sending a man to the Scottish wars, and of the lords of the manor. The Lay Subsidies were taxes collected in each vill and in 1334, 13,089 place-names were recorded, substantially the same number as in 1086. This shows that there were fewer parishes than vills; but townships, if they could be listed, were much more numerous than either. Parish boundaries reflected many stages in the development of English society.

PART ONE

PATTERNS

CHAPTER ONE

FOUNDATIONS
OF THE PARISH

The supremacy of Canterbury cathedral as the head of the church in England reflects Augustine's crucial importance. It was never supplanted despite its position on the farthest south-eastern peninsula of the country, nowhere near the centre of the country; London and York were better centres for communications, though Canterbury was closest to the continent. The cathedral is just inside the Roman walls of the city; rebuilt and restored, the walls still follow the original course. The elusive but increasingly accepted Roman foundations of the English church are one strand in the establishment of Christianity of particular relevance in Kent, a county which uniquely had a Roman name, *Cantium*, or the Latin version of a British one. Bede recorded in the *Ecclesiastical History of the English People* that King Ethelbert of Kent gave Augustine a church 'built by the ancient Roman Christians' to serve as his cathedral, which he dedicated to Our Saviour, alternatively Christ Church. Immediately outside the city walls to the east, Augustine had already been given a more expansive site for a monastery, because he led about forty monks and priests on the mission which arrived in England in 597. The monastery was dedicated to St Peter and St Paul, but later known as St Augustine's, and Augustine and Ethelbert were buried there. The proximity of the two great churches led to considerable rivalry. Two paths, of monastic retreat and devotion on one hand and worldly work on the other, were present in the church from the beginning in monastery and cathedral. Canterbury also shows the crucial role of Anglo-Saxon kings in the adoption of Christianity, a religion initially imposed from above; progress was made through royal patronage - or that is the recorded story.

LEFT: *Canterbury cathedral from St Augustine's gateway*

BISHOPS AND KINGDOMS

It can be argued that the identity of England was created by Pope Gregory when he entrusted to Augustine the conversion of the English, and later made him 'archbishop of the English people'. The Venerable Bede's *Ecclesiastical History of*

Canterbury, Kent - The main gate to St Augustine's monastery was built by Abbot Fyndon between 1287 and 1300, during a period of great prosperity when there were at least eighty monks. Crenellation needed the permission of the king, and was a sign of status. The most ancient monastery in England was also one of the wealthiest; in 1086 only four were wealthier. What remains are ruins, and mainly nineteenth century buildings used for an Anglican college and now The King's School.

the English People, Historia Ecclesiastica Gentis Anglorum, finished in 731, was based on the concept; the book was quickly recognised as a major work of scholarship and it has preserved the history and influenced understanding of the early Anglo-Saxon church ever since.[1] Bede was born near Jarrow about 672 or 673, and when he was seven was given to the care of the abbot of a new monastery at Monkwearmouth, moving to Jarrow when it was founded about seven years later. At the end of the History he wrote that 'amid the observance of the discipline of the Rule and the daily singing in the church, it has always been my delight to learn or teach or write'. He wrote many books, and corresponded widely to collect information for the *History*, which he finished four years before his death, and for which he is still revered more than a millennium later. Bede recorded the story of the fair-haired slaves in Rome's market place, 'not Angles but angels', who were seen by Pope Gregory and stimulated the mission, though he admitted to some scepticism about it as 'handed down to us by the tradition of our ancestors'. Gregory's focus on the English suggests an appreciation that a British church and British bishops already existed, and he wrote to Augustine 'we commit to you, my brother, all the bishops of Britain' but British bishops were not willing to be dominated. When Augustine arrived, there were at least seven rival Anglo-Saxon kingdoms. Boundaries were not stable, and territory was gained and lost in a series of conquests and shifting alliances. Before any political unity existed, the

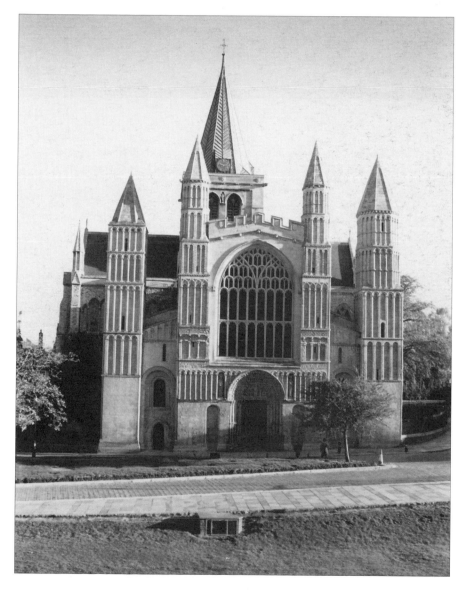

Rochester, Kent - the second Kentish cathedral was again placed in a Roman town by Augustine. To the Anglo-Saxons, Rochester was simply the Caester. *The surviving Norman cathedral was built by Bishop Gundulf who was the architect of the castle, close by, controlling the mouth of the Medway, and also of the Tower of London.*

English church's organisation linked the Anglo-Saxon kingdoms together and created a sense of identity and from 672, when a general council of bishops met at Hertford, 'canons' or rulings on practical and doctrinal matters were issued.

Augustine had less than twelve years in England, perhaps much less; he died possibly as early as 604 and no later than 609 and it is surprising that Bede did not know the year of his death, in view of his importance. But Augustine had instituted three bishoprics including Canterbury within seven years of his arrival. King Ethelbert built a cathedral dedicated to St Andrew at Rochester and one dedicated to St Paul in London. Like Canterbury, these sees were based in Roman towns. The division of the kingdom of Kent between Canterbury, the 'borough' or 'burh', and Rochester, the 'castle' or 'chester' of early records, possibly reflected real differences between the peoples of East and West Kent, the 'Men of Kent' and the 'Kentishmen'.[2] London was in the kingdom of the East Saxons which acknowledged Ethelbert as overlord. Augustine might then have moved to London to fulfil Gregory's plan, but his political base was more secure in Canterbury and the East Saxon conversion did not survive the Kentish king's death, although the see of London was re-established sometime before 669. Gregory had made Augustine personally superior to all other bishops, but had not envisaged Canterbury being forever superior to London and York.

Anglo-Saxon kingdoms were the first parishes, each under the care of a bishop. Pope Gregory had sent Augustine a scheme dividing the country into two provinces or archbishoprics, London and York, with twelve bishops in each; he wished there to be many bishops, close enough together that three or four could easily meet to ordain a colleague, but the plan was never fully implemented. Most dioceses were very large, reflecting political realities, and the fact that there were more kingdoms in the south of England than in the north influenced ecclesiastical geography for nearly a millennium. In Wales, Ireland and Scotland, in contrast, the church's organisation was not based on the territories of such powerful kings; there were consequently more bishops controlling small tribal areas.[3]

Royal support was crucial to the progress of conversion, as the story of Birinus illustrates. Birinus was sent by Pope Honorius, and was consecrated a bishop before he left; nothing is known about his life before this. He arrived in England in 634, and intended to travel 'beyond the dominions of the English', perhaps into Wales, but found the Gewissae in the Upper Thames valley 'most confirmed pagans', so he set about preaching and teaching there. He rapidly secured the conversion of King Cynegils, who was baptised 'with his people'; a king's conversion carried with it the nominal conversion of his whole kingdom. Oswald, King of Northumbria, was conveniently at hand as sponsor, and gave his daughter in marriage to the king soon afterwards. Birinus was given Dorchester on Thames for his see, again a Roman town, but the focus of this kingdom soon shifted southwards, becoming Wessex, and the bishop's seat was moved to Winchester in 660 or 661. Birinus appears more as a diplomatic ambassador than a missionary, and the marriage cemented an alliance between Northumbria and the Gewissae. Adherence to Christianity, and accepting a

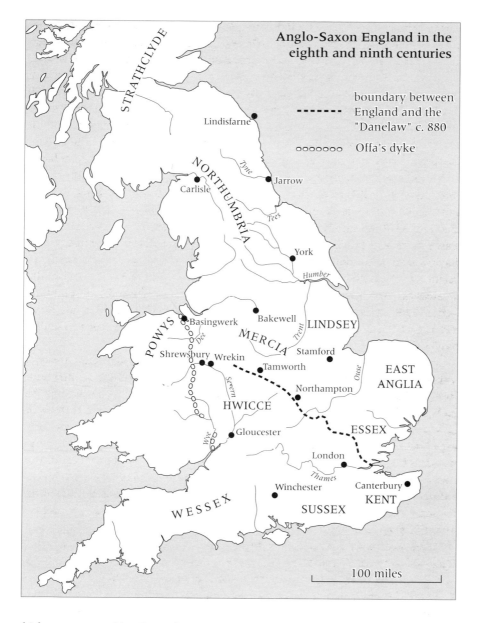

Anglo-Saxon England in the eighth and ninth centuries

- - - - - - boundary between England and the "Danelaw" c. 880

ooooooo Offa's dyke

STRATHCLYDE

Lindisfarne

NORTHUMBRIA

Tyne

Jarrow

Carlisle

Tees

York

Humber

POWYS

Basingwerk

Dee

Bakewell

LINDSEY

MERCIA

Trent

Shrewsbury   Wrekin

Stamford

Tamworth

EAST
ANGLIA

Severn

Northampton

Ouse

HWICCE

Gloucester

Wye

ESSEX

London

Thames

Winchester

Canterbury

KENT

WESSEX

SUSSEX

100 miles

bishop sponsored by Canterbury or consecrated in Ireland, Scotland or Francia, was a carefully calculated political move in the struggle for domination between the Anglo-Saxon kingdoms.[4]

Northumbria became Christian under King Edwin in 627, when he married a Kentish princess, daughter of king Ethelbert. Paulinus acccompanied her to the north, and might have become archbishop of York. But there was a brief interruption after Edwin was killed in battle, and when Christianity was restored in 635 by King Oswald, who was already Christian, a bishop was placed at Lindisfarne; York did not become the seat of a bishop again until about 663. If York Province initially echoed *Britannia Secunda*, the most

northerly of the four provinces of early fourth-century Roman Britain, its southern boundary was the Humber in the east and the Mersey in the west; the name Mersey derived from the Anglo-Saxon word for boundary. But the Mercians pushed beyond the Mersey as far as the Ribble, which became a linguistic and diocesan boundary.[5] A bishop of the East Angles was established about 631 when Felix came from Burgundy, and with the succession of a Christian king to the expansionary midland kingdom of Mercia in 654, a great part of England had been converted. The South Saxons were last; the king married a Christian princess before 680. By the time Theodore reached England in 669 to be archbishop of Canterbury, the foundations for seven dioceses had been laid but only three bishops survived in office, and the church was far from secure.

Three kingdoms were dominant by the late seventh century. In the north, Northumbria stretched from the estuary of the Humber as far as the Roman Wall and beyond; part of this kingdom became the shire of Northumberland and a larger part became Yorkshire. In the middle of England was Mercia, centred in the later county of Staffordshire and lands immediately to the east; at its greatest, Mercia reached from the Thames to the Ribble and from Offa's Dyke to the Wash. Along the south coast was Wessex, the kingdom of the West Saxons, centred on Hampshire; Wessex expanded westwards to the Tamar, and northwards to the Thames. Four small kingdoms maintained independence for a considerable time: Kent, Sussex (the South Saxons), Essex (the East Saxons) and East Anglia (the Angles of Norfolk and Suffolk). Eventually, in the tenth century, kings of Wessex became the rulers of England. Northumbria was the last kingdom to give up its independence, in the mid-tenth century, though it did not fully accept integration and remained liable to repudiate the authority of southern kings.

Theodore set about furthering Gregory's scheme, persuading the rulers and bishops of Mercia, East Anglia and Northumbria to accept division of their areas, so that by the time of his death in 690 the number of bishops had been increased to thirteen or fourteen. The division of East Anglia, with a bishop for Norfolk and one for Suffolk, was not permanent, but may have shaped the later counties. Two small kingdoms in the west which had been absorbed by Mercia were made separate dioceses by 680, with the bishop for the Magonsaete at Hereford and for the Hwicce at Worcester. A bishop for the heartland of Mercia was placed at Lichfield, a few miles from the royal palace at Tamworth. Lindsey was separated from Northumbria to which it had recently been joined. But not all Theodore's work endured: a bishop for the Middle Angles at Leicester and two more in Northumbria, at Hexham and Ripon, were shortlived.[6] In 705 Winchester diocese was divided and a bishop for the land west of Selwood placed at Sherborne. There was no archbishop in York until 735 and archbishops struggled to retain their position during the Viking conquest.

The church was disrupted by waves of pagan Viking invaders from Norway and Denmark during the late eighth and ninth centuries who plundered the churches and murdered monks and nuns. The bishop of Leicester moved to Dorchester on Thames, to the very edge of his territory and his see was

LEFT: *Lichfield cathedral, Staffordshire - the heavily carved west front was completed in 1327 and has statues of saints and Biblical figures which were originally gilded; the architectural period is known as 'Decorated'. The stone steeples, too, are fourteenth century. In 669 Bishop Chad placed the see for Mercia in the church of St Mary at Lichfield, at the centre of a vast multiple estate; the cathedral dedication is now St Mary and St Chad.*

eventually combined with Lindsey, making the Norman bishop's move to Lincoln logical. Other bishoprics disappeared. The monks of Lindisfarne heeded Cuthbert's request not to submit to conquest but to move his bones 'wherever God may send you'. Cuthbert had reluctantly became a bishop as well as prior of Lindisfarne, and was buried there in 687. The monks moved with his coffin to the mainland, and in 883 they settled at Chester le Street. They moved again in 995 to a strongly-defended site above the River Wear at Durham. The generous grants of land which built up the princely powers of the bishop from the late seventh century were made partly out of veneration for Cuthbert and also to secure the loyalty of this area.

Durham cathedral - is considered the 'finest example of Early Norman architecture in England' with remarkable spiral and zigzag carving inside. The wealth and power of the community of St Cuthbert were already well-established when surviving members moved to Durham in 995. The Norman cathedral, built between 1093 and 1133, is on the hill top above the gorge of the river Wear, adjacent to the castle built by William the Conqueror which became the bishop's palace.

Kings of Wessex provided the leadership to stop the Danish advance. A treaty about 886 between King Alfred of Wessex and the Danish Guthrum of East Anglia partitioned England: south and west of a boundary running from the Thames to Bedford, and along Watling Street to Tamworth, was controlled by Wessex, and east and north of this line was allocated to Guthrum. Beyond was the Danish kingdom of York, and only the extreme north of Northumbria remained unconquered. Early in the tenth century the 'Lady of the Mercians', Aethelflaed, daughter of King Alfred, organised a system of fortified towns or *burhs* in Mercia on the Wessex pattern, each drawing on a defined territory. Wessex had been divided into 'shires', possibly even before 700, each under an 'ealdorman'. When Aethelflaed's brother, Edward the Elder, became king of Wessex, he may have introduced shires to Mercia or perhaps they were not formed until the end of the tenth century; the timing is uncertain.[7] The Danes organised larger shires for a similar system of defence and Yorkshire and Lindsey were sub-divided into thirds, the 'Ridings'. After the Danes were defeated in the early tenth century, the land between Ribble and Mersey, later forming the core of Lancashire, was detached from York and transferred to Lichfield diocese and so to the Province of Canterbury. Later in the tenth century, Nottinghamshire was transferred to York Province, bringing the boundary to the River Trent and a little beyond. These arrangements lasted until 1542.[8]

The shires in Wessex formed the basis for new dioceses in the tenth century: Winchester was confined to Hampshire and Surrey, and Sherborne to Dorset; Wells (Somerset), Ramsbury (Wiltshire and Berkshire), and Crediton (Devon) were instituted. Just before 1066 Devon and Cornwall were combined and the bishop moved to Exeter, and Sherborne and Ramsbury were combined.[9] But the same principle was not applied to the Mercian shires, and some notable and durable anomalies resulted. Shropshire, based on Shrewsbury, extended on both sides of the River Severn; but most territory south of the river was in Hereford diocese and north of the river was in Lichfield. The diocese of Worcester related to Worcestershire, and also to most of Gloucestershire and part of Warwickshire. London diocese comprised Essex, Middlesex and part of Hertfordshire. In 1066, there were thirteen bishoprics in the south but Durham and York were the only sees in existence in the northern province.

Norman bishops, as they took over their English sees, were not in sympathy with cathedrals in rural locations and they moved to larger towns. They were also keen to increase the status of their bishoprics with ambitious schemes of rebuilding; some moved to well-endowed monasteries which had the further advantage of giving control over their powerful abbots. The names of the sees changed, but there were few boundary changes. In 1075 the bishop of Lichfield moved to St John's, Chester and subsequently to the monastery at Coventry about 1087; the bishop for Sussex moved from Selsey to Chichester; and the bishop of Sherborne with Ramsbury moved to the fortified hill-top of Old Sarum or Salisbury, but early in the thirteenth century planned an entirely new town round a second new cathedral at New Salisbury. Dorchester was on the very edge of the nine and a half counties in the see and before 1086 the bishop

English dioceses in 1133, with earlier sees also shown

------ boundaries of English dioceses

● cathedral city

▲ earlier sees

Lindisfarne

Hexham

CARLISLE

DURHAM

Ripon

YORK

COVENTRY & LICHFIELD

LINCOLN

Leicester

Elmham

NORWICH

ELY

HEREFORD

WORCESTER

Dorchester

Dunwich

Ramsbury

LONDON

ROCHESTER

BATH & WELLS

SALISBURY

WINCHESTER

CANTERBURY

CHICHESTER

Crediton

Sherborne

Selsey

Bodmin

EXETER

St. Germans

100 miles

had moved to Lincoln. The bishop of Wells moved about 1090 to the monastery at Bath. There was one bishop of East Anglia; he failed to move into the powerful abbey of Bury St Edmunds but went from Elmham to Thetford, a town which spanned the border of Norfolk and Suffolk, and then in 1091 to the city of Norwich. The new cathedrals were built defensively: Salisbury was in a hill-fort, Lincoln was a fortress-church, strongly defended at the west end, Rochester had a free-standing fortified tower and a castle nearby, and Durham, too, shared its site with a castle.

The Normans created only two new bishoprics: the small diocese of Ely for the county of Cambridge in 1108, reducing slightly the huge Lincoln diocese, and Carlisle in 1133; the 'lands of Carlisle' were not part of the English kingdom at the time of the Norman conquest but were conquered by the second Norman king, William Rufus, in 1092. The boundary was not fully defined for centuries, and there was frequent pressure from Scots kings. The counties of Cumberland and Westmorland, created in 1176-7, ignored the quite recent diocesan boundary. From this time the diocesan structure remained unaltered for four hundred years.

A tidy system of archdeaconries based on the shires was introduced by the Normans. Archdeacons were assistants to the bishops. Their primary business was the church's buildings, including parsonage houses, which they inspected

Ely cathedral, Cambridgeshire - the west front is Norman and originally had five towers. An abbey was founded in the seventh century on an island in the fens, and from 1108 its considerable wealth helped to support the status of a new Bishopric; it was second only to Glastonbury in 1086. Barnack stone was used in its construction.

to see that they were sound and properly maintained, and that churches were properly equipped for services. The archdeacon's courts gradually came to handle not only business concerned with church fabric but also with parishioners' wills and their tithe payments to the church. Rural deans were a second step between bishop and parish, also systematised by the Normans. The rural dean convened meetings of the clergy, and if needed, secured their testimony as to lands belonging to the church; he communicated the bishop's and archdeacon's orders, assessed taxation and the amount due for dilapidations of the parsonage house by an outgoing incumbent. One church in a deanery had to be large enough for meetings of churchwardens and parishioners, when bishop or archdeacon conducted a visitation; it was often an old foundation, sited on a royal manor.

ARRANGEMENT OR CHANCE?

A bishop's role was crucial in extending the Christian church: he ordained clergy and consecrated churches; he consecrated the oil and balm, the 'chrism', for use in baptism; he preached to convert pagan Anglo-Saxons and to teach the faith, and carried out mass baptisms; he confirmed. A bishop was also more than a pastor - he was a major political figure in the kingdom; he joined the chief landowners in the king's councils, and often witnessed charters dealing with transfers of land. Bishops provided the written documentation which helped to change the Anglo-Saxons from warring tribes into legally organised buyers and sellers of land. When a kingdom was converted, the bishop must immediately have tried to ordain priests and build churches to give the conversion real substance. Paulinus baptised people in the River Swale because 'they were not yet able to build chapels or baptisteries' and Birinus 'built and consecrated churches, and by his labour called many to the Lord'. It is difficult to imagine a bishop refusing to consecrate a church in the first centuries after the conversion, and equally difficult to imagine tight control. For example, churches were founded by individual missionaries like Fursa, an Irishman, who arrived in East Anglia soon after bishop Felix, and was given a site for his church; he was already a bishop, and so quite independent of Felix. Similarly Bede mentioned another Irish missionary called Dicuill who was established at Bosham although the South Saxons were not yet Christian; typically, his church was on the site of a Roman building. Bede also recorded the name of an Irish bishop in Kent and there must have been others whom he did not mention, like Maidubh at Malmesbury.[10]

The contemporary word for a major church foundation in Latin was *monasterium*, monastery, in Anglo-Saxon *mynster*. An early 'minster' was not necessarily a community of monks living under a rule, as the word 'monastery' later implied. 'Minster' was appropriate to an enclosure separating a religious site from the community at large; it might have housed priests, deacons, monks or nuns, or a mixture.[11] There was a head or 'father' called the abbot or abbess, and a prior who dealt with practical administration. On the continent the distinction between cloistered monks following a rule like St Benedict's and secular communitites of priests and deacons concerned with pastoral care, and under the bishop's supervision, was clearly recognised by mid-eighth century but not until the tenth century in England. Minsters could be sited in town or village, or in an isolated situation like Lindisfarne. They were centres of learning and of teaching, especially for intending clergy, places of hospitality for the king and the bishop, of adminstrative organisation for collecting tax and for the control of important communication routes, especially bridges, and they provided the venue for ordinations and meetings of the clergy. Information on early churches inevitably relates to minsters which became monasteries. They were generously endowed, and had charters or written grants of land. Fragile papyrus was used for the first Kentish charters, but parchment came into use in the late seventh century and was durable, in a few cases even lasting into the twentieth century. Less ambitious foundations, oratories or chapels without an enclosure, did not need royal charters; their landholdings were comparable with those of village farmers. Monasteries also had libraries where documents were copied in order to preserve them, and monks wrote histories of their houses.

Many minsters were founded in the second half of the seventh century. The impetus came from three sources. Firstly, kings were important; they worked with their bishops to provide a number of churches associated with their centres of administration, the royal vills.[12] King Oswiu's vow in 655 to give twelve ten-hide estates for the founding of six monasteries in Deira and six in Bernicia, the sub-kingdoms of Northumbria, seems to show an attempt to institute a framework of organisation, and the foundation charters of Gloucester and Pershore, which gave wide powers of collecting tribute or church scot, appear in a similar light. Gloucester abbey, founded about 679 by Osric, ruler of the Hwicce, was given the territory of three hundred tributarii; Osric's sister is said to have been the first abbess. A parallel transaction gave Pershore in Worcestershire the territory of three hundred cassati. The two Latin terms need not show that Roman taxes on countrymen's estates were still collected but that church tax was related to the land of a free man.

'Minster' place-names in west Wessex, particularly in Dorset, seem to indicate a group of major churches founded under King Ine, who ruled between 688 and 726. Ine issued a law code 'marked by a definite purpose of advancing Christianity' and he resigned at the end of his life in order to go to Rome. He instituted the bishopric of Sherborne, and the 'minster' names suggest that these churches were founded to support the new bishopric. Their territorial responsibilities were seemingly defined by rivers: Sturminster was on the River Stour in Dorset, Axminster and Exminster in Devon on the Ax and Exe rivers, and Warminster in Wiltshire on the River Were. These were all royal manors. Charminster and Ilminster are also named with reference to rivers, and Beaminster and Yetminster in Dorset and Bedminster in Somerset were named by reference to particular people. Ine's sister is associated with the founding of Wimborne Minster in Dorset in 718; Wimborne was a royal manor on a stream or bourne called the Wim, and this church retained a special status for centuries as a 'royal free chapel' independent of the bishop.

A second group of founders were landholders, large and small. Benedict

Biscop, the founder of Monkwearmouth monastery in 674 and of Jarrow two years later, in which Bede lived and wrote, is an example of a wealthy private founder who had the cooperation of the Northumbrian king; Biscop travelled widely on the continent to collect books and pictures, craftsmen and teachers, and holy relics for his new foundations, and the buildings at Jarrow were of stone 'in the Roman manner', with stone-slated roofs and window glass. The twin monasteries in 716 were large enough to have been in effect a town, with six hundred 'knights of Christ', and eighty others who went to Rome with Abbot Ceolfrith.[13] Other founders who provided resources for a building and a priest to minister to family and inhabitants of their estate may have been humbler and their churches undocumented but numerous. Bede referred, as if it was a matter of course, to 'the oratory of the village' where a man prayed after recovering miraculously from a fatal illness.

Thirdly, men and women founded monasteries which they ruled personally. Bede regarded some private monasteries as no more than a way of avoiding public duties; but some were founded for kings' daughters for whom they offered a career. Mildburg, the daughter of Merewalh, king of the small western kingdom of the Magonsaete, purchased land at Wenlock for a monastery about 685 and became the abbess. Her mother was a member of the Kentish royal family and probably the first abbess of Minster in Thanet. The Kentish royal family is notable for no less than fourteen saintly royal daughters, at least six in charge of important churches probably founded for them; these include one generation of daughters at Lyminge and Folkestone about 630 and another generation at Minster in Thanet and Minster in Sheppey about 670. Bishops struggled to gain control of the churches in their dioceses. At the end of the seventh century, a royal command made eight Kentish 'minster' churches subject to the archbishop of Canterbury's control; they had presumably been independent hitherto.[14]

The place of minsters in the origins of the parochial system is a matter of debate.[15] Could the three hundreds from which Gloucester or Pershore collected church scot be termed parishes? Were minsters essentially parochial at all? The 'minster hypothesis' sees a comprehensive network of minsters in control of other churches in their territories, to which slowly and reluctantly over the next several centuries they gave up parochial authority and sources of income. Parishes therefore evolved from the break-up and decay of minster territories. But the hypothesis appears to make the early church too tidy, and with too tight a definition of parochial responsiblity. It also ignores the possibility of several existing churches drawn into subordination to one superior church at a later date. A council of English bishops which met in 747 at a place called *Clofesho* (an Anglo-Saxon place-name which is no longer identifiable), agreed to canons exhorting bishops and priests to carry out their duty of pastoral care without mentioning institutions like 'minsters'. In Kent, a recent historical study by Alan Everitt concluded that the attempt to find a comprehensive and tidy pattern of superior minster churches fails; 'enigmas and eccentricities' show that church foundation was not wholly a matter of royal or episcopal organisation and some one-time important churches appear

Brixworth, Northamptonshire - All Saints' church may have been built in the seventh century by a king of the Middle Angles; it has been suggested that this was Clofesho, *where a council of English bishops met in 747. The church was like a Roman colonnaded market or* basilica; *the great arches shaped in Roman bricks once led to side chapels. This is 'the most impressive pre-Viking church still standing in England'.*

later in anomalous positions. Early church organisation was very fluid; superior churches could be displaced, relocated to new sites, or even given as endowments to new foundations. Beaminster, for example, was given to Gloucester abbey soon after its foundation and Iwerne Minster was given to the new Shaftesbury abbey on its foundation by King Alfred, a keen reorganiser of churches.

The ninth canon of *Clofesho* asked that priests with duties of care for 'places and regions of the laity' be diligent in preaching, baptising, teaching and visiting'. Did 'places and regions' have specific territorial meaning? Regio, 'region' now has expansive connotations, but areas described as regions varied considerably in size, and 'territory' or 'district' might be a better translation. Bede recognised a hierarchy of areas, using *provincia* for a kingdom and *regio* for an area less than a province, which perhaps might be a sub-kingdom, as when he wrote that Northumbria and Mercia were made up of *regiones*. In the early eighth century, a grant of land for a minster at Wootton Wawen in Warwickshire was described as in the region 'which from ancient times is called the *Stoppingas*', that is 'belonging to Stoppa's people' who might be regarded as a tribe. If Wootton Wawen were central to the region, these people were located in the area of the River Alne, in the triangle between Redditch, Leamington and Stratford upon Avon. Surrounding the modern parish of Wootton Wawen are ten smaller parishes, each with intricate boundaries, but together forming a territory with simpler boundaries.

The Rodings in Essex appear to have formed a similar region. Eight parishes, all existing by 1291, have Roding as part of their name, and sixteen holdings were identified simply as Rodings in Domesday Book. The name referred to 'Hrotha's people'.[16] Small kingdoms and tribal areas like these were gradually brought together in the English kingdom led by Wessex, and a new territorial organisation devised. As early as the eighth century in Wessex and probably the tenth century elsewhere, settlements were grouped into hundreds, which did not always respect the earlier teritories. Wootton Wawen's territory was divided between two hundreds along the River Alne; the Rodings were mainly in Dunmow Hundred but partly in Ongar Hundred. Each hundred in turn appears to have had its major church, sometimes confirming the status of an older church, but sometimes displacing it with another in a more convenient position.[17] The later pattern of parishes contains elements of the earliest foundations, interwoven, amended and overlaid by later development.

'Place', *locus*, seems to have meant then what it still does and was a useful maid of all work. Bede used 'place' when he did not choose something more specific like 'city', 'town', 'royal vill' or 'estate'. It must often have meant 'township'. From at least the late seventh century, bishops were entrusting small areas or places to the care of individual priests. About 690 Theodore required that a priest should continue to minister in any place where there had been a monastery if it moved to another site. Breedon on the Hill in Leicestershire was given to the monastery of Medeshamstede (Peterborough) in the late seventh century, on condition that the monks appointed 'a priest of good repute to minister baptism and preaching to the people assigned to him'. On the continent 'parish' was being used in this context about 600, but in England not for another hundred years. A life of St Cuthbert written about 700 recorded that he dedicated a church in a 'parish called Ovington' which belonged to Whitby Abbey. Bede used the *Life*, but he avoided the word parish and wrote 'possession' instead, having an exact sense of the historical meaning of the word, and the third canon of *Clofesho* similarly stated that a bishop should travel round his parish once a year and call people together and teach them, especially those who rarely heard the word of God, prohibiting pagan practices such as sortilege or casting lots.[18]

As Stenton concluded 'The development of a parochial system is the central thread of English ecclesiastical history in the generations following the arrival of Theodore, but it is virtually ignored by contemporary writers ... In the general history of the English church the monasteries of this period are of less significance than the obscure parish churches which remained as the permanent basis of English ecclesiastical organisation'.[19]

PATTERNS OF PASTORAL CARE

Several early patterns of pastoral care influenced the eventual pattern of parishes. A minster community might have sent priests out to serve chapels in the villages and hamlets in its area, the classic 'minster pattern'; it might have appointed priests or deacons to live locally and serve chapels; or there might have been numerous independent, smaller church foundations. The alternatives might be categorised as Roman or British, Gallic, and Irish.

The 'Roman' pattern: St Helen's, Worcester
Pope Gregory I assumed that towns should be centres for the church's

organisation, as they were in Italy, and it is notable that when an Anglo-Saxon king was converted, a bishop was placed in a former Roman town. Britain had become Christian in the period of the late Roman Empire; had Christianity survived? Bede accused the Britons of a great failure in not attempting to convert the Anglo-Saxons, but it was no doubt difficult for a man who was in fear of losing his land, and possibly his life, to convert his new masters, nor would the new rulers have wanted British churchmen in positions of authority.[20] But on the western side of the country, particularly, it is possible that the British did convert them; they came late to the area and within a short time had become Christians.

It seems possible that a church and a Christian community survived in Worcester.[21] When Bishop Bosel arrived about 680, it seems he may have found at least one church in the former Roman city, and perhaps two, and some elements of the Roman organisation apparently still in existence. The evidence is an eleventh century dispute between the priests of the churches of St Alban and St Helen. Both churches were sited within Worcester's Roman defences: St Alban's was at the northern end and St Helen's was in the centre, beside the Roman road which ran through the city; the cathedral occupied the southern end. The dedications are characteristic of very early churches, and neither is common in the Worcester area.

Wulfstan, the bishop in 1092, found the dispute of such importance and long continuance that he summoned 'all the wisest men' from the three counties in the diocese, Worcester, Gloucester and Warwick, to a meeting in the crypt of his new cathedral. The bishop commanded 'the old men, and those with the greatest knowledge of the ancient rights and customs of the churches and parishes of Worcester to declare the truth concerning the ancient customs and

Worcester cathedral - sited on a cliff above the River Severn and within the Roman fort which Anglo-Saxons recognised in its name, it still rises above the modern town. Theodore placed a bishop here about 680 for the small kingdom of the Hwicce. The Normans built a castle nearby, and in 1084 Bishop Wulfstan began a new cathedral. What stands today is mainly thirteenth and fourteenth centuries, but Wulfstan's crypt survives, where wise men met in 1092 to discuss the position of a rival church in the town.

parishes, not only of the two churches named, but of all the churches in the city of Worcester'. He wished to establish that the cathedral was the 'mother church' of Worcester but its status was apparently challenged by St Helen's. There were implications for the cathedral's income, as the mother church would be able to claim various payments from the city's inhabitants. The phrasing of the Synod's findings was ambiguous: 'they affirmed that there was no parish in the whole city of Worcester but that of the Mother church'; however, 'the church of St Helen, in truth, had been a vicarage of this Mother Church from the days of King Ethelred, and Archbishop Theodore, who founded the See at that time and placed Bosel there as first bishop in the year of our Lord's Incarnation 680'. It was extremely unlikely that St Helen's was founded as a parish church with a vicar at the same time as the cathedral. If the vicarage was so ancient, the cathedral must actually have displaced St Helen's, appropriating its revenues and its position. The inferior position of Evesham abbey, which held St Alban's, was established along with St Helen's.

The relative positions of the bishop and prior of Worcester were also at stake. About 969, Wynsius the priest serving St Helen's, and other clerks, had been persuaded by Bishop Oswald to join the newly-founded priory when he turned the cathedral establishment into a Benedictine monastery. Wynsius 'surrendered the keys of the church', together with lands, tithes, burial fees and all other customs and ecclesiastical rights, and he became the first prior soon after. Through his control of St Helen's, the prior could claim a certain superiority over the bishop. Eventually, in 1234, the prior surrendered the patronage of St Helen's to the bishop. St Helen's still had seniority over other town churches. In 1291 six churches 'within the city' all paid a small sum of money to the priory, but not St Helen's, which was listed separately. In 1535, it was the first of the city's churches listed, and its ancient superiority was remembered and reported by Leland. Not until 1938 was St Helen's reduced to a chapel of ease, being united with four other Worcester churches, and it is now used by Worcester Record Office.

St Helen's parish might indicate the territory assigned to the Roman town. It extended on both sides of the River Severn, and controlled the crossing of the Severn at Worcester where a network of roads and lesser 'ways' converged on the bridge built in Roman times; to the west and south, the boundary was the Teme as far as the junction with the Severn, and to the east, the Bow Brook. Altogether it stretched some thirteen miles from east to west. Parts of this territory were in the cathedral's parish, interspersed with St Helen's. The priory's cartulary contained a record about 1113 of the 'things which pertain to the church of St Helen's, nine houses around the church suggest that there had been nine canons. Twelve chapels belonged to St Helen's.[22] Only one, Martley, had its own priest; otherwise, the chapels must have been served by clerks from Worcester. Surprisingly, six of the chapels were in the bishop's manor of Northwick near Worcester. It must have been particularly annoying to the bishop to find that he could not appoint the priest in one of his most substantial estates, Wick Episcopi; not until 1370 was a bishop able to close Wick church, then conveniently said to be 'half deserted and attended by very few', and to create a parish church of St John, Bedwardine, in its place. The hold of an ancient church on its chapels was tenacious.

The 'Gallic' pattern: South Elmham, Suffolk

The English church, especially in the south-east, may have been influenced strongly by practices across the channel.[23] The conversion of the kingdom of the East Angles was achieved by two men who had strong links with Gaul: King Sigeberht of East Anglia spent some time as an exile in Gaul, and had been baptised there; he invited Felix, a Burgundian who had been consecrated a bishop in Gaul before he came to England, to lead the church in his kingdom. In Gaul, it was accepted that oratories or chapels in the territory of a mother church should have their own priest or deacon; early in the sixth century a council at Vaison, on the border of Burgundy, described a rural clerk as one who lived in the countryside and said the divine office, he and his people going to the mother church on the great feast days. Such chapels might more easily have become independent parish churches than those without a resident priest.

The 'Saints' or the 'Nine Parishes' of South Elmham in Suffolk, on the border with Norfolk, might have developed from such a Gallic arrangement. South Elmham had an administrative unity, possibly of Roman origin; the element ham in a place-name seems to indicate an early manorial centre, often near a Roman road.[24] Elmham was described in Domesday Book as a 'Ferding', that is, a fourth or quarter part of the Hundred of Wainford. It forms a strikingly rectangular tract of land. Nine churches and a fraction of a church were recorded and in 1291 eight churches were taxed and Flixton church was a small monastery. Seven Elmham parishes are identified simply by the saint to whom the church is dedicated, not by the name of a settlement; the other two parishes in the 'Ferding' are Homersfield and Flixton, both close to the River Waveney. Elmham St Margaret appears to be most central, but to the south-west there are the ruins of a church called simply 'the Minster', situated within an earthwork enclosure, and with an unusual ground plan. Near it is the bishop's manor house of Elmham Hall. The East Anglian bishop claimed jurisdiction over the whole of South Elmham in 1086, and directly controlled two thirds of the land, with its many small freemen's holdings. He held a second Flixton, fifteen miles away, and the coincidence of two Flixtons which were both episcopal possessions has prompted the suggestion that the name was derived from Felix, rather than from a Norseman called Flik. South Elmham could well have been an early endowment of the bishopric. Curiously the bishop had a second large estate called Elmham in Norfolk, which was the East Anglian bishop's see about 1076. Five South Elmham churches show Norman architectural details, and All Saints has a characteristic East Anglian round tower. The average size of the parishes as recorded in 1831 was less than a thousand acres: the smallest, St Nicholas, was 450 acres, the largest, St James, 1530 acres; by this date one church had been demolished and the total population of the nine parishes was 1550, but there were six clergymen.

Adjacent to the 'Nine Saints' are the 'Seven Parishes' of the Ilketshalls, Mettingham and Bungay, through which a Roman road ran to the crossing over the Waveney which gave the hundred of Wainford its name. Seven churches in this area were recorded in Domesday, five entered under the king's manor of Bungay; a small amount of land was noted under Ilketshall, but a large amount under Bungay, together forming a coherent unit. Six churches were recorded in 1291. The Seven Parishes made up a second quarter of Wainford hundred, and similarly may show 'Gallic' influence. Four parishes are distinguished by their saints' names. St Lawrence is a long, thin stretch of land on either side of the Roman road, and the church is in a Roman station; St John's, only 800 acres, is near the Roman road. St Andrew's has a primitive eleventh century round tower and St Margaret's and Holy Trinity Bungay also have round towers; Bungay's appears to be the oldest. All the parishes were under 2000 acres in 1831, and excluding the two churches in Bungay there were 1500 parishioners and five clergymen. If an early establishment of many chapels with their own priests were widespread in East Anglia, it could be one explanation for the many parish churches recorded in Domesday Book.

The 'Irish' influence: Gilsland in Cumbria

Ireland had become Christian in the fifth century. Irish missionaries began to travel widely before the end of the sixth century; to leave family and home was a form of penance, and the Irish Christians' urge to evangelism was a notable characteristic. Christians in Gaul were strongly affected by them, and they also went to Germany and to Scotland; Columba's monastery of Iona existed before 597, and governed the churches in the northern part of Ireland as well as Scotland. From Iona, missionaries went to Northumbria and further south.[25] The Irish church was organised in relation to the many small kingdoms or territories, each the land of a kindred and named from the family concerned. A bishop was responsible for each territory, and his church provided for the education and training of priests; there were possibly as many as 150 Irish bishops in the seventh or eighth century. In addition, numerous small churches were built in the countryside, served by a local priest with perhaps one assistant, and by the eighth century there was a developed system of pastoral care: people knew to which church they belonged. Irish laws show that in return for pastoral care, the community paid dues including tithes. There was also enthusiasm for the contemplative life, monasteries often being founded in remote places.

Irish influence was particularly strong in Northumbria, mediated by Iona, and for about two hundred years the Northumbrian kingdom included modern Cumbria. When Northumbria was weakened by Viking attacks, much of Cumbria was absorbed into the British kingdom of Strathclyde, and subsequently into the Scottish kingdom. It was not subject to Danish control from York after 866-7, nor to English control when reasserted over south Cumbria in 927. For several centuries northern Cumbria was 'beyond the frontier of Latin Christendom' and was 'predominantly Celtic'. The most northerly part, Gilsland, was unique in not being controlled by the Normans when the lands of Carlisle were taken over after 1092, and it did not become English until 1158.

In the Celtic fashion, Gilsland is known by a family name.[26] About 1158 Gille son of Bued was named as the previous owner of the barony of Gilsland; his name was Irish-Norse, or Gaelic. Gilsland barony contained about 138,000 acres, much of it forested, fenny or high moorland; Tyndale fells in the south reach nearly 2000 feet (621m.). It is bisected by the River Irthing and Hadrian's Wall, which follows the high ground immediately north of the river. Its boundaries split the parish of Stapleton in the north-west along the River Lyne, and the parish of Croglin along Croglin Water in the south; Croglin church to the south of the river was within the area controlled by the Normans about 1100. Earlier, the high ground of King Harry Common had probably defined Gilsland. The parochial pattern in Gilsland was of independent parish churches and, in the most northerly part, a monastery at Bewcastle which does not appear to have had any authority over other churches. The elaborately carved Bewcastle cross incorporates a sundial on one face which would have been in a monastic enclosure, enabling the community to calculate the date of Easter; the decorative interlacing patterns on the sides, though worn, have been compared with illuminations in the Lindisfarne gospels, and the cross has been dated to the first half of the eighth century. It was within a Roman fort also the site of a well-known pagan shrine. Though linked by a Roman road to Birdoswald on Hadrian's wall, Bewcastle in its remoteness fits a typical Irish situation for a monastery. The church is dedicated to St Cuthbert, like Ruthwell which also has a carved cross of about the same period. The monastery effectively guarded the Northumbrian frontier and its foundation would fit with the extension of Northumbrian authority to the area in the seventh century. Many minor place-names in Gilsland are British or Scandinavian, but parish names are predominantly Anglo-Saxon, which suggests that they were organised during the Northumbrian period. Eight parish names end in *ton*. British churches appear to have been made subject to Anglo-Saxon foundations: Cumwhitton and Cumrew to Hayton, Triermain to Walton, and Cambeck (Kirkcambeck) to Askerton.

Several church dedications in Gilsland seem to reflect Celtic missions. Denton, like Bewcastle, is dedicated to St Cuthbert. While he was bishop of Lindisfarne between 685 and 687, Cuthbert travelled to Carlisle several times and his importance in the area is evident from the fifteen churches dedicated to him in Carlisle diocese.[27] Another church in an abandoned Roman fort at Brampton to the south of Hadrian's wall, was dedicated to St Martin but popularly associated with St Ninian and with a holy well called 'Ninewells'; the dedication to St Martin is unique in Cumbria and rare in England, but Bede linked St Martin of Tours with St Ninian. Ninian founded the church dedicated to St Martin at Whithorn in Galloway in the fifth century, and ministered as a bishop in northern Cumbria. A church at Brougham dedicated to Ninian, and popularly known as 'Ninekirks', is also in a Roman fort. Across the River Irthing from Brampton, Irthington church is dedicated to St Kentigern or Mungo, the late sixth century bishop of Glasgow; there are seven or eight dedications to him in the Cumberland area.

An Augustinian priory was founded at Lanercost between 1158 and 1169, soon after Gilsland became part of England. The 'land of Lanercost' was between the 'old wall' or Roman wall and the River Irthing and much of the priory's land was in the parish of Walton; Lanercost and Walton formed one vill in 1334.[28] The churches of Walton, Brampton, Irthington, Farlam, and Carlatton were all given to the priory. A possibly Celtic pattern was converted to something more 'Roman'.

FIXING PARISH BOUNDARIES

If at the beginning of the nineteenth century when the first national censuses were taken there was uncertainty about what constituted a 'parish', there was much more indefiniteness in Anglo-Saxon England. Gradual elaboration of the church's laws took place over several centuries and 'parish' acquired a clearer meaning in two stages, widely separated in time. The first was the enforcement of tithe payments by the king in the late tenth century, and the second was a clear definition of pastoral responsibilities in the twelfth century.

Churches relied on a variety of sources of support in addition to any endowment of land, and they received offerings from penitents, from pilgrims, and from those to whom they ministered. Some payments were enforced by royal government in so far as it was possible. Tithe was the most important of these. Very early it was an accepted moral obligation for Christians to pay one tenth of their year's produce to the church where they were baptised, initially used by the bishop for charitable purposes. 'Tribute' was mentioned by Theodore about 690, 'levied according to the custom of the province'; tribute was a general term for tax and included tithe, and it is notable that from the beginning practice varied from place to place. Bede criticised the fact that tribute was paid to the bishop by remote villages whose inhabitants had not so much as seen him for years. At the end of the sixth century, some dioceses in the Frankish church began to enforce payment of tithe with the threat of excommunication and by the late eighth century, the emperor had placed his authority behind payment.[29] Already tithes from parts of an estate were being granted to different churches, and a generation later reforming councils were held which agreed that tithes belonged to local churches and their clergy. It would have been difficult to enforce payment if there were no certainty about which church should collect them; 'Every church should have a boundary of the estates from which it receives the tithes'. This was a 'definitive regulation', and might have influenced England once the period of political instability was over.

About 930, English laws stated that payment of tithes was obligatory, together with church scot, plough alms, and soul scot. King Ine's laws in the early eighth century had referred to church scot, which was paid from each dwelling at midwinter, St Martin's feast day or Martinmas (11 November). It was occasionally noted in Domesday Book: at Pershore it was a packload of corn at Martinmas from each freeman with a hide of land in three hundreds in the county, closely reflecting the late seventh century foundation charter. The other payments may have been as ancient; plough alms was a penny a plough team paid after Easter, and soul scot was possibly a Christianised pagan custom of paying for the benefit of the soul after death.[30]

Soon after Edgar became king of England in 959, he made the law on tithes more effective by introducing penalties for non-payment. Tithe was associated to some extent with the cure of souls, since a thegn or landowner could give one third of the tithes from his own land to his local church if it had a graveyard, but not to a 'field church' without a graveyard, which would later be called a chapel. All other tithes from freemen's land were to be paid to the old, or superior, minster 'to which the obedience pertains'. By the beginning of the eleventh century, three grades of minster were recognised, the head minster or cathedral, the medium minster and the lesser minster, and more than 300 churches can be identified in Domesday Book to which 'medium' or 'lesser minster' might be appropriate, even though the record was certainly not complete.[31] Edgar's law prevented wholesale redirection of tithes without the consent of the superior church, but encouraged the provision of local village churches for which tithes were a means of funding a priest without the need for an endowment of land. In the century following Edgar's laws, landholders were energetic in building churches on their estates; the share of tithes claimed by existing churches was no doubt greater or smaller depending on the status and power of their patrons or owners, involving bargains and perhaps some conflict between pastoral responsibilities and status. Tithes eventually became a form of property separated from pastoral responsibility, and could be bought, sold and leased. They became a subject of enormous legal complexity. Gratian's collection of church canons about 1140, the *Decretum*, reinforced their territorial rather than their pastoral aspect; he helped establish that tithes should be paid to the church within whose parish the land was situated, whether or not the landholder himself lived there.

The concept of a parish was also refined. The bishops' policy in their councils was to protect the rights of older churches and to resist any increase in lay power. It was established that only one parish church could have responsibility for the cure of souls of a group of inhabitants; 'within one boundary there are not to be many baptismal churches, but one, with a number of chapels', and that the parish church should have a permanent endowment of glebeland, tithes, and offerings which constituted the 'title' of that church. Burial rights, baptismal rights and tithes became the 'normal definition' of a parish church.[32] This meant that 'strict parochial boundaries of the kind familiar to us today can never have existed before the twelfth century'. From this time change became much more difficult as a church had to be compensated for alteration of its title. 'The canon law laid its cold hand on the parishes of Europe, and froze the pattern which has in many parts subsisted ever since'. In 1237, after almost a century of discussion, Pope Gregory IX issued the *Decretals* which became the classic formulation of canon law. The freezing of the pattern of parishes explains the close correspondence between the *Pope Nicholas Taxation* of 1291 and the *Valor Ecclesiasticus* of 1535, and medieval canon law continued to be the basis of the Church of England after the break with Rome, until new laws were created by parliament in the nineteenth century.

CHAPTER TWO

THE PATTERN
IN THE SOUTH

The irregular honeycomb of parishes which covers southern England was constructed on a base of even more numerous manors and small estates, through which the countryside was governed, manpower mobilised for defence, and taxes collected. Some parishes simply matched a manor, but many reveal signs of more sweeping and artificial organisation. Late Anglo-Saxon England had a well-developed administration in which churchmen played a key role, and it would be surprising if this did not influence the church itself. When the Norman overlords visited their new fiefs which they took over from defeated Anglo-Saxons, they found a countryside dotted with churches built in the previous one hundred years. According to Goscelin of St Bertin, the Pope was told by the bishop of Ramsbury in 1050 about 'England being filled everywhere with churches, which daily were being added anew in new places'. His testimony is particularly credible because he came from Flanders before the Norman Conquest and lived at Ramsbury with Bishop Herman for twenty years.[1]

LEFT: *East Lexham, Norfolk - St Andrew's church*

Possible signs of late Anglo-Saxon workmanship have been identified in some 300 churches. Amongst the more enigmatic are the round towers of East Anglia. They give an impression of great antiquity, but are difficult to date precisely; in some, Anglo-Saxon building techniques are found in conjunction with Norman, but 'by far the greatest number belong to the late eleventh and the first half of the twelfth century'. At East Lexham, the round tower almost certainly pre-dates the Norman Conquest; at West Lexham, where there is also one, it may be slightly later. Domesday Book recorded a church in Lexham, not distinguished as East or West but connected with the larger of the two Norman landholdings, and Lexham Hall is not far from East Lexham church. Round towers are mostly attached to simple, small buildings because larger, more affluent communities rebuilt their churches in later sophisticated architectural styles. W.J.Goode in *East Anglian Round Tower Churches* listed 120 standing in Norfolk in 1993, nine in ruins and at least twenty more known to have existed;

West Lexham, Norfolk - St Nicholas's tower is probably a little later than East Lexham's about a mile away. West Lexham's larger population of freemen in 1086 may have built it soon after. There was a scatter of cottages and houses near the church about 1600; by 1800 only a few were left, but the church heeds the request of Jesus in John 21 verse 16, 'Feed my sheep'.

there were forty-two in Suffolk and a small number elsewhere in England and some in Ireland. The main concentration is along the the Yare and Waveney rivers in the east of Norfolk, where there is also a concentration of Scandinavian place-names, and the style has been traced to trading connections with areas bordering the Baltic and the North Sea where similar round towers can be seen, a renewal of links made by earlier settlers.[2]

DISTINCTIVE PARISH NAMES

East and West Lexham in Norfolk are examples of a common feature of parish names throughout the south: two or more contiguous places share a basic name and are distinguished from each other by what Maitland called a 'surname'; in Gloucestershire, typical examples include Great Barrington and Little Barrington, South Cerney and North Cerney, Aston Subedge and Weston Subedge, Upper Slaughter and Lower Slaughter, Shipton Oliffe and Shipton Sollers, Ampney St Peter, Ampney St Mary, and Ampney Crucis. East and West, North and South, are common and so are Great and Little, or Magna and Parva. Sets of shared names are prolific in East Anglia and in Essex; for example, thirty-one parishes in Essex have 'Little' in their name, twelve in Norfolk, nine in Suffolk and eight in Buckinghamshire.[3] Other distinguishing 'surnames' were the land-holder's family name, or his or her position: King, Queen, Prince, Duke, Earl, Child, Sheriff, Bishop, Abbot, Prior, Monk, Nun, Friar, Canon, White Ladies, Maids. There are certainly hundreds, and probably thousands, of examples, of this type of place-name. Shared place-names may often imply division of an earlier territorial unit.

In 'The surnames of English villages' in the *Archaeological Review* in 1889, Maitland entertainingly discussed place-names of this sort. He commented on some unusual ones like 'Zeal Monachorum, Ryme Intreseca, Toller Porcorum, Shudy Camps and Shellow Bowells but did not point to former pairings: Ryme

Extrinseca, Toller Fratrum, Castle Camps and Shallow or Shellow Jocelyn which was an alternative name for one of the Rodings. Of thirty-seven later place-name pairs in Norfolk, Domesday indicates that at least twenty-two pairs of manors existed before 1086 although the distinguishing surnames are not often recorded in Domesday Book.[4] Maitland suggested this implied that named land units had been divided not long before 1066 and that 'On the whole the inference that the map suggests is that these surnames of our villages did not become stereotyped before the end of the thirteenth century'.

The Manningfords, a little to the south of Pewsey in Wiltshire, nicely fit Maitland's theory. Three manors and townships called Manningford were recorded in Domesday Book, later to be distinguished as Manningford Abbots, Manningford Bruce and Manningford Bohune.[5] The settlements are on the gravels in the valley of the River Avon and crossed by the road from Pewsey to Devizes which runs parallel to and south of the river. The Avon ford which helped to identify the estate was on a road running north and south, now disused. The Manningfords form an oblong block of territory four-and-a-half miles long and one and three quarters wide, reaching from downland in the south-east where sheep were once pastured, across the river valley where the arable land was concentrated, to the commons and woods on the greensand in the north-west. This territory was split into three long, thin strips of land, each one on average only half a mile wide, and of approximately a thousand acres. The boundaries are so nearly parallel that it seems they were made simultaneously, in or before 987. At that date the eastern strip, of ten hides, was granted to the New Minster in Winchester (later Hyde Abbey after a move to a site outside the city walls); sometimes called Little Manningford, by the late thirteenth century the name Manningford Abbots was established. The western half of Manningford, also amounting to ten hides, was divided into two long,

Manningford Bruce, Wiltshire - St Peter's church is small and simple. It stands close to a Roman villa, and seems likely once to have served all three Manningfords. The nave without aisles, and the rounded chancel or apse appear to be Norman; but tall, narrow entrances, and flints laid in herringbone pattern, revealed when external plaster was removed in 1882, suggest a date about 1000.

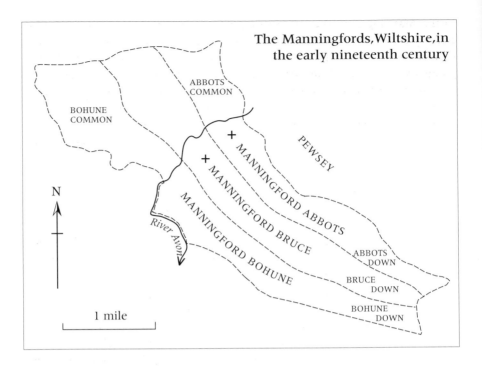

The Manningfords, Wiltshire, in the early nineteenth century

thin manors of six and a half and three and a half hides. The king appears to have made the division, because before 1066 he had the lordship of one of the townships and had granted the other to a servant. The western-most township passed shortly after 1086 to Maud and Humphrey Bohun; the middle strip eventually passed to William de Breuse in 1275 and about that time these two place-names also became fixed.

In 1291 there were two parishes, Manningford Bruce and Manningford Abbots; they were combined in 1926. The two parishes formed one civil administrative unit or vill in 1334. Manningford Bohune was a separate vill. At one time all three townships had a church. St Peter's in Manningford Bruce may once have been the church for the whole area. Not only was it central, and has stylistic features possibly of the tenth century, but church and rectory house are close to a Roman villa site and the ford is in the parish. Manningford Bohune had a church with a large amount of glebe in the early twelfth century, but it lost parochial independence: the Bohun family, created Earls of Hereford in 1200, held the adjacent estate of Wilsford and made Manningford Bohune a chapel in Wilsford parish, absorbing the glebeland themselves. Six hundred and fifty years later, in 1859, a chapel was built on Manningford Bohune common. The township and parish maintained its separate boundaries until 1939 and then the southern half was united with the other two Manningfords, nearly re-creating the early Manningford estate. The Manningfords show how parishes reflected township and manorial divisions, though not every one established its independence.

On the other hand, an interesting set of places sharing a common name in the valley of the River Piddle or Puddle in Dorset may show the opposite process to the Manningfords; the name appears to have related to a possibly tenth-century administrative district drawing together the valley's townships, rather than an earlier estate which was broken up. This would be comparable with the gradual snowballing of smaller territories into larger regions and lathes which is Alan Everitt's view of Kentish administrative development. The Piddle valley stretches about ten miles from Piddletrenthide at the source to Turner's Puddle on the lower reaches. Townships generally reached across the valley from hillside to hillside and appear to have been ancient; the folded chalk downlands and narrow valleys have many signs of dense pre-Roman occupation, while 'the Saxons came so late to Dorset that it cannot have been they who created the complex arrangements of estates and land units which covered the county by the ninth century'.[6] The relationships between townships, manors, parishes and place-names were complicated.

There were thirteen Domesday Book entries for 'Piddle' or alternative spellings, and only two 'surnames': Affpuddle, and Little Piddle. Later there were twelve vills and eleven churches, but in 1291 only five parishes and in 1535 eight, six with Piddle or Puddle in their name. Puddletown parish, over 8000 acres and much the largest in the valley, comprised the estates of several Domesday holders as well as of the king. Piddletrenthide parish, 4500 acres, contained three tithings and fitted to the framework of manorial ownership as did Piddlehinton, under 3000 acres. Affpuddle parish, 5000 acres, included the township or tithing of Bryant's Puddle. Burleston, Tolpuddle and Turner's Puddle were all long, thin strips of land forming parishes of less than 1000 acres

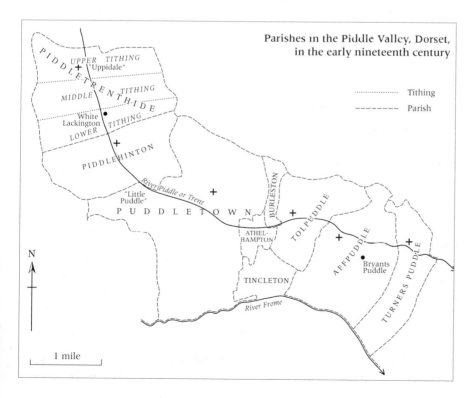

Parishes in the Piddle Valley, Dorset, in the early nineteenth century

.... Tithing
— — — — Parish

which corresponded with Domesday holdings. Aethelhampton was a tiny parish of only 290 acres. Of these four very small parishes, only Tolpuddle was independent in 1291. Puddletown is central to the area, and was the king's estate in 1086, the *villa regalis* and head of a hundred; this was Hardy's Weatherbury in *Far from the Madding Crowd*. Puddletown parish contained four vills but six tithings. This church was the only one in the valley recorded in 1086. Puddletown appears from Domesday to have been a new town which had drawn on the lands of six surrounding townships to provide the king with an extensive block of arable land. It can hardly be coincidence that four of the six townships have deserted villages and Aethelhampton has just one large house close to Puddletown, and appears likely to have been the royal manor house.[7]

Several estates in the Piddle valley had been conveyed to the church in the tenth century, and charters name some townships. In 934, Burleston and Little Piddle were given to Milton abbey. Both were later tithings in Puddletown parish. But Burleston in Domesday Book was identified simply as 'Piddle'. It remained a separate vill. Little Piddle was a vill, a small part of which was conveyed to Milton abbey; there were two larger parts, both identified in Domesday as Little Piddle. Another estate, 'Uppiddle', was transferred to Shaftesbury abbey in 966. The boundaries of Uppiddle show that it was at the head of the valley, as its name suggests; this township did not continue as a separate vill but by 1086 had been joined into a larger estate which became

Piddlehinton, Dorset - St Mary's church is in one of the larger parishes in the Piddle valley. After the estate was confiscated from the French monastery which held it in 1086, it was given in 1442 to Eton College; the tower, the oldest part of the church, was built soon after and is similar in style to Affpuddle's, built about 1462.

known as Piddletrenthide and was held by St Peter's, Winchester. Estate and parish were made up of three tithings but two former manors, one called White Lackington. The name Piddletrenthide has obscured the earlier township names. It could have two origins; in 1212 it was recorded as *Pidele Trentehydes*, and in 1314 as *Pudele thrittyhide*. The fact that the tax assessment was thirty hides appears to explain it; other names were formed in this way, like the several Fifields which were originally 'Five hides'. But 'Hyde' may alternatively refer to Hyde abbey, as the New Minster at Winchester became, and 'Trent' may have been another name for the Piddle river; Leland when he crossed the bridge at Wareham called it the Trent *alias* 'Pyddildour'. 'Dour' is also a river name.

Two more Piddle estates transferred to the church became identified by the name of their last lay owner. Aethelmaer, a man with ducal powers in Dorset, founded Cerne abbey in 987, and with his wife Aeffa, or Aelfridus in full, endowed it with a Piddle estate. By the time of Domesday *Affapidele* was the recognised name. The parish also included Bryant's Puddle, held by one of the king's thegns. This 'surname' changed with each change of lay owner. It was *Prestepidel* about 1100, reflecting the fact that it was held by Godric the priest in 1086; between 1238 and 1334 it was Piddle Turberville, from a different owner, and had become Bryant's Puddle by 1465. Tolpuddle, famous because of the early nineteenth century labourers who were punished for swearing an oath to band together for the improvement of their working conditions and pay, acquired its prefix soon after 1086; just before 1066 Tole, the widow of Urk, had transferred the estate to the newly founded abbey of St Peter's, Abbotsbury. Piddlehinton was also a monastic estate before 1086, and this name referred to the *ton* of a religious community.

Other Dorset parishes sharing a name may have originated in the same way. There were three Winterborne parishes which together comprised eight townships along a tributary stream of the Stour. Their nearly parallel boundaries stretched across the valley on both sides of the river, marked by continuous hedges which suggests that they were early. The 'surname' of two of the parishes is the name of the township with the church: Winterborne Stickland, the northernmost, contained Stickland and one other township; Winterborne Clenston, in the middle, contained two townships besides Clenston; while Whitchurch, the southernmost parish, also contained two other townships.[8] 'Winterborne' was the Domesday name for all the estates and before 1086 nine were held by the count of Mortain. Winterborne Whitchurch, like Puddletown, appears as a later focus for the valley, while the other seven townships were all gradually deserted.

After administrative districts had been built up by increasingly powerful and sophisticated Anglo-Saxon kings, they were subject to a contrary process of fission into manors and small free estates owing military service to the king, and encouraging more intensive cultivation of the land. A surge of surviving written material for the tenth century, wills, leases, grants of land, may give a misleading impression of how many new units were being created; some like the three Manningfords were perhaps new, but others were much older townships. Parish names have obscured the townships from which they were created.

CELTIC SAINTS AND PARISH NAMES

To an unusual extent, Cornish parishes are known by the name of the saint to which the church is dedicated, not by the name of the township in which the church was situated. In the 1334 Lay Subsidy, a hundred parishes, well over half, were known by their saint. One third, mainly in east Cornwall where Anglo-Saxon influence was stronger, are saints 'universal' throughout the western church, like Peter or Michael or Mary; but even more unusually, two-thirds are Celtic. In Cornwall, 'The candle lit by the early saints still burns'. Most of these Celtic saints are known also in Wales and Brittany, but some are unique to Cornwall, like St Ewe, St Just and St Ladock, who were recorded in an early tenth century manuscript with another thirty of known Cornish significance. Even where a modern place-name does not include 'St', it may refer to one, as in Gerrans, Phillack, Philleigh and Probus, originally 'St Gerent', 'St Felec', St Filii' and 'St Propus'; these four names are also recorded in the tenth century. So general were place-names based on saints that a few were popularly invented, like St Murther to explain Merther, 'place with relics', or St Dennis to explain a name probably originally *dinas*, hill-fort.[9]

There are strong links with Brittany, with Wales and indirectly with Ireland in the early history of the Christian church in Cornwall.[10] Migration from Cornwall to Brittany had begun probably in the fourth century and missionaries travelled backwards and forwards in the following centuries. Missionaries from Wales came to Cornwall in the late fifth and sixth centuries; some may earlier have come from Ireland, as suggested by memorial stones in Irish 'ogam' script. There are hints of these links in the few surviving lives of early Cornish saints. St Winwaloe lived about the end of the fifth century, but the story of his life was written four centuries later. He was said to have been born in Brittany and is patron of the church of Landevenneck; he came to Cornwall and four churches are dedicated to him: St Winnow on the River Fowey, Landewednack on the east side of the Lizard peninsula and the chapel of Gunwalloe on the west side, and the chapel of Towednack on the Lands End peninsula. A 'pet' form of his name was To-Winnoc. He is supposed to have founded fifty churches and two monasteries.

A second saint, Samson, whose Life was probably written in the early seventh century, was a Welsh nobleman's son from Dyfed who became a monk and then a bishop in the early sixth century. He travelled to Cornwall, where the church of Golant is dedicated to him, and he visted the monastery of Docco, in the present parish of St Kew; Docco or Doghow was at one time associated with Kew in the dedication of the church, and the nearby farm called Lanow preserves the name of the *lann* or enclosure of Doghow. Samson then went to Brittany where he founded the monastery at Dol. There was also a story about the missionary activity of men and women called sons and daughters of King Broccan; Broccan was said to have spent many years in Ireland but his name is perpetuated in Breconshire. One of the sons was St Nectan; two Cornish chapels are dedicated to him and the church in Hartland in Devon, where the surviving fourteenth-century copy of his Life was made which tells the story of Broccan's children. Eleven Cornish parish churches are dedicated to 'sons and daughters', mainly in the north-east of the county, and a Welsh version of the legend adds two more. These stories suggest a significant number of churches were founded in Cornwall at a period when Anglo-Saxons were still fighting for control of parts of England and before they had accepted Christianity.

Naturally early Celtic missionaries came to Cornwall by sea, and found sheltered sites by harbours and river estuaries along the long rocky coast where they established a settlement within an enclosure or *lann*, as at Landewednack. There may have been a need to provide for defence and for quick escape from hostile inhabitants. Nearly two thirds of the churches to which the word *lann* has been applied in the past are near navigable water and sometimes missionaries took over existing burial grounds. *Lann* is probably a good indication of an early church as the word went out of use before the eleventh century and 'quite possibly a good deal earlier'. It has been found referring to about fifty church sites, mainly in east and mid-Cornwall, and sixteen parishes retain this element in their name, like the former county town of Launceston, the *lann Steffen*, to which *ton* has been added. Excavations at two chapels, Lanvean in St Mawgan in Pydar and Helland in Mabe (*hen-lann* meaning old lann), demonstrated that both were early religious sites; Helland was disused before the Norman Conquest. About fifty more place-names which contain *lann*, like Lanow in St Kew, no longer appear to refer to a church. Apart from dedications, the use of this word is the commonest evidence for an early Cornish church, though the enclosure was not necessarily a monastery as later understood.

Cornwall was the last part of England to be conquered and colonised by Anglo-Saxons. Their progress across the south was halted in the seventh century and not resumed again for a hundred years, and later penetration was slow and largely confined to the east and north. Between 815 and 838 the king of Wessex subdued the Cornish, and one consequence was that their bishop was forced to submit to the authority of the archbishop of Canterbury; the bishopric was amalgamated with Devon's from the early eleventh century. Fully effective English rule dated from 936 when Athelstan suppressed a rebellion and established the Tamar as the county boundary. Parishes were probably organised following Athelstan's conquest.[11] The tenth-century list of saints may support this, because many names were ordered as if on a journey round their parishes and the list could have been written to record these significant saints out of a 'myriad' of Cornish religious sites. For example, there were three times as many chapels as there were parish churches before the Reformation, and many were dedicated to Celtic saints. There were also many burial grounds which became disused as parish churches established their monopoly of burials. A few dedications to Celtic saints were replaced by the Anglo-Saxons, like the church of St Kew which is now dedicated to St James, but the survival of so many ancient Cornish names shows how well-established the churches were. The names survived also because the Cornish language was

Gunwalloe, Cornwall - the chapel of St Winwaloe is nearly on the beach on the west side of the Lizard peninsula and in the parish of Breage. It is probably dedicated to the same late fifth-century missionary as Landewednack near the tip of the Lizard. The separate tower built into the rock is older than the main church.

St Just in Roseland, Cornwall - the church of St Just and St Mawes is on the west side of the Roseland peninsula, and close to St Just Pool, a bay in Carrick Roads. Near the church is St Just Well, a spring from which the water for baptisms was drawn, for the nearby rectory house and probably for boats anchored in the Pool.

a living one until the late eighteenth century; the last sermon preached in Cornish was said to be at Landewednack near the tip of the Lizard peninsula in 1670 and Cornish was spoken longest in the farthest south-west.

The regular pattern of Cornish parishes suggests they were organised by an overlord. They may have matched Anglo-Saxon and Norman manorial organisation, but particularly in west Cornwall the saints' churches were not side by side with the manor house as they were in some parts of England. For example, the deserted site of Tybesta, a Duchy manor, was some distance from the parish church of Creed - St Crida was named in the tenth-century list - and from the market borough of Grampound founded by a Norman lord in the same parish. Similarly, the bishop of Exeter's manor of Tregaire covered the Roseland peninsula, but was remote from the two Roseland parish churches of St Just and Gerrens, also established by the tenth century. There were no outstandingly large parishes which might have been early 'minsters', except possibly St Stephen's, Launceston, which significantly is close to the Tamar in the Anglicised part of Cornwall. The average parish size based on 161 churches in the *Valor Ecclesiasticus* was eight square miles and seven square miles in Devon, a little larger than in other parts of southern England.[12]

Cornish parishes typically contain many small and scattered hamlets; moreover at least 750 medieval settlements are now deserted.[13] In five parishes covering three Duchy manors, there were fifty-seven places named in the fourteenth century and 203 messuages or houses, half of which were in small groups of two, three or four. Nucleated villages were unusual, and the Normans were responsible for founding seven or eight of the market towns, doubling the number which probably existed. Over much of Cornwall settlement names typically begin with *tre*, comparable with the Welsh *tref*, 'estate, farmstead', but in Anglicised areas apparently replaced by *ton*. Such dispersed settlements were well-served by many small chapels, and perhaps there had once been an attempt to provide a chapel to every four farmsteads; Padstow and St Merryn parishes, for example, contain twenty-seven *tre* place-names, four churches and a number of chapels, and the Roseland parishes of St Just and Gerrens contain sixteen *tre* places and two chapels, St Mawes and St Anthony. The older pattern of many small Christian sites brought religion in Cornwall close to where people lived, but the parish churches provided a thin network and by the early nineteenth century, as population and industrial centres grew, it gave scope for an explosion of Methodism.[14]

PATTERNS ON THE MAP

It is intriguing to notice patterns in parish boundaries: the set of spokes radiating from the crossroads called 'Six Hills' on the Fosse Way in Leicestershire, for example, or from Dunsmore Common in Warwickshire further south along the same Roman road, or the circle of parishes surrounding North Walsham in Norfolk, or the series of narrow strips laid out across a river valley like the Avon, the Piddle or the Winterborne in Dorset, or the ladder of near-rectangles on either side of High Dyke, the Roman road running north from Lincoln. These examples suggest a sweeping authority able to partition the countryside systematically. Because parishes were structured on the more ancient patchwork of townships, they have fossilised this pattern. Less regular patterns of parishes can also reveal something about the story of parish formation.

There are two markedly different patterns of parishes in Kent. The contrast is not between Canterbury and Rochester dioceses, or between East and West Kent, but between what Everitt termed the 'Original Lands' or the 'old arable lands', and the Weald. The areas of earliest settlement and greatest fertility were

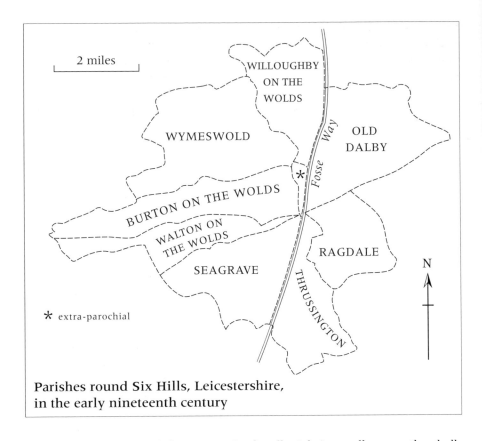

Parishes round Six Hills, Leicestershire, in the early nineteenth century

in the north and east of the county, in the alluvial river valleys, on the chalk Downs, and along their narrow southern border of greensand. This region was crossed by the Pilgrim's Way and Roman Watling Street which went from London to Canterbury, and then to Richborough or Dover. Settlements were focused on the rivers: Medway, Darent, Cray, Great and Little Stour, Swale and Rother. The Original Lands were quite intensively cultivated by 1086. Most parishes were small; about 300 averaged 1570 acres, but sixty parishes of superior or minster churches averaged 4000 acres. The pattern of parish boundaries was often intricate and untidy. In contrast, the clay-capped Weald in the south-west was thickly wooded and thinly populated, the average size of fifty-two parishes was 4500 acres, and many were rather larger. Here parish boundaries were simpler and comprised coherent geographical blocks of land.[15]

Kent had a continuous Christian tradition from the time of Augustine's arrival in 597, and in the 'Original Lands' the case for continuity is strong between the Romans and the Jutes, the particular Anglo-Saxon invaders of Kent. King Ethelbert's Frankish wife, Bertha, who was a Christian, was allowed to worship in a church on the east side of Canterbury which Bede said was a Roman building. It is outside the Roman walls of Canterbury and is dedicated to St Martin, a saint of particular significance to the Frankish kings. Bede also said King Ethelbert 'recovered' a Roman church for Augustine's cathedral. About fifteen early important churches in Kent can be identified in addition to the two cathedrals, and all were in the 'Original Lands. They were sited on royal estates, close to or on the sites of Roman buildings, and near major Roman roads or the Pilgrims' Way. Archaeological evidence also supports Romano-Jutish continuity; 'Roman brickwork and parts of Roman structures are incorporated in perhaps more parish churches in Kent than in any other county'. At the same time, there was continuity with pagan sites; Pope Gregory wrote to Augustine to tell him

> what I have decided after long deliberation about the English people, namely that the idol temples of that race should by no means be destroyed, but only the idols in them ... it is essential that they should be changed from the worship of devils to the service of the true God.

Denser settlement, surviving early churches and many small freemen's estates all will have contributed to the pattern of parishes in this part of Kent. A group of ten parishes around Faversham, mostly very small, strikingly illustrate the intricate arrangements which occured in the 'Original Lands'.[16] There was an extraordinary interlocking of parish boundaries, with detached parts in some instances traceable to grants of land in the district or *regio* of Faversham to the archbishop of Canterbury or to the chapter of the cathedral of Christ Church during the ninth century, when it appears that common marshland pastures were being divided into separately-owned blocks. Faversham is near the north coast of Kent on the River Swale, and separated from the Thames estuary by the Isle of Sheppey; a harbour is near and there are extensive riverside marshes. The area, intersected by Watling Street, was intensively settled in the Roman period. Faversham seems to have been named from the Latin *faber*, or smith, and evidence of Roman iron working has been found. The church is sited on or near a Roman building; when the tower collapsed in 1755, it revealed many reused Roman bricks. In the immediate neighbourhood there are also many signs of Roman occupation: the ruined church of Stone incorporates part of a Roman mausoleum and Stone and Preston churches were both sited close to Watling Street; there is a Roman site in Buckland; Ospringe had a Roman cemetery and late Iron Age pottery; and evidence of Roman cremations has been found in both Oare and Graveney. Davington is situated on the pre-Roman trackway to the north of and parallel with Watling Street.

Ospringe was the largest of the ten parishes, nearly 3000 acres, and was the head of the deanery.[17] The place-name may possibly be Celtic, or be related to a word meaning 'god'. At one time the church had a round tower. Faversham parish was 2270 acres, and consisted of the borough, stretching between the creek and Watling Street, and five separate portions of land. Buckland was 1340 acres. The place-name indicates it was an estate originating in a royal charter or 'book'. Most Kentish parish churches of the eleventh century have been categorised by Everitt as 'bookland churches', founded on small private estates of which Buckland next Faversham is typical. They were particularly common in the Downland areas and had parishes averaging 1570 acres or two

Preston next Wingham, Kent - St Mildred's church shows Saxon workmanship in the nave and the lower part of the tower, and the dormer windows may date from before 1300. Preston, a 'priest's town', was recorded in Domesday Book; the manor belonged to St Augustine's abbey, but the dedication suggests it had once belonged to Minster in Thanet where Mildred was abbess. There was a passage across the Wantsum channel to the small port of Stourmouth nearby. The church was recorded about 1100.

and a half square miles. The other eight parishes around Faversham were very small; six were under 1000 acres and Goodnestone was only 140 acres. Graveney had three isolated fields and one larger piece of ground, all separated from the main part of the parish, and these had probably resulted from royal grants to the archbishop in 812. Preston parish also included two detached portions.

Eight of the ten parish names in the Faversham area were in Domesday Book, and churches were mentioned at Preston, Luddenham, Oare (one and a half churches), and Norton (three churches which might well have included the unnamed Davington and Stone). Four and perhaps five appear to have been typical bookland estates, but since 1066 had become part of the vast interest of Odo bishop of Bayeux. There was no mention of a church at Faversham although, apart from his controlling position in the boroughs of Dover and Canterbury, it was one of only four royal vills in Kent which the king kept in his own hands in 1086. The others were Aylesford, Dartford and Milton.

Preston is particularly interesting. Hasted noted that Preston manor extended into the parishes of Davington, Luddenham, Stone and Buckland, emphasising how the parishes did not correspond with manorial structure.[18] St Catherine's church, Preston, was within Faversham borough, in a rectangular section of Roman streets resembling a city 'ward'. The parish included a detached block of marsh or 'Hamme' north of the Faversham creek which had been sold to the archbishop of Canterbury in 815, and another block of land

1. Cutsdean, Gloucestershire - called a 'little vill' when it was transferred to Bredon minster church in 780, it gives an insight into a medieval village: four farmhouses round a pasture ground on a slope above the 'dean' or valley which helped to identify it, and surrounded by arable fields and pastures which were farmed in a shared system until divided by enclosure act in 1777.

2. The church of St James is approached through Manor Farm yard. The tower is medieval; the rest of the church was rebuilt in 1863, but the site is probably ancient as Domesday Book recorded a priest here. Cutsdean rectory was annexed to Bredon as a result of arrangements made in the eighth century. The small building on the left is said to be where the rector put his trap after driving over to take Sunday service.

3. Escomb, County Durham - the church has no known dedication. It was built before 800 and suggests Irish influence. It has a round churchyard and was built with stone from the Binchester Roman fort; two original windows are visible high up in the south wall, and the walls taper. When first recorded it was a chapel of Auckland. Local initiative saved it in 1863 when a new parish church was built; in 1970, it was restored as the parish church.

4. The Heath, Shropshire - the chapel is in the parish of Stoke St Milburgh. The pilasters or thin buttresses suggest that it was built before 1066, but the decorated, round-arched south doorway is typical Norman period. It was not altered as parish churches were: no aisle was added, the chancel was not lengthened, large windows were not inserted, though some small ones were cut through the central pilasters at east and west ends, and no tower was built.

south of Watling Street containing the manor of Copton, conveyed to the archbishop in 821. It is surprising that Preston church was not dependent on Faversham, but its early status is suggested by the place-name whch means the 'priest's town', and the land in the 'Hamme' was said in 875 to be adjacent to 'land of the brotherhood belonging to Preston', a reference to a religious community of some sort. Copton and land south of Watling Street became known as South Preston, and the Hamme as North Preston, which in the later nineteenth century became the parish of the Brents after a benefactor built a church and vicarage to serve the growing population of brick-makers.

The contrast of the Faversham area with Wealden parishes is marked. No early minster churches appear to have been established in the Weald unless Tonbridge was one, and there are no early Anglo-Saxon place-names.[19] As its name implies, the Weald was a forest, *Andredsweald*, covering a folded landscape of small hills and valleys. The soil was so wet that in winter roads were impassable because of mud, and in summer the ruts were baked and dusty; such complaints were common until the dramatic improvement in road surfaces in the nineteenth century. In the seventh century it was the preserve of herdsmen and pigs and was heavily wooded still in 1086. More than a hundred manors situated in the north and east of Kent had their particular 'dens' within the Weald, special areas where their pigs fed in the autumn on the oak and beech mast.[20] There were at least 700 dens; 130 are named in pre-Conquest charters, and it is possible to locate a large number of these. For example, the men of Ospringe had a den fifteen miles away at Tilden, in Headcorn parish, and a droveway can still be traced linking the two. The forest was penetrated by numerous droveways from the earlier-settled and more tractable lands, and it has been estimated that perhaps 60,000 swine enjoyed the seven weeks of the pannage season which finished at the feast of St Martin on 11 November. Pigs feeding under an oak tree are carved on a misericord appropriate to October and November in the church at Ashford, on the edge of the Weald.

The exploitation of *Andredsweald* was surprisingly regulated; manors had dens according to a geographical rationale: the manors furthest west, for example, had the westernmost part of the forest. Consequently the Weald was divided between the dioceses of Rochester and Canterbury. The men of Rochester, the *Caestrewara*, had rights in the northern parts of the forest and the men of Canterbury, the *Burgwara*, had rights in the south. Dens gradually became permanent settlements, the origin of a pattern of dispersed farmsteads rather than village clusters; Hasted frequently noted that Wealden parishes were collections of hamlets built round greens or forstalls, and in the 5400 acres of Smarden parish there are still sixty-two separately named farmsteads on the Ordnance Survey map. Wealden settlers were freeholders owing only tenuous loyalty to distant lords of the manor, hence later the large number of 'yeomen' farmers.

A tidy system of parishes was imposed over the fragmented pattern of settlement, manorial claims and administrative hundreds. Parish names like Tenterden, Biddenden, Bethersden, and Benenden, show that the church in a particular den became the focus of a parish. Tenterden, the den for the men of Thanet some forty miles away, has a church dedicated to St Mildred, one of the royal saints associated with Minster in Thanet, and this could be one of the earlier churches in the Weald; it has been suggested that it was founded before the Minster community was destroyed in 840 by Danish raids, or the dedication could be a later reflection of the connection. Parishes could not be based on manorial claims. For example, eight dens belonging to Little Chart, named in a charter of 843, formed a chain of pastures leading westwards from the parent manor deep into the Weald; they became parts of the parishes of Pluckley, Smarden, Biddenden, Bethersden and Cranbrook, and a den called *Hilgaringden* was divided between three parishes.[21] Wealden parishes were replete with many overlapping jurisdictions which show their synthetic nature; Headcorn was divided between five hundreds and two of the larger administrative subdivisions of Kent, the lathes.

Cranbrook dominated communications throughout the eastern Weald; it was on the road from Rochester through Maidstone to Hastings, and close to the junction of four of the main droves which came into the forest. It was also an administrative centre for a large hundred. Cranbrook church was dedicated to St Dunstan, the late tenth-century archbishop of Canterbury, one of only three such dedications in Kent. Because of its strategic position, Cranbrook could have been founded as a superior church for part of the Weald. Tonbridge similarly dominated an important road from London, where there was a bridge over the Medway and the parish extended on both sides of the river. The larger and better-known Tunbridge Wells grew up much later on the south-west boundary of Tonbridge; Hasted said that the chapel of King Charles the Martyr stood 'remarkably in three parishes': the altar was in Tonbridge, the pulpit in Speldhurst and the vestry in Fant in Sussex. Tonbridge's name is unusual in placing ton before 'bridge', making it probable that it was an early royal manor controlling the important bridge, and the church is dedicated to St Peter and St Paul, also a hint of an early foundation.[22] A church here would have been convenient for eminent travellers.

Tonbridge was the largest parish in Kent; in the nineteenth century it was nearly 15,000 acres or twenty-three square miles, and had formerly been more extensive, including the parishes of Bidborough and Leigh. The parish included many of the dens attached to Wrotham manor, the archbishop of Canterbury's major estate in Rochester diocese, so king and archbishop had cooperated in founding an important church for that part of the Weald. Tonbridge saw Harold's soldiers march southwards in October 1066 and, soon after, the victorious Normans march northwards. It was only incidentally recorded in Domesday Book, but William I had placed a trusted Norman companion there, Richard de Clare, who built a castle from which he controlled the 'Lowy', an area more extensive than the parish, consisting of numerous dens belonging to twenty-four different manors; it served to reduce the power of the Saxon bishop of Rochester, while Richard de Clare and the Norman archbishop of Canterbury formed a partnership for the control of Kent.[23]

Domesday Book recorded 'pannage', a due collected by lords of manors for pasturing a herd of ten pigs, but dens were rarely named; the only hint of Little Chart's dens was the terse statement that there was 'pannage for 35 pigs'. Correspondingly, many places in the Weald were not mentioned. Five churches were recorded out of the twenty-four in the deanery of Charing in 1291, which covered mainly Wealden parishes, and there was no mention of Tenterden nor of six other 'den' parish names, nor of Cranbrook, Headcorn, Hothfield and Sandhurst; seventeen places and seven churches were noted out of twenty-seven in the Rochester deanery of Malling. Occasional references to fourteen hundreds show that the Weald had been divided administratively, but it would appear largely unpopulated if it were not for lists of churches preserved amongst the archives of Rochester and Canterbury cathedrals and St Augustine's abbey, in the *Textus Roffensis*, the *Domesday Monachorum*, and the *White Book*. They were apparently made close in time to the Domesday survey, probably at the behest of the Norman archbishop Lanfranc, but based on Anglo-Saxon records. Approximately 300 churches were named, not every one definitely identified with a modern place-name, compared with 186 churches known from Domesday Book.[24] All twenty-four churches in Charing deanery were recorded and two more in addition, and twenty-six out of twenty-seven in Malling deanery; Tonbridge was listed first in the Rochester list, showing its importance. The Kentish parochial system was already largely formed; there were 353 parish churches in the *Pope Nicholas Taxation*, and 414 in Hasted's *History of Kent* published at the end of the eighteenth century.

Wealden churches often stood isolated from settlement, as at Horsmonden, East Peckham, Pembury and Sandhurst they still do. They were sited to be convenient for a group of dens. A hilltop was common, perhaps chosen to be visible amongst the trees. The church towers at Goudhurst, Cranbrook, Hawkhurst, Rolvenden and Tenterden were all sites for Armada beacons. Furley wrote in 1874 that

Stone in Oxney, Kent - the former vicarage is a typical 'Wealden' house. Although this Stone was not mentioned in Domesday Book, St Mary's church was in the 'White Book' of St Augustine's abbey, and the monastery agreed to build a house for the vicar in 1347; the church was rebuilt after a fire in 1464, and possibly this house also dates from then. Plentiful oak and considerable prosperity encouraged the building of many houses like this in the Weald.

The one at Tenterden was long preserved; it hung at the end of a piece of timber eight feet long, placed at the top of the church. It resembled an iron kettle, and held about a gallon, with an iron ring, or hoop, at the upper part, to hold more coal, resin etc.[25]

Other Wealden churches like Tonbridge, Bethersden, Headcorn, Leigh, Penshurst, Marden and Staplehurst were sited at river crossings, or, like Cranbrook, Rolvenden and Benenden, on droveways. Villages were later settlements, either planned near the church, or attracted to it by the opportunity for trade at the Sunday gathering. The de Clares had a market adjacent to their castle in Tonbridge before 1100, there were shops in the high road at Tenterden close to the church, markets at Edenbridge, Headcorn, Brenchley, Marden and Cranbrook were encouraged with charters and in the next century at Hawkhurst, Smarden and Goudhurst. The exceptionally large churchyard at Headcorn was probably the market place, with a regular set of house plots laid out along its sides. At Horsmonden, market development was centred on a crossroads and a highway or a river crossing had more attractive power than the church.

When were the Kentish Wealden parishes defined and by whom? A possible time was while Edgar was king of England, from 959 to 975, and Dunstan was archbishop of Canterbury, from 960 to 988. These two powerful men worked closely together. About 960, Edgar issued the ordinance which required a proportion of tithes to be paid to the old minsters. Armed with this ordinance, Dunstan would have been able to arrange support for each new church through some part of the tithes of many small free estates. The manorial situation did not obstruct a planned layout of parishes because the 'paramount' manors in the old settled lands belonged overwhelmingly to the king or to the church.[26] Wealden parishes were necessarily large, to enable rectors to collect enough tithes for their support from the small patches of arable under cultivation and from the offerings of scattered parishioners. As population grew, and prosperity was increased by cloth and iron-working, rectors and vicars had good incomes so long as offerings were regularly paid; unfortunately for the clergy, after the Reformation these payments tended to collapse.

MONASTIC REFORM OR PARISH FORMATION?

'It looks very likely that the tenth century and especially the later part of it, was the key period in parish history.'[27] Three men, with King Edgar, were important. All were men of high social position, all were monks, and all became bishops about the same time. Dunstan became archbishop of Canterbury in 960, Oswald bishop of Worcester in 961 and Aethelwold bishop of Winchester in 963. Oswald also became archbishop of York in 972, while still retaining his see of Worcester. Prior to 960, Dunstan had been abbot of Glastonbury for fifteen years, and had devoted himself to promoting a strict ideal of the monk's life. Oswald had spent some time at the monastery of Fleury in France, which was a great influence on both continental and English monasteries, and he brought Abbo of Fleury to teach in his new foundation at Ramsey in

Huntingdonshire. Aethelwold had been a monk at Glastonbury, and went as abbot to restore monastic life at Abingdon; he was later responsible for convening a council at which representatives of continental monasteries were present, which drew up a code of practice for English monastic life called the *Regularis Concordia*.

Oswald and Aethelwold promoted the reformed monastic ideals of Fleury by placing communities of monks in some English cathedrals in place of more informal groups of canons. Aethelwold created communities of monks at both the Old and New Minsters at Winchester; Oswald similarly created a monastic community at Worcester, drawing into it the powerful priest of the town's church of St Helen. Where the change was made, it created resources for worship, for scholarship and for education. The displacement of the canons was not always welcomed. They had either to become monks, or to move out, perhaps into the countryside to live near the chapels which they had previously served while members of the cathedral community. The motives behind the reform may not have been wholly monastic idealism and piety; the bishops also sought a method of separating a cathedral's two functions, that of powerful religious centre on the one hand and of provider of pastoral care within an area on the other, with the aim of encouraging religious life in the countryside. Reform also facilitated the reorganisation of a cathedral's resources, part providing a fund for the community and part for the bishop.

Parish formation may have been as much a part of the tenth-century reformers' aims as monastic reform. Archaeological and architectural evidence often points to the first stone church being of tenth or eleventh century date. The development of a parochial system meant founding and funding many modest-sized churches, each with its own priest. Just as Dunstan had immersed himself in monastic life while he was an abbot, so as archbishop he seems to have taken on the responsibilities of that position. His first biographer, himself a monk, concentrated on his early monastic reform at Glastonbury, and on his personal piety, while saying little about his work as archbishop of Canterbury. Dunstan was no doubt often occupied with attending royal councils; but a pastoral concern was hinted at by the brief mention of how he founded and endowed new churches and 'was indefatigable in the work of instruction, gathering young and old, men and women, clerk, monk and lay, to listen to his teaching ... and thus all this English land was filled with his holy doctrine, shining before God and men like the sun and moon'.[28]

Bishop Aethelwold may have been responsible for creating a compact block of twenty parishes in the countryside around Winchester, perhaps the 'territory' of the Roman town. Sixteen of the churches were recorded in Domesday Book and it is suggested that the other four were also in existence, all twenty representing 'a once-and-for-all systematic foundation of churches' in all the settlements of Winchester's *parochia* in the late tenth century.[29] Not all were of equal status; in 1291 several were chapels. The twenty parishes were mostly small, especially those close to the River Itchen. Their tidy and generally compact nature contrasts with the more usual Wessex situation where 'the later parochial system is nothing but a mass of complex anomalies and illogicalities' with a few very large parishes, and many with detached parts separate and distant from the main part of the parish. As Winchester was the capital city of the kings of Wessex, who had made themselves kings of all England, Aethelwold's work in the region would have demonstrated royal policy towards the creation of a small-scale parochial system.

When Oswald became bishop of Worcester he was hindered from creating independent parishes through the strongly entrenched position of St Helen's church, which remained in control of most of its chapels. But after he became archbishop of York he may have created parishes in the archbishop's Wessex manor of Mottisfont in Hampshire; there were seven churches in 1086, of which six were chapels with full parochial rights of baptism and burial, and later there were ten churches, so that again almost all settlements had one. But Oswald's main contribution seems to have been in the county of Huntingdon, outside his episcopal jurisdiction.[30] It was a small county, recaptured from the Vikings by the Wessex king Edward early in the century, and drawing Huntingdonshire into the diocese centred on Dorchester on Thames. Oswald, of Danish descent, came from the Fenland. Here there was a more regular manorial framework than faced Dunstan in the Kentish Weald. He founded Ramsey abbey about 969 in cooperation with Ealdorman Aethelwine, whose family were prominent landholders, and was nominally abbot for twenty-four years. His personal connections secured further lands for the foundation. By 1086 Ramsey was the tenth richest monastery in the country, with an annual income of £358; the abbot of Ramsey held twenty-four manors and had authority almost equivalent to a bishop. During the same period, bishop Aethelwold was active in re-establishing monastic life at Ely and Peterborough; he also founded a monastery at Thorney, and assisted a relative of Oswald's in founding Crowland. In 1086 Ely was the second richest monastery in the country with an income of £769 and Peterborough was eleventh with £323; Thorney and Crowland each had incomes of only a little over £50.

The co-operation and large family interests of Ealdorman Aethelwine assisted Oswald in what seems to have been a comprehensive organisation of parishes carried out in step with the foundation of Ramsey abbey. In 1086, there were fifteen churches on the abbey's estates; on the less numerous Thorney estates there were six churches. Although it had been part of the Danelaw, Huntingdonshire had an insignificant number of freemen in 1086, but a high percentage of ecclesiastical manors. Domesday Book records a church and priest in fifty-three out of eighty-three places, representing nearly two-thirds of the late thirteenth-century total. The average size of parishes in Huntingdonshire in 1291 was relatively small, 3000 acres or four and a half square miles, though Ramsey's parish was much larger, nearly 18,000 acres.

If Dunstan was responsible for creating a parish structure in the Weald of Kent, and for giving impetus to the creation of parishes elsewhere, the appointment of Aelfgar, one of his personal assistants or chaplains, as bishop of Elmham in 1001 would probably have furthered the process of parish formation in East Anglia. There were social ties between Kent and East Anglia, and respect for the archbishop is illustrated by two substantial bequests to his church either during Dunstan's lifetime or shortly afterwards; between 961 and 995 Aethelric willed Bocking in Essex to the cathedral monastery of Christ Church, and Hadleigh and Monk's Eleigh in Suffolk were given by Brihtnoth in 991.[31] These estates thereafter formed a Canterbury 'peculiar' outside the jurisdiction of the bishop of East Anglia.

A LANDSCAPE FULL OF CHURCHES

The landscape of Norfolk and Suffolk is still thickly studded with churches, and in the past was even more so; there are still at least 1000 medieval parish churches. When Bishop Suffield of Norwich surveyed his diocese in 1256, he noted 782 benefices in Norfolk, more than in the *Pope Nicholas Taxation*, making the average parish size a little over two square miles (1500 acres), the smallest in the country. In Suffolk, he recorded 484 churches.[32] The medieval diocese of Norwich, therefore, covered nearly 1300 parishes, one seventh of the number in the whole country. The social structure of East Anglia was in very great contrast with a county like Gloucestershire where there were almost no freemen except lords of the manors, and was an important reason for the emergence of an exceptionally large number of parishes, which in turn partly explains why many simple early churches survived without substantial later rebuilding.

A large number of churches were recorded in Domesday. In Suffolk there were perhaps as many as 436 churches, located in 345 villages and seven towns, and some 639 places were named. It appears that in Suffolk an uniquely full census of churches was made, with a note of the amount of each church's glebeland. The commissioners' treatment of churches across the country was by no means uniform; it may have been accidental that they chose to collect comprehensive information in Suffolk or it may indicate that special circumstances relevant to the Inquest made it appear necessary. Norfolk, larger

Little Snoring, Norfolk - The tower of St Andrew's church was originally joined to the nave; the conical roof was added about 1800. Domesday Book recorded two freeholders with a church here, so the tower is potentially Anglo-Saxon. The church is away from the village, and supports John Betjeman's view of Norfolk as 'a fleet of churches on undulating pasture, meadow and breck'.

though not so densely populated, had a similar history and social structure, and the Domesday survey was made by the same set of commissioners, but fewer churches were noted; one estimate is 217 rural churches (and about sixty in towns) and another is 241. There were 726 vills. No reference does not mean there was not a church, as the explicit statement 'All the churches of all Hermer's land are assessed with the manors' indicates. Thirty-five churches confirmed to St Benedict's, Holme, in 1047, were not recorded, and systematic omission seems likely in the two hundreds with only one church noted in each. Yet in Thetford thirteen and a half churches were referred to and in Norwich at least forty-nine, seven in one street (St Benedict's Street). If each church was no more than a small room the number in Norwich may not have been excessive to accommodate a population which may have exceeded 5000.[33] There are many entries like Thetford concerning fractions of a church, which make counting East Anglian Domesday churches particularly difficult. The men and women holding part of a church provided a similar proportion of the priest's income, which was the tithes from their landholdings. The fractions undoubtedly contributed to patterns of tithing 'so intricate that they resisted attempts at consolidation until the later nineteenth century'.[34]

The territorial structure of East Anglia was extremely complex by the time of the Domesday survey. Townships were frequently divided between several lords and groups of freemen, and manors did not coincide with townships.[35] Parishes reflected that complexity. In a small area six miles square round Barton Bendish, near Swaffham in south west Norfolk, there were once twenty-three churches; now there are twelve parish churches, one redundant church, the ruins of three, and seven are 'lost'. Twenty-one parish churches were recorded in 1254. Barton Bendish and Beechamwell each had three churches; several places had two; at West Dereham, two churches stood in the same churchyard. The Domesday survey of Beechamwell notes only one church associated with one substantial landholder and three freemen. At Barton Bendish to the west there were two principal landholdings before 1066, each of two carucates or ploughlands: the assets of Thorketel's holding included sheep, a church with twelve acres, and pigs; the wealthy lady Aethelgyth had a church with twenty-four acres. A church was often sandwiched between sheep and pigs as part of a manor's sources of income, and of these two, one is disused and the other demolished. The Barton Bendish church which is still in use was not recorded, but archaeological evidence suggests that it existed in the eleventh century, and in 1291 it was the best endowed of the three; there were another fifteen Domesday freemen who may have been responsible. To the west again is Fincham; here one quarter of a church was recorded but the other three quarters are not traceable, though there were many groups of freemen. Next is Stradsett, where in 1086 two churches each had thirty acres, one noted with the cob, heads of cattle, pigs and sheep, and one held jointly by thirteen freemen whose 210 acres were said to be counted as a manor. Separate returns of communicants were made in 1603 from all three churches in Barton Bendish, whose combined population was in the region of 300, and from two churches in Fincham, population also about 300. The three churches in

Beechamwell were combined in one return and had about 375 people. Stradsett had only 100.[36]

Two or even three churches sharing one churchyard epitomises such dense provision. There are 36 examples in Norfolk, three or four in Cambridge and Suffolk, and one in Essex.[37] Each parish had its priest or share of a priest and its particular tithe-paying lands. In most cases, the physical evidence of one or more of the Norfolk churches has disappeared, but survived in the eighteenth century when Blomefield and Parkin, two local rectors, were collecting historical material, and their diligence may account for the large number of known examples. At Reepham in Norfolk two churches survive, but there was once a third; Hackford church was burnt down in the sixteenth century and was never rebuilt. All were in the same churchyard and served the three parishes of Reepham, Hackford and Whitwell. The boundaries of the three parishes almost converged on the churchyard. Reepham, to the east of the church, had a neck of land linking it to its section of churchyard; Whitwell, to the south-west, had an island of churchyard quite detached from the rest of the parish; Hackford parish adjoined the west side of the churchyard. Reepham was only incidentally mentioned in Domesday, its inhabitants attached to Kerdiston, where half a church was noted and two freemen with half a priest. There was a chapel near the manor house; 'No part of it is now standing', Blomefield commented, 'being carried away at times to build and repair neighbouring houses'. The other half church was not mentioned but clearly was St Mary's, Reepham. In Whitwell, half a church was attached to one group of two freemen and the other to a second group of two freemen. No church was recorded at Hackford, although it was centrally placed in the group of four townships and became a market town. Division of a territory centred on Hackford into several separate parishes seems to have led to the shared churchyard and glebeland.

In other places in East Anglia, two churches stand close together though not actually in the same churchyard. A site may have had special significance. Two churches, St Mary's and St Martin's, stand side by side at Trimley in Suffolk, and the name Trimley probably meant 'tree-cross island', probably referring to an early wooden cross.[38] Both churches were in Domesday, one with twenty acres and the other with eight acres, strangely both attached to the same landholding. An arrangement made not long before 1086 at Thorney in Suffolk was described in Domesday Book. Four brothers, who were freemen and parishioners of the existing church, had built a chapel on their own land close to the cemetery because the mother church 'could not take in the whole of the parish'; the mother church had agreed to take half the burial fees and a quarter of the alms collected in the new church, but later disputed that it had surrendered part of its land. The church of St Mary, Thorney, is 'now no more than a scatter of rubble on the edge of Stowmarket St Peter's churchyard'. A somewhat similar situation must have existed at Fordley, whose parish church stood over a mile away from its parish on the edge of Middleton churchyard; like St Mary's, Thorney, Fordley's church is now no more than a scatter of rubble. Twenty-seven and a half freemen occupied Fordley in 1086, and shared half a priest, and half a priest belonged to Middleton, which appears to have been the original church for both communities. These examples show that Domesday fractions of a church could indicate physically distinct buildings but a shared priest.

Two factors could be relevant to the well-filled landscape of East Anglian churches. One was the relatively dense population in the eleventh century; Suffolk was the most densely populated of any English county, Norfolk was the most populous. The second and perhaps more important was the exceptional numbers of 'free men'; Lincolnshire was the only other county with comparable numbers. Freemen and sokemen accounted for between one third and a half of the Domesday population in East Anglia and Lincolnshire, but counts vary because it is not possible to know how many men held land in more than one place. The two terms used in Domesday, 'freeman' and 'sokeman', may sometimes have been interchangeable; freemen probably paid the king's taxes personally and not through a lord of the manor, and a group of freemen could be assessed collectively. There is some correspondence between the distribution of freemen and of small parishes.[39]

The origins of some groups of freemen may be in late Roman settlements. East Anglia is remarkable for the large number of place-names ending in *ham*: 77 in Norfolk, 70 in Suffolk, and there were more names ending in *ingaham*: 48 in Norfolk and 16 in Suffolk. These place-names frequently appear to indicate Roman estate centres, and at some *foederati* were settled, those north European war bands invited to protect parts of Britain from the depredations of their fellows after the Roman legions were no longer able to defend the island. Seventeen of the thirty-eight places noted by Warner with shared churchyards are places named *ham*, including Reepham. Scandinavian settlers were probably not numerous enough to have influenced the social structure extensively. In Norfolk the greatest concentration of Scandinavian place-names, in the hundred of Flegg, does not coincide with an area of notably small parishes, and in three hundreds in West Suffolk only one per cent of place-names shows Danish influence, though one in twelve personal names was Danish in the later eleventh century.[40]

Anglo-Saxon society had a number of groups which merged into each other. Freemen, or ceorls, came between the highest class of thegns or nobles and the villeins or unfree peasant farmers; below them again were the bordars or smallholders and the slaves. Thegns were men of status, with military obligations and holding at least five hides, a very substantial landholding of about 600 acres.[41] King Edgar's laws stated that a 'thegn' should have a church on his land and it was said that a ceorl with five hides of land and

church and kitchen

bellhouse and gatehouse

seat and office

in the king's hall

could call himself a thegn and claim noble status. Freemen with much less than five hides of land between them may have protected their free status by jointly becoming the patron of a church or part of a church, particularly when under

Lavenham, Suffolk - St Peter and St Paul's church is decoratively built of flint and dressed stone; the tower, 141 feet high, was started in 1486. Cloth merchants were financing magnificent churches at this period. Two benefactors were responsible in Lavenham: a famous clothier, Thomas Spring; and John de Vere, Earl of Oxford, whose ancestor already held the larger of the two manors in the parish in 1086.

pressure from tightening manorial structures. 'Many men' had given the sixty acres of land held by the church of Swanton in Norfolk. Parishes were based on men's economic relations; tenants of one lord in East Anglia worshipped in a different church from tenants of another lord or from groups of freemen. The freemen's churches were probably small wooden buildings, just large enough for them, their families, and possibly a few tenants and servants, to stand out of the wind and rain. Later generations took on the responsibility with great enthusiasm, building expensively in stone so that their churches have withstood the passage of many centuries.

As a result of the very irregular structure of landholding, each man's land, and with it the church's tithe, was 'inextricably intermixed with its neighbours and consisted of many detached fragments'. There were more than twenty small but independent holdings in some townships, and as many as thirty-three in Coddenham, Suffolk. In Norfolk, 'in many parishes there is no obvious 'village' at all, and even the church stands isolated in the midst of arable fields'. In the Suffolk landscape, the church 'focuses most of our attention and captures most of our imagination ... often solitary, away from the farmsteads, surrounded only by the fields'. In a few cases a settlement has moved away from the church, but more often, as in the Kentish Weald, the church was placed to be convenient for the scattered farmsteads, perhaps at a crossroads. In these circumstances, parishes were not compact territories; the coincidence between the names of Domesday Book vills and the names of parishes misleads. Gradually, and in a piecemeal fashion, parish boundaries were consolidated. There was also a gradual accumulation of estates and of manors in fewer men's hands which led to the decay of some settlements and of their churches; by 1650, seventy per cent of Norfolk and Suffolk townships contained only one manor and at least one hundred and thirty deserted villages are known in Norfolk.[42] Map making, and reorganisation and enclosure of the fields, made parish boundaries more precise and created some of the patterns now observed.

CHAPTER THREE

THE PATTERN
IN THE NORTH

Hope Cross in Derbyshire stands seven feet high beside the Roman road which crosses the Kinder Scout area of the Peak District. The Hope valley penetrates the Pennines deeply on the eastern side and the road ran from here to the top of the Snake Pass and then down the now disused track called Doctor's Gate to Glossop on the north-west. The faces of the square stone on the top of the monolith have Glossop on the north and Hope on the south sides and Sheffield and Edale on the east and west sides; at one time there would probably have been a head stone above and no directions. Hope Cross is about two and a half miles from Hope church, and is close to the boundary with Edale township and chapelry which follows a stream along Jagger's Clough; it is also at the point where a track from Edale crosses the Roman road and then goes steeply downhill to a crossing of the River Ashop, which now feeds Ladybower reservoir. This is a typical site for a stone cross.

Stone crosses are particularly symbolic of the church in the north. In mountainous countryside, settlements in sheltered valley sites shared great tracts of rough moorland grazing and woods without needing to define each share precisely; a cross provided a strong and sufficient statement. Parish boundaries were made without the aid of maps and were defined by men walking across the countryside; the simplest, making use of rivers and streams, tracks, hill tops and ridges, are likely to be the earliest. In more cultivated countryside, use could be made of hedges and ditches, woods and trees, and furrows drawn by the plough through arable fields. In default of obvious landmarks, boundary stones, wooden posts or crosses were erected at key points. The investment in effort to construct a boundary like Hadrian's Wall or Offa's Dyke was only justified by the importance of the division; moreover, these were boundaries chosen as strategic lines, and few parish boundaries follow them.

Crosses may have been significant in ceremonies of 'beating the bounds', an example of christianising the pagan custom of Rogation-tide processions which

were acknowledged as important by the church as early as 511.[1] Churchmen were particularly inclined to mark their territories in this way. The area round Ripon, Yorkshire, 'on ilke syde ye Kyrke amyle', which constituted St Wilfrid's League, was made a sanctuary and freed from geld by Athelstan at the beginning of the tenth century; it was marked with eight stone crosses, one of which survives two miles north-east of Ripon. The abbey of Lanercost marked its estate with crosses cut in oak trees. Lilla Cross, on the boundary of Whitby abbey lands, appears in an early twelfth-century charter and still stands. The abbeys of Fountains and Sawley settled an argument about the boundary of Fountains Fell by a perambulation after which 'it was marked with crosses sunk in the earth'. The Maiden Cross on the Maiden Way was on the boundary of Cumberland and Northumberland and the Rere Cross on Stainmore on the boundary of Westmorland and Northumberland, but both also marked the dioceses of Carlisle and Durham and York and perhaps more anciently had indicated the Anglo-Saxon dioceses of Lindisfarne and Hexham.[2]

Because of the shortage of written evidence, stone crosses may provide valuable evidence of early churches in the North. The cross at Eyam in Derbyshire, for example, is dated by the carving to about 800. Ward Lock's *Red Guide to Buxton, the Peak and Dovedale* of 1912 records that: 'it is said to have been found on the moor and removed to the churchyard, where it lay uncared for until it attracted the attention of Howard, the philanthropist, who caused it to be erected in its present position'. A church at Eyam was not mentioned in 1086 though the rectory was listed in 1291, but the cross demonstrates that the origins of this parish were much earlier (the eleventh-century font was given to the church in the nineteenth century). A sense of its historical significance probably prompted its removal to the churchyard. Similarly Bakewell cross was

Eyam, Derbyshire - the fine decorated cross in St Lawrence's churchyard at Eyam is dated to about 800, and is notable because it has its head. The cross suggests that church and parish are more ancient than any written source shows. It seems too elaborate to have been a boundary mark, yet apparently once stood on the moors.

moved to the churchyard from high on the moors above Darley near Matlock, and the remains of a cross from Ollerenshaw, comparable with a Bakewell fragment, were moved to Chapel en le Frith churchyard about 1920. Many fragments of carved stones, were found when Bakewell church was restored in 1841, some of which might be earlier than the cross and one of the few surviving Derbyshire charters, dated 949, concerns the endowment of a monastery there.[3] The churchyard cross, thought to be about 1000, may have been erected a little earlier to mark the monastery's territory.

CONQUEST AND LORDSHIP: THE PEAK DISTRICT

Although the name of the Peak survived attached to the upland part of Derbyshire, and to a great tract of royal forest, the ancient district was more extensive. *Pecsaete*, Peak dwellers, were included in a seventh or eighth century list of peoples under Mercian control. Their district was probably bounded by an ancient line, 'The Lyme' or 'The Lyne', reflected in a number of place-names, and included part of Cheshire. But an important political division took place about 877 when the Danes won the territory to the east of the River Etherow; consequently Derbyshire was assessed for taxation in Danish carucates and was divided into wapentakes and Cheshire was assessed in Anglo-Saxon hides and divided into hundreds. The two counties were probably created in the late tenth century, placing the townships of Mottram, Hollingworth and Tintwistle, which were in the valley of the Etherow, in Cheshire.[4] The later deaneries of High Peak and Ashbourne and the wapentakes of High Peak and Wirksworth largely corresponded with the Derbyshire portion of this ancient district.

The Peak was not specifically named nor the Forest described in 1086 but William Peveril does appear to have been the King's Forester. He built a castle at Castleton, and Domesday noted that two former landholders had been displaced to make way for it; the name 'Peak' crept into Domesday Book inserted above this entry. The bounds of Peak Forest were first recorded in 1286, and were very simple: the Rivers Goyt, Etherow, Derwent, Bradwell and Wye, and the Tideswell brook. They cut across parishes. A legal forest was not all wood nor uninhabited, but was an area within which game or wild beasts were protected and special law applied, forest law. The common rights of inhabitants existed side by side with the royal privilege of preserving deer; when Peak Forest was enclosed in the seventeenth century, the king was entitled to half the communal grazing and the commoners to half, but the king's share in the 'purlieus' or outskirts of the forest was only one third.[5] There were freeholders within the forest, but they were not lords of the manor supervising other small farmers. It was not a situation in which numerous parish churches would flourish.

The stone crosses with round shafts which are found throughout the ancient Peak may be evidence for churches before 1086; though not readily datable unless carved, they are considered to be tenth century. Sometimes they occur in pairs, like the oddly-named Robin Hood's Picking Rods, also called the 'Maidenstones', two pillars set in a large base stone beside a track leading over the Pennine edge from Ludworth to Plainsteads and Glossop. Four townships met there, and the manor of Glossopdale, given to Basingwerk abbey, with the Peak forest lordship of Longdendale; now they are on the edge of the Peak National Park.[6] The 'Abbot's chair', not far away, is the broken base of another round-shafted cross, like a worn chair, and was so named in 1640; the name indicates a popular association with Basingwerk abbey, which controlled Glossop church from the mid-twelfth century until it was dissolved three hundred years later.

There were many other stone crosses in the Peak. Plans of the Forest of 1640 were decorated with sketches of crosses and show that more then had head stones, lost to natural decay and unheeding re-use in the intervening three hundred years. The Revd J.Charles Cox studied the maps at the beginning of this century and 'during three rambles with the old plans in our hands in three successive years' found parts of a dozen crosses.[7] He demonstrated that only one, at Edale Head, related to divisions or wards of the forest. This cross, since moved a short distance, stood at the highest point on a trackway from Hayfield over Kinder into Edale, on the watershed of the Mersey and the Humber river systems. The three wards of the forest met here: Longdendale, the Campagna, and Ashop and Edale; the alternative name, 'Champion Cross', reflects a connection with the Campagna, the 'champaign' or arable district of the forest. The cross also marked a parish boundary between Hayfield, which was a chapelry of Glossop, and Edale which was a chapelry of Castleton. Cox argued that the crosses marked parochial divisions. They asserted churches' rights over the great common of Kinder, which was not enclosed until 1840 - when the creation of a private estate set the stage for the mass trespass by walkers nearly one hundred years later.

A typical northern pattern of parishes existed in the Derbyshire Peak and one also typical of forest areas; much territory was extra-parochial and the central area of the Peak did not become a parish until the nineteenth century. The pattern might date from an ancient period of simple minster church organisation, but it is also possible that it was an authoritarian imposition by late Anglo-Saxon or early Norman kings; it is customary to think in terms of fission of early units but an opposite process of fusion is equally plausible. Large royal manors in the Peak in 1086 contained several formerly independent smaller manors, also many subordinate townships called berewicks; a berewick was a 'barley farm', an out-lying township belonging to the central manor. Many berewicks had a chapel. Parish boundaries and estates overlapped but did not correspond, suggesting that they were organised at different times, and two periods, one after the defeat of the Danes and the second the period of Norman repression after 1066, may be relevant. In 1086, Bakewell manor with its eight berewicks was grouped with Ashford and Hope to make an obviously artificial unit of thirty vills and fifty carucates or ploughlands; and Ashbourne with six berewicks was linked with Darley, Matlock Bridge, Wirksworth and Parwich to form a second thirty vill and fifty carucate unit.

Bakewell, the chief manor in High Peak wapentake, is situated in the wide valley of the Wye, Ashford is two miles up the River Wye, and Hope is about

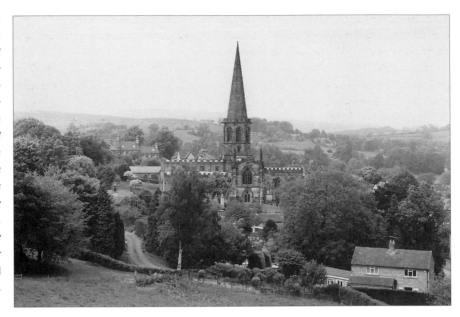

Bakewell, Derbyshire - All Saints' church is on rising ground dominating the bowl or 'well' in the hills to which the place-name may refer, although a warm-water well supplying a Roman bath may also have been its origin. The church was largely rebuilt in the nineteenth century. Bakewell was the inspiration for 'Lambton' in Pride and Prejudice.

ten miles to the north in the valley of the River Noe. Hope and Ashford were already linked early in the tenth century when the estate was said to have been bought from the heathen, that is, the Danes; the purchase represented a peaceful handover of control of the area. Bakewell was chosen by Edward the Elder, king of Wessex, in 920 for the site of a defensive *burh* in his drive to recover control over Mercia, and in 949 Eadred, 'king of the English, ruler of the Northumbrians, emperor of the heathen, and protector of the Britons', as he was comprehensively styled, transferred Bakewell to Earl Uhtred to endow a monastery. A reference to 'old land charters' which were not to be used in evidence hints at reorganisation.[8] In 1086 Bakewell manor had two priests and a church endowed with three times as much land as Hope church, which had one priest and was a separate parish. No church was recorded at Ashford but with its twelve berewicks it was in Bakewell parish; later there was a chapel at Ashford. Bakewell parish also covered four other Domesday manors and altogether there were twenty townships, and seven dependent chapels were recorded in 1280. In the nineteenth century the parish was 40,600 acres but could have been larger if it once included Youlgreave and Edensor; parochial organisation divided Wardlow, shared with Hope, and Harthill, shared with Youlgreave.[9] This structure could have followed the foundation of the tenth-century monastery.

Hope parish covered the southern and eastern part of Peak Forest and was as extensive as Bakewell, with at least twenty townships including Tideswell, a Hope berewick in 1086, which later became an independent parish covering four townships.[10] Tideswell church became known as the cathedral of the Peak after a large building was erected, probably with the income from lead tithes, perhaps at the same time as the vicarage was established. A church at Glossop controlled most of the north-western part of the Forest and had a similarly extensive parish. It would have been logical to place a church at each end of the Roman trans-Pennine road, at Glossop and Hope, and the place-names show the *hop* or valley had significance.

The north-western part of Peak Forest was called Longdendale, and it included Kinder Scout, the highest of the moors. Longdendale is the name for the long, narrow valley of the River Etherow; it was also the name of the king's Domesday manor: three overlapping but not corresponding areas. Mottram in Longdendale, distinguished from Mottram St Andrew in Prestbury parish a few miles away, might have been the first church of the dale; it is on a hill where the 'moot' or meeting once took place, and commands a view of the valley. The parish stretched to Woodhead at the top of the dale and included Hollingworth and Tintwistle; the Cheshire lord of Longdendale in 1320 held the advowson, or right of presentation, but Mottram had been cut off from the rest of the dale through the Danish conquest.[11] The Derbyshire manor contained twelve Domesday vills, of which Glossop was one, all in Glossop parish. Added as an afterthought to the name Longdendale in Domesday was the name of Thornsett, showing that the manor reached southwards beyond the Etherow valley as far as the River Sett; Thornsett is now the name of a hamlet on the north bank of the Sett and Ollersett is to the south.

Glossop was sited near the confluence of several streams flowing into the Etherow and other settlements in the parish were scattered thinly along the rivers and streams in twenty-one townships and hamlets, but after industrial development of cotton spinning started in the later eighteenth century, population was concentrated at new Glossop, leaving the parish church at Old Glossop to one side. There was no sign in Domesday Book that Glossop was a centre of administration, and there is no record of a church until about 1157 when part of Longdendale, 'namely Glossop with the church that is there', was detached from the forest to form the manor of Glossopdale granted to the Welsh abbey of Basingwerk, which was situated at the northern end of the Welsh Marches. The terms of the grant make it likely that a similar estate had been placed in William Peverill's possession by Henry I. This manor contained ten of the twelve Domesday vills.[12] The rest of Glossop parish remained within the forest until the general disafforestation of the seventeenth century.

There are signs that Longdendale was reorganised by the Normans. William the Conqueror had acquired total authority. The twelve Longdendale vills were said to be manors held by freemen in 1066, but these men had no successors in 1086; former landholders' names were known to the Domesday commissioners, so they had been displaced not long before 1086. They also recorded 'all Longdendale is waste'. This did not necessarily mean that the land was uncultivated but that there were no longer independent tax-paying landholders.[13] Following the Northern rebellion in the winter of 1069-70 in favour of a Danish claimant to the throne, there had been punishing devastation in the Conqueror's 'harrying' of the North. A vigorous reorganisation could have applied to the manors and the churches.

Chapelries may hold further clues to the history of the Peak parishes. There is an important early indication in the grant by William II to the bishop of

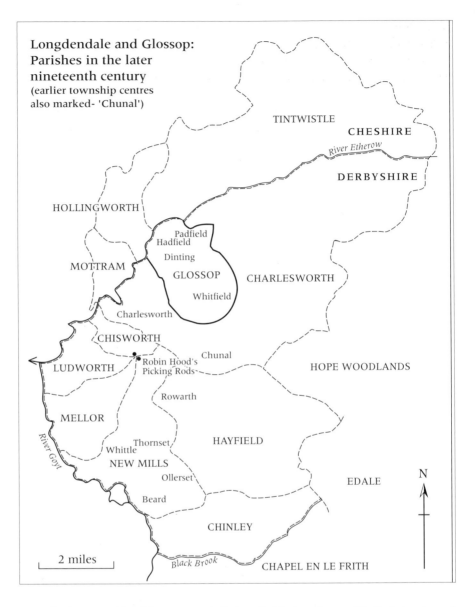

Longdendale and Glossop:
Parishes in the later
nineteenth century
(earlier township centres
also marked- 'Chunal')

TINTWISTLE

CHESHIRE

River Etherow

DERBYSHIRE

HOLLINGWORTH

Padfield
Hadfield

Dinting

MOTTRAM

GLOSSOP

CHARLESWORTH

Whitfield

Charlesworth

CHISWORTH

Chunal

Robin Hood's
Picking Rods

HOPE WOODLANDS

LUDWORTH

Rowarth

MELLOR

River Goyt

Thornset
Whittle

HAYFIELD

NEW MILLS

Ollerset

EDALE

Beard

N

CHINLEY

2 miles

Black Brook

CHAPEL EN LE FRITH

Lincoln in 1093 of Ashbourne and Chesterfield churches, with their lands and tithes as they existed at the time of Edward the Confessor and all the chapels in the berewicks. The implication is that some and perhaps all of the berewicks had chapels before the Norman conquest. In 1240, when an ordinance for Ashbourne vicarage was made, there were nine chapels and all were in townships named in Domesday Book; four were in berewicks of Ashbourne, out of the six belonging to the manor, but six were in other manors or their berewicks. One of Ashbourne's chapels was at Ballidon. A newly-discovered charter of 963 is a grant by King Edgar of an estate at Ballidon in the 'District of the Peak-dwellers' and its boundaries appear to match the later chapelry.[14] The pre-Conquest lord was named in Domesday but was no longer in possession and church and lord together had perhaps been deprived of independence by the Normans.

Glossop parish contained two chapelries, Hayfield and Mellor. The chapelry districts extended Glossop parish boundary some eleven miles southwards from the parish church well beyond the Sett to the Black Brook, the boundary with Chapel en le Frith. A road runs the length of Glossop parish from north to south, providing a spine of communication which also marked a division between the more settled areas close to the Etherow and the higher moors. Hayfield and Mellor chapelries contained four of the twelve Longdendale vills. Neither was named in Domesday. In fact, Hayfield was not a township, and the name does not appear in administrative lists like the Hearth Tax in the 1660s nor in the early nineteenth-century censuses. The settlement spanned the River Sett; part was north of the river in the township of Great Hamlet, while the church was to the south in Phoside.[15] It was the administrative centre for a constablewick in Peak forest known as Bowden Middlecale, corresponding with the chapelry and there were ten townships, which invites comparison with the ten vills in the manor of Glossopdale. There was a tradition that Hayfield church had been moved from Kirksteads in Kinder in 1386; Cox noted that the 'information has reached us from several sources'. It was also said that the church was built by Robert of Kynder in 1420 at his own expense, but perhaps in fact rebuilt. These traditions may reflect the earlier significance of Kinder; it was a British name, probably meaning hill, to which Norsemen added 'scout' also meaning hill.

Mellor, too, is a British name. Mellor church is on a hilltop with an extensive view over the Goyt river valley, a position somewhat similar to Mottram in Longdendale. Three surprising dates are recorded in a scating plan of Mellor church of 1868: 'Font erected 1018. Tower erected 1140. Old Pulpit 1360'.[16] The sources of the information are unknown, but might reflect the history of the chapelry. The Domesday townships of Ludworth and Chisworth were in Mellor chapelry and also in the manor held by Basingwerk abbey; they would

Glossop, Derbyshire - Robin Hood's Picking Rods are situated on the moor beside a well-defined track. They marked the meeting point of four townships and of the chapelries of Hayfield and Mellor, and were still useful in the seventeenth century to describe enclosures in the Forest.

Chapel en le Frith, Derbyshire - the church of St Thomas Becket. The dedication is a clue to its history. Enterprising freeholders of Bowden in Peak Forest built a chapel some fifty years after Becket was murdered in Canterbury cathedral; they, too, were once in dispute with their lord the king. Although called a chapel, the freeholders claimed it was an independent parish church, but this was not fully accepted until the eighteenth century; at that time the church was 'refashioned'.

surely have been in Glossop church's own parochial area if the chapelry had been created after Glossop manor was granted to Basingwerk. Robin Hood's Picking Rods may originally have marked the boundary between the churches of Mellor and Kinder, made subservient to Glossop about 1066.

Chapel en le Frith epitomises the anomalous and uncertain situation of churches in the Forest. Nominally it was in Hope parish. It was in the township of Bowden, and was alternatively called Bowden chapel until the nineteenth century. Bowden was to the south of the River Sett and its tributary the Kinder, and the boundary is marked still by Bowden Bridge a short distance above Hayfield. Bowden was not in Domesday Book but in the *Lay Subsidy* of 1334 it was a relatively wealthy vill, and in 1431 there were eight yeomen and two gentlemen prosperous enough to be taxed individually; each was the owner of a 'Hall', a free or independent farmstead, and eight Halls of historical interest remain.[17] The predecessors of these and other freeholders had apparently founded the chapel between 1224 and 1238 and arranged to pay the minister. Upwards of forty 'foresters, verderers, keepers and freemen' in 1318 asserted that it had been endowed with a burial ground and the right to baptise, two privileges which made it 'parochial'; but this was not accepted by subsequent bishops and consequently it was not included except incidentally in surveys of parish churches in either 1291 or 1535. There were also doubts about the chapelry boundaries when the Forest was enclosed in the seventeenth century.

The right to appoint the minister of Chapel en le Frith was frequently disputed. The king at first claimed the presentation in right of his royal estate in the forest, and the dean and chapter of Lichfield claimed it because Bowden was in their parish of Hope. In addition, the Priory of Lenton in Nottinghamshire had been granted certain tithes from Peak Forest by Peveril and for three centuries disputed the dean and chapter's interest.[18] The king gave up his claim, but the dean and chapter did not; as far as they were concerned, the church was a 'chapel' still. The survey of dean and chapter property made under authority of the Commonwealth parliament in 1650 noted that the parishioners had the right of presentation and donation, 'as they affirme', and that it 'hath been so beyond all memory of man'. It was a 'donative' because twenty-seven inhabitants could grant the living without needing the bishop's approval. The dean and chapter were disputing this as late as 1747, when twenty-seven freeholders, nine from each 'Edge' into which Chapel en le Frith was divided, Bowden, Bradshaw and Combes, won confirmation of their right to choose their minister. After some 500 years, Chapel en le Frith was finally recognised as a parish church.

The long-term effect of the parochial structure in Peak Forest was to deprive it of a reasonable number of well-supported rectors. Sometime after 1157 half the small tithes and all the great tithes of Glossop church were appropriated to the support of the monastery of Basingwerk. Hope church, together with Tideswell and Bakewell, was transferred to the bishop of Lichfield in 1192 and thence to the support of the cathedral dean and chapter. Most of the area of Peak Forest was left with two vicars having modest incomes from parishioners' offerings and from the less important agricultural produce of the area, who served the two great parishes of Hope and Glossop, while the enterprise of inhabitants provided for their own local ministers in chapels like Hayfield, Mellor and Chapel en le Frith.

PARISHES AND 'SHIRES'

'Shire' was the word used of the major divisions of the kingdom of Mercia. Cheshire was mentioned in the *Anglo-Saxon Chronicle* in 980, the first known reference to a Mercian shire. Perhaps the divisions had been made earlier in the century, following the success of the kings of Wessex in winning control from the Danes, or they may have been mainly early eleventh century and not all

were defined simultaneously. Subdivision into hundreds, wapentakes and Ridings was organised about the same time.[19] The three Ridings centred on York were apparently organised by the Danes; Yorkshire was a very large shire indeed. The shires were named in relation to their central town or settlement which was a defended *burh* and facilitated defence and control. The reeve of Chester, as Domesday stated, could call one man from each hide in the county to repair the city wall and bridge. The shires also provided a comprehensive network for collecting taxes. By 1086 the word was also used of smaller territories. In the Domesday survey of Yorkshire, there was Borghshire on the east side of the West Riding: a wapentake based on Aldborough, a former Roman capital in the territory of the Brigantes, later superseded by Knaresborough; and there was Cravenshire: a region on the western edge of the same Riding, with a Celtic name perpetuated as the name of a deanery and attached to fifty-three place-names. There was also mention in the City of York of 'Six shires besides the archbishop's'. By the twelfth century, 'shire' was being regularly applied to certain areas much smaller than a county, like Blackburnshire and Salfordshire in Lancashire, Sowerbyshire, Hallamshire, Richmondshire and Howdenshire in Yorkshire. The word was also used of single parishes in Yorkshire like Coxwold, Gilling, Masham and Ripon, which implies some distinct perception of the integrity of those areas.[20] Generally it described areas which contained only one or two parishes.

Sowerbyshire was closely related to the parish of Halifax, which was the largest parish in the historic county of Yorkshire, 118 square miles. Like other large parishes, Halifax's territory was based on a major river, the Calder and its tributaries. Churches in the western half of Yorkshire were sparsely recorded in Domesday Book, but Halifax was not named at all. Nothing is known concerning the origins of the parish, and the first record of Halifax's name in the early twelfth century concerned the church; yet its history implies that the church was older than this. Halifax was part of the vast royal estate centred on Wakefield in the late thirteenth century; surviving records of the manor court show it was in the graveship of Sowerby, or Sowerbyshire, one of twelve graveships or bailiwicks in the manor.[21] In 1086 Sowerby was a Wakefield berewick; a court met at Wakefield until 1430 and either at Sowerby or Halifax from 1433 onwards. Much later, there were chapels at Sowerby and Sowerby Bridge, but Sowerby once had more importance; notably it is on the River Calder, whereas Halifax is on a tributary.

It is usually assumed that the mother church of the huge Wakefield manor was Dewsbury, with which its parish largely corresponded, but Halifax was a second possibly early church in the region. The church was given to Lewes priory in Sussex sometime after 1106, when the second earl William de Warenne become lord of the manor of Wakefield, and before 1147 when the

Wensley, North Yorkshire - Holy Trinity church controlled a river crossing and the parish was based on the upper reaches of the river Ure, which was known as Wensleydale by 1150. It included Bolton castle higher up the dale. Carved stones are evidence that a church existed here before 1000.

gift was confirmed. It is unlikely that the Normans had established the church and then so quickly given it away, and the name itself referred to an Anglo-Saxon site that was 'holy', *halig*. The secular adminstration of Halifax remained under the earl's control, and according to the Hundred Rolls was incorporated into the forest of the sixth earl of Warenne in the early thirteenth century. The gift of the valuable patronage of the church only made sense if the church was owned by an hereditary priestly family who stood outside the earl's jurisdiction; by this means the priest's power was reduced. Before 1273 Lewes priory had appropriated the rectory and the archbishop of York required that a vicarage be instituted, 'on account of the great produce and revenue of the Mother Church of Halifax (which church together with its chapels and dependencies, has been for a long time in the patronage of foreigners, who were more eager for the milk and wool, than for the salvation of souls, and have shamefully neglected its spiritual concerns)'. The vicar was to live in the parish, and have a sufficient income for hospitality and for the other burdens 'on so rich a benefice'; he had to provide for the service of the chapels.[22] The great tithes of the nineteen medieval townships in Halifax parish went to the priory until 1537, and after the dissolution of the priory, to the Crown.

Where were the chapels referred to about 1273? Like Glossop to the south, Halifax parish was divided between the parish church and two chapelries, Elland and Heptonstall, a recurring northern pattern. As described by John Crabtree, gentleman, in the early nineteenth century, Halifax church itself had a parochial district of ten townships, including Halifax itself and Sowerby, and the inhabitants of these ten townships had to maintain the parish church; the parochial chapelry of Elland had six medieval townships (later eight) and Heptonstall had three (later five). Heptonstall was not a separate vill but was part of the medieval manor and vill of Halifax. Crabtree commented that 'When this arrangement took place, we have nothing to shew, the subdivisions of the great Saxon Parishes form one of the most obscure subjects of English antiquity'. Both Heptonstall and Elland chapels had rights of baptism, marriage and burial, hence were 'parochial'. Elland was reputed to be the oldest of Halifax's chapels and the presence of a knightly family from about 1200 may seem significant as a chapel would have been a natural adjunct to Elland Hall; but at Heptonstall there was no equivalent secular lord. Elland is on the River Calder, and Heptonstall is on a steep cliff above the river. A theory of the evolution of Halifax parish might involve the establishment of a major church at Dewsbury, where an early sculptured fragment has been interpreted as having preaching and pastoral significance, and a 'holy place' as a centre for a large moorland area, and finally the definition of its parish to include two other churches and parochial subdivisions in the late tenth or early eleventh century.[23]

Just as Halifax church related to Sowerbyshire, Ecclesfield church, east of the Pennines, at one time had superiority over Hallamshire, which covered some 72,000 acres, and like Halifax had three parochial divisions, Ecclesfield, Bradfield and Sheffield. The three names shows that 'field' had first been appropriate to a territory systematically divided rather than to an agricultural feature. The southern boundary of Sheffield was particularly significant: the River Sheaf divided Northumbria from Mercia, York diocese from Lichfield, and Yorkshire from Derbyshire; it may also have defined the southern boundary of the British kingdom of Elmet.[24] The first part of Ecclesfield's name, *eccles*, strongly implies a continuity from the late Roman period; Ecclesall, the church 'hall' or manor, was in Sheffield. Hallamshire in 1066 was a twenty vill unit; Domesday recorded that the lord's hall was in Hallam, a large composite manor with sixteen berewicks, and the manors of Attercliffe and Sheffield were said to be the lord's own lands. There was no mention of a church in Ecclesfield but, typically, it was transferred soon after the Conquest to a Norman monastery, St Wandrille's priory near Rouen, together with two thirds of the tithes of Sheffield; one third of Sheffield tithes, with the advowson of a church or chapel, went to Worksop priory. The tithes remained divided thereafter. Bradfield continued to be a chapelry in Ecclesfield parish into the nineteenth century and St Wandrille's in 1188 claimed that Sheffield was a chapelry, too, but Worksop priory maintained a vicar in Sheffield, and the market and administrative centre for Hallamshire established parochial independence.

Hallamshire is an unusually good example of the possible survival of an ancient territory. If all parishes termed 'shires' were as old, the principal church in each could be very early and the parishes reflect early estates. Hexhamshire, for example, now in Durham but for centuries attached to Yorkshire, which covered some 82,000 acres, was probably the land of thirty 'families' given to Bishop Wilfrid in the 670s. It would be natural for territories like this to be incorporated into a later system of hundreds and parishes. Perhaps they could be described as multiple estates, consisting of townships organised systematically for the provision of food taxes for the King and his household, and for effective exploitation of moorland and lowland; particular townships were required to undertake specialised functions like horse breeding or cattle rearing. The king held the chief township.[25] They were more comparable with a southern hundred than with a manor, in which typically one township provided both the lord's own land and the land of the villagers; the multiple estate was suited to the less intensive cultivation of an upland region. Estates of this kind existed in Wales and across the Scottish border, and the large parishes in Northumberland and Durham referred to as shires seem similar. Aucklandshire in particular had a structure of obligations to the lord, the bishop of Durham, showing close similarity with early Welsh estates. Gilling is a Yorkshire example of a parish which might also have been a multiple estate, in which there was 'an Apple-by, a Bar (barley) -ton, two Lay (vegetable) -tons and a Cow-ton'. But on the whole 'place-names do not give much evidence in Yorkshire for the resources and composition of an estate'.

In Lancashire it is suggested that the Domesday hundreds were constituted by combining two multi-settlement groups or 'estates'. Six hundreds in south Lancashire were known as shires and there is some indication that each in 1086 had two principal churches.[26] They had probably been organised after the land 'Between Ribble and Mersey' was detached from the Danish kingdom about 930. In Domesday Book this area was surveyed with Cheshire. Both hides and

Whalley, Lancashire - a Viking age cross, one of three in the churchyard of St Mary and All Saints. The monks of Whalley abbey, whose ruined church is nearby, called them 'Crosses of Blessed Augustine'. The carving of this cross seems an attempt to imitate metal craftsmanship. St Mary's was an important land-holding church in Domesday Book, and was the basic endowment of the later monastery.

carucates were used in tax assessments, and the hundreds were sometimes also described as 'manors', so that there was confusion about how best to categorise them. All were in the king's hands. Before the Conquest there had been many small manors in each hundred, but in 1086 the numbers of freemen had been much reduced; this would have facilitated the parallel organisation of two main churches controlling others in the area.

The two churches and parishes in Blackburn hundred or Blackburnshire were Blackburn and Whalley. This was the shire which retained its integrity for longest. There are no signs that Blackburn was an ancient settlement, but the church at Whalley, situated on the River Calder, had a much larger endowment of land in 1086, and has some Roman antecedents and three pre-Conquest crosses. Newtonshire appears to have been a new unit, as its name suggests, which approximately matched Winwick and Wigan parishes. One church in the hundred was described in Domesday as 'St Oswald's of the vill' and the other, without a dedication, as 'the church of the manor'. Winwick church was dedicated to St Oswald so that the other church would appear to be Wigan, which was centrally placed. There is some evidence in surrounding place-names that a British population had survived here for some time and conceivably churches, too; both Wigan and Winwick churches have round churchyards, and Winwick, like Whalley, has a surviving pre-Conquest carved cross.[27] Where appropriate, existing churches would have been used as the centres for new administrative areas. Similarly, there are indications of two churches in West Derby hundred and two in Salford hundred. Domesday referred to St Mary's and St Michael's in Salford hundred, both said to be 'in Manchester'. Manchester had been of importance since Roman times and had a church dedicated to St Mary, and Ashton under Lyne church was dedicated to St Michael. But strangely there was no mention of Eccles, whose name strongly suggests Roman origins and whose very large parish occupied much of the western half of Salford hundred. Had the church been temporarily suppressed? Or was St Mary's at Eccles one of the two churches indicated?

There is some evidence of systematic construction of parochial units of six vills, and larger units of multiples of six.[28] The twelve vills of Longdendale in Derbyshire fit into this pattern and the thirty vills in each of the two groups of royal manors in the south Peak. In 1311 Blackburn and Whalley together contained sixty vills, twenty-two in Blackburn parish and thirty-eight in Whalley. Blackburn had ten townships in its parochial area and two chapelries, Walton le Dale and Samlesbury, each with six townships. Walton le Dale, an important Roman base, had the normal endowments of a parish church: land, tithes and oblations, although it had the status of a chapel, and the hundred boundary made a detour to include it in Blackburn. Whalley had six chapelries in 1296; Whalley's own parochial district contained twelve townships but the chapelries were less regular. Three plain crosses of the tenth or eleventh century probably marked parochial sub-divisions, and in the churchyard at Haslingden, one of the chapels, there is the base of a double cross.[29] There were twelve Domesday vills in the parish of Prestbury in Cheshire, although the 'priest's manor' itself was not named. Ninth or tenth century round-shafted crosses from different locations again seem to reflect parochial sub-divisons. Hexham was divided into six wards and Staindrop in Durham when it was given to the church in the eleventh century had eleven dependent townships or 'appendices'. Lanchester in Durham was divided into eighteen constablewicks and had three chapels, and Chester le Street into twelve constablewicks and two chapels. There could not be a greater contrast with the south, especially with East Anglia. The dispossession of local landholders from the time of the Norman Conquest favoured a strong organisation of large parishes under royal control, but it is difficult to say when a systematic organisation of six vills to a chapelry took place.

THE SIGNIFICANCE OF 'KIRKBY': CUMBRIA

'Kirkby' is a place-name of Scandinavian origin, meaning 'church-place' or 'church-town', *kirkja-by*, and is found almost exclusively in the north of the country.[30] The pagan Vikings, pirates from Denmark and Norway, started to come to England at the end of the eighth century as raiders, burning churches and spending the winter in nunneries, but then they came to settle. They also went to the Northern Isles and Caithness, from where they spread southwards to the western isles, Ireland and north-west Britain; the Earldom of Orkney remained within the Nordic world until the later fifteenth century. Some of the evidence of Viking atrocities comes from Irish sources. A more systematic invasion of England started in the later ninth century; a Danish king in 875-6 won York, and the Danes were converted to Christianity. They ruled most of the north of England for about fifty years before their control crumbled under pressure from the southern English kings of Wessex; the first king of all England, Athelstan, established his control of Cumbria as far as the Eamont River when he met rulers from further north at Dacre in 927.[31]

Norse speakers migrated in sufficient numbers for their vocabulary to influence dialect particularly in the Lake District and to be reflected in many minor place-names in Cumbria. But few parish names in the area are Scandinavian, making the Kirkbys more notable: Kirkby Thore, Kirkby Stephen, Kirkby Lonsdale and Kirkby Ireleth are names in use; Kendal was formerly Kirkby Kendal; Cartmel, St Bees and Newton Arlosh were called Kirkby in medieval sources, and there was a *Kirkeby Crossan* near Workington. Most and perhaps all these places had churches with wide responsibilities, their parishes containing numerous townships and chapels. It is most unlikely that the Kirkbys and Kirbys were settled for the first time in the tenth century. Many occupy attractive and strategically important sites commanding road junctions and river crossings. Churches, too, most likely existed at these places before the Scandinavian incursions, especially as in Cumbria continuity of religious practice from Roman times is a possibility. Kirkbys, therefore, were renamed, as is increasingly seen to be the case in other places. 'Kirk', on the other hand, entered the vocabulary and was in use long after the Scandinavian period; Kirkcambeck, Kirklinton and Kirkbampton were simply Cambok, Levington and Bampton until the late thirteenth century.

A small part of Cumbria was under English control in 1086, and was surveyed rather perfunctorily in Domesday Book. *Cherchebi* occurred three times with no other qualifying name: one certainly related to Kirkby Kendal, the second to Kirkby Lonsdale, and the third is taken to be Cartmel, though in this case 'Kirkby' early dropped out of use. Rather surprisingly, there was no specific mention of a church at any of the three, and similarly no church was mentioned at thirteen out of sixteen Kirkbys in Yorkshire.[32] Nonetheless, these churches appear soon after in records of Norman reorganisations.

Cherchebi or Cartmel, in the extreme south of the Cumbrian area, is a good example of 'Kirkby' referring to a church already existing when Scandinavian speakers were naming English places.[33] In 685, Cartmel 'with all the Britons belonging to it', was given to bishop Cuthbert; this estate probably corresponded with the later parish, just as a generous grant of land in and around Carlisle corresponded with the later parish of St Cuthbert's Without. The gift hints at an existing Christian centre in Cartmel, but even if one did not exist, a church or monastery would then have been founded, just as Cuthbert founded a second monastery in Carlisle. An Augustinian priory was founded in the late twelfth century which took over the earlier church's endowment; an existing church became the south choir of the priory church. Cartmel parish covered the peninsula which overlooks the sands of Morecambe Bay referred to in the second part of the name, *melr*, sandbank; it had other naturally defined boundaries at the River Winster in the east, and the River Leven and Lake Windermere in the west, and was 36 square miles. It was divided into four quarters, as recorded in the sixteenth century, when the Augustinian canons served four chapels in the parish, and the priory church was near the meeting-point of four township boundaries. By 1831 there were seven townships. Cartmel could be an example of an estate which maintained its integrity at least from the late seventh century, and the use of 'Kirkby' indicate recognition by Scandinavians of the important church in that area.

Kirkby Ireleth similarly might have been the church for the Furness peninsula, west of Cartmel; these two areas were linked later in a deanery. Ireleth was named in Domesday but it was not called Kirkby nor was there an indication of a church; nonetheless the name was probably in use as indicated by minor place-names: Kirkby Pool is the stream meandering through one of the sandy inlets of the Duddon River separating the peninsula from Copeland, and Kirkby Moor and Kirkby Park Wood are in the same area. Kirkby Hall,the old manor house, was formerly called 'Crosshouse' and the remains of the cross were visible nearby in the early nineteenth century. Kirkby Ireleth manor was part of the endowment of Furness abbey, founded in 1127, but Kirkby Ireleth church and its lands were claimed by the archbishop of York, perhaps an indication of an earlier significance. It remained a parish church for an extensive area, 43 square miles, but lost its overall importance in Furness.

Kendal and Kirkby Lonsdale were the other two places named *Cherchebi* in Domesday Book. Roman fort, Anglo-Saxon church and Norman motte all show the antiquity and significance of Kendal. This *Cherchebi* was in the manor of Strickland, and the parish did not match the manor. The parish was based on the valley of the Kent, and covered all the south-eastern valleys of the Lake District. In 1831, it contained twenty-seven townships and 107 square miles, but had once been even larger; the boundary to the west had been Lake Windermere: Windermere and Grasmere churches, serving eight lakeside townships, achieved independence before 1291. Leland, writing about 1540, found Kendal parish particularly notable, recording that there were above thirty chapels and hamlets belonging to the 'head church', that the parish

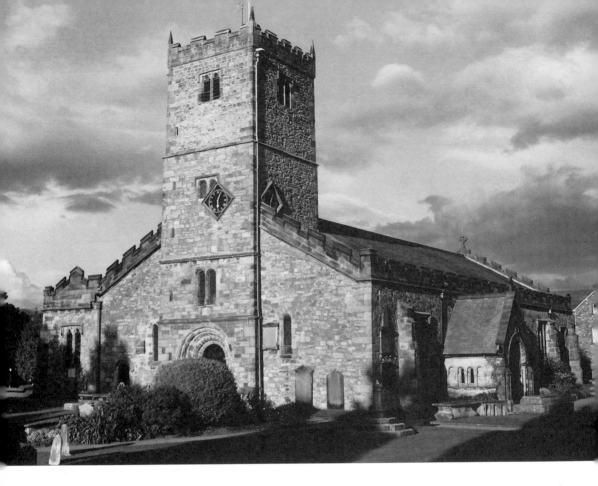

church was beside the River Kent, and that Kirkgate was the main street in the town; the focus has since shifted northwards. Leland commented also on Kirkby Lonsdale that it was 'a very great and famous parish' and he called it simply 'Kyrkby'. Kirkby Lonsdale was half the size of Kendal in 1831, covering nine townships and some fifty-three square miles. As at Kendal, the church was sited near a river crossing, and a Roman fort lay across the river at Casterton. Its area of authority may once have been the upper Lune and its tributary valleys, reaching as far as Austwick, the *ost* or east wick of an earlier estate; the later Lonsdale deanery covered this area. Kirkby Lonsdale itself in 1086 was in the manor of Austwick, which consisted of twelve former manors and fourteen scattered townships; this was typical of estates in southern Cumbria. Like Kendal, too, manor and parish did not correspond: the parish was a smaller, compact unit of seven Domesday vills, of which three were in Whittington manor. No attention was paid to the church's boundaries in forming the Domesday manors nor, nearly a hundred years later, in fixing the county boundaries; Kirkby Lonsdale was placed in Westmorland; Austwick and other parishes in Lonsdale deanery were in the West Riding of Yorkshire and Whittington with other parishes were in Lancashire.[34]

There were several equally large 'Kirkby' parishes which confirm the significance of the name, but which were not in the area surveyed in

5. Lincoln cathedral - is on the top of a hill, facing the castle. It, too, was fortified at the west end, although later embellishment has partly obscured the machicolations or gaps in the three great arches through which stones could be dropped on the heads of attackers. The first cathedral was built by bishop Remigius, a Norman monk who had been with William the Conqueror at the battle of Hastings; he transferred his seat from Dorchester on Thames to Lincoln, which from Roman times had a Christian history.

6. *Lanercost Priory, Cumbria - is close to the river Irthing, where the valley widens. The north aisle was the parish church and now the restored nave is, too. The priory gave hospitality to travellers and bemoaned more than once the ruinous cost. It also suffered Scottish attacks. Edward I stayed here when campaigning against the Scots; in 1306-7 he was ill and unable to leave for a whole winter. Numerous carts with supplies for his large party wound along the narrow roads.*

7. *Tewkesbury, Gloucestershire - the abbey church was saved by the townsmen agreeing to buy it from Henry VIII because they said they had no parish church. The abbey was one of the richest and last to be dissolved. The monastic buildings were on the south side, despite the risk of flooding from the Swilgate river, and were nearly all demolished, although the abbot's house became a private house, and was bought for the vicarage in 1883 by public subscription.*

Domesday. St Bees was called *Cherchebi* in an early twelfth-century record, *Kirkebi-beccoh* in a late twelfth-century, and *Kirkeby Becok* in the *Valor Ecclesiasticus*.[35] There is a relatively narrow strip of fertile ground between the sea and the upland containing the highest Lake District mountains of Great Gable and Scafell, and settlements are small and widely scattered; the only pass to the east is Wrynose through which the Romans had built a road with a fort at Hardknott at the end of the long valley of Eskdale. St Bees position, on the extreme west coast of Cumbria where Wainwright's 'coast to coast' walk begins, is remote for overland travellers but more accessible from the sea. An Irish missionary and saint called Bega, to whom the church is dedicated (not the same as 'Begu' referred to by Bede) founded a small monastery at St Bees; in legend she was held to have been given as much land as was white with snow on Midsummer's Day, which was miraculously extensive. The parish included the harbour of Whitehaven and significantly the prior of St Bees was a baron of the Isle of Man and collected tithes from the island. As the point from which to reach with Christianity into this isolated land or to control it administratively, St Bees was well-chosen, and a small monastery was a very practical solution to the challenge of how to maintain a centre providing education as well as religious services.

Bega fits with a period of colonisation in this area about 900 by settlers of mixed Irish and Scandinavian origins, and St Bees was probably the centre of control. There was a *konungs haugr*, a king's mound at St Bees, a parallel to *Hougun*, the mound near Kirkby Ireleth which was the centre of the Norman barony of Millom. St Bees' parish related to the Norman barony of Copeland, a name meaning 'the bought land'; like Ashford and Hope in Derbyshire and Amounderness in Lancashire it appears to have changed hands peacefully. The centre of the Norman barony was at Egremont, a chapel of St Bees until about 1200, and the forest of Copeland as it existed about 1200 was attached to St Bees' parish. Five churches scattered through Copeland deanery, from Workington in the north to Whicham in the south, paid a pension to St Bees in 1291, suggesting they had once been subordinate. When St Bees was transferred to St Mary's abbey, York, about 1100 by William Meschin, he required that six monks and a prior should always be maintained there; this implies that a small monastery survived. It was dissolved with the abbey in 1539. In 1831, including Loweswater, the parish contained 115 square miles and thirteen townships, and like Cartmel there were four chapelries; Loweswater chapel is documented as early as 1125. St Bees church was appropriately in Preston Quarter, the 'priest's area'. To the north of St Bees, *Kirkeby Johannis*, later called Newton Arlosh, was possibly a similar church centre; there is a local tradition that it was founded by St Ninian in the late fourth century. It was displaced by Holme Cultram monastery in the eleventh century, but the church at Newton Arlosh continued to be the parish church until after the abbey was dissolved.

Kirkby Stephen parish controlled the head-waters of the River Eden and contained ten townships and 50 square miles. Early medieval relationships with neighbouring churches suggest that this Kirkby had once controlled Brough,

with its chapel at Stainmore, and Crossby Garret.[36] The long, thin stretch of
Great Musgrave parish appears to have been separated from Kirkby Stephen,
too, and the church's dedication to St Theobald, a French hermit who died in
1066, supports a relatively late date for the parish, while Little Musgrave was
in Crosby Garrett; the two Musgraves were united in 1894 to form one parish.
Kirkby Thore, lower down the Eden, was named from a Scandinavian lord. It
formerly included Temple Sowerby but even so was not a large parish. These
two Kirkbys were south of the Eamont in territory won by Athelstan, but in
Carlisle diocese when it was established after the Normans pushed the
boundary of English territory significantly further north. The diocesan
boundary followed the watershed between the Eden flowing north and the
Lune flowing south, the same boundary as had once separated Lindisfarne
diocese from York.

The question is not so much when the Kirkby churches were founded but
when their great parishes were formed. Their name might surprisingly imply
that these parishes were constituted during the period of Danish control. Three
languages have contributed to the place-names of Cumbria, Cumbric or British,
Anglo-Saxon and Norse. Although since 1974 Cumbria has become the name
of the whole region, few parishes have Cumbric names. Most parish names are
Anglo-Saxon, though only a quarter of minor place-names - of hamlets and
farms. It seems to indicate that the majority of parishes were organised during
a period of Anglian control from Northumbria before the Danish conquest,
rather than being a reflection of large-scale Anglian settlement.[37] The use of the
Norse 'Kirkby' for a few places, on the other hand, may imply that the Danish
rulers of York used churches as centres for their administrative areas, a parallel
with the organisation of the hundreds in the south. Mountainous areas were
difficult to supervise, but a superior church might aid in this task and a river
provide a clear organising principle. Lonsdale and Kendale also have the Norse
'dale', meaning river valley, in their names. The Danes were organisers through
military necessity, and the Kirkbys all occur within the Cumbrian area under
their control and claimed by Athelstan in 927.

As in East Anglia, the Scandinavian invasions destroyed northern
monasteries and their stores of documents, so that there are few surviving land
charters. The north was not touched by the Benedictine monastic movement of
the tenth century, either, although Oswald was archbishop of York from 971 to
992; the Normans reintroduced monasticism. The Norman Conquest brought
further disruption. By the time of the Domesday survey, lordship was so
concentrated that compared with the south there were few men with influence
and wealth to safeguard or make their estates independent parishes. Where
king or bishop had control, lordship and parish sometimes coincided; but in
other cases a parish's rationale was as a coherent group of townships,
disregarding manorial structure. It has been suggested that a fully parochial
system on the southern pattern 'never really developed in Cumbria before it
was imposed by reorganisation in the nineteenth and twentieth centuries'.[38]
This might seem true of much of the north, though less so if account is taken
of parochial chapelries.

CHAPTER FOUR

A VARIETY

OF STRUCTURES

The narrow cobbled street and timber-framed houses in Fish Street, Shrewsbury, create something of the atmosphere of a medieval town. At the end of the street is St Julian's church. The lower stages of the tower are medieval, built probably about 1200; the rest of the church was rebuilt in mid-eighteenth century. St Julian's was one of six churches in Shrewsbury recorded in Domesday Book. Four are in the centre of the town, three have suffered misfortunes in the last two centuries. St Julian's is now a craft centre. Immediately behind it, St Alkmund's, rebuilt except for the tower at the end of the eighteenth century, is still in use. St Mary's, not far away, with its carved Norman south doorway and two-story porch, was the most important of the central churches at the time of the Domesday survey; now it is open through the devotion of local people and The Churches Conservation Trust, and is only occasionally used. St Chad's, south-west of St Julian's, was the most important church to the medieval townsmen; five guilds had chantries there: Weavers, Mercers, Tailors, Skinners and Shoemakers, and about 1540 Leland noted that it was the principal church. St Chad's tower fell in 1788 and following this nearly all the church was demolished. A new church in fashionable classical style on a circular plan was built on the edge of the town above the River Severn, looking across to Kingsland; recently this church was the most thronged with congregation.

In addition to these four Shrewsbury churches, Domesday Book recorded St Michael's at the Castle, which no longer exists, and the important monastery of St Peter which was being built in the eastern suburbs; part of this church remains to serve the parish of Holy Cross. It was not unusual for there to be several or many churches in a town, but Shrewsbury was unique in having six holding land; in comparison, Winchester and York had four and Canterbury three.[1] Shrewsbury's churches display a variety of parochial structures. St Alkmund's and St Chad's were collegiate about 1066, and St Mary's may also have been, or perhaps it was made collegiate when the church was rebuilt in

LEFT: Shrewsbury, St Julian's church and Fish Street.

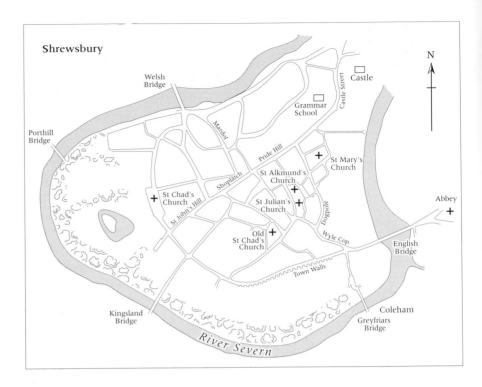

the first half of the twelfth century. St Julian's was portionary, an arrangement common in the western part of Britain and possibly ancient; in 1228 three portions were referred to, but not long afterwards St Julian's and St Michael's were combined. St Mary's, St Michael's and St Julian's were 'free' chapels, independent of the bishop's supervision. The typical pattern of one rector caring for a parish and serving the parish church was hardly present in Shrewsbury in the eleventh century.

The six Shrewsbury churches each had parts of the town in their parish, and parts of the surrounding rural area from which they collected tithes and where there were subordinate chapels.[2] Probably twelve chapels existed by 1291. Three, Astley, Broughton with Yorton, and Clive (entered under Broughton), had priests in Domesday; Broughton chapel was still 'open to adjoining fields' in the early nineteenth century. There were also chapels at Little Berwick, Fitz, Ford and Uffington, and probably Albrighton where there is an ancient font, Preston Gubbals which has an old south doorway, and Albright Hussey. The *Pope Nicholas Taxation* recorded a poorly-endowed church at Upper Rossall or The Isle, later regarded as a chapel in St Chad's parish, because St Chad's collected the tithes and Little Eton chapel was attached to the new parish of Little Pitchford in the early twelfth century; St Chad's continued to collect the tithes here, too.

The parochial district served by the six churches once took in four huge meanders of the River Severn but one meander round the island of Coton has since disappeared; it stretched seven miles north to Clive (St Mary's), five miles west to Ford (St Michael's), two and a half miles east to Uffington (St

Alkmund's) and Emstrey (St Peter's) and south to Betton and Hanwood (St Chad's) and Pulley (St Julian's). Astley (St Mary's) was appropriately the 'east ley' or east clearing, disafforested in 1300, and the two Preston's, Preston Gubbals and Preston Montford, both 'priest's towns', were settlements either founded by a church or named because owned by one: St Alkmund's held both manors in 1086. A circle drawn to encompass the six parishes would also include, to the south of the Severn, the parish of Meole and the chapelry of Sutton, the 'south ton' but attached to Much Wenlock, both in Hereford diocese.

There was an unusually complicated and interlocking pattern of boundaries; of the six churches, only St Peter's abbey had a compact parish. Owen and Blakeway noted in their *History of Shrewsbury*, published in 1825, that there were numerous 'insulated portions' of one parish within another's territory. The parish of St Michael's at the Castle had four discrete parts, three in or immediately north of Castle Foregate intermingled with St Mary's, and one at Ford to the west; St Julian's parish included most of the settlement of Shelton, though St Chad's parish included the township's fields and two insulated portions within the village. Other townships were split: Harlescote and Albright between St Alkmund's and St Mary's; Coton between St Mary's and St Michael's; Pulley between St Julian's and Meole; a small part of Meole was St Chad's. St Alkmund's had a very small town parish and rural territory to the north which was quite detached. Hadnall, north of Shrewsbury, was an 'insulated portion' of the parish of Middle.

When might the complicated parochial pattern have emerged? Shrewsbury might have been a major early Christian religious site, enclosed in a loop of the river and comparable with Evesham and Pershore churches which are sited in meanders of the River Avon. Early monasteries had more than one church within their enclosure, each with its religious function in the calendar of worship; at Twynham in Hampshire, Ranulf Flambard is said to have demolished nine churches standing round the churchyard in order to make room for the grand new building of Christchurch.[3] But Shrewsbury's churches do not appear to relate to each other in this way.

The dedication of St Julian's, more correctly St Juliana's, hints that it is the most ancient church in Shrewsbury, although it appeared the least important in 1066; St Juliana was martyred in 303 during the persecutions of Diocletian, in Nicomedia in Turkey across the Straits from Constantinople, and this is the only known English dedication to her, though her feast day was celebrated by the early English church. There is the possibility of Christianity surviving from Roman times in the area; St Andrew's church within the Roman city of Wroxeter is five miles down the Severn. After the area became part of Mercia, Shrewsbury may have become an administrative centre which replaced Wroxeter. The bishop of Lichfield was then given a site for a church with other lands, so giving assistance in the development of the town; archaeological evidence suggests that a church on St Chad's site, on the highest point of the Shrewsbury peninsula, was built soon after Chad's tenure of the see between 669 and 672. St Chad's church was outside the oldest town wall but its parish

Wroxeter, Shropshire - St Andrew's church stands in the south-west corner of Viroconium Cornoviorum, the fourth largest town in Roman Britain, beside the road leading to a crossing of the river Severn, and near the upthrust hump of hill called the Wrekin. Two Roman columns have been set up as gateposts, and Roman masonry was reused in the church. Four priests were recorded here in Domesday Book, and seven villagers. In 2000 it is one of the 'Millennium' churches of the Churches Conservation Trust.

extended across Welsh Bridge to Frankwell where in 1086 the Frenchmen's forty-three houses were. St Julian's church, just inside the earliest town wall, fitted with the property boundaries of Wyle Cop, a densely populated street leading to English Bridge, in the middle of which its parish met Holy Cross parish, but St Julian's included nearly all Coleham on the further side of the Severn with which it was linked by a ferry. This matched the pattern which has been found in East London, where parishes extending beyond the town walls were associated with gateways.[4]

The first written reference to Shrewsbury was in a charter issued in 901 by Aethelred and Aethelflaed, rulers of Mercia, granting land to Wenlock monastery while *in civitate Scrobbensis*, 'in the city of Scrobb'; coins minted in Shrewsbury in the tenth and early eleventh centuries most commonly had 'Scrobe' or 'Scrobr' on them, but a series of changes in spelling and pronunciation have led to the modern name, and a misreading gave the abbreviated 'Salop'.[5] Aethelflaed, the Lady of the Mercians, who died in 918, was traditionally said to have founded St Alkmund's church, and the dedication may support this. Alkmund or *Ealhmund* was a Northumbrian prince murdered about 800, an obscure saint for a Shrewsbury church, but Aethelflaed may have sent relics from Derby, where Alkmund was buried, following her capture of the town from the Danes in 917. In the same way, she took the relics of St Werburgh, a Mercian princess but one of the 'cousinhood' of Kentish saints, from Hanbury to Chester. St Alkmund's church was built on part of St Julian's site - the King's market in 1261 was held 'in the cemeteries of Saints Alkmund and Juliana' - and perhaps was given much of St Julian's endowment. St Alkmund's church has the later conventional east-west orientation, but St Julian's has not. St Alkmund's was supposed to have been further endowed by King Edgar who created prebends.

Edgar was also regarded as the founder of St Mary's, the second royal church. The central part of Shrewsbury was fortified about that time and the first reference to Shrewsbury's shire is in the Anglo-Saxon chronicle in 1006. St Mary's was close to the northern boundary of the *burh*. It has been suggested it was a minster church for land north of the Severn, with Meole a minster for south of the Severn.[6] But Meole church was in the diocese of Hereford, a striking divergence from the major part of its proposed territory, while a jagged boundary between St Mary's and St Alkmund's points to a late division, St Alkmund's giving up territory to St Mary's. In 1086, St Alkmund's and St Mary's parishes appear to have a systematic basis: as well as their own manors each included two adjacent manors on the edge of the Shrewsbury area and one elsewhere, and two freeholders' estates, one under the control of the earl, one under the sheriff. The organising hand could have been King Edgar's, allocating the tithes between the Shrewsbury churches, or it could have been closer in date to Domesday.

The Normans built a castle close to the Anglo-Saxon defences and fifty-one houses were demolished to make room for it; St Michael's, the third royal church, was at this northern gateway. As Leland observed 'The castle of Shrobbesbyry is set so that it is in the very place where the towne is not defendid with Severne, els the towne were totally environyd with water'; the southern sweep of the river remained a barrier only crossed by ferries until the late nineteenth century. In 1086 Shrewsbury was called a city. Of the sixteen towns given this description, ten were bishops' sees, twelve were Roman in origin and fourteen were centres of Anglo-Saxon 'shires'. Shrewsbury's boundaries were those mapped for the old municipal borough in 1832, almost 750 years later, with the exception of Shelton, in 1086 said to be in the city but later in the 'Liberties' administered with Shrewsbury.[7] The Liberties were extended in 1495 to include the areas within the parishes of the central churches, so rationalising a little the complicated pattern.

Shrewsbury, Shropshire - the south porchway of St Mary's dates from about 1200, with a fine carved doorway; the upper room was remodelled in the late fourteenth century, perhaps for the priest who took the services, as dean and prebendaries were customarily absent. The outer doors were made out of the former rood screen dividing the chancel from the nave. The church was closed in 1987, and became 'the cathedral of the Redundant Churches Fund', now The Churches Conservation Trust.

CANONS AND PREBENDARIES

Collegiate churches like St Alkmund's and St Chad's in Shrewsbury by 1066 were not primarily concerned with the pastoral care of a parish, which was delegated to a vicar or chaplain; rather, a college was a way of using the resources of a parish in land and tithes for the support of important royal, episcopal or noble servants, and of creating an institution bringing honour and prestige to the founder. The status and dignity of a church was raised by having several canons, as well as priests, clerks, vicars choral who sang the services for the canons, and probably choristers and a school. One clue to an unusually large and elaborate chancel in a parish church is that it was built for a collegiate establishment.

The collegiate pattern had its origins in the Christian ideal of a communal life, but by 1066 had developed into something more individualistic and worldly.[8] As long as most of the people were pagan, it was necessary to give support to a Christian priest with at least one clerical companion, or a larger community of clerics. An early Anglo-Saxon bishop had a community at his cathedral known as his *familia*. In the early fifth century, a rule was formulated by Augustine, bishop of Hippo on the Mediterranean coast of Africa, for the daily lives of his staff of priests who lived in a 'monastery of clerics' and were active in the world, which led to a recognised Augustinian order. The rule was made a little less strict after 1118 and a number of English houses of 'regular canons' were founded after this to follow the rule. In a general sense all priests lived according to the church's rules, but 'canon' became the accepted term for a priest with a communal situation, or 'secular canon' because he was a man with worldly possessions. 'College' was the community's legal expression: members or fellows of a college held its property in common. There was a guardian, master, dean or provost at the head of a college, and the canons were subject to his authority. As a corporate legal body, a college had a seal to validate its transactions concerning land.

Before the Norman Conquest, a pattern was emerging in which property was divided and each canon was allocated part as a 'prebend' for his lifetime. Prebend meant 'that which is provided', like 'provender'. A prebend was originally the food and clothing distributed from a common fund, and later money, not necessarily in equal shares but reflecting a hierarchy; but individually held estates became so usual that this is what the term usually meant by 1066.[9] Other collegiate property remained in common, and buildings like a refectory, as well as the church itself. King Edgar reputedly created ten prebends for St Alkmund's church, Shrewsbury, before 975; he could have enlarged the church's endowment to support more canons or have reorganised the endowments into individual estates. Other collegiate churches claimed Edgar as their founder, for example Southwell, Derby, Leicester and Tamworth and these were reorganisations. Prebendaries usually had their individual houses: In the city of Chester Domesday Book recorded thirteen houses belonging to the warden and twelve canons of St Werburgh's church; similarly twelve canons' houses belonged to St Alkmund's in Shrewsbury, and sixteen houses let to townsmen in 1086 by the bishop of Chester must formerly have accommodated the sixteen canons of St Chad's. Holy Cross, Waltham, which Earl Harold founded in 1060 by the River Lea in an area of new settlement in the forest, was generously endowed with estates and the dean and twelve canons had their individual prebends and houses. After Harold claimed the throne, he prayed at Waltham and then rode to meet the Norman armies near Hastings.

Prebends were sinecures, without cure of souls in the parish; two or more could be held without violating the canon law which prohibited the holding of more than one living. The college of St Martin le Grand in London, founded

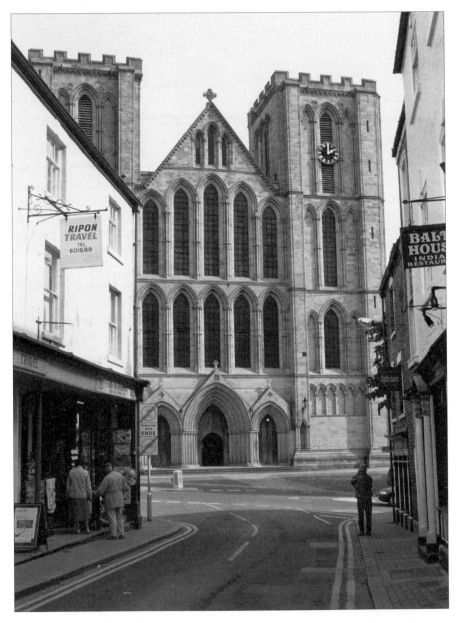

Ripon cathedral, North Yorkshire - Archbishop Walter de Gray built the west front in mid-thirteenth century, adding to his predecessor's nave. St Peter's church was one of the three great collegiate churches in York diocese, and was founded in 672 by the rich and overbearing St Wilfrid. Although suppressed, the college was refounded between 1604 and 1606 with six canons. In 1836 Ripon became the first new cathedral for three hundred years.

about 1068 by William the Conqueror, was in effect 'a college of civil servants'. The canons of St Martin's in Dover were an important community of clerks situated at the main English port, who must have discharged many useful services to both the bishop and the king. Further along the south coast a similar royal prebendal church existed at Twynham, west of Southampton, later called Christchurch. Domesday Book gave a detailed, if problematic, account of St Martin's, which exceptionally was described before the king's lands in Kent. It recorded that before 1066 the prebends were in common, but Odo, bishop of Bayeux, divided them into individual shares. The details which follow contradict the obvious interpretation because twenty out of the twenty-two canons in 1066 had named predecessors, each holding a separate estate of usually one sulung or about 200 acres. Three had been in possession of their prebends before 1066, five had inherited from their fathers or in one case a brother, one prebend continued to belong to the abbot of St Augustine's, the archbishop of Canterbury had given his to his archdeacon, and Spirites' prebend had been transferred to Nigel the doctor who had taken his lands nearly everywhere. Odo's 'division' seems to relate to legalities: instead of a single assessment for the church, each canon paid tax individually.

Either before 1066, or soon after, prebends existed in nine cathedrals and in the archbishop of York's near-cathedral churches at Southwell, Beverley and Ripon. Canons could be supported by the revenues of other well-endowed parish churches. For example, Edward the Confessor just before 1066 granted the church in his royal manor of Axminster in Devon as a prebend for two of the seven canons in York minster.[10] Axminster church had existed before 786, and was a college of seven priests in the early tenth century. The two canons held the church in common, which meant that each had half the income and alternately nominated a vicar to serve the parish; what had once been a well-endowed minster now became a relatively poor vicarage. Prebendaries were required to reside in the cathedral community for part of the year. If prebendaries were not often resident, the tenth century movement to replace secular canons in cathedrals by monastic communities was perhaps stimulated by a need to secure permanent attendance in the church. The numbers of cathedral prebends were much increased by the Normans and by the thirteenth century Lincoln, York and Salisbury each had more than fifty canons. Nine cathedrals were served by monastic communities, which was an English oddity, and Carlisle was founded late enough to follow the Augustinian rule.

Anglo-Saxon collegiate churches rarely survived the Norman period. The college of Waltham was given to Durham cathedral after 1066, and the nave pillars with the deep zig-zag patterns which were intended to be filled with bronze, are like the design used in Durham cathedral itself. Later Waltham became an Augustinian abbey and was the very last of the monasteries to be dissolved. St Alkmund's college in Shrewsbury was dissolved in the 1140s when its endowments were used to found an abbey of Augustinian canons on the largest of its prebendal estates at Lilleshall near Newport, some sixteen miles from Shrewsbury; the dean of St Alkmund's was one of the founders. A vicar carried out the church's parochial duties in Shrewsbury. But the collegiate ideal never lost its appeal, and other churches were given similar constitutions before the Reformation again destroyed them.

PORTIONARY CHURCHES

The endowment of a portionary church like St Julian's, Shrewsbury, was divided between two or more rectors who were usually concerned with the pastoral care of the parish; there was one parish church, and possibly some chapels in other townships. The arrangement would misleadingly be interpreted as collegiate. It might have been the result of dividing a church's resources to create separate rectories but not separate parishes; it might have resulted from the absorption of two or more churches into a single parish; or it might from the beginning have been the way those parishes were organised. Two portioners was an ancient ecclesiastical pattern found on the continent, and was not unusual in England in 1066, but the resources of such large parishes were sometimes reorganised at a later date to endow collegiate churches, for example in Wingham in Kent and in Lanchester, Chester le Street and Auckland in County Durham.[11]

The pattern was characteristic of the western part of Britain. In Shropshire, three portionary churches survived into the nineteenth century and two into the twentieth: Westbury had two portioners until 1862, Pontesbury had three until 1909, reduced to two in the late twentieth century who became the nucleus of a group ministry, and Burford had three until 1974. Westbury and Burford had two priests in 1086, suggesting the antiquity of the arrangement. Alberbury had four portioners in the twelfth and thirteenth centuries, until absorbed by Alberbury priory, and here, too, traces of the earlier organisation were still evident in the nineteenth century. Other Shropshire churches which were possibly portionary in 1066 were Stanton Lacy with two priests, and Wroxeter with four.

Alberbury, Westbury and Pontesbury are contiguous parishes on the western border with Wales and the coincidence of these three portionary churches all centred on a 'bury' points strongly to simultaneous organisation.[12] All are in the diocese of Hereford and were in the hundred of Rhiwset. Was 'bury' a translation of 'Llan' and had the Anglo-Saxons adopted an existing Welsh system? Alberbury had a Welsh name - Llanfihangel-yng-Nghentyn - St Michael's in the Lowlands, and there is a circular enclosure in Pontesbury and a near circle at Westbury marked by the road pattern reminiscent of that associated with some churches in South Wales. In North Wales, a number of portionary churches existed in 1291. The organisation could have been linked with the tenth-century organisation of hundreds.[13] Each parish contained a number of townships and hamlets and there are signs of a systematic regularity in the Domesday pattern of manors, with one manor held by the Earl, two or three other manors, and one or two minor free holdings. In Burford and Pontesbury two portions were nearly equal in value and one was half the value, an arrangement which appears designed for two priests and a deacon; Westbury had a third, smaller portion allocated to a 'sacristan'. But the internal arrangements for the portions were not the same in each parish.[14]

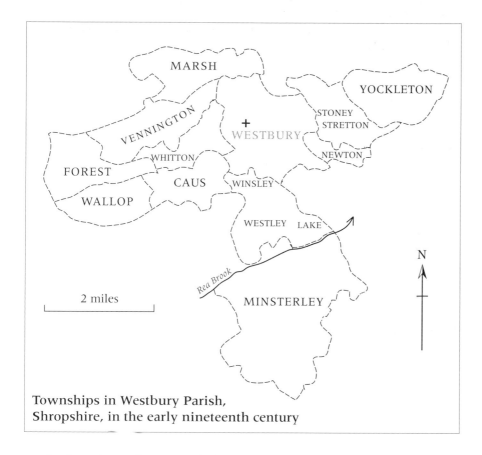

**Townships in Westbury Parish,
Shropshire, in the early nineteenth century**

Westbury is to the west of Shrewsbury, by reference to which it was probably named, and is mainly north of the Rea brook, with the township of Minsterley south of the brook appearing like a later addition to an otherwise fairly compact stretch of territory. Minsterley was a royal manor in 1066 and most of the tithes from the township were not paid to Westbury's rectors. The tithes of the other townships were divided equally between the two rectors. The township of Westbury itself consisted of Westbury Dextra (right) and Westbury Sinister (left) indicating the physical division of the church building. Until 1859 there was only one rectory house; then Yockleton became a separate parish and the second portioner became its rector and moved there.

Pontesbury is mainly to the south of the Rea brook, but with a line of townships on the north side. The tithes of Longden, a large block of land in the south-west of the parish, were held jointly by the second and third portioners; a chapel there is documented about 1221, and it remained a benefice without parochial responsibilities. Tithes from a group of townships in the north of the parish were almost entirely the second portioner's, and Pontesbury, Pontesford and several adjoining townships were divided between all three: approximately two thirds of the tithes belonged to the first portion, while the third portion had a larger share than the second. Each portioner had glebe in one only of the three divisions. Until 1840, the rector of the first portion had responsibility for services in the church for twenty-six weeks in the year, and the second and third portioners for thirteen weeks each. The consecration of a chapel at Cruckton in 1840 led to the bishop specifying parochial areas for each portioner, not without considerable argument, while the pattern of church duties remained the same. There were three rectory houses, two close to the church and one a little distance from it. The first portion house was known as the Deanery but was demolished in 1965; the second ceased to be the parsonage in 1910 and is now called the Manor House; the third is the Old Rectory.

Alberbury is immediately to the north of Westbury, and is bounded by the River Severn. The church was given to Shrewsbury abbey in the mid-twelfth century but soon after was assigned to Alberbury priory, which gradually acquired the patronage of all four portions. The priory appropriated all the tithes and endowed a vicarage in 1289, and also made provision for a priest and a deacon. In 1414 the priory and its estate passed to All Souls College, Oxford, which continued to appoint a Welsh speaking sexton or vicar's priest; after the Reformation parishioners asked for this arrangement to continue and a curate was provided. When the tithes were commuted, All Souls was allotted ten times more income than the vicar, and the parish clerk, presumably the successor to the sexton, had a quarter as much as the vicar. All three had some share in the tithes of the six divisions of the parish.

Portioners might appear like prebendaries, and indeed Pontesbury was described as prebendal in the *Valor Ecclesiasticus*, but the origins of the portionary churches seem to lie in a different concept. Similar parochial arrangements might explain why, in some places in the Eastern counties, two or even three parish churches were built in one churchyard, or there were two churches side by side like the two thatched naves of Pakefield in Suffolk which had two rectors until 1743.[15] Portionary churches were not colleges 'in an incomplete state of development', as thirteen jurors emphasised in 1384 when asked about the status of Ledbury parish church, in Hereford diocese, another portionary church which lasted into the nineteenth century: the portioners 'have no common seals, common chests, common bells, common buildings or chapter-houses for consultations. Nor have they a dean, provost, master or warden, or any other person as principal chief in the same'.

Portionary churches were sometimes reconstituted as colleges. In instances in Kent and Durham, the archbishop of Canterbury and the bishop of Durham wanted opportunities for patronage. Both were restricted by the monastic constitutions of their cathedrals which meant there were no prebends to give their staff and political supporters; Durham cathedral had become a Benedictine monastery in 1083 and Christ Church, Canterbury, by the early eleventh century.[16] Bishop Anthony Bek of Durham instituted a college at Lanchester in 1284, at Chester le Street in 1286, and at Auckland, where the bishop had a country house, in 1294. Together, these three parishes formed a continuous sweep of territory to the west of Durham. According to the *Pope Nicholas Taxation* all three were portionary churches before Bek's reforms. The portioners had looked after the chapels in each parish; Lanchester had three chapelries and Chester le Street two. Under Bek's constitutions, the dean of each college had the cure of souls of the whole parish, collecting small tithes and altar dues; he paid two assistant curates to serve the parish church and to provide matins for parishioners each day before they went to their labours; a prebendary was responsible for providing a substitute curate for each chapel. Bek transferred to the deans the 'messuages, courts and lands' belonging to the chapelries, and the prebendaries were allocated only a sufficient area of the courtyard 'in which they may sell their corne'. So Bek had created several non-resident prebends; perhaps he had also clarified who had responsibility for the cure of souls. By 1535, the deans had engrossed the lions' share of the available resources and after the colleges were closed, chapels and parish churches were left with poorly-paid perpetual curates.

Wingham in East Kent was the archbishop of Canterbury's largest and most valuable Kentish manor, which in 1291 provided nearly a fifth of his substantial income drawn from Kentish estates; it may have been one of the earliest bequests to the church of Canterbury, although little is known about it before 1066. The manor covered about 20,000 acres of fertile arable and marsh along the course of the River Stour and the rapidly silting-up Wantsum channel. Attached to it was a tract of wood on the downland to the west at Womenswold - the wold of the men of Wingham. There was no mention of church or priest in Wingham in Domesday Book but the *Domesday Monachorum* listed six churches which 'pertained' to Wingham church: Ash, Nonington and Womenswold were later chapels of Wingham; two churches became disused, and the sixth, if correctly identified as Elmstone, became an independent parish before 1535.[17]

In the *Pope Nicholas Taxation* Wingham was a portionary church with a provost and vicar for Wingham itself, and one portioner serving Ash with its chapels, a second Goodnestone, and a third Nonington with the chapel of Womenswold. Ash was the wealthiest of the four portions, substantially wealthier than Wingham itself. The archbishop planned to convert the portioners into a college in 1274; the deed was confirmed by the Pope in 1287, and the first head inducted, and by Edward I in 1290. The college was to consist of a provost and six canons: two priests, two deacons and two sub-deacons. The archbishop's chaplain was the first provost, his lawyer and advocate at the Papal court was given a priest prebend, and his nephew a sub-deacon prebend. Relatives of later archbishops were similarly given prebends, and the last provost, Edmund Cranmer, was appointed by his brother, archbishop Edward Cranmer.

The foundation charter declared:
We...have turned our eyes to the church of Wingham as it were to a fruitful vineyard filled with branches and fruits, which cannot be easily cultivated by the labours of one husbandman, nay, further, by the labours of two, from the great extent of the parish as well as its numerous population, and its revenues are sufficient to furnish the payment of more labourers. And it seems very much opposed to the divine plans that what is quite enough for more soldiers of Christ should be pressed into one purse.

It stated that Wingham was being divided into four parishes. In practice the archbishop was not making parishes but altering relationships. In particular the status of Ash was reduced by assigning the chapel and tithes of the manor of Overland to the college provost; Overland 'borough' - or tithing - nonetheless remained in Ash parish. The other parochial divisions, in addition to Wingham itself, were Goodnestone with the hamlets 'which from the earliest times have belonged to the church of Goodnestone', and Nonington; these were areas 'which the vicars are known to have so far held without hindrance', showing it was not a wholly new arrangement.[18]

The provost had responsibility for the whole parish; his house was the former rectory next to the church. The canons' prebends consisted of land and tithes in particular areas of the parish. They did not have to reside in Wingham all the year round although three large timber-framed houses survive; like the provost each was to appoint a resident vicar and fourteen stalls were provided in the chancel of the church, enough for all. In 1535 the college paid seven stipendiary priests or curates to serve the churches, two for Wingham and one each for Ash, Overland, Richborough or Fleet, Nonington, and Womenswold.[19] Fleet was the one vill in Wingham manor named in Domesday; it included Richborough Roman fort, within which was one of six ancient churches in Kent dedicated to St Augustine, perhaps dating from the seventh century. On the other side of the Wantsum is Ebbsfleet, traditionally where Augustine landed in 597.

Wingham, Kent - the fifteenth century 'Wealden' house in the main street, now called the Old Vicarage, was occupied by the vicar at some time although also associated with a series of medical practitioners. When Wingham college was dissolved, the perpetual curate had no house. In 1797 Revd Thomas Hey DD, inherited the former college property; he endowed the curate with £100 a year and a house and a little land, perhaps this house.

Monasteries in the Parochial System

Between 1100 and 1135, the number of monasteries in England and Wales doubled and by 1216 it had doubled again to approximately 700; at its peak about 1300, there were between 800 and 1000. As English bishops informed the Pope at the end of the twelfth century, 'hitherto canon law and English custom alike permitted a man to erect a conventual church in his own fief'.[20] A monastery lent prestige to a large manor and provided many facilities; the founder gained influence as a benefactor, and he secured prayers for his soul. Norman monastic foundations like St Peter's abbey, Shrewsbury, were communities of monks following the Benedictine rule, or a variation of it. Like a collegiate church, a monastery was not primarily concerned with pastoral care of parishioners; on the other hand, the work of serving God in daily prayer could as well, or better, be continued in a monastery than in a parish church.

There were several possible relationships between a monastery and the parish in which it was situated. It might replace an existing church whose revenues supported the new foundation, and so have cure of souls in the parish: the parish church might continue in use, or the monastery church become parochial; alternatively a monastery could exist within another church's parish. When the monasteries were dissolved between 1536 and 1540, the royal commissioners deemed most monastery churches to be non-parochial and so they were destroyed; in a few places where one served as a parish church, perhaps by default, parts of the building were allowed to survive.

The abbey of St Peter, Shrewsbury, replaced a parish church, and the abbey church contained the special altar of Holy Cross for the parish. The Domesday jurors explained that Earl Roger, a powerful Norman lord who was probably a kinsman to William I and held nearly all the king's lands in Shropshire, had granted to his new abbey an existing monastery of St Peter 'where there was a parish church of the city'. Ordericus Vitalis wrote a near contemporary account

Shrewsbury, Shropshire - the south side of the former abbey church. When the abbey was dissolved, the nave was preserved as the parish church of Holy Cross; 'stumps' of the destroyed south transept are visible. The monastic buildings were on this side, but nothing survived the cutting of the London to Holyhead road in 1836 except the Refectory pulpit which still stands in the car park.

of the foundation. He was the son of the priest of St Peter's at the time, and was baptised in 1075 in the nearby church of Atcham and educated locally. He said that the existing St Peter's church was outside the city's east gate in the area called the Foregate. This was part of the city of Shrewsbury, with thirty-nine burgages, although divided from the rest of the town by the Severn; a gate controlled the entrance to the bridge, near to or on the site of English Bridge.[21] Ordericus Vitalis said that his father had begun to rebuild St Peter's church in stone, and when he gave it to the abbey he entered the community together with one son, but half his father's property was retained for another son; this appears to be the endowment of 'the vicarage of the altar of Holy Cross, the parish church of Monks' Foregate'. No record of a vicarage ordination exists, but an agreement between a vicar and abbot John, sometime between 1278 and 1291, described which lands paid tithe to the vicar, including all crofts and curtileges in the Foregate. Apart from what is now Abbey Foregate, the parish of Holy Cross was mainly in the township of Emstrey, which is puzzling. The church at *Eiminstre* or Emstrey - the name meant minster on an island or by water - had disappeared before the time of Domesday; St Peter's, sited nearer the town, may have replaced it. After the abbey was dissolved in 1540, the western part of the abbey church was preserved for Holy Cross parish.

The old parish church of Tewkesbury in Gloucestershire continued in use when the newly-founded abbey took over the earlier church's substantial estates and responsibilities. Tewkesbury abbey was founded in 1102 by Robert Fitz Hamon, a Norman companion of William II. It was sited close to the new market borough which had been given a charter by William the Conqueror's Queen, Maud. Tewkesbury abbey continued to receive benefactions from the wealthy men who were patrons, and the church, with its massive scale and splendid tower, reflected their status and wealth. The abbey's relations with townsmen were not always good. In 1367 the monks complained to the king of the town's hostility. There was a dispute concerning payments for the re-consecration of their church, which the townsmen probably thought the abbey should meet as it collected all the tithes and offerings. As a result, 'the said parishioners rashly withdraw tithes and oblations due to the said church, go about with armed force, lie in ambush day and night to wound and ill-treat the abbot and monks and their servants and threaten them in life and limb so that they dare not go outside the abbey gates to serve the said church or do other business'. Eventually the old parish church ceased to be used. When the abbey was dissolved in 1540, the townsmen claimed that they had no parish church, and they were allowed to purchase the abbey church.[22] Legally it then became parochial, and the townsmen's success has preserved it as one of the largest parish churches in the country. But there was no rector or vicar, and only gradually was the curate's position made satisfactory.

The Augustinian abbey of St Mary at Cirencester, in Gloucestershire, was founded by Henry I about 1117 'for the good of the souls of my parents and ancestors, and for the remission of my sins, and for the welfare and safety of my kingdom'. Like Tewkesbury, the new abbey absorbed an existing church's lands and tithes. Leland wrote about a 'great chirch of Prebendaries' prior to the abbey's foundation. There is little indication of this in Domesday Book, but Henry I's charter confirmed that the church was collegiate, providing that the secular canons' prebends should pass to the abbey when they died, and excavation in 1965 showed that the new abbey church had been built on top of what is considered the longest Anglo-Saxon church in the country.[23] As well as the monastery church, Henry I built a parish church of St John the Baptist next to the market place. It was extensively rebuilt in the early sixteenth century. Here there was no need to preserve the abbey church when the monastery was dissolved in 1539 but, like Tewkesbury, the parish was left without either rectory or vicarage.

The new monasteries drew revenues from many parishes, often at a considerable distance away. The Normans made an 'immense number' of donations of tithes to their foundations, at first mainly in Normandy, but in the twelfth century to their English foundations.[24] They felt free to transfer two thirds of the tithes of their own land, the amount previously reserved to the minster church, and in many cases these tithes were not supporting the local village church. They also gave the advowsons of many churches to their monasteries, which could mean tithes and all other sources of revenue; sometimes the monastery claimed the tithes for itself at a later date. Tithes were a tax which could be used in accordance with changing priorities. But in time, the monasteries' wealth greatly over-balanced that of the parochial clergy. Earl Roger's donations to Shrewsbury abbey before 1086 included five churches in important manors in the immediate region: Wrockwardine, Baschurch, Hodnet, Morville and Corfham; these were five of the six hundredal manors listed first in the Domesday account of Earl Roger's holding. Condover, the sixth, was given to Shrewsbury abbey soon after 1086. This primary group of six manors and hundreds looks like the heartland of the *Wreocensaete*, the people who took their name from the Wrekin and from Wroxeter, forming the

Diddlebury, Shropshire - St Peter's is notable for Anglo-Saxon masonry: the unusual western arch, supported in the twelfth century with a lower arch, once provided an imposing entrance, and the mounded-up and round churchyard is a sign of an ancient church. It was the church for the Domesday manor of Corfham, at the centre of two hundreds.

nucleus of Shropshire. The churches in Shrewsbury town centre were not his to give to the abbey. Tewkesbury's foundation charter gave the abbey the churches of Fairford and St James' in Bristol, as well as lands in Sussex, Devon, Dorset, Shropshire and Wales, but by 1535 it had appropriated the revenues of no less than twenty-one churches. The endowment of Cirencester abbey consisted of the priest Regenbald's property. Regenbaold, or Reinbold, was called dean of Cirencester and Leland saw his tomb in the abbey church; effectively he served Edward the Confessor and William I as a 'chancellor'. He held property in Cirencester and elsewhere in the county, and twenty churches in the south and west, one of which was Bray in Berkshire where, as a consequence, there was later to be a flexible-minded vicar.

It is surprising that lords of the manor chose to give up their power to choose the parson by transferring the advowson of so many churches to monasteries, but in practice their patronage was valueless because the son of a married priest was able to succeed his father. Lords were also powerless where the church was collegiate and the canons admitted new members to the community and elected the master. The Normans naturally disliked independent clerics of Anglo-Saxon parentage, who could be a focus for hostility or even rebellion. 'The parson (and his heir) had to be prised out. A change could sometimes be made when he died, but such disinheritances upset local society'. Transferring the advowson to a monastery was possibly the only acceptable way of interfering. A church council at Lillebonne in Normandy in 1080 outlined a procedure: after the death or resignation of an incumbent, the monastery was to present a new candidate to the bishop for approval; if he chose not to live in the monastery with the monks, he was to be provided as a vicar with a suitable maintenance out of the church's revenues. Either he gave up his church's independence, or he lost a proportion of the church's income. Imposing celibacy was another way of removing married and hereditary parsons, and of the bishop asserting control over parish clergy. The council of Westminster in 1102 agreed that the sons of priests should not be heirs of their father's churches, and this was repeated in 1175. Hereditary succession was gradually eliminated. A late case concerned Bradbourne in Derbyshire; in 1214, after years of litigation, the canons of Dunstable ejected a rector and vicar who were sons of former incumbents and were themselves married.[25] Celibacy sharpened the distinction between clergy and laity.

The neglect of pastoral care became so serious that the bishops formulated canons requiring monasteries to provide their churches with vicars and with permanent endowments, sometimes with a requirement also that the vicar be resident. By about 1184, perpetual vicarages existed in more than half the English dioceses, and in the next thirty years they increased in step with the great increase in appropriations; it is estimated that by 1200 a quarter of all English churches were in the hands of religious houses. A Lateran Council in 1215 agreed: 'Since therefore it is not lawful to muzzle the ox that treads the corn, but he who serves the altar should live of the altar: we have ordained ... a sufficient portion be assigned for the priest'. As a result, differentiation of great tithes from small and personal tithes emerged. The great tithes, of corn and hay, were usually retained by the monastery; the small tithes might be given to the vicar, and the personal tithes and offerings of parishioners nearly always were, and these became 'a substantial portion of the priest's endowments'.[26] Of 8000 churches taxed separately in 1291, 1500 were vicarages; by 1535 the number had more than doubled. When the monasteries were dissolved, many parish churches were left with little endowment and some with no regular minister.

CHAPELS IN THE PAROCHIAL SYSTEM

Characteristic Romanesque or Anglo-Norman architecture and decorative detail is evidence of the energy directed to church building during the century following the Norman Conquest. In Worcestershire, nearly two thirds of the churches and chapels with medieval fabric have Norman period features, 102 out of 161. In Shropshire, Herefordshire, Oxfordshire and Gloucestershire, more than half the medieval churches and chapels contain Norman masonry, though the proportion is about one third in Warwickshire and Staffordshire. In many cases, timber buildings were probably being replaced with stone. Rebuilding was not only instigated by Norman lords; Wulfstan, Anglo-Saxon bishop of Worcester from 1062 to 1095, was active in building churches on his estates as well as rebuilding his cathedral, and he brought pressure to bear on other landowners in his diocese to do the same.[27]

Their architecture shows that chapels as well as parish churches were built, like The Heath in Shropshire, a centre of worship for a small community and apparently highly regarded. In Worcestershire it is notable that by far the majority of surviving Norman buildings, about eighty, were chapels; the twelve chapels of St Helen's, for example, all have evidence of construction in this period. In itself this may suggest that the distinction between parish church and chapel was not yet clear. By the end of the twelfth century, as the parish became more sharply defined, chapels ceased to attract so much attention; but parish churches were rebuilt, a response to their status and income, to fashions and prosperity, and perhaps to a larger number of churchgoers. Some chapels became parish churches over the next several centuries and were rebuilt; but many continued in use without extensive alteration.

Hubberholme, North Yorkshire - the Norman tower of St Michael and All Angels was perhaps the 'chapel and chamber' given to Coverham abbey in 1241. A graveyard was consecrated in the late fifteenth century because inhabitants claimed the river Wharfe in spate and winter snow prevented them reaching their parish church in Arncliffe. This was J.B.Priestley's favourite church.

The word 'chapel', Frankish in origin, gained currency in William I's laws for what in Anglo-Saxon England was a 'field church', that is one without a graveyard. It is not easy to know how many chapels there were at any date; they were not regularly recorded as the 'mother church' was the tax-paying unit, but they were not uncommon. The list of 152 churches in Rochester diocese in Kent copied into the *Textus Roffensis* about 1115, but perhaps dating from thirty to forty years earlier, specifically named twenty-four chapels; it also contains evidence of changes in status.[28] The list recorded annual payments for 'chrism', the oil used in baptism: nine old pence from a church or six pence from a chapel, so typically these chapels had baptismal rights and the large number of Norman fonts which have been preserved show baptism took place in many churches.

From the early twelfth century bishops' registers and monastic cartularies seem to record the consecration of chapels, but a study of the Shropshire parish of Morville shows that when, about 1138, the bishop of Hereford consecrated five chapels out of the seven then in the parish, in at least three cases, Astley Abbots, Aston Eyre and Oldbury, it was actually a graveyard, not the chapel itself.[29] The apparently unique dedication of Astley Abbots chapel to St Calixtus, an early third-century pope whose martyrdom was described in the seventh century, suggests it is much earlier than its Norman-style architecture or the record of consecration. Aston Eyre church, built by the Norman lord, Robert Fitz Aer, has a tympanum rated 'the best piece of Norman carving in Shropshire'.

Shrewsbury abbey's appropriation of Morville church coincided with these chapel or churchyard consecrations. The bishop required the abbey to provide for the service of the church, and the chapels were made parochial probably as a much less expensive method of fulfilling the obligation than creating vicarages, which would have meant giving up at least some tithes. But some thirty years later, Aston Eyre lost its burial rights, and before the end of the century the abbey took over the presentation to the chapel and confirmed to

Farmcote, Gloucestershire - the chapel of St Faith is beside an old road climbing the Cotswold edge from Hailes. It is little altered since the Norman period, except that the apse at the east end has gone - the blocked chancel arch is visible. It was once parochial; in 1551 'an exceptionally ignorant man' ministered to about thirteen communicants. It became attached to Guiting Power church, some miles away, where the same family was lord of the manor.

itself burial fees and mortuaries. In the early thirteenth century Astley Abbots was treated similarly. Aston Eyre formally became a parish at the end of the nineteenth century. Of the other chapels, Oldbury and Tasley became independent rectories by 1291; Billingsley, a third chapel with Norman architecture, was a rectory by 1535. Aldenham was a private chapel for Aldenham Park, and Underton became a Bridgnorth prebend.

The freezing of parishes as they existed by the early thirteenth century led to a tightening up of relationships. Defending his right to be admitted parson of Altham in Lancashire in the late thirteenth century, Henry of Clayton claimed that it 'had always been a parish church, with rights of baptism and burial, and all other rights which distinguish a parish church from a chapel'; but he lost his case to the powerful rector of Whalley who collected the tithes. Nonetheless Whalley abbey, which was founded soon after and held the rectory, paid £20 in 1301 for a successor at Altham to surrender his claim. Altham became a parochial chapel, but without even a parochial district until given one again in 1866. A contrary case, however, was Tideswell in Derbyshire. During an enquiry by Papal Commissioners in 1252 into the status of the church, said to be a chapel of Hope, a priest who had served the church for several years was asked to say how he knew that it was parochial. He replied that 'all the children born in the parish of Tideswell he baptised in the same church, and all who died ... in the said parish, he buried in the churchyard ... he also made paschal tapers in it; and performed in it the hallowing of the font on the vigils of Easter and Pentecost'.[30] Tideswell was accepted as a vicarage.

After the thirteenth century, chapels were hardly ever made independent parish churches The last bishop to make parishes in the diocese of Winchester was Henry of Blois. Between 1161 and 1170 he created vicarages in three of the village chapels held by the canons of the collegiate church of Christchurch in Hampshire, turning them into appropriated parish churches; these are among the oldest surviving formal vicarage endowments in England. Neither the king nor the archbishop of York could create parishes. King John in 1207 made an important port and borough at Liverpool on the Mersey to aid him in his invasion of Ireland, but as Leland observed some centuries later: 'Lyrpole, alias Lyverpole, a pavid towne, hath but a chapel. Walton, a four miles off nat far from the se, is paroche chirch'. The archbishop of York in 1310 visited the king's new town of Kingston upon Hull, 'and found a funeral procession winding along the Humber to a distant burial church, between a high tide and a gale; with a great effort he succeeded in arranging burial rights for the chapel of Holy Trinity, Hull; but this church, one of the greatest of medieval parish churches, was only truly made a parish church by Act of Parliament in 1661'.[31]

Chapels nevertheless continued to be founded throughout the medieval period, modifying the rigidities of the parochial system. A statement in 1233 referred to the chapel at Windlesham in Surrey: the vill had been very small, 'no more than three men who were parishioners of the church of Woking', but then it grew, and 'an oratory was instituted in which the chaplain of Woking would celebrate and read the Gospel'. This would appear not to have been parochial. In Lincolnshire, chapels were founded on newly-settled land. Four

Wigston Parva, Leicestershire and Wibtoft, Warwickshire - the two chapels of the Assumption of Our Lady were in the parish of Claybrooke in Leicestershire until Wigston Parva was transferred to Sharnford in 1904. In 1221 it was arranged that a chaplain should serve each chapel on alternate weekdays. Wigston Parva chapel, beautifully cared-for by the chapel warden, is in an enclosure like a churchyard, but was not parochial and the ground is a vegetable garden.

Wibtoft chapel is south of Watling Street in a square moated enclosure, perhaps the original site of the toft or 'curtilege' which belonged to a Dane called Vibbe. Large foundation stones are old but the fabric is mainly of the last two centuries.

'thorpe' places in the parish of Edenham appear as new settlements in a woodland area, and each at one time had a chapel. Round the Wash, there was intensive reclamation in the eleventh and twelfth centuries, both of fen and sea marsh. A group of parish churches on a ridge of higher land, including Spalding and Holbeach, Fleet and Whaplode whose names reflect their situation, controlled at least eight chapels established for new settlements. At Whaplode Drove, the chapel was for 'the easement of those who guard the banks of the rivers and ring the bells as a warning'.[32]

New foundations were often chapels of ease. They existed by permission of the rector or vicar of the parish, who might serve the chapel himself or might appoint a curate. The parishioners of Bakewell in Derbyshire complained to the archbishop of Canterbury in 1280 that the dean and chapter of Lichfield cathedral were not keeping the seven chapels in the parish in repair. The chapter replied that they were only chapels of ease and that it was as a great favour that the inhabitants were allowed to have them. Nonetheless Lichfield was required to provide suitable chaplains and pay each of them two and a half marks (£1.69), the parishioners to supply the remainder of the stipends. The chapter was also to find books and ornaments, while the parishioners had to repair the naves and chancels and find a chalice and missal for each. Chapels of ease could be parochial, with a font and less often a graveyard, but there were an unknown number of other chapels, with and without parochial functions, independent of the rector or vicar of the parish. Many were apparently founded to supply frequent and convenient services but did not take baptism or burial away from the parish church. Bishops continued occasionally to grant parochial rights to such chapels. The chapel yard of Didsbury was consecrated in 1352, in response to the inhabitants' difficulties during the Plague years, the only one of the six chapels in the parish of Manchester to be made parochial before 1540, and the appropriately named Newchurch in Rossendale in Whalley was made parochial in 1511 because the mother church was twelve miles away over a road 'very foule, painfull, and hillous', through country 'extreamly and vehemently cold in the winter'.[33]

It was probably the practice for a deacon to minister in many chapels. A deacon can baptise and bury, read morning and evening prayers, preach and teach but it needs a priest to say mass, and a chapel had to be consecrated for mass to be said in it. Mass was essentially the priest's token eating of bread and drinking of wine, with perhaps occasional participation by some of the congregation in eating the bread. Easter was the one obligatory communion in the year - the essential festival amongst the forty or fifty feast days in the medieval church calendar when parishioners in chapelries were obliged to attend the parish church. Considering the distances involved for people in the townships in northern parishes, it is clear that attendance at the mother church could only have been an occasional festival, but frequent attendance at mass became a medieval ideal. Marriage was not an essential function of the parish church: by mid-twelfth century, it was accepted that marriage was contracted following a mutual declaration by the partners, and the church did not establish a monopoly until the mid-eighteenth century.

CHAPTER FIVE

PRIVATE ENTERPRISES,
PUBLIC DUTIES

The churchwarden of Stanton Lacy in Corvedale in Shropshire personally takes care of this ancient church: a lunchtime conversation on a summer day in 1997 interrupted his work of repairing a leaky roof. The continuing repair of the fabric by past generations of churchwardens has preserved this largely Anglo-Saxon church. The pilaster strips on the west end are an eleventh-century feature, and are comparable with the Northamptonshire church of Barnack. Stanton Lacy church is close to the River Corve, towards its southern end. A legend associates its foundation with St Mildburgh of Much Wenlock who was saved from a pursuer by a sudden rise in the river and vowed to found a church in thanksgiving. But its dedication is to St Peter and a Roman villa north of the church might suggest more ancient foundations. Domesday recorded two priests here, implying an important church. Stanton manor probably reached as far as the confluence of Corve and Teme and the border of Shropshire, where de Lacy lords built a castle and planned the market town of Ludlow. As Leland noted about 1540, Corvedale was 'plentiful of corne' and 'strecchith from abowt Wenlock to Lodlo'. Ludlow became an independent parish and the success of the new town no doubt drew the attention of the lord of the manor away from Stanton Lacy church, leaving the small rural community without the financial means to rebuild it in later medieval style.

LEFT: *Stanton Lacy, Shropshire, and churchwarden.*

The responsibility of the local community for maintenance of their parish church was specifically stated during the thirteenth century throughout Western and Central Europe. In 1287, a synod of the English church at Exeter ordered that inhabitants should contribute according to the amount of land held in the parish. The increasing fragmentation of manorial structures probably made this necessary, as parishes related to several manors and one lord of the manor or patron could not enforce contributions from all. A church rate was collected in 1325 in the hamlet of Wembdon in Bridgewater parish, Somerset, for rebuilding its ruined chapel, and two rates were collected in Bridgewater in 1367 to pay for the new spire of the parish church. No parliamentary statute enforced payment, but church rates were accepted as customary and part of common law. Customarily, too, the rector maintained the chancel; parishioners maintained the nave and usually the tower, and in London and Norwich the chancel as well.[1] The assessment and collection of contributions, and the husbanding and use of resources, both required delegation to a small number of people, the churchwardens.

A response to the church's fixing of responsibility on parishioners was that they began to bequeath property to their parish church to help discharge the burden, and gifts and legacies were sufficient in some places to obviate the need for rates for some centuries. Churchwardens were trustees of such property, but only in towns did this constitute a large part of their revenue and church rates rather than bequests of property were likely to have encouraged the institution of churchwardens everywhere. Fund-raising was widely undertaken, through entertainments and church ales on festive occasions, when the churchwardens organised the brewing and sale of ale. A church house was sometimes purchased or given for the purpose – an early village hall; an inventory for the church house at Nettlecombe in Somerset shows that it contained a variety of vats and cauldrons for brewing.

Churchwardens were chosen 'by the hole assent of the paryssh', and each township might have its own warden; in Shipton under Wychwood, for instance, there were six wardens, one each for Lyneham, Milton, Ramsden and Leafield and two for Shipton itself. The township was the natural agricultural unit for raising money assessed on land. In non-agricultural parishes, churchwardens might represent occupations; Brighton parish in 1570 agreed that two churchwardens should be substantial fishermen, and one a landsman. The choice of churchwardens was a matter of local custom and was not regulated until 1571, when church canons required that they be elected annually by minister and parishioners jointly. The role of the minister was strengthened in 1604, and if there was disagreement, the minister was to have the choice of one warden. This practice became fairly usual thereafter, but altered the previously democratic basis of the wardens.

From the mid-sixteenth century, churchwardens became the vital instruments for enforcing legislation concerning church furnishings and church attendance and they were asked to undo much of the enterprise of previous generations of parishioners. The English reformation much strengthened the formal parish organisation, but religious life was seriously affected. The attraction of resources from parishes to monasteries over many centuries was made irrevocable after they were dissolved; the suppression of collegiate church foundations affected few parishes; but the suppression of chantries and guilds, which formed widespread but 'informal parts of the structure of the parish', and were still being founded in the 1530s, a decade before they were abolished, removed the means by which numerous private individuals had built up services for ordinary people. After the restoration of king and episcopal church in 1660, churchwardens had to enforce uniformity, an unenviable and ultimately impossible duty. Their duties as agents of central government overshadowed their earlier, democratic origins.

EXTENDING THE PARISH'S SERVICES: CHANTRIES

As the name implies, a chantry was a financial provision for the 'chanting' of masses by a priest in memory of the founder.[2] At its simplest, a bequest paid a priest to pray for a short while, perhaps five days following the funeral, or more generously for a 'trental', thirty masses on thirty consecutive days. John Fortey, 'woolman' of Northleach in Gloucestershire, who was responsible for building a substantial part of the present church, left six shillings and eightpence in 1458 to each of 120 churches round Northleach for their fabric 'that the parishioners may have me commended in their prayers'.[3] A larger fund could provide masses for a year, or even in perpetuity, and, more expensively, for a priest to devote himself to this purpose alone. The peak of chantry provision was a 'college' of priests. A chantry was most often founded to pray for an individual or family, but some were cooperative, in the form of guilds; the priest or

Stoke by Nayland, Suffolk - the Guildhall and St Mary's church tower. There were four guilds in the parish and the Guildhall was built about 1400; above was a room for meetings and feasts, and the ground floor was partly a commercial venture with at least one shop. The church was rebuilt soon after, owing much to the wealthy Howard family; Stoke by Nayland was already associated with a lordly family in the tenth century. The tower is mainly brick and was painted over-arched by a rainbow by John Constable.

chaplain of the guild regularly 'minded' or recalled the names of past members, referred to as 'bidding the bedes'. Guilds also had social functions. Schools and almshouses were also chantries; in the almshouse founded by John Estbury at Lambourne in Berkshire, prayers at midday were to be said for his own soul, and for 'the sowls of his parents, auncestors, frendes and all Christian sowles'.

A chantry endowment extended the services available in the parish in a number of ways. Chantry priests frequently helped in the administration of communion at Eastertime. They also provided more occasions on which parishioners could attend mass - bequests were sometimes designed to provide the early morning 'morrow mass' for the benefit of working folk; there was a very full daily round of prayer in churches before the Reformation, which meant they were used much more than now seems possible. A chantry was often associated with a particular altar in the parish church, or with a chapel specially constructed within the church. But in a substantial number of cases, an independent chapel was built in which, with the agreement of the bishop, the chantry priest ministered to local inhabitants. It meant that a priest rather than a deacon served the chapel, in order to say mass. The Chantry Commissioners said in 1547 that mass was said daily in the chapel of Padiham in Whalley; in Burnley chapel in the same parish it was celebrated 'but three times in the week'. A chantry could also be a response to a church's loss of income through the appropriation of its revenues by other religious bodies. A chantry endowed at the end of the twelfth century in the chapel of Monyash in Bakewell in Derbyshire, for instance, for which the dean and chapter of Lichfield had responsibility, supplemented the two and a half marks a year they paid to the chaplain. A chantry was the most usual but not the only means of providing services in a chapel. In Cumbria, inhabitants in some townships collectively provided an endowment for a priest. The inhabitants of Old Hutton in Kendal parish agreed in 1470 to provide ten marks (£6.69) for their chaplain to be raised by a rate on land, and in Burneside or Burnshead ten marks was raised by a charge on seats; in Kentmere, another Kendal chapelry, inhabitants were assessed at one shilling on every half mark of 'Lord's Rent'.[4] These payments constituted a legal contract and were later held to be obligatory.

Chantries were of considerable importance in the large parishes in the north, as the history of the chapels in Prestbury in Cheshire illustrates.[5] The monastery of St Werburgh in Chester had been granted the church of Prestbury towards the end of the twelfth century and appropriated the rectory early in the thirteenth; about 1291 the vicar was required to provide the chapels in the parish with 'fit service'. Two chapels were recorded earlier than this, and chapels at Taxal and Gawsworth gained independence about this time. By 1547 there were nine chapels in Prestbury parish. The most important was a chapel of ease at Macclesfield, first documented in 1278; Edward I in 1261 had made it a market borough with burgesses and a merchant guild, but could not make a new parish. The priest, called an 'assistant', was appointed by the vicar of Prestbury. Thomas Savage, archbishop of York in the early sixteenth century, who was born in the town, built and endowed a chantry chapel and intended to create a collegiate church in Macclesfield, but his aim was not fulfilled; he

8. Much Wenlock, Shropshire - Holy Trinity is the parish church, while close by are ruins of the monastery founded for St Mildburg in the seventh century. The church was derelict in 1101, and was rebuilt soon after. The priory encouraged the growth of a market town; the sixteenth century market hall, on the western side of the churchyard continues the traditional link between market place and church.

9. Aylesford, Kent - the bridge over the River Medway is dominated by St Peter's church. The bridge is about six hundred years old, and built of Kentish ragstone; the church was founded probably in the seventh century, and the tower is largely Norman. Aylesford was a royal vill or estate and the river crossing made it a good centre for meetings of the Lathe. There is an important Roman villa in the parish, at Eccles, Latin for church, and notable megalithic burial chambers.

10. Landewednack, Cornwall - St Winwallo's is the most southerly church in the country, near the tip of the Lizard peninsula. It is probably dedicated to a late fifth-century missionary to Cornwall; typically it is close to the sea and beside the path leading down to a sheltered cove. The church has a twelfth-century doorway. The tower is later, built of granite and the local serpentine stone.

also advised Sir John Perceval, a Lord Mayor of London, on the foundation in 1502 of a grammar school 'for gentlemen's sons and other good men's children', to be taught by a chantry priest who would pray for the founder's soul. In 1548 four chantries existed in Macclesfield chapel, and there were five priests as well as the 'assistant'. The abolition of chantries closed the grammar school but it was refounded in 1552.

Chelford chapel was recorded about 1280, when it was transferred with the manor to St Werburgh's monastery by Robert de Worth; he asked the monastery to find a chaplain to pray 'for the souls of himself and his ancestors and successors for ever, and to celebrate mass there on Sundays and two days in each week at the pleasure of the Abbot, and the remaining four days in the mother church of Prestbury'. The chaplain was to be paid six-and-a-half marks. Poynton chapel was recorded in 1312 because of a dispute about the advowson between Nicholas de Eton and his wife on one side and the abbot of St Werburgh's on the other; the abbey was probably trying to assert control over the whole parish. The chapel was near Poynton Hall, and had an enclosure or yard but no burial rights; it was made parochial in 1674. Marton chapel was endowed by Sir John Davenport in 1370 with sixty acres of land to maintain a chantry priest for ever. Bosley chapel was given parochial rights of baptism and burial by Papal Bull in 1402 'on account of the high hills, the deep valleys and the swollen rivers' which made it dangerous to reach Prestbury church; it is certainly a considerable distance away, on the far side of Macclesfield. Bishop Gastrell recorded an inscription in the building: *facta fuit* 1430, 'built in 1430', which appears to be the date of a new building to celebrate its new status. Siddington chapel existed by 1474 and like Poynton, had an enclosed chapel yard though no burial rights; it was not made parochial until 1721. A chapel at Newton was mentioned in 1536 when it was endowed with two mills by Humphrey Newton.

Pott Shrigley chapel existed before 1492, when Geoffrey Downes described in his will 'all things that I will have done in a chapple of my foundation called Downes Chapple in Pott Shrigley'. Geoffrey Downes of London, gentleman, brother of the owner of Shrigley Park, provided an income for two chantry priests, but arrangements had already been made by Dame Jane Ingoldisthorpe, possibly his wife, for one of the two. Downes' priest was to keep 'noe horse, ne hawke, ne hounde, ne nothing that should destroy or lett him from the service of God', a reminder that Pott was in Macclesfield forest. The priest, to be nominated by the owner of Shrigley Park and his successors, was to live in Pott, to teach, to look after the vestments kept in the chapel, and 'goe priestly arrayed with his gown and his hood'. He was not to be connected with any Cheshire gentry family. He was to pray for Geoffrey Downes and Dame Ingoldisthorpe, and also for the brothers and sisters of the Fraternity in the chapel. Membership of the Fraternity cost six shillings and eight pence; poor people could pay in instalments or might be forgiven, so inhabitants collectively could share this chantry. In 1548 three chantries and four priests were recorded at Pott; two chantries were in the Downes chapel and the third was perhaps connected with the Berristall chapel.

None of the chantries or chapels in Prestbury parish was recorded in the *Valor Ecclesiasticus*. But at the visitation in 1548 twenty-one priests were named: six under the heading of Macclesfield, four under Pott and eleven under Prestbury itself. The abolition of chantries was probably not immediately disastrous, because existing priests were paid pensions and could continue to serve the chapels during their lifetimes, but eventually the number of priests in the parish was approximately halved. Inhabitants had to organise fresh means to maintain their local ministers. In 1550 the inhabitants of Newton paid the priest's wages but, although they attempted to raise money for repairs of the chapel, it was in ruins by the early eighteenth century. The inhabitants of Marton bought the chapel and the chapel yard, which indicates that alone of the Prestbury chapels it had not been considered independent of any chantry and had been taken over by the crown; they continued to support a priest into the eighteenth century, but there was 'no settled minister' because no regular endowment. The large and prosperous town of Macclesfield was left with the 'assistant'. In 1606 an additional priest was provided as a King's Preacher, to be appointed by the mayor, and the appointment of the assistant became the responsibility of the mayor and corporation. In the early seventeenth century one more chapel was built, at Wincle, so that ten existed in 1648 when the parliamentary committee ordered that ministers' stipends should be increased with the income from Prestbury tithes, which after the dissolution of St Werburgh's monastery and creation of a new bishopric had been given to the dean and chapter.

As Prestbury shows, the *Valor* is a poor guide to chantries; most were not 'benefices', and therefore not taxable; in Devon, the *Valor* included no more than a third of those discovered by the chantry commissioners a decade later. Over the whole country, it recorded 2374 chantries. Yorkshire was exceptional; in eight deaneries, the Valor recorded 282 parishes and 235 chantries, and an unusual number of village churches were served only by chantry priests; they were particularly numerous in the Old and New Ainsty, or York deanery, (forty-four rectories and vicarages and fifteen churches served by a chantry) and in Doncaster deanery (fifty-six rectories and vicarages and eighteen chantry churches).[6] In contrast, in the six deaneries in Lincoln diocese in the archdeaconry of Leicester, corresponding with the county, a mere thirteen chantries were recorded in the Valor but 190 rectories and vicarages.

CHANTRY COLLEGE AND GUILD CHAPEL IN STRATFORD UPON AVON

The rectory and manor of Stratford upon Avon both belonged to the bishop of Worcester, but he was not responsible for the college founded in the early fourteenth century, though he gave his consent. The church was an ancient foundation, at the centre of a large estate of nearly seven thousand acres which had been given to the bishopric before 709; included was woodland about ten miles to the north of Stratford where the bishop of Worcester pastured his pigs, which became a detached part of the parish. The bishop of Worcester planned a new town about 1182 near the ford over the Avon and the earliest masonry

RIGHT: *Stratford upon Avon, Warwickshire - the medieval Guild of the Holy Cross maintained a chapel, hospital or almshouse, and grammar school on the western edge of the borough. The Guildhall on the left dates from 1473, and had council chamber, library and grammar school on the first floor. Adjoining it are almshouses. On the right is the early fifteenth-century schoolmaster's or Pedagogue's House, and behind there is the house provided for the Guild's vicar, the chapel is just behind.*

in the church shows it was rebuilt about the same date. The town or borough bounds did not include the church, and the area round it became known as Upper or Old Stratford. The town and six agricultural townships were in the parish and rural parishioners, relatively few in number, were later to object to paying rates for the relief of poor townsmen, eventually successfully.[7]

A chapel in the new town was built by local men who founded the Guild of the Holy Cross in 1269. The Guild acted as a town council, which the bishop had not given his new town; it maintained a priest or chaplain, a hospital or almshouse for ten aged poor people, and probably from the beginning also a grammar school - the bishop's register records a schoolmaster in 1295. Robert de Stratford was instrumental in founding the guild, and became the master.[8] He had two sons who were prominent clerics and politicians. They perhaps felt it necessary to aggrandise the parish church to counterbalance the Guild. The elder, John de Stratford, was rector of Stratford until 1319, when he resigned in favour of his younger brother. He had a prebend at Lincoln and York, became dean of the Court of Arches, the senior church court in the province of Canterbury, and he served Edward III as chancellor. In 1323 he became bishop of Winchester and in 1337 archbishop of Canterbury. He had obvious

Stratford upon Avon, Warwickshire - the late medieval chancel of Holy Trinity church is seen best across the river Avon. It was built for the collegiate church's clerks and choristers, and contains their carved misericord seats. William Shakespeare was buried in the chancel, showing the social position he had achieved in the town. The spire replaced a shorter, wooden one in 1763.

opportunity for the accumulation of considerable wealth. John de Stratford founded a chantry college at Stratford in 1331, to consist of a master and assistant and three chantry priests, and rebuilt the south aisle of the parish church with an altar for the chantry dedicated to St Thomas of Canterbury. His position of authority must have helped him persuade the bishop of Worcester to sell him the advowson of Stratford rectory, which he gave to the chantry college, and the tithes of the whole parish. From 1340 the college warden was also the rector. However, the bishop of Worcester appointed both the warden and sub-warden, so did not lose his valuable patronage.[9] The college increased the church's status, redistributed the rector's large income, and secured more priests for church services which townspeople could attend.

Meanwhile the younger brother, Robert de Stratford, was also accumulating church and cathedral prebends, and finally became bishop of Chichester and was consecrated by his brother. Robert was responsible for securing grants of the market tolls to the burgesses of Stratford, enabling them to pave the streets. John died in 1348 and Robert in 1362. The brothers' nephew, Ralph, also a cleric, became bishop of London in 1340; at that point, three members of the family were bishops. Ralph died in 1354, but the year before he had begun to build a college house for his uncle's chantry priests on the north-west side of the churchyard. Leland about 1540 described the college as an 'ancient pece of worke of square stone'. It was demolished at the end of the eighteenth century, but nineteenth-century development of College Street and College Lane commemorates the building.

In legal terms the chantry college at Stratford was separate from the rectory of the parish church until 1415, when a royal charter combined them. At the end of the century Dr Thomas Balshall, master for many years, built the splendid new chancel in which he was buried in 1491. The Guild chapel was rebuilt about the same time by Sir Hugh Clopton, Lord Mayor of London in 1492, who provided the stone bridge over the Avon and built a house for himself, New Place, later purchased by William Shakespeare. In 1515 the master of the college, Dr Ralph Collingwood, gave an endowment for four choristers. He required the boys to assist daily in divine service, entering the choir two by two; they were also to wait on the College at dinner and supper, but on no account to enter the buttery to draw beer either for themselves or for others. After dinner they were to go to Singing School. 'They should not be sent upon any occasion whatsoever into the town'. They said prayers for Collingwood and also for Master Thomas Balshall, described as a special benefactor. On the north side of the chancel there was a two or three storey building - accounts vary - with a vaulted lower chamber and a priest's chamber or minister's study above, and the upper room was divided for the four choristers to sleep in, two in a bed. It sounds like a pele tower, perhaps an earlier rectory house, but was demolished in 1799. The effect of this series of developments at Stratford was that in 1535 one curate discharged the parochial duty of the church, the baptisms, marriages and burials of parishioners, but the rectory revenues supported five other clergymen; the warden's income was nine times greater than that of his deputy, or of the curate and chaplains.

Rushford college, Norfolk - founded by Sir Edmund Gonvile in 1342, who founded a Hall in Cambridge; the master was rector of the parish and there were five fellows or chaplains. The communal building, now a private house, is south of the church. The college was dissolved in 1529.

St John the Evangelist's grand tower shows how the church was built in fitting style for the college. After 1529 parts were destroyed; the tower, and nave much reduced in height, were saved by the small community of about 100 inhabitants. It is one of the few thatched churches remaining in Norfolk.

The indexes of religious houses in the *Valor Ecclesiasticus* recorded seventy-four colleges in England, in addition to the nine secular cathedrals. Another thirteen churches were called colleges in the returns, and prebends or prebendaries were referrred to at a further six, which makes a total of ninety-three. Forty-five chantry colleges have been identified. This may be an underestimate. Colleges were spread fairly evenly through all counties and ranged from a tiny one like Ruddington near Nottingham, with a master and two chaplains barely justifying its title, or Rushford in Norfolk, to the near-cathedrals at Southwell, Beverley and Ripon, and the prestige institution of St George's, Windsor. Perhaps a quarter dated from the Norman period, although some later foundations had reconstituted once important Anglo-Saxon churches like Tamworth in Staffordshire, Maidstone and Wye in Kent and the two colleges in Shrewsbury in Shropshire; Crediton in Devon had briefly been the seat of an Anglo-Saxon bishop.[10] The colleges survived the dissolution of the monasteries, but a decade later they, too, were closed by the Protestant reformers.

The suppression of chantries, guilds and colleges

It was inevitable that as Protestant ideas took hold, chantry priests would be prevented from saying traditional Catholic masses for the dead, whether in parish churches and chapels, hospital or guild chapels. The Protestant perception was that the prayers of others were not the means of salvation, which must rest on personal faith and actions. Chantry endowments were nothing like as extensive as those of the former monasteries, perhaps a quarter of the value, and their confiscation was probably not the principal motive for suppression; in Devon in the short term, pensions to former chantrists more or less balanced revenues, and in Cumbria chantry estates were each a few pounds in value at most.[11] Numbers of unbeneficed clergy fell very sharply after the abolition of the chantries.

An act of parliament in 1545 instituted the first survey of chantries and guilds with a view to suppression. Then Henry VIII died. A second Chantries Act in 1547 authorised the suppression and a second survey was organised. More chantries were discovered, but the government was still suspicious, with some reason, that endowments were being concealed. The act included a statement that it was not intended to close 'any chapel made or ordained for the ease of people dwelling distant from the parish church'. In Lancashire it is suggested that the act was interpreted generously, in so far as chapel buildings were not generally seized. Other commissions of 1547, 1549 and 1552, to discover and ensure the removal of popish vestments, chalices and ornaments, did not ignore the chapels, and deprived them of their small amount of riches. The government took no notice of the commissioners' pleas about the value of chantry priests. At Lavenham in Suffolk, the 'curate could not possibly serve the cure without the help of the priest of St Peters Guild'; at Mildenhall, which the commissioners noted was a large and populous town, they observed the 'sundrie hamletts dyvers of them being chapples distante from the parishe chirche oone mile of twoo whear the seide preist dyd synge mas sundrie festivall dayes and other holy dayes and also helpe the curatte to minister the sacraments, who withoute helpe werre not able to discharge the cuer'. It was not unusual for chantry priests also to be schoolmasters, as at Lavenham, Clare and Long Melford. Two hundred and seventy chantries were noted in Suffolk alone.[12]

As a consequence of the Chantries Acts, many chapels in the south went out of use, especially if they had no 'settled' income; some were demolished, or became houses or barns. Natural processes of population movement had already led to the decay of some chapels, as noted by the Chantry Commissioners, and in 1545 there was permission to demolish a church building if it stood within a mile of another, or if the inhabitants could not raise nine marks a year for its priest; a few chapels were probably closed for these reasons. In Hampshire, eighty disappeared, one fifth of the existing 'public' churches and only six chapels of ease in rural areas survived; in Worcestershire, of 180 medieval chapels which are documented, 100 do not survive. In Surrey 'a large, ill-recorded and now largely vanished class of chapels may be dimly

perceived'; and in Shropshire over a hundred 'destroyed chapels' were listed by Dukes in 1844. In the sparse parochial skeleton of the North, chapels remained important, and were an important legacy from the medieval period. Local inhabitants sought to maintain their ministers, an important preparation for the independent chapels which sprang up in the eighteenth and nineteenth centuries. The Church of England had no overall plan to redirect confiscated resources to chapel ministers or even to vicars, and was unwilling to face the problem of how to alter its parochial structure and redistribute income in line with changing circumstances. It 'stuck grimly to its obsolescent parish boundaries'.[13]

The Chantries Acts affected colleges, hospitals and guilds bound to pray for the departed. As enclaves of self-governing clerics not closely supervised by the bishops as parish priests were, colleges were able to resist religious changes. They also showed some lack of concern for pastoral responsibilities. About 1547, Thomas Cromwell was informed by a local man, Raymond Harflete, that Ash in Kent had always had a vicar, 'till for the last twenty-two years the said canons have usurped the vicarage to their own use'. For a rent, he wrote, the canons of Wingham college let the vicarage to temporal men; they put in unsuitable curates, obtained 'best cheap', so that 'within a quarter of a year we have had seven curates, which has caused much strife, as we are 500 residents'. The archbishop of Canterbury had compelled the canons to appoint a vicar, but they kept tithes of wool and lamb from him, and 'without them he cannot maintain hospitality'.[14] Such complaints reaching the government helped to justify closing the colleges. Exceptions were made only for colleges in

Ripon, North Yorkshire - the Old Deanery was built when the college was refounded by James I. Like other colleges, it had been closed in 1547. The dean ceased to live here in the mid-nineteenth century and moved to the house previously reserved to the canon in residence, and since the 1960s to Minster House. The photographer was here captured at work.

cathedrals, for twenty-six educational colleges at Oxford and Cambridge, for Eton and Winchester, for St George's, Windsor, and for almshouses without chaplains. The four prebendaries of St Endellion, Cornwall also survived, and Tiverton, Devon was not formally suppressed.

Though not numerous, closing the colleges was important for the parishes concerned. Three chapels in Wingham college's care, Ash, Nonington and Wingham itself, were provided with a perpetual curate paid a fixed stipend but the fourth, Goodnestone, had no assured provision. None of the curates was provided with a house, not even Wingham's, despite the considerable amount of college property in the village, including three timber-framed houses built for the canons, which was all sold. Kirkoswald college in Cumbria had been in existence for only 24 years and was not even finished when royal commissioners arrived to take possession. The master and fellows refused to 'conforme themselves for the alteration of that College to another use'. They were summoned before the Privy Council, which made them give in. Vicars of the parishes concerned, Kirkoswald and Dacre, were deprived of their churches' revenues, and were paid stipends unaltered thereafter for many years. The vicar of Kirkoswald also lost the Rectory pele tower, at the centre of the buildings erected for the college fellows; the college was leased until 1590, when it was sold with the Kirkoswald tithes to Henry Fetherstonhaugh of Dacre, in whose family it has remained ever since. Few were able like John Dacre, provost of Greystoke, to fight the suppression in legal terms, claiming that when the college was founded in 1382, it had not been merged with the rectory, a claim supported by the entry in the Valor: 'Rectory and College'.

Parson Dacre was supported by Lord Dacre, Lord President of the Council of the North, a powerful figure. The provost won, and kept the endowments and the building, though not the five chantry priests.[15]

The college at Manchester was one of the very few to be refounded, within a decade of its closure, by the Roman Catholic Queen Mary. It had consisted of a warden and eight fellows or vicars, four clerks and six choristers. There were also seven chantry priests and five curates attached to outlying chapels. The parish was very extensive, nearly sixty square miles, and there were thirty townships including Manchester itself. The warden and fellows were ordered in 1537 to preach 'every Sunday in the Church of Manchester or in one of the chapels'; two curates did the 'duty' of the parish. A memorandum to the chantry commissioners noted that Manchester was 'so great a parish, and so great a circuit, that many times the rest of the priests be enforced to minister sacraments to the said parish when the curates are overcharged'. The population was perhaps a little under 2000.[16] The warden received £85 a year, the two curates £13 each. The college was refounded, threatened with extinction the following year when the Protestant Elizabeth I came to the throne, and assured of continuity by royal charter from Elizabeth in 1578. Elizabeth I's charter provided for a smaller establishment of a warden and four fellows, four men and four boy choristers, but made no substantial alteration to the work of the parish: two chaplains or vicars were to visit the sick, administer the sacrament and other divine services. They collected 'surplice fees', the dues paid for baptisms, marriages and burials, as remuneration; in a populous parish, this could be quite a large sum of money. Preaching was still the responsibility of the warden and fellows, who occasionally rode out to preach in the chapels; they were expected to have higher levels of education than those concerned with pastoral care. The rectory tithes and lands were returned to the college but the former college building remained in private hands; in 1656, it was given for

Manchester - Chetham's College. When the college was founded in 1421, the manor house was adapted for the warden and eight fellows, and some buildings survive including the great hall. Given for a grammar school and library in 1656 , now they are used by Chetham's School of Music. Overshadowed by modern building, they are an oasis of calm.

a school and library, following the plan and bequest of Humphrey Chetham and now is used by the innovative School of Music. The opportunity to fund ministers in the chapelries and create new parishes was missed, while the college continued to provide incomes to clerical politicians.

The suppression brought opportunities for local enterprise. Stratford upon Avon college and the Guild of the Holy Cross were both dissolved in 1547, and in 1549 the bishop of Worcester was required to exchange his manor of Stratford for another source of income.[17] The townsmen's position was then much altered. In 1553 they petitioned for a royal charter of incorporation, and the council was successful in purchasing Guild property and some part of the college's, including some tithes; Shakespeare later leased half those tithes, giving him the right to burial in the chancel of the church. A vicarage was endowed and the new Corporation charged with paying the stipends of the vicar and an assistant minister, and providing the vicar with a house; a schoolmaster and a reading minister for the Guild chapel were similarly provided for. The stipends were rather more than the College had paid its curates, but as the value of the great tithes increased, the council was pressed to increase them, which it did to some extent. Most deleterious in the long term, personal tithes had also been granted to the Corporation, so that they would appear as a tax to support the council rather than the church.

Former church property was used during Edward VI's reign to found a number of grammar schools by royal charter, which became known by the king's name. Some were new enterprises, others replaced schools which had been sponsored by monasteries, colleges or chantries. Other schools endowed with former church revenues included Christ's Hospital (1553), Repton (1559), Merchant Taylors' (1561), Rugby (1567), Uppingham (1584) and Harrow (1590). Shrewsbury (1552) was typical. Soon after the dissolution of Shrewsbury abbey, the borough secured a charter of incorporation and the council petitioned Henry VIII to make the abbey available for a grammar school, but this was not granted, partly because the king was planning to set up a bishopric there. Following closure of St Chad's and St Mary's colleges, two prominent citizens successfully petitioned for the college property to be made available for the purpose of a school. St Chad's property consisted mainly of tithes of lambs, wool and flax from the town and suburbs, and St Mary's tithes of pigs, geese, apples, onions and garlic in the town and Castle Foregate and Coton - a glimpse of the rural nature of a town, evident too in the Corporation's order in 1538 that 'hedges of thornes that stand in any street' should be removed. Easter dues were included in the school endowment and as in Stratford upon Avon, became a council tax.[18] The relationship between churches and parishioners was not strengthened by this secularisation of the small tithes.

THE DUTIES OF THE PARISH

Through the amazing reversals of religious policy of the mid-sixteenth century, churchwardens more or less dutifully carried out orders respecting their churches.[19] Henry VIII died early in 1547; Edward VI's reign was remarkable for the extreme Protestant sympathies of those controlling the government for the young king. There was a ruthless attempt to extirpate traditional Catholic practices in worship. Mass was abolished; communion in both kinds, bread and wine, was substituted for as many as possible in the congregation on at least three occasions a year. Processions were forbidden with the exception of one at Rogationtide. The confidence of the Protestant reformers is breathtaking. At St Michael's, Gloucester, the churchwardens' accounts record payments to labourers for taking earth out of the church in order to lower the floor where the new communion table was to stand in place of the old altar. The churchwardens bought the new *Book of Common Prayer* in 1549, with the whole liturgy in English instead of Latin; a second and further reformed Prayer Book was issued in 1552. The rood-screen was taken down, the walls of the church whitewashed to cover the wallpaintings or 'images' and new pews and a pulpit installed.

Protestant reforms came to an abrupt end with the accession of Mary, daughter of Catherine of Aragon, in 1553. England reverted to Roman Catholic ways of religious observance, though Mary did not try to restore chantries or encourage masses for the dead. The restoration was welcomed by some; the vicar of Much Wenlock in Shropshire wrote in his Register Book 'the people made great joy, casting up their caps and hats, lauding, thanking and praising God Almighty with ringing of bells and making Bonfires in every street'. Parishioners of St Michael's, Gloucester, paid for the expense of 'restoring' the church. Six parishioners who had bought vestments and altar silver from the churchwardens during Edward VI's reign sold them back to the church. A haulier brought the earth back into the church, but after the accession of the Protestant Elizabeth I it had to be removed once more. Mary died in 1558; Elizabeth, daughter of Anne Boleyn, had been brought up as a Protestant and was committed to Henry VIII's reformation if not to Edward VI's. A new rood screen at St Michael's was only just finished when it was dismantled and sold. More whitewash was applied to the walls. All the reversals of policy must have had a disastrous effect both on belief and on unquestioning acceptance of the Church. What ensured such obedience? The punishment for non-compliance could be severe: Bishop Hooper was burnt at the stake in his own cathedral town of Gloucester in 1554.

It would be understandable if there were no conviction that Protestantism would endure when Elizabeth I succeeded to the throne, but as her reign lengthened, the Protestant Church of England became more secure. In the south and east particularly, Protestantism became well-established and there was demand for more reform by those labelled 'Puritans'; parishes were small, the number of clergy correspondingly high in relation to the population, and often educated at the universities of Oxford and Cambridge where they were influenced by reforming ideas. In the north, settlements were scattered and often isolated, parishes large and the number of clergy in proportion to the population smaller; it was easier in these circumstances for families to maintain their Roman Catholic allegiance, and pay the fines required of recusants. Cumbrian chapels, for example, continued for some time to be staffed by men uninfluenced by Protestant ideas; Skelsmergh, Selside and Greyrigg in Kendal parish were under the patronage of Catholic families, and remained 'obstinately unreformed'. It is notable that the commissioners for church goods found remarkably few in Cumbria. Were they all very poor? Or had the chalices and holy ornaments been hidden away? In Crosthwaite, the parish including Keswick and three other chapelries the newly-appointed reforming bishop of Carlisle produced an extensive inventory in 1571, of the 'popish reliques and monuments of superstition and idolatrye as presently remain in the said parish'.

Churchwardens were the key to enforcement of Protestant ideas. Their duties were extended and formalised in Canons issued in 1571 and 1604. They were charged with much more than seeing that churches in their care were 'diligently and well-repaired', clean, whitewashed from time to time and 'decked with chosen sentences of the holy scripture'. It was their responsibility, too, that the churches were properly furnished with communion table, pulpit and font, and with necessary service books. They reported on those who 'obstinately for religion' refused to attend church, and warned vintners and victuallers not to open their taverns during service time; they saw that parishioners received communion 'as the laws and statutes do command'.[20] They were charged with maintaining good order in church and presenting to the church courts anyone who disturbed the peace with 'noisy or unseemly conduct', which led them to prevent entertainments like church ales and to keep the churchyard free of markets, merchants, pedlars, beggars and vagabonds. They had to keep a close eye on parishioners' morals and present those who refused to mend their ways. They could even check up on the minister, that he was duly authorised by the bishop and conducted himself and the services in church in a satisfactory manner.

The Reformation coincided with an increase in the parish's civil responsibilities imposed by parliament. Initially priests, parish clerks, churchwardens and constables were the agents of adminstration. From 1536 parishes were asked to provide for their poor, whether orphan, aged, sick, disabled or for some other reason impoverished. From 1538, baptisms, marriages and burials had to be recorded in parish registers and when it was realised that paper registers were not durable, parish clerks and priests were enjoined to use parchment, and to copy existing paper registers at least from the date of Elizabeth I's accession. Consequently many parish registers start with law-abiding exactness on 17 November 1558. From 1555, each parish was made responsible by act of parliament for the repair of highways within its bounds. Local, able-bodied men worked for four and later six days a year on this task, and a new set of parish officials was introduced, the surveyors of the highways, chosen by the ratepayers. In 1572 overseers of the poor were added to the parish's officers and the Elizabethan Poor Law of 1601 gave real authority to overseers chosen by ratepayers, in cooperation with the churchwardens, to raise and spend money on poor relief. The records of these responsibilities are well-known. The association of the church with the Old Poor Law cannot have endeared working men to the church. From the mid-sixteenth century until the nineteenth century, the parish provided the framework of civil administration. There was no other comparable nationwide organisation with literate persons of authority in at least 9000 places. These were the centuries when the parish was all-important.

PURITANISM AND PAROCHIAL REFORM

'Puritanism' emerged during the reign of Elizabeth I as it became clear that there was no encouragement from the queen for further church reform. Puritans considered that the Protestant reformation had not gone nearly far enough. They understood that the attempt to create a church of all believers had been frustrated, and that the Crown had managed to retain control from above through bishops and parochial clergy, even though abrogating the authority of the pope, not one built from below through congregations. This is the meaning of the statement that the Church of England is both Catholic and Reformed.

Puritans placed particular emphasis on preaching, which was the means of teaching the new ideas. But there was a shortage of properly qualified clerical teachers, and a shortage of well-paid benefices to attract them. Local enterprise again sometimes filled the gap. The town of Kendal in Cumbria became keenly Protestant following two strongly Protestant vicars between 1551 and 1562. In 1578 it was recorded:

> That the whole parish will resolve to provide and find a learned preacher (whereunto they are exhorted) to join with the vicar of the said church that by them two they may have every Sunday in the year a sermon to their great comfort and edifying. That all such stipend and portions of money as were wont to be given to the organ player and other unnecessary clerks be wholly employed to the stipend of that preacher and the rest to be supplied by the contribution of the well-disposed parishioners of the said parish.

There had been forty-five clergy in the parish before the Reformation, a large number even taking into account twelve chapelries and six chantries in the parish church, and though not formally collegiate, services must have had some of that style.[21] But Kendal was an exception in the Lake Counties.

Elizabeth I's first archbishop of Canterbury, Matthew Parker, recognised the problem consequent on the serious reduction in numbers of chapel curates through the abolition of the chantries. Immediately after his appointment in 1559 he instituted an order of 'Readers' who, like the old chaplains, could read the service of the day and a homily, but not administer any of the sacraments or preach. 'Their services were extensively used in the Lake District during the next two centuries', though not always highly regarded. A group of puritan preachers in Lancashire in the 1590s said that

> The chapels of ease, which are three times as many as the parish churches and more, are utterly destitute of curates, many of them supplied with lewd men, and some bare readers. By means whereof most of the people refrain their parish church under pretence of their chapels, and having no service at their chapels come not at all, but

many grow into utter atheism and barbarism, many enjoy full security in Popery and all popish practices.

They exaggerated, but there was some substance in their comments; there were nearly twice as many chapels as parish churches in Lancashire by 1552: 100 chapels and 59 parishes and the number of clergy in the county was a quarter of the pre-Reformation figure.[22] Richard Bancroft, who was archbishop of Canterbury between 1604 and 1611, said that parishioners 'grudge in their hearts to be driven to go five or six miles to the church both winter and summer', and that he had experience of 'great suits in law for the maintenance of a chapel of ease within half a mile of the parish church'.

Limited reform was achieved during Elizabeth I's reign by making chapels 'parochial', and it seems that this was done quite widely. There are at least nine examples in Cumbria.[23] At Holme Cultram the abbey church was made parochial about 1555, but the church of Newton Arlosh was downgraded to a chapel in consequence. There were four chapels in the parish of Greystoke: Threlkeld and Watermillock existed by the early thirteenth century and Threlkeld had long been parochial; Watermillock was made parochial in 1558 and Matterdale in 1580. Mungrisdale may have been the most ancient chapel, if the name refers to Mungo or St Kentigern, but was the last to be made parochial; the baptism register dates from 1774. Grants of parochial status meant that boundaries were drawn to define which people could use the chapel, usually on the basis of existing townships. The chaplains might then have a share in parochial income drawn from fees. Chapelries were as anxious to guard their incomes as parish churches; when a chapel for Hugill in Kendal parish was built at Ings in 1546, the inhabitants still had to pay £2 to the chapel of Staveley, and pay for seats and christen and bury there.

The agreement of the patron and of the rector or vicar was necessary for a chapel to be made parochial. Trinity College, Cambridge, became patron of the huge parish of Kendal after the dissolution of St Mary's, York. The College surveyed its new property in 1563. The vicar was required to pay two curates

Newton Arlosh, Cumbria - St John's church and tower were built together in 1304 by Holme Cultram abbey. In 1573 a jury said: 'A strong peile called Newton tower hath been ever a notable safeguard and defence ... which tower is now decayed in the roof'. When it was restored in 1843 only parts of the walls were standing.

for Kendal church, but despite the fact that each hamlet had its own chapel and a priest

> to minister divine service by reason they are so far distant from the parish church yet the vicar is not charged with the stipend of any of the said curates. And none of the said hamlets may marry, christen or bury or administer any sacrament but the same are to be ministered by the vicar and his curates at the parish church'.

In the 1580s, Troutbeck successfully petitioned for parochial status, on the grounds that the way to Kendal was 'very dangerous', and so did Staveley because of 'frequent overflowing of waters', a common reason in such petitions, but Kendal went to court to 'unchurch' this chapel.

A petition from Killington and Firbank in Kirkby Lonsdale in 1585 referred to the distance of the chapel from the parish church and to floods in winter making it difficult to take 'little ones' for baptism and corpses for burial. Killington is about seven miles up the valley of the River Lune, which was crossed twice to reach Kirkby Lonsdale, so the floods were not just rhetorical. There was probably a close connection here between the local determination to make the chapel parochial and the Killington farmers' newly-acquired status of freeholder: the freeholds of the farms, together with a proportion of moors, waste, and rights to pasture, according to their customary rent, were sold by the lord of the manor about that time.[24]

Chapelry inhabitants still had to attend the parish church for the three communions required by the Prayer Book. The curate at Greystoke wrote up the parish register for the rector between 1597 and 1609 in unusual detail; he noted that parishioners in the chapelries would attend for a 'general communion' accompanied by their curates. A similar arrangement was made in the act of consecration of Soulby chapel in Kirkby Stephen, Cumbria, in 1663, where the inhabitants, 'in token of their subjection to the mother church', were to go three times a year to receive the sacraments in Kirkby Stephen church. Soulby is about two miles from Kirkby Stephen and a second chapel, which appears to be in origin a Norman building, is five miles to the south at Outhgill in Mallerstang, a narrow valley of the River Eden between high fells. Canon Simpson, vicar of Kirkby Stephen between 1863 and 1886, described how 'within my own recollection' the vicar took duty at Soulby chapel on Good Fridays, and at Mallerstang on Easter Tuesdays; on Easter Sunday he claimed the traditional assistance in Kirkby Stephen church of the two chapel curates. For this reason the mother church had two large pewter flagons for the communion wine, each holding upwards of three quarts. The interaction perhaps fostered the sense of community in both chapelry and parish.

Parochial reform slowed in the early seventeenth century, especially under Archbishop Laud, who even prevented a group of private individuals buying tithes which were for sale and using them to improve the incomes of ministers through an organisation called the Feoffees for Impropriations. Not until parliament took arms against the king in the Civil War was there a dramatic opportunity for change.

PART TWO

THE PARSON'S PLACE

CHAPTER SIX

PARISHES AND LIVINGS

Easter is the central festival of the Christian year, and in the past it was also the occasion for vicars to collect from their parishioners an important part of their income. At Shipton under Wychwood, Oxfordshire, several eighteenth-century Easter books have survived in which payments due from the parish's households were recorded. Two old pennies were paid for each communicant, generally of the age of sixteen or above, and one penny for a garden. The vicar, or perhaps his curate or the parish clerk, noted whether a household had cows, calves, lambs, colts, pigs, eggs, fruit, or 'sweetware', or had pastured sheep or cattle in the parish during the year, so that appropriate dues could be paid. Even though pennies were not collected from poor households, the many small contributions and a few substantial ones from larger landowners or farmers amounted to £40, four fifths of Shipton Vicar's income. He also received £10 a year from the Professor of Civil Law at Oxford University, who had been allocated the great tithes of this large parish by James I; earlier they had been paid to a canon of Salisbury Cathedral. For this modest but regular stipend the vicar looked after some 385 households in 1734 in the six townships of the parish. Perhaps the vicar collected his dues in the church porch, where parish business was often transacted. In Hope in Derbyshire young folk paid their pennies 'at ye chancell gate', in Kirkby Stephen in Cumbria Easter dues were left on the 'Truppstone' in the churchyard, and in St Just in Cornwall, on the 'vannte stone'.[1]

LEFT: *Shipton under Wychwood , Oxfordshire - the vicar in the church porch on Easter Sunday*

THE PARSON'S DUE

The tradition of giving an Easter offering to the rector or vicar was ancient. Written evidence about the practice starts in the twelfth century, and Easter books survive from many parts of the country from the mid-sixteenth century.[2] They display numerous, confusing differences in detail and nomenclature, but the same general patterns. Three types of payment may be included in an Easter book: small tithes, personal tithes and offerings. All were governed by local 'lawdable customes', and the date when each was established might vary from parish to parish.

Small tithes, which were shares of the multifarious produce of the earth, were important to a country clergyman and from a large agricultural parish brought a substantial income; they were paid by all those actually living in the parish. 'Great tithes' of corn and hay were directly related to land not people and were therefore paid in the parish where the land was situated. Both were legally termed 'predial' tithes. When Easter books were compiled, small tithes were generally paid, money instead of actual produce. In many places a penny was paid for a garden, as at Shipton under Wychwood; at Darley in Derbyshire it was a 'garth' penny, and a penny for 'glebe' went to the bishop which elsewhere might have been called a 'plough' penny. 'A penie yearlie called a smoke penie by every householder in lieu of firewood' was paid at Rowington in Warwickshire and at Exeter about 1600 a smoke penny was paid for houses with a kitchen, chimney and hall, and poorer dwellings paid a halfpenny. Tithable items included lambs and wool, cows and horses, apples and pears, bees and hives, chickens and pigeons, onions, hemp, woad and flax, and other produce which had been significant enough in a parish for the parson to have established that it was tithable. New items were added to the list from time to time if the parson was energetic in pursuing his rights.[3]

Personal or 'privy' tithes of profits and wages were particularly important to the town clergyman, but were difficult to assess and collect. By the mid-fifteenth century in London they were left to the 'good devotion and conscience of the parishioners'. An act of parliament in 1548/9 limited them permanently to what had been customary for the last forty years, and day labourers were exempted from payment. It seems a surprising measure for the Protestant Edward VI's reign, because it left clergy dependent on voluntary payments and deprived them of a share in the increasing commercial wealth. Where it was well-established, the collection of personal tithes continued. At Ledbury in Herefordshire, Easter books between 1598 and 1607 include conventional sums for a man's 'trade', his 'gaynes', and his 'hands', thus covering profits from buying and selling, income from handicrafts, and wages. Occasionally attempts were made to revive personal tithes; for example, Parson Sampson of Clayworth in Nottinghamshire in 1683 tried but failed to collect one farthing in the shilling of servants' wages, as his predecessor had told him was his right.[4] For at least one place, Oundle in Northamptonshire, Easter books show some elements of personal tithing surviving as late as 1869.

'Offerings' or 'oblations', sometimes called communion silver, meal silver or altarage, met the costs of church services. A possibly mid-sixteenth century manuscript at Darley Hall in Derbyshire, records traditional practices: each household provided every Sunday a penny for a white loaf and a halfpenny for wine, except at Easter when the parson provided them; at Easter a special payment was due of a 'wax farthing' for tapers or candles to light the altar and a 'chadd farthing' to 'hallow the fonte for christening of children and for oyle and creame to anoyle sycke folkes'.[5] Darley church was in Lichfield diocese, and Chad was the first bishop, so the chadd farthing appears to be the continuation of the early church practice of payments to the cathedral at Easter for 'chrism', the holy oil supplied to local churches. In many parishes, Easter books suggest that households gave two pennies for a communicant member, being a half-penny for each of the four main festivals of the year - the 'offering days' or 'quarters'; the Ledbury Easter book of 1597 indicated which young folk were receiving communion for the first time, and so did Ludlow's early eighteenth-century books. When all contributed a few pennies, parishioners related strongly to the parson and the church, and sometimes the parson's income depended to a surprising extent on these personal contributions.

Offerings could appear inequitable, for example in London as early as the thirteenth century, in face of the great wealth of some citizens, and an arrangement was made for payments according to rental values, described as a tithe on houses. Other towns also had rating systems, including Canterbury, the date of introduction not being known, and Coventry by a special act of parliament of 1558. This method, called 'Quarterage', was used to raise the wages of the curate and parish clerk in St Michael's, Chester, towards the end of the sixteenth century; in Cumbria contributions of this sort were called 'prescriptions'. A quarterly 'contribution' offered by the parishioners of Earl's Colne in Essex in the 1640s induced Ralph Josselyn to become minister of the parish. He was promised £15 a year from approximately 200 households but he rarely received as much, 'even with much calling upon'; 'a man or 2 is willing, but not any other are willing so much as to gather it up from others', he wrote in his diary, 'but people are regardles and careles of the worship of god, as if they could well spare it'. Walter Hook's experience was similar, nearly two centuries later; while vicar of Holy Trinity, Coventry, he wrote to a friend in 1831 that 'while by my rate here, at the lowest valuation, I ought to receive £498 a year, I only in fact receive £250'. His collector blamed him because he too readily forgave folks their payments.[6] Careful accounts kept by clergy enabled them to answer accurately the bishop's or archdeacon's questions about their incomes, but did not reveal the inevitable fluctuations from year to year nor the contractual relationships between clergy and parishioners. Because of the need for close contact with parishioners if all these small sums were to be collected, they were usually granted to a vicar, while the simpler and more valuable great tithes were retained by the rector.

Each parish had its own particular customs about how great tithes were collected, too. It was the parson's task to arrange to gather his share from the fields. Where the arable land of the parish was extensive, he would need a large tithe barn to hold his stock until it was sold or used. The Clayworth *Rector's Book* shows how it was done in one Nottinghamshire parish. Wheat, barley and peas were tithed 'off the ridge', the great rolling curves of land in open field areas; the tithingmen drew up several ears of corn in every tenth stook to show it was the parson's. Parson Sampson had a long-running battle with his parishioners over tithing pease. Each handful as it was cut was called a 'reap'. He noted in 1677

Some began to leave the pease in reaps in the Furrow, never turning them up to the rig before they were tithed: which I, looking upon as a new device the better to defraud the Church of its due etc, went into the field myself, and ordered the tithing men to set out the tithe out of those upon the rig, and then, out of those reaps left in the furrow.

This dispute, and his claim to a tithe of servants' wages, no doubt led to the resistance encountered by the churchwardens in 1685 when they tried to record the church's lands and tithes in a new Terrier, and a 'most scurrilous' anonymous letter meant 'nothing could be done in it'. The importance of tithes compared with other sources of income was plain from his yearly accounts. In 1676, for example, they were worth £115 out of his total income of £155; the Easter reckonings were £3.12s.6d.[7] His house and land he valued at £13.6s.8d. The value of crops from glebeland was not an important source of income to most clergymen compared with one tenth of the produce of a whole parish.

Tithing was peculiarly complicated, it varied from parish to parish, and it was frequently the subject of dispute. Local custom ruled everywhere. Changes did occur in individual parishes, but they were strongly resisted if they led to more tithe being paid; when land use changed or new crops were introduced, a sharp question about tithes immediately arose. For the parish clergyman, there was nothing like the uniformity of economic situation present in the modern Church of England.

ORDAINED INEQUALITY: THE *VALOR ECCLESIASTICUS*

The *Valor Ecclesiasticus* in 1535 revealed the very unequal resources of parish clergymen across the country. At the simplest, there were two classes of churchmen: an upper class consisting of bishops and archdeacons, cathedral deans and canons, and a lower class of parochial clergy. But there was also an important division within the parochial clergy between the more affluent, that is most rectors and some vicars, and the poor, that is a few rectors, many vicars, and a mass of chaplains and curates.

No other group in the past has been so often the subject of enquiry into its income as Church of England clergymen - by bishops carrying out visitations, by parliamentary commissions during the Civil War period, by the Governors of Queen Anne's Bounty - or so comprehensively as in 1535 and 1835 by royal commissions. There is an enormous mass of information, but even so it is not easy to compare figures of clerical incomes at different periods. In 1535 not all sources of income were equally well documented, and the details given differed from parish to parish and from deanery to deanery; for some areas, there is simply a figure for gross income and taxable income. Values of livings may well have been underestimated. There were omissions; in 1535 the majority of chapelries were not recorded and some churches were not specifically referred to in a cathedral or monastery's accounts. But the collection of so much information across the whole country was a good demonstration of the effectiveness of the church's organisation.

The motives for the enquiry in 1535 were simple: Henry VIII and his government were in financial difficulty, and the church offered notable, or

Hadleigh, Suffolk - The Deanery Tower is an impressive brick gatehouse built in 1495 by a rector who was chaplain to Edward IV and held several clerical offices. There is no Deanery of Hadleigh but the rector is also Dean of Bocking in Essex. In 1535 both together were worth £81.

even notorious, taxable wealth. The king first took over the taxes known as First Fruits and Tenths paid to the Pope. First Fruits, or 'annates', were a proportion of a clergyman's income in the first year after presentation to a benefice, and Tenths were a fixed annual sum calculated on the 'profit' of a living after essential expenses had been allowed for. New valuations for these taxes were secured in 1535, later recorded in the King's Book or *Liber Regis*.

More than half the livings overall in England and Wales in 1535 were valued at less than £10; a third were between £10 and £20, and just over a thousand livings exceeded £20, sometimes by large amounts.[8] Ten deaneries across the country show some typical variations:

Valuations in ten deaneries in the *Valor Ecclesiasticus* 1535

Deanery and county	Valuations			Numbers of		
	Up to £10	£10-£20	Over £20	Rectories	Vicarages	Total
Charing, Kent	4	9	11	14	10	24
Brisley, Norfolk	19	10	1	24	6	30
Ludlow, Shropshire	8	7		9	6	15
Wenlock, Shropshire	15	4	1	15	5	20
Stow, Gloucestershire	13	8	5	18	8	26
Rothwell, Northamptonshire	10	22	9	31	10	41
High Peak, Derbyshire	5	6		3	8	11
Kendal, Cumbria	2	1	6	5	4	9
Kirkby Lonsdale, Cumbria	4	3	3	5	5	10
Pontefract, Yorkshire	5	10	12	8	19	27
Total	85	80	48	132	81	213
%	39	38	23	62	38	100

Land was generally insignificant both for rectors and for vicars, especially as the valuation included the parsonage house. But there was a contrast between north and south. In Pontefract, Kirkby Lonsdale and Kendal deaneries, both rectory and vicarage incomes were generally higher than in the south and twelve out of eighteen rectories had some land; few but large parishes made good livings. In the south, land either had little value or there was none at all attached to the livings.

Wealthier livings were usually the product of the great tithes, but the *Valor* revealed how many had been directed from parishes to monasteries, and to a much smaller extent to bishoprics and cathedral deans and chapters. The monasteries controlled about half the assets of the church, or about a tenth of the wealth of the country; three quarters was land, their 'temporal' estates, but about a quarter was their 'spiritual' estates, the rectories of parish churches. There were at least 3850 parishes where the rectory land and tithes had been appropriated out of 8840 parishes in the *Valor* and 3347 had vicarages. In Yorkshire and in the diocese of Lincoln, of a total of nearly 2000 livings, two thirds had been appropriated, in Kent and in the diocese of Chester more than half.[9]

Rectors as well as vicars everywhere relied to a striking extent on the personal contributions of parishioners. In some deaneries the *Valor* specified small tithes, personal tithes and offerings, or referred to the Easter book, Easter roll or in Hereford *debita paschalia*. At Ludlow in Shropshire, where Easter books survive from 1601, 'privy and divers small tithes' brought the rector nearly the

whole of his £20 income. Similar payments were mentioned in four parishes in the deanery of Charing in Kent. The parson of Hawkhurst received £12 from the Easter book and £5 from offerings, and his income was doubled by corn tithes. The vicar of Rolvenden collected small tithes and offerings worth £9 and had a small plot of land. At Cranbrook, the vicar had £19 from personal tithes and £7 from four offering days, and very little other income, and at Tenterden the vicar's small tithes and personal tithes, together worth £33.10s., constituted the whole of his income.

The same was dramatically true of the vicarage of the vast and populous parish of Halifax in Yorkshire. The vicar's house, garden and adjacent shops were valued at only eight shillings and two shillings were paid by a mill, but his income of £100 was made up of oblations and small and personal tithes. The great tithes were collected by Lewes priory in Sussex and were worth £133. Privy tithes and oblations were always itemised in the deanery of Pontefract and in six parishes they provided over two thirds of the vicars' income, in thirteen over half. Kendal in Cumbria is another example where the vicar's very large income of almost £95 was largely made up of the Easter book, small tithes, oblations, and personal tithes. These vicars were amongst the wealthiest parochial clergy in the country. In contrast, in the Cotswold upland deanery of Stow in Gloucestershire, small and personal tithes and oblations, though frequently mentioned, provided rector or vicar with generally less than £1. These parishes had small populations, and the largest Easter Book, of less than £2, was collected by the vicar of Longborough whose total income was only £6.10s.

Had unbeneficed clergy serving chapelries been included in the *Valor*, the overall picture would have been much more weighted to the poorest group, but curates were excluded because they did not pay clerical taxes. Economically curates were at the bottom of the clerical hierarchy. Stipends had often been fixed in much earlier times and were substantially lower than £10. An act in 1545 authorised the demolition of chapels if the inhabitants could not raise nine marks (£6) for the curate's salary, which shows what was considered acceptable. Curates must have had other means of livelihood. William Harrison in *A description of England* in 1577 noted that 'a glover or a tayler will be glad of an augmentation of 8 or 10 pound by the yere' through becoming a minister. Comparisons with late twentieth century non-stipendiary ministers spring to mind.

The *Valor* figures were quickly made out-of-date by inflation, and where great tithes and land were the main sources of income, the clergy's income rose as it did for other farmers and landowners; inequalities between the minority of good livings and the rest grew proportionately wider. Nonetheless the *Valor* figures continued to be used as the material for argument and decision for the next two centuries, and prevented realistic discussion of the clergy's status and needs; the criterion for holding more than one living remained £8 as recorded in the *Valor* until 1803.

Very soon after the *Valor* survey the confiscation of church property began in what has been termed 'the Age of Plunder'.[10] In just over a decade, 1536 to

1547, the wealth built up over nearly 1000 years was dramatically reduced, as first the smaller and then all the monasteries were closed, followed within a few years by the colleges and chantries. All their land, commercial property and tithes were transferred to the crown. At the same time there was a less well-developed attack on the property of bishops and cathedral deans and chapters. Some bishops were as wealthy as the richest monasteries. They had to 'exchange' some of their estates for some of the monasteries' 'spiritual' estates - advowsons and tithes - or, as a later commentator wrote, 'King Henry the eighth ... stole the sheep and gave not so much as the trotters for God's sake'. Elizabeth I continued the policy of 'exchanges' of episcopal estates.

A very small amount, less than three per cent of the church's property, was given away. A few estates were given to Oxford and Cambridge colleges, a few were applied to charitable uses, some were given by the crown to endow new bishoprics. The majority were sold to laymen, in this way entrenching the dissolution firmly amongst influential men in all counties. Elizabeth I and James I sold 3669 lots of parish tithes; local gentry, or men with money to invest, bought them and became impropriators.[11] Occasionally a man of conscience used former religious estates to endow a church, a college or a charity school. It was a massive transfer which was to be an important influence on the Church of England in the next three centuries.

An unprecedented opportunity for modernising the church's structures and improving the value of forty per cent of parochial livings by endowing them with great tithes was not taken. The only reform was the creation of six new dioceses. A scheme for more cathedral and collegiate churches, apparently drafted by Henry VIII in his own hand, envisaged thirteen new sees based on

Dorchester, Oxfordshire - the old grammar school is one of the few abbey buildings to survive and was probably the guest house; parts are fourteenth and fifteenth century. It was converted to a grammar school in 1652 by the owner of the abbey estate and the parish tithes; the pupils' small wooden drawers can still be seen. The master lived on the first floor and as he was also the minister, it was the parsonage, too. The church tower was rebuilt in 1602.

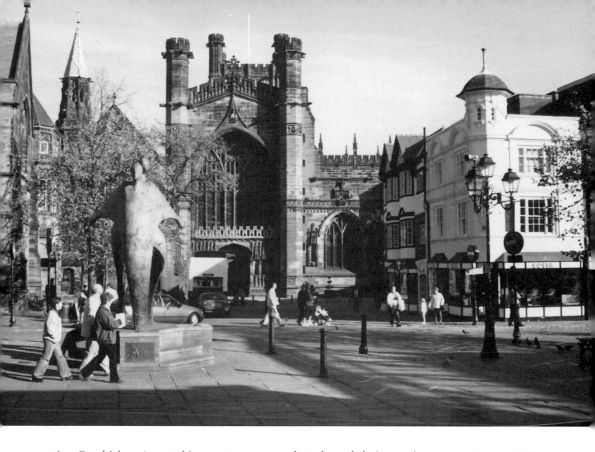

counties. But bishops' vested interests were an obstacle and their acquiescence in the reformation so far achieved was important. Six dioceses were created of which five survived: Bristol, Chester, Gloucester, Oxford and Peterborough; the cathedral of Westminster lasted only until 1550. The very large dioceses of Lincoln and York in particular were reduced a little in size. Chester was as unwieldy as any of the older dioceses; it contained Lancashire, formerly part in Lichfield diocese and part in York; also Cheshire and the archdeaconry of Richmond, both taken from York. Colleges of secular canons were created to support the new cathedrals and the old cathedrals whose monasteries had been closed were refounded as secular colleges.

NARROWING THE GAP: QUEEN ANNE'S BOUNTY

Reform of parochial finance was discussed frequently in the seventeenth century, and during the Civil War a real effort was made to transfer more ecclesiastical income to parish priests, particularly chapel curates, but it stopped with the Restoration in 1660. The first enduring reform was by Queen Anne's Bounty.[12] In 1704, parliament agreed to a scheme to help the poorer clergy by using the Crown's income from clerical taxes of First Fruits and Tenths, as had briefly been tried during the Civil War period. Radical alternatives were also discussed: to restore tithes to parish clergy, or at least to compel their lay owners to pay better stipends to vicars and perpetual curates. Members of Parliament quickly approved the less radical reform which made the richer

Chester cathedral - the west end is seen from the Town Hall across Northgate Street. The monastic church was saved through Henry VIII's creation of a new see in 1541. Aethelflaed, Lady of the Mercians, refounded a church of St Peter and St Paul and dedicated it to the Mercian St Werburgh; in 1092 the Earl of Chester made it a Benedictine abbey.Church and monastery occupied a quarter of the walled town.

Kettlewell, North Yorkshire - The Vicarage is a demonstration of changing attitudes. It is dated 1647. In 1741 Queen Anne's Bounty augmented the living to match a benefaction, and two years later a parsonage house was exchanged for this one. It was thought 'unfit' for the vicar in 1835; his income was then £120. In 1901 it was sold, described as 'only a small cottage'. It was repurchased by the church and the vicar moved back in 1947.

clergy finance improvements to the incomes of the poorer. The corporation set up to administer the scheme was called 'The Governors of the Bounty of Queen Anne for the augmentation of the maintenance of the poor clergy'. The clerical taxes were still based on incomes recorded in the *Valor Ecclesiasticus*, and although there was talk of revaluation, they remained unchanged until abolished in 1926; the Bounty's revenue from this source was fairly stable at about £13,000 a year. It took the Governors several years to sort out administrative problems involved in the collection and distribution of their revenues, and the first augmentations were not made until 1714.

The Governors first asked the bishops for up-to-date information on livings under £80 a year. This says much about the meaning to them of 'poor clergy'. Their returns showed 5082 livings in England and Wales below this figure; 3826 were under £50 and about 500 under £20. The results were presented to the Queen in December 1707. By this time the Governors had found it impossible to collect First Fruits and Tenths from clergy with incomes below £50 a year, and parliament agreed in 1707 to exempt this group, which led to a second return of eligible livings; 3839 were 'discharged'. These returns were published in 1711 as *Liber Valorem et Decimarum* by John Ecton, one of the Bounty Board's principal officers and the 'certified' valuations of 1707 were used for nearly a hundred years before the Bounty was authorised to update them in 1805. Like the *Valor Ecclesiasticus*, the first two surveys for Queen Anne's Bounty did not expose the real extent of poverty amongst parochial clergy because they generally ignored chapelries, but information was gradually accumulated, especially after 1715 when it was confirmed by parliament that curacies and chapelries were to be augmented, and in 1736 the published

Return Made by the Governors of the Bounty of Queen Anne listed 5638 livings worth under £50 and included 1678 chapelries. Poor livings continued to be 'discovered' and more were created as new churches were built. In 1786 an up-to-date *Liber Regis* was published by John Bacon, Receiver of First Fruits, with much additional historical information.

The Governors gave a capital grant of £200 to buy land, in order to bring a small but regular income to the incumbent of a poor living. All over the country over the next century numerous small plots of land were transferred into the church's ownership. At first the Bounty's grants were given to livings under £10, selected by lot, provided they were benefices; this policy excluded chapelries unless they were 'perpetual', otherwise the Governors saw no guarantee that their augmentations would be securely in church ownership. The qualifying income was raised on several occasions. Many chapelries were given some parochial functions and became perpetual curacies in order to receive Queen Anne's Bounty. Livings could receive more than one augmentation. A second policy was to offer £200 if a private benefactor was willing to give a similar amount, and this proved popular; at first a living under £35 a year qualified, also raised at intervals thereafter. After 1715 benefactors could become patrons. The vicar of Whalley in Lancashire, who was patron of the chapelries in his parish, found it advantageous to sell some of his advowsons; in 1722 five of his chapels were made independent, and two more later in the decade. Generally patrons did well out of the Bounty, because the value of their advowsons rose as the livings were improved.

Rectors and vicars who supplemented their incomes by serving one or more chapelries were not allowed to hold an augmented curacy. The vicar of Bakewell in 1786 wrote a long account of the injustices of the Bounty's rules which prevented him from receiving augmentations which had twice fallen by lot on Monyash chapelry in his parish, which he held; he pointed out that his vicarage was under £50 and was itself eligible for augmentation. His financial problems were not unrelated to his quiverful of children: 'I am straining every nerve in the support of a wife and a numerous Family, having upwards of twenty Children, & in daily expectation of an Increase.' The Bounty Board was unmoved. He was also frustrated in the same way with respect to Chelmorton chapelry. In 1807 he was still writing to request the augmentations and then had twenty-five children.[13]

Altogether Queen Anne's Bounty made more than 5000 capital grants during the eighteenth century, and the Church of England received endowments totalling about £1.5 million. This is a counter to the view, given focus by John Wesley's campaigns, that the eighteenth-century church was weak and unpopular, and highlights the large number of laymen willing to endow a local church, and of men willing to take poor livings even if they would have to eke out their incomes with teaching in a local school. In 1809, during the Napoleonic wars, £100,000 was voted to Queen Anne's Bounty, and the grant was repeated ten more times. Slightly different rules were drawn up for distributing this money: higher income limits, much larger grants, and a sliding scale of stipend relative to parish population. Between 1801 and 1840 the Bounty was consequently the means of transferring a further £2 million to poorer livings. At the same period £1.5 million of taxpayers' money was transferred to the church through the Church Building Commissioners, which added up to a substantial addition to the Church of England's endowments.[14]

The results of the long years of Bounty augmentations were noticeable. In Derbyshire, augmentations between 1772 and 1832 doubled the incomes of many livings, and sometimes increased them much more; the vicarage of Ashbourne, for example, was valued at £45 in 1813 and £148 in 1831, the vicarage of Hathersage at £49 in 1813 and £100 in 1824. Most clergy could hardly be described as poor by the time the Ecclesiastical Revenues Commission was appointed in 1831. Nonetheless, they did not regard themselves as well paid. The vicar of Alfreston in 1829 thought £149 'insufficient for a maintenance, and the suport of my professional character in such a public situation, when through age, infirmity or sickness, I am under the necessity of employing a curate'. Like a colleague in Bakewell, his hope to persuade the Bounty to bend its rules for him was in vain.

There were criticisms of the Bounty's work. Augmentation could be blocked by a patron refusing to make a living into a perpetual curacy, or refusing to improve his contribution to a clergyman's pay. Some curacies could not be augmented because they would remain too poor to support an independent minister as the Bounty required. The Governors could have chosen to husband the Bounty's moneys and make annual grants of income which would have given more flexibility, whereas small pieces of land could not always be managed effectively. No account was taken of the population of a parish or the situation of the church. It might have made more sense to give money to parishes where the population was large even if not 'poor' by the Bounty's reckoning. Bishop Wake of Lincoln, from the viewpoint of his diocese with its

Glossop, Derbyshire - the vicarage was endowed solely with Easter dues and surplice fees. It was valued at £13 in 1535, and qualified for Queen Anne's Bounty. In 1817 it was augmented with the parliamentary grant, raising it to £122 by 1835; there were then nearly 8000 parishioners. In 1850 the Bounty helped to build this house. In 1986 another was built in the garden where there have been summer parties.

many small parishes, as early as 1713 suggested that poor benefices might not need augmenting at all if they were united with others, as had happened briefly in the mid-seventeenth century. He proposed that the bishops prepare lists and a comprehensive act of parliament be passed to sanction all suggested amalgamations. It would have greatly improved the parochial structure, but both inertia and the fear of offending patrons prevented action.

The establishment of the Ecclesiastical Commission in 1836 with powers to augment stipends and establish new parishes altered the Bounty's situation. From this date its grants were restricted to parishes where private endowments were offered and which were too small for the commissioners' attention; its fund was clearly inadequate to meet the need for urban churches though in 1843 it was required to lend the commissioners £600,000 for new parishes. For over a hundred years Queen Anne's Bounty had principally strengthened the rural church and worked within the traditional parish framework.

ABOLISHING TITHES - BIT BY BIT

Even while Queen Anne's Bounty was quietly and modestly raising the incomes of the poorest livings by securing small endowments of land, at the opposite end of the parochial scale rectors throughout the Midlands and North were agreeing to, or actively promoting, large transfers of land to the church by means of enclosure acts in order to extinguish tithes.[15] Where this occurred, it made a big alteration to their relationship with their parishioners; they ceased to be tax-collectors and became landowners. Between 1757 and 1835, 2220 enclosure acts were passed which extinguished or commuted tithes, and at least 185,000 acres passed into church ownership. This land formed a significant further endowment of the Church of England In the short run those parochial clergy involved were raised to gentry status, but the implications were probably not sufficiently appreciated until later; in the long term one basis of the established church was undermined.

Enclosure involved large-scale reorganisation of the fields and could not proceed without the agreement of the tithe owner. In the open field system, cultivators shared the local resources of the land, cooperating in their style of husbandry to the general good, and having the right to graze animals on the commons. After enclosure, each farmer had complete control of his own land all the year round; the fields were hedged, fenced or walled to show where one man's land ended and another's began. Such dramatic reorganisation obviously posed a problem for tithe collection, as no long-sanctioned custom would support the new arrangements: old arable fields would be put down to permanent pasture, and old permanent pasture would be ploughed up. A great deal of expense was involved which the tithe-owner did not share, but as a result of which he could expect to draw one tenth of the enhanced value of the produce, and clerical allotments were fenced at the charge of the other owners, an advantage which remains to those lands. Occasionally tithes continued to be collected from new enclosures, in twelve out of fifty-five Derbyshire acts, for example, and sometimes old enclosures were not included in an act but remained subject to the traditional payments.[16]

The majority of enclosure acts extinguished all tithes in the parish. Though neither comprehensive nor unambiguous, there is a great deal of information in the returns of 'lands assigned under enclosure acts in lieu of tithes' requested by parliament in 1864 and published in 1867.[17] Clerks to the peace were asked to list lands allotted to clerical incumbents, to ecclesiastical corporations and to impropriators. The clerk in Carlisle wrote 'In reply to your circular of 12th inst. ... I have to state that there are above 100 awards enrolled in my office, comprising some thousands of skins of parchment, and therefore I am unable to prepare and furnish the return called for'. The diligence of other clerks or their assistants can only be gratefully acknowledged. In counties like Cumberland, where enclosure mainly concerned rough grazing, it was in any case not usual to extinguish tithes; downland and moorland were not directly tithable, although compensation might be given for tithes on animals pastured in the parish. In Staffordshire, three quarters of enclosure acts dealt with commons and waste, and only a quarter mentioned tithes. By contrast, in Oxfordshire where enclosure was largely of open fields, three quarters exonerated tithe.

In counties where open fields were widespread, considerable transfers of land were made to incumbents, notably 31,750 acres in Lincolnshire and 24,016 acres in Northamptonshire; in each of the Midland counties of Bedford, Cambridge, Nottingham, Oxford, Warwick and Worcester, they gained something in the region of 7500 to 10,000 acres, in Gloucestershire, about 12,000 acres, and the returns were not complete. For example, Bourton on the Water was not in the Gloucestershire return. In lieu of tithes, the rector there

Hallaton, Leicestershire - the former rectory house of dark yellow ironstone is mid-nineteenth century. Until 1728 there were two rectors, one for the 'North Mediety' or half of the parish, and one for the 'South', corresponding with the two principal manors; they were united through the marriage of the patrons. At enclosure in 1771 the rector was allotted 470 acres in place of about 100 acres of glebeland and the tithes, making him a significant landowner.

11. Otham, Kent - St Nicholas's church, beside a droveway leading from the Weald to the earlier settled lands to the north-east, may once have been a traveller's halt and shrine. A church was recorded in 1086. Its isolated position in a parish of scattered farms is typical of many in Kent, but the main manor of Gore Court is close by. The tower appears to have been built first, and a priest could have occupied the upper room; a similar church tower-house is seen not far away at Leeds.

12. Great Musgrave, Cumbria - St Theobald's church is by the River Eden; a packhorse bridge stood close to the church but was swept away by floods in 1822 and a new road bridge was erected a short distance away. It is a unique dedication. The rectory house was beside the river to the left and was often flooded. The parish had fewer than 200 inhabitants in 1845 when the church was rebuilt; the rectory was demolished in 1883 and only an old walnut tree is left.

13. Duntisbourne Rous, Gloucestershire - a note in the porch of St Michael's church reads 'For a thousand years this little church has given comfort to generation after generation. There are today only thirty parishioners, nearly half of whom are children or old age pensioners. We are trying to maintain the church for the use of future generations'. It has a beautiful setting above the valley and stream which gave several places their name.

14. The rectory is beside the church, a house 'fit for a gentleman'; in 1834, when the rector built it, there were 126 inhabitants in the parish. After thirty-one years, he was said 'never to have resided', preferring Yarnton in Oxfordshire; a succession of curates lived here. It was a good but not a wealthy living and the patron was Corpus Christi College, Oxford, since its foundation in 1516. The house was sold before 1939.

was given 209 acres and 259 acres in the neighbouring Lower Slaughter in his parish; two new farms, Lower Slaughter Farm and Bourton Hill Farm were built, and the barns removed from near the rectory where they had been for centuries. Another omission was Hazleton, where the rector had 82 acres of glebe, to which 188 acres were added for tithes. These tithe allotments made a big addition to the rector's existing landholding, and a few rectors could *ex officio* be seen as 'small' landowners, defined as those with 1000 acres and £1000 income; at Withington in Gloucestershire, 859 acres in lieu of tithes were added to 212 acres of glebeland to bring the rector into this category.[18] Withington was the bishop of Worcester's manor, and any land given up by the manor to extinguish tithes passed to another part of the church. At Stanton in Gloucestershire, the rector was lord of the manor and patron of his own living; in his own right he had eighty acres allotted for tithes and seventy-three acres was allotted to the rectory. In this case, as long as there was a son to inherit the benefice, land given by the manor to the rectory was not lost to the family.

Enclosure added to the gap between clergy and their parishioners. It stimulated an 'extensive building of houses which were appallingly apt symbols of the new status they assumed and which have been a millstone round their necks ever since'.[19] A gap between rich and poor clergy perhaps became clearer, too, as their sources of income became more strongly differentiated. On the other hand, in Derbyshire it appears that rectors who continued to collect tithes in the years of agricultural prosperity during the French and Napoleonic wars in practice gained more than those renting out newly-enclosed land.

Quite as much or even more land in place of tithes was given to the impropriators, men whose predecessors had purchased rectories belonging to monasteries, and to appropriators, the ecclesiastical corporations, bishops, cathedral deans and chapters and other ecclesiastical bodies. The Oxford clerk to the peace noted difficulties in making the proper distinctions; the bishop of Oxford and the dean and chapter of Christ Church were called impropriators in the enclosure documents; should they have been entered under the heading of ecclesiastical corporations, he wondered? Lessees, like the owner of Bibury manor estate who leased the tithes from Christ Church, Oxford, were sometimes named as impropriators. But the general situation is clear. In Derbyshire enclosures between 1775 and 1846, laymen gained over 7000 acres, incumbents close to 2000 acres. Three dukes were pre-eminent in the county: Devonshire was allotted over 3000 acres, Rutland 2250 and Portland 1130. It was not surprising that these great county landowners promoted enclosure. In Leicestershire, lay impropriators received 10,000 and incumbents 8000 acres. In Worcestershire, on the other hand, about 8000 acres went to the bishop and other ecclesiastical bodies, incumbents were allotted about 9600 acres, and about 4000 acres went to laymen; in Gloucestershire incumbents received about 12,000 acres and laymen not more than 8000 acres.

The enclosure movement demonstrated that tithes were not an inevitable charge on the land, and so increased the pressure for their general abolition which became fierce when agricultural prosperity collapsed after the end of the Napoleonic wars. It was further increased when some tithe owners, faced with falling income, attempted to reassert rights which had been in abeyance for many years, or to extend tithing to new crops like potatoes. Trinity College, Cambridge, encouraged all its lessees to reassert such rights and after enclosure in Scalthwaitrigg, a township in Kendal parish, a legal dispute started in 1817 which lasted for seventeen years and ended with Trinity paying for a private act of parliament to establish its claims.[21] Enclosures which extinguished tithes also extinguished any hope that lay owners would ever return them to the church. But had lay ownership not been substantially reduced before 1836, abolition rather than general commutation of all remaining tithes might have been demanded.

Three quarters of the £4 million worth of tithes commuted after 1836 were in church hands. The Tithe Commutation Act of 1836 substituted payments in cash for remaining tithes, whether collected in kind, or in money compositions negotiated between farmers and tithe owners.[22] Personal tithes and Easter offerings were excluded from the act but in practice were frequently included by agreement of those concerned. In most parishes some tithes were still being paid by particular farms or townships even after enclosure. At Naunton in Gloucestershire the enclosure act in 1778 had referred to 'several open and commonable fields, hills, downs, pastures and commonable lands called Naunton fields'. The rector had received the largest allotment, of 444 acres in lieu of tithes. Some old-enclosed land, including Upper Harford and Ayleworth, was also discharged from tithes but Harford Hill farm and Lower farm, which belonged to Corpus Christi college, Oxford, Roundhill farm and some other holdings were still tithable. After commutation, the rector received initially a rent charge of £140 from these.[23]

The request of the commissioners for tithe commutation for a general survey and mapping of the whole country was unfortunately refused. Tithe maps relate to about four-fifths of England and Wales but only a third were approved as a valid legal record. The commissioners divided the country into 12,275 tithe districts and in more than half, 7147, a voluntary agreement was arrived at which meant that a certified map of the district was not needed before claims could be settled. In each district, the value of tithes was averaged over seven years, 1829 to 1835, and was standardised by assuming that one third of the sum was used to purchase wheat, one third barley and one third oats. In future, a tithe rent charge would be indexed according to the current average price of those quantities of grain. Valuers divided the rent charge for each parish between the tithable lands, taking into account soil, situation and cropping, and this was the difficult part of the process. Once fixed, the farmer could calculate how much he would have to pay each year: less if prices had fallen and more if they had risen. During the middle years of the nineteenth century prices held fairly steady, but after 1879, in the Great Depression, the value of the tithe rent charge was eroded by a sustained fall in prices.

Parliamentary returns of tithes commuted under the 1836 act were made on several occasions.[24] Commutation was obviously most important in counties unaffected by enclosure, like Devon, Essex, Hampshire, Kent, Norfolk and Suffolk, Sussex, Somerset and Wiltshire; in all these counties, well over

£100,000 a year was allocated in rent charge, and in Essex, Kent and Norfolk, well over £200,000. But the most striking aspect was that three fifths of the rent charge for the whole country was due to incumbents; the other two fifths was divided nearly equally between appropriators and impropriators. This emphasises how impropriators had promoted the extinction of tithes at enclosure. Monasteries, it seems, had been particularly likely to be given lands and tithes in open field parishes, which had been sold to local gentry after the dissolution. Commutation saved something for the church of this ancient source of income for another hundred years. Abolition would have effectively disestablished the church and left many parish clergy without a reliable source of income. Commutation removed some of the annoyance of tithes collected in kind and it gave clear state backing to their continued payment; it formed part of the general revision of the constitutional position of the Church of England in the 1830s but it avoided real modernisation of the church's financial support, leaving it still dependent on the agricultural community. In 1936, a hundred years after the Commutation Act, the rent charge, too, was abolished, with some compensation to the church from the taxpayer.

TOWARDS EQUALITY: THE ECCLESIASTICAL COMMISSION

Three hundred years after the *Valor Ecclesiasticus* a second comprehensive survey of clergymen's incomes was made by a royal commission. The motive was church reform, stimulated partly by religious feeling and partly by fears of social unrest. The French Revolution, and the riots and demonstrations in England in the early years of the nineteenth century, were a warning of what could happen if discontent grew; there had been a large increase in population, especially in towns, while the parochial system was largely unchanged; the weak attachment of the poor to the church had been exposed by preachers such as John Wesley and Evangelicals in the Church of England; and the country's constitution, of which the church was part, was thought by many to be out of date. Parliament had started to acquire some facts and figures of a limited nature in 1803 concerning incumbents who did not live in their parishes or in their parsonage houses, and thereafter in most years a return was made to parliament on one aspect or another of parochial arrangements. When a majority of Whig members of parliament was elected in 1830, after a long run of Tory governments, a spate of reforming ideas was released.

Much of the energy of the first year of Whig government was directed to parliamentary reform, altering the long-outdated ways in which members of the House of Commons were chosen. But church reform was also a prominent Whig concern, and more so after twenty-one out of twenty-six bishops in the House of Lords voted against the Whig's second attempt to pass a Reform Bill. This action identified the Church as Tory and against democracy. In 1831, the Whigs established a royal commission to enquire into ecclesiastical revenues in England and Wales, as a preliminary to change.[25] Over the next few years, they carried several acts indirectly affecting the position of the Church of England: in 1834 the Poor Law Amendment Act, which moved responsibility for support of the poor away from the parish to unions of parishes; in 1836 the Tithe

Commutation Act; and in 1837 an act instituting civil registration of births, marriages and deaths using the machinery of the new Poor Law Unions for registration. The Whigs also attempted to abolish church rates in 1834 and again in 1837-8, but were defeated by a combination of Dissenters, who did not want to pay so much compensation, and churchmen who wanted more.

The royal commission of 1831 surveyed all churches with a regular maintenance for the minister, whether parish church or chapel, and a few without, and it also enquired into bishops, deans and chapters. Returns were requested from every clergyman of his income averaged over the three years 1829 to 1831. Information was also required on whether he held more than one living, if he paid an assistant or substitute curate, whether there were a suitable parsonage house and money had been borrowed on mortgage for it, who was the patron and the owner of the tithes, what was the population of the parish and the seating capacity of the church and any chapels in the parish. Returns were received from 10,540 incumbents, of which sixty-two were 'sinecure' rectors omitted from the commissioners' analysis because without parochial responsibilities; 178 failed to make a return, and about twenty-four benefices were not separately itemised because annexed to a 'superior preferment' like an archdeaconry. The number of returns was not equivalent to the number of parishes; many new town churches had no defined district, as in Liverpool where nearly all were within the one Borough parish, and many chapelries had districts but were not parochial, as in Leeds and Manchester. Population figures had to be calculated, the report noting that the 1831 census did not always reflect parish boundaries. It took four years to prepare a report.[26] The information was tabulated and the distribution of benefice incomes analysed. Those holding more than one benefice did not always point this out and the commissioners did not attempt to analyse how many clergymen were pluralists, or the actual incomes which resulted; nonetheless the evidence was clear enough to ensure acceptance of the Pluralities Act.

Malpas, Cheshire - a rectory house built about 1700 for the Higher Moiety or half of the parish. It was a large parish of twenty-five townships, with one in Wales, and each rectory was over £1000 in 1835. The two halves were united in 1885 and this house continued as the rectory until recently.

Barnack, Cambridgeshire - the former rectory house is mainly mid-nineteenth century; very old parts of the house have been demolished. The rectory income was over £1000 in 1835. The garden has been developed as 'Kingsley Parkland' because Charles Kingsley's father was rector here, and a new rectory house built in 1950.

The 1835 report showed a steep hierarchy of wealth on a wide base. At the top end of the scale, 254 benefices, or 184 after clerical taxes were paid, brought their incumbents more than £1000 a year; 507, about a twentieth of the total, brought £750 or more. In general, the same rectories were wealthy in 1835 as were in 1535, but there were cases where the values of livings had been dramatically increased. The richest living in the country in 1835 was Doddington in Cambridgeshire. It was a large marshland parish, and in 1535 brought a competent income of £22. The fens were drained, the land was enclosed, and most significant, the rector successfully went to court to establish his right to tithes from newly-cultivated land. By 1815, Doddington was worth £5000, by 1835 £7306; only six bishoprics were worth more. Stanhope, in Durham, was the second richest benefice in the country, and here, too, a change in tithes had increased the value. The living had been a good one in 1535, valued at £67, but after the restoration, Charles II granted the rector a new tithe on 'clean lead ore'. Lead had been mined in Weardale since at least the mid-twelfth century, when the mines had been granted to the bishop of Durham whose estate included most of the dale.[27] In the early nineteenth century, bishop and rector negotiated with the London Lead Company to increase their royalties and tithes. Consequently, in 1835 Stanhope rectory was worth £4718. By comparison with the notable if few wealthy livings, no wonder the clergy as a whole felt themselves poor.

About half of the benefices in England and Wales were under £220, and the average gross income was £303. As livings worth up to £200 were eligible for the Bounty's help, the scale of values had changed little since the sixteenth century, when half the clergy were considered shamefully poor. A third of livings, 3528, were under £150; this was the income given to incumbents of new parishes formed after 1843 under Peel's Act. On the other hand, the Governors of Queen Anne's Bounty had nearly achieved a minimum of £50;

297 livings were still at or below this amount. For the 4224 curates standing-in for absentee incumbents, the average stipend was £79, but reform of their position required moral pressure on incumbents to pay more. The largest numbers of livings under £150 were to be found in the dioceses of York (638), Chester (366) and Lincoln (386). Chester also had the largest population of any diocese and the highest ratio of people per benefice (3434); Durham was a close second (3100). The lowest ratios were in three eastern dioceses, Lincoln (693), Norwich (678) and Peterborough (642), and in Oxford (668). By an unfortunate historical irony, where ancient patterns of small parishes existed, population growth had not overwhelmed the parochial ministry, while the very areas where the pattern was least adequate were those with the largest population growth.

The bishops together drew a little under one twentieth of the church's total revenues; their average gross income was £6727, or £5936 net. Deans and chapters and collegiate churches drew twice as much of the church's total revenue as the bishops. Non-resident prebends brought good incomes to those already well-provided with exceptionally good parochial benefices. For instance, four prebendaries in the small diocese of Rochester who were drawing £600 apiece from the cathedral were also parsons. All four held two or more parish livings and three of the four held at least one other cathedral prebend too; one was also Provost of Oriel College, Oxford. They paid curates to do the duty of the parishes and where they actually lived was a matter of choice; the size of a parsonage house sometimes reflected an income drawn from a much wider area than a single parish. One Rochester prebendary's income was nearly £4500, equivalent to a poorer bishop. Attention was easily focused on these men, and a campaign to reform such situations distracted attention from more general issues, but even so substantial help for poorer clergy was not going to come very quickly from appropriating their sources of wealth.

Before this great volume of information was published and the Whigs had time to digest it, they were temporarily out of office, and Sir Robert Peel became prime minister. He defused the demand for church reform which the Report was going to fuel by setting up the Ecclesiastical Duties and Revenues Commission charged with proposing reforms. A partly secular commission appointed by the government was taking power from the bishops, and in the long-run, the results of Peel's action were more revolutionary than he could have foreseen. Peel had also been involved in the removal in 1828 and 1829 of some of the civil disabilities of Dissenters and Roman Catholics, which weakened the church's established position.

The first report of the new commission concentrated on the bishoprics, and the second on cathedrals and collegiate churches. The third report recommended setting up a permanent church commission, and in 1836, with the Whigs back in office, an act was passed turning the Duties and Revenues Commission into the Ecclesiastical Commission, to continue drafting reforms. The commission was given authority to make Orders in Council which it had merely to lay before parliament every January. It was an early quango, on the pattern of the Poor Law Board set up two years previously. The Ecclesiastical

Commission's semi-autonomous position, answerable to parliament, and its clerical and lay members, were a nice example of the checks and balances which were thought typical of the English constitution, ensuring that there was no position of absolute power.

The Ecclesiastical Commissioners were given power to determine the bishops' incomes. The concept of a bishop's position was still lordly and incomes ranging from £4000 to £15,000 for the archbishop of Canterbury were considered appropriate. Surplus revenues from their estates after this amount was deducted were paid into the commissioners' 'episcopal fund', to be used to create new sees. Durham was the prime target of reformers and between 1837 and 1850, the bishopric contributed £150,000 to the Commissioners' episcopal fund, used to endow both Ripon and Manchester; the bishop was allowed £8000 a year. The cathedral dean and chapter was also wealthy. Dean and chapter estates contributed £96,000 to the commissioners' common fund, more than one sixth of the total. Durham was much aggrieved that its endowments were used all over the country and not in the county.

The act reforming cathedrals and collegiate churches, which was to release funds for parochial reform, was passed in 1840. All 290 prebends with no requirement for residence were abolished, and canonries for which occasional residence was required were reduced from 230 to 127. The minimum income for a dean was to be £1000; a canon's income varied between £500 and £1000. About forty per cent of the cathedrals' income was transferred to the commissioners during the nineteenth century, between £70,000 and £80,000 a year in terms of the 1835 report; if applied to the 3000 poorest clergy it could have provided about £25 each.[29] This illustrated the argument of defenders of

Rievaulx abbey, North Yorkshire - was surveyed by Sir George Gilbert Scott in 1854 for the Cathedral Commission 'in case of the erection of additional sees'. He considered the choir and transepts 'readily capable of restoration'. In considering new dioceses, he wrote, 'historical associations should not be lost sight of', in order to 'connect the future with the past'.

Truro cathedral - was designed by J.L.Pearson in 1880 and finished in 1910. It was the first new cathedral built since the Norman period. It was fitted into a constricted town site and part of the parish church of St Mary was incorporated as the south aisle. Now it dominates the town from many angles. The revival of a Cornish diocese in 1877 was a response to the failing position of Anglicanism in Cornwall: more than twice as many Methodists went to church as Anglicans in 1851.

the establishment like Sidney Smith, who wrote in the Edinburgh Review, the journal he had helped to found, that the dissolution of cathedral chapters would contribute very little to solving the church's financial problem, but would remove an incentive for an ecclesiastical career. 'What were the purposes for which colleges were instituted, and to what purposes might they not now be put? Was the parochial ministry so overwhelmingly important, after all?', he asked. The questions were brave ones, of continuing relevance.

The commissioners used these funds to augment poorer livings and provide for new. Their policy was to pay what was required to achieve a minimum stipend on a scale related to population; this policy led eventually to the commissioners becoming the central stipends authority. Initially they set a target of £150 a year for parishes with a population of 2000 and over. As progress was made in raising the income of the clergy in larger parishes, the scheme was extended to smaller and smaller ones, so losing concentration on the problems of the urban ministry, though by 1907 the commissioners were checking if parochial benefices could more sensibly be combined before augmenting them. Like the Bounty, the commissioners also encouraged private benefactions by making capital grants. They made a distinction between livings in 'public' patronage, that is in the hands of the Crown, the bishops or other clerical bodies, and livings in private patronage; 'family' livings were only eligible for grants where offers of endowment were made, and the commissioners tried to persuade owners to transfer the patronage to the relevant bishop. An unwillingness to increase an advowson's value to a patron who might sell it meant that populous parishes were not necessarily given the help for which the commission was instituted. The work of the Ecclesiastical Commission overlapped more and more with Queen Anne's Bounty. In 1920 the commission took over the work of making capital grants to livings under £200. The Bounty's long-continued sources of revenue, First Fruits and Tenths, were abolished in 1926 and amalgamation with the Ecclesiastical Commission, which had been recommended more than once in the preceding hundred years, was carried out in 1948 and the new body was renamed the Church Commission.

The influence of the Ecclesiastical Commissioners over the Church of England was profound but almost accidental. Their concept of their duties was necessarily limited: the financial management of the surplus assets of bishops, deans and chapters and their use to augment poor but populous livings, to create new urban district parishes, and to build or improve parsonage houses. It was the responsibility of each bishop to determine the overall shape of the parochial ministry within his diocese. The debate on the Church of England's organisation was limited by this division of responsibility. Arguments were strongly traditional; it was assumed that the framework of parishes, archdeaconries and dioceses would remain, tying the Church to its ancient territorial structure. In an expansionary period, the mismatch between rural and urban provision was not apparently too pressing; in the second half of the twentieth century, under the depressing influence of contraction, the historical framework has been more obviously in need of large-scale revision.

CHAPTER SEVEN

POOR AS CHAPEL MICE

Ripponden is at a crossing of the Ryburn stream which flows into the River Calder; the land rises steeply on either side, the banks are heavily wooded. The name shows that in early times there was a streamside settlement or 'den' within the forest. The modern road through the narrow Ryburn valley follows the stream closely to its junction with the Calder at Sowerby Bridge, but from at least Roman times an important route linking York and Chester passed along Blackstone Edge, dropped down to Ripponden and crossed the stream, continuing on the other side towards Halifax and York. This was the route followed by small wool dealers or broggers delivering wool and collecting yarn or cloth from the many, scattered farmsteads in habitable spots amongst the moors. Celia Fiennes travelled the road in 1698; three miles from Elland she described 'a great precipice or vast descent of a hill as full of stones as if paved and exceedingly steep ... the end of this steep was a little village all stony alsoe; these parts have some resemblance to Darbyshire only here are more woody places and inclosures'. The 'little village' was Ripponden, then on the Elland or Barkisland side of the stream, though now the settlement is more extensive on the other, Soyland side. A writer in 1958 remembered seeing the pavement before the road was repaired.[1] The Romans may have paved the road at Blackstone and perhaps they built the first bridge at Ripponden but the earliest written evidence is in the court rolls for the manor of Wakefield in 1313. A chapel on this site could have been very ancient, providing shelter for travellers and a minister to look after the bridge. There was a local tradition that the early seventeenth-century church could be entered from the bridge. The present church, the fourth known, was built in 1868 a little further from the stream.

Ripponden is representative of many northern chapels, displaying local enterprise and piety and the importance of ecclesiastical niceties. Its history has been described in three articles by J.H.Priestley in the *Transactions of the Halifax Antiquarian Society* in 1932, 1935 and 1958. Ripponden was a chapel in the enormous parish of Halifax, and its minister was a curate. It was not a

LEFT: *Ripponden - St Bartholomew's church, West Yorkshire*

township, but was in Barkisland in Elland chapelry district. Great tithes paid by the inhabitants went to the rector of Halifax; small tithes went to the vicar of Halifax; fees for baptisms, marriages and burials went to Elland's chapel curate. Church rates were paid for the upkeep of Elland chapel, and money collected at communion services at Elland was distributed to inhabitants of Ripponden and of all the townships in the chapelry .

Ripponden was a 'free' chapel outside the normal parochial organisation. It was licensed by the bishop in 1465 for 'low masses' for the convenience of worship by the inhabitants of Barkisland, Rishworth and Soyland - that is for ordinary services, but not for 'high mass', which was reserved to the parish church of Halifax, together with the other sacraments; it meant that Ripponden could not be a chantry chapel, because the names of those who had asked for prayers after their deaths were recited at High Mass. The year after the bishop's licence, Edward IV noted 'the great distance that his tenants in Sowerbyshire were distant from the church' and granted to four representatives of 'the whole number of our tenants there, eight marks (£5.34) for the salary of such chaplain whom it may please them to accept to celebrate divine service in the chapel', to be paid out of the revenues of the royal manor of Wakefield, so the inhabitants, and not the vicar of Halifax, had the right to choose their minister.

The Reformation, in particular the suppression of the chantries in 1547, ended the payment of the salary, and other endowments were also lost; although not founded as a chantry chapel, later endowments must have had this character. The chapel continued in use and an almost unbroken list of ministers exists from 1561; in that year the curate was provided with a 'chamber', and several bequests were made soon after which helped to repair the chapel. In 1566 a thoroughly Protestant minister was chosen, who in his will gave 'humble thanks to God, in that it pleased His goodness not to suffer me to perish in the pit of popery and idolatry'. At the end of the century, a house and ground were given to trustees for the use of the chapel's minister and the site continued to be occupied by him until the late twentieth century. The curate received a payment of two shillings a year for each pew or seat, a common means of financing a minister. Early in the seventeenth century a new chapel was built.

A survey of church ministers and parishes, undertaken in 1649-50 by parliament to assist in the reform of the church, recommended that Ripponden should become an independent parish, together with seven other chapels in Halifax parish; it found that Ripponden's minister had 'No settled maintenance'.[2] Shortly after this, probably in 1653, the chaplain was given two cottages at Bridgend, the income from which was to pay for a sermon in each of the five summer months of April to August. The cottages became the Old Bridge Inn. From about the same time other bequests were made to pay for sermons, so adding to the curate's income. The inhabitants of Ripponden during the Civil War accepted a minister ejected from Prestwich rectory for refusing to accept church reform, but their next minister was a Puritan who at first refused to accept the 1662 Act of Uniformity. This act provided a check to the old democratic choice of minister for Ripponden by requiring vicars to ensure that curates under their parochial control conformed to the restored Prayer Book: the vicar of Halifax made use of this to secure nomination of men acceptable to himself.

Ripponden curate's position was improving. He had income from the Bridgend cottages as well as from pew rents and in 1697 the three townships of Barkisland, Rishworth and Soyland agreed to provide £40 a year for his salary. The chief inhabitants were to choose the minister, always subject to agreement with Halifax's vicar. The newly-constituted Board of Queen Anne's Bounty in 1707 surveyed 'poor' livings; Ripponden was valued at rather less than the inhabitants had agreed to provide. In 1724 the Bounty provided an endowment to match a locally subscribed sum of money, and £500 was invested for the benefit of the curate. The living became a perpetual curacy. The much improved status of the curacy was accompanied by a decision to rebuild the chapel a little higher above the bridge; a flash flood had damaged part of the church two years previously. The new chapel was a simple eighteenth-century classical building with a tower, and it seated 716 in pews arranged in meeting house fashion facing the pulpit not the altar. The system of pew rents continued. By 1743 there were 553 families in the three townships, so the population was between 2000 and 2500, two thirds of whom were engaged in the clothing trade as weavers, clothiers or dressers; 140 received communion that Easter of 1743.[3] There followed a series of well-qualified and notable graduate ministers: two wrote histories of Halifax town and parish. The private means of Ripponden's curates in mid-nineteenth century enabled them to employ two assistant curates, and the parsonage house was extended, it was said to house a private school. Some years later the old bridge was going to be demolished, but there was local protest and in 1802 it was declared public property and is now a scheduled ancient monument. The steep and narrow cobbled street, the bridge and the inn have some of the atmosphere of Ripponden in the past. In 1864, it was decided to build a new chapel in Gothic style to seat eight to nine hundred and abolish the ownership of pews, and in 1876 Ripponden chapel finally cast off its subordination to Elland; although the Civil Registration Act had enabled marriages to be celebrated in the chapel, half fees had still been paid to Elland for baptisms and burials. Not until the very end of the century was the link with Halifax broken and patronage of the chapel removed from the vicar to the bishop of Wakefield.

SHORT-LIVED REFORM: 1642-1660
In 1642 the Lords and Commons declared

> that they intend a due and necessary reformation of the government and liturgy of the church; ... they will therefore use their utmost endeavours to establish learned and preaching ministers, with a good and sufficient maintenance throughout the whole kingdom; wherein many dark corners are miserably destitute of the means of salvation; and many poor ministers want necessary provision.[4]

A 'competent' income was stated in 1649 to be £100 a year, a difficult target even a hundred years later, but parliament was paying its army chaplains £146 a year. Action was not possible until Charles I had been defeated. In 1645 the Committee for Plundered Ministers started to augment clerical incomes from the confiscated property of Roman Catholics and of 'delinquents', who had fought for the king. Episcopacy had been suspended in 1643 and abolition was confirmed in 1646, and the income from tithes held by bishops, deans and chapters was also used. It was an immense undertaking to try to organise the transfer of tithe income, returning it, as a general principle, to ministers in the parishes from which it was drawn. The administrative machinery did not exist, grants depended on local knowledge prompting application for help, and property rights were strongly respected: lessees customarily paid a small annual rent with a large sum on renewal of a lease and they were not required to pay more realistic rents to finance poor ministers. Some royalists regained possession of their estates by 'compounding', that is by paying lump sums to parliament, in which case payment of augmentations stopped, and some ecclesiastical estates were sold by parliament to raise money. A minister fortunate enough to be granted an augmentation one year did not necessarily receive the money, nor the same amount each following year.

Not until December 1649 was a survey determined on by parliament 'for the discovery of the value of the several livings in the respective counties'. It was typical of the new situation that the survey was organised by county not by diocese, and that in recording numerous northern chapels, with or without cure of souls, it reached deeper into the parochial system than Henry VIII's commission for the *Valor Ecclesiasticus*. A further objective of the survey was to recommend suitable parochial reorganisations, either by amalgamating or by splitting parishes. Such far-reaching reforms were not seriously considered again for over two hundred years.

The Derbyshire commissioners in 1650 recorded 112 benefices; one quarter were assessed at under £20 and nearly half at under £40.[5] They also noted

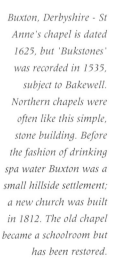

Buxton, Derbyshire - St Anne's chapel is dated 1625, but 'Bukstones' was recorded in 1535, subject to Bakewell. Northern chapels were often like this simple, stone building. Before the fashion of drinking spa water Buxton was a small hillside settlement; a new church was built in 1812. The old chapel became a schoolroom but has been restored.

nearly eighty chapels in use, while stating the income of only seventeen; of these, the curate of Longstone in Bakewell received £45, but the others less than £15, and it must be assumed that the ministers in the other sixty-three chapels relied on the voluntary offerings of the inhabitants, like the curate at Beeley in Bakewell who received £8 'Gratuity of the Parishioners'. By the time of the survey, thirty-seven augmentations had already been received, but sixty-seven orders had been made; eventually seventy-four livings, many of which were chapelries, received augmentations during the period 1645-1660.

Glossop rectory, once a monastic possession, had been bought after the dissolution of Basingwerk abbey by George Talbot, Earl of Shrewsbury and passed through marriage to the Howards, Earls of Arundel and Dukes of Norfolk; Thomas Howard was both delinquent and Roman Catholic. The revenue from the rectory was estimated at £350, out of which the vicar was paid £30. The vicarage of Glossop and the three chapels in the parish were given augmentations out of this fund, and enough was left to be applied outside the parish to other needy ministers. The tithes of Bakewell were appropriated to the dean and chapter of Lichfield; their income from this parish alone was estimated to be nearly £1000 with tithes on lead ore; from this handsome sum £53 was paid to the vicar and nothing to any of the nine chapel curates; the clerics of the cathedral had not thought it their responsibility to see that the chapels were adequately staffed or the curates remunerated. In one of the earliest grants, made in August 1645, the parliamentary committee used Lichfield revenues to augment all nine Bakewell chapels, but Sir Edward Leech, a lessee, needed several reminders before he paid some of the curates concerned. Bakewell's vicar also received a grant of £50, in consideration of the size and populousness of his parish - there were 1000 communicants, about 1400 people. Later, his living was valued at more than £50 and the grant was reduced. After the revolutionary changes of the Commonwealth period were undone by the restoration of the king in 1660, it was not surprising that nearly all these Derbyshire chapels appeared on eighteenth-century lists of poor livings.

There is no doubt that those giving information to the commissioners thought chapelries should be made independent. 'Fit to be a parish church' was a frequent comment. They put forward many suggestions for ironing out anomalies of the medieval inheritance, sometimes in spite of augmentations already made; for instance it was suggested that Charlesworth should be united with the mother church of Glossop, and Beeley in Bakewell with the parish of Edensor. Hayfield and Mellor, the other two chapels in Glossop, were thought fit to be parish churches and the inhabitants of Beard, on the very southern boundary of the parish, who wished to build their own chapel, should be allowed to; Brownside township should be transferred to the parish of Chapel en le Frith, as it was near that parish church. On the other hand, it was not suggested that the historical boundary between Hope and Bakewell should be altered, although Fairfield chapel on one side of Ashwood Dale stream and Buxton on the other were close to each other; both chapels were recommended for parochial status. Otherwise, Hope parish was to be broken up, and many of its townships transferred to four surrounding parishes; this threat may have prompted the survey made in 1658, and preserved in Lichfield's archives, of Easter payments owed by Fairfield chapelry and by 627 households in nineteen townships in the parish. In the third great Peak district parish, of Bakewell, seven out of nine chapels were considered fit to be parishes, and the proposal was actually approved in January 1659, but the reform was of short duration; by this date the government was in turmoil following the death of Cromwell, and Charles II returned to England in the spring of 1660.

The same recommendations to break up large parishes were made in other northern counties. Seven of the twelve chapels in Halifax were thought suitable to be become parishes, including Ripponden. It appears that inhabitants of most of Halifax's chapelries were withholding their small tithes from the vicar, presumably to pay their local ministers. In Leeds four of the seven chapels were recommended to be parish churches and a new church was proposed on a site central to four townships. In Lancashire, there were 118 chapels and 64 parish churches; the implication was that two-thirds of the parochial clergy were probably not receiving 'a good and sufficient maintenance'. At least forty-four chapels had no settled endowment and thirty-six had less than £4 a year. In Lancashire and Cheshire together, the average income of 51 curates given augmentations was just under £9.[6] Fifteen gentlemen gave evidence in Salford Hundred, which included Manchester parish. They did not estimate Manchester's population, but £100 was raised through the Easter roll, which might indicate at least 3000 and possibly twice that number.[7] The warden of Manchester collegiate church with one fellow and one minister were the 'pastors' and were 'all painfull godly preachinge Ministers'. The tithes of the large parish brought an income of £550 but out of this none of the nine chapel ministers was paid a salary; with the exception of Salford's chaplain, they were dependent on the contributions of the people. Some inhabitants in recent years had witheld their tithe payments, for instance at Newton, and paid their minister £40 instead.

Only Didsbury of the nine chapels was parochial.[8] Didsbury and Denton had been regarded as chantry chapels in 1547, and confiscated by the crown, but the inhabitants redeemed the buildings. Stretford, Blackley, and Chorlton also existed before 1547 and perhaps Gorton. Two more chapels had been founded at the end of the sixteenth century at Birch and Newton, in response to a growing population, and Salford's chapel was described in 1650 as 'lately erected' by Mr Humphrey Booth, a fustian dealer; fustian was a coarse cloth of cotton and flax, and this beneficence shows the importance already in the mid-seventeenth century of the cotton business in Manchester. His widow was paying the minister £20 a year. Five chaplains had houses, in some cases recently provided by the inhabitants. Eight of the nine Manchester chapels were described as 'fit to be a parish', including Salford which, as the jurors said, was within a quarter of a mile of the parish church but had 'a competency of inhabitants and communicants there within itself'. The commissioners also proposed one new chapel half way between Reddish and Heaton Norris to serve both townships, which were some six miles from either Denton or Gorton chapels. Heaton Norris did not get its chapel until 1765.

The story at Whalley was very similar. Seven chapels had existed before the end of the thirteenth century, one was fifteenth century and six were sixteenth century; Newchurch in Pendle and Newchurch in Rossendale had both been built following the enclosure of the Forest in 1507. Two chapels had been redeemed by the inhabitants after the chantries were abolished. Formerly a possession of Whalley abbey, in 1547 the Crown had required the archbishop of Canterbury to exchange one of his landed estates for the tithes of the enormous parish with its thirty-five townships, and to take on the obligation to pay the vicar and six curates.[9] In 1650 the glebe and tithes were 'farmed', that is, leased. New ecclesiastical owners of rectories were no more willing than the monasteries had been to give their income to parish priests; even the Easter offerings went to the farmer until Archbishop Juxon in 1660 gave them to the vicar and curates. The vicar was paid £38, and the six curates either £10 or £11.10s. Five more curates or chaplains were supported by the inhabitants. The jurors stated that the income from Whalley parish was £600 from tithes leased to a local landowner and £100 from glebeland. The stipends of the vicar and six curates used about one seventh of this amount; if the church's revenues had been spread amongst the fourteen chapels, each would have had £50. Unlike Manchester, ten of the fourteen chapels were parochial; Marsden was omitted from the survey. In most of the chapelries and townships there were more than 100 families, and in Colne more than 400. Apparently an exact census was taken in Padiham, showing 232 families and 1106 persons, and family size was 4.7. If this was typical, some 3300 families in the parish altogether suggest a population of 15,000. Despite their small stipends, three curates were Masters of Arts. The parliamentary committee had already ordered nine to be given grants, making their income up to £40. For each chapelry the same formula was repeated : 'the Inhabitants humbly desire it may bee made a parishe Church and competent maintenance allowed'. Suggestions were made to adjust boundaries and to erect a new chapel to serve the townships of Briercliffe and Extwisle, where there were said to be above one hundred families.

Fairfield, Derbyshire - The Vicarage dates from the seventeenth century, and is one of the older parsonages in Derby diocese. Reputedly it was once an inn. In 1794, when it was renovated by public subscription, it was called 'Fairfield Parsonage', but it is not known for how long the perpetual curate had lived here. It was not officially a glebe house because it was owned by trustees until 1927,

In the south, large collections of chapelries in one parish were unusual. Nonetheless proposals for reorganisation were made. A considerable list of anomalies in parish boundaries was presented in Gloucestershire. Suggestions included the transfer of farms and hamlets to parishes where the churches were nearer, and amalgamations of small parishes like Shipton Oliffe and Shipton Sollers where the two churches were half a mile apart, and the parishes were intermingled within one village. Of thirty-three chapels, independence was suggested for twelve, balanced by about the same number of amalgamations. Notable mismatches of status and importance were Stroud, a chapel of Bisley, and Moreton in Marsh, a chapel of Bourton on the Hill. Though on a smaller scale than in industrial towns in the north, new and growing market centres had not been recognised by the parochial system.

With the return of Charles II in 1660, plans for the augmentation of poor livings and the reorganisation of the medieval parish structures were abandoned. The independent spirit encouraged during the Civil War period, however, continued. Familiarity with self help in the chapelries, and the freedom to pursue new ways of religious observance which had been enjoyed during the Civil War, encouraged small groups to continue regardless of the restoration of the Church of England. Quakers, Baptists and Presbyterians or Congregationalists, although persecuted, survived as independent sects. The inhabitants of Charlesworth in Glossop were allowed by the Howard family to use that chapel for Presbyterian meetings and it has remained a Nonconformist chapel; an Anglican church was not built until 1849. In Birch in Manchester, Colonel Thomas Birch endowed an existing chapel in 1640 and after 1660 his son and succeeding trustees appointed Presbyterian ministers. Some inhabitants withdrew their contributions for his maintenance; eventually, in 1697, the Presbyterian minister was ejected and a Church of England minister substituted.[10] Nonconformity after the Civil War undermined the basis of those local initiatives which had been taken a century before, when all believed in the same church.

If all the proposed reorganisations of the Commonwealth period had taken place, the Church of England's parochial structure would have been revolutionised. There was another implication. Inhabitants of chapelries who paid their chapel ministers and appointed them, either collectively or through trustees, were effectively outside the bishops' supervision. Had chapelries become parishes, they would have been drawn into the episcopal framework. Some supervision was achieved in 1662 by making chapel ministers subject to the approval of the parish's rector or vicar, and this principle was extended in the eighteenth century through the conditions for grants imposed by Queen Anne's Bounty.

THE BREAKDOWN OF UNIFORMITY

On the fell-side above the Lune valley, along a narrow, winding road which preserves its peace and seclusion, Killington Hall stands beside a stream which feeds the Lune, sheltered by trees and hills. The Hall was the focus of a community of farmers scattered across the fells wherever shelter could be found by a springside; adjoining it are the ruins of a fortified tower house or pele with windows fourteenth century in style. In front of the Hall is the chapel. A dispute in Killington at the end of the seventeenth century provides insight into the difficulties which could be encountered by chapel curates who were paid by their congregations. Killington was in Kirkby Lonsdale parish. When the chapel had been made 'parochial' in 1585, land holders in the two townships of Killington and Firbank had agreed to contribute towards the salary of the curate according to the amount of their lands. Such arrangements were common in Cumbria. In 1671 and 1675, several Quakers in Killington were accused of refusing to pay their shares of his wages, or to make an Easter offering. It is easy to understand the Quakers' objections. They were not of the congregation, but went to the Quaker Meeting at Brigflatts near Sedbergh, which was not far away; at just this date they were raising money to build their Meeting House.[11] Why should they pay towards the Church of England minister? The trouble continued. William Sclater had become 'clerk preacher' of Killington in 1671, and it was probably his son who became curate in 1685, and twelve years later secured the appointment of a commission to investigate his case.

The commission met in Kendal early in 1697 and fourteen men gave testimony. They confirmed that there was an old chapel in Killington, kept in good repair, and that 'time out of mind' the inhabitants heard divine service and sermons there given by the curate, whose wages were paid by the owners and occupiers of houses, lands and tenements in the township. A record survives of the evidence given by Thomas Hebblethwaite of Killington. He was aged 56, and drew not only on his own knowledge but also on the recollections of his father and of several other 'ancient men'. He knew the chapel well, it was 'the first place where he went to school'. He thought that the occupiers of Killington Hall did not contribute to the curate's stipend because they had provided a site for the chapel and its burial ground. Conveyances of property in Killington included details of the payment to the curate, and also of a 'modus', a payment in lieu of tithe corn, to the parson of Kirkby Lonsdale. The Quakers had conspired to defeat this by destroying a deed referring to the payments, and two brothers had exchanged pieces of land and were cultivating them together 'Hotch pott' to obscure the obligation on specific plots. The commission found for the curate in June 1697, but the Quakers were not finished and they appealed. The case dragged on for nearly four years. Most inhabitants were for their curate and were contributing to his costs in the case; as his salary was about £8, this was just as well. William Sclater finally won and was paid arrears owing to him. He was succeeded in turn by his son in 1724, who died in December 1778 - making over a hundred years of ministry by the family. Such persistence suggests other ties in the area, in particular some land, and this may further explain why the Quakers were not disposed to pay the curate money which was a supplement to his farming income.[12]

It seems likely that William Sclater wrote out the names of the inhabitants, with their 'Degrees, Titles, Qualifications and Estates', for a new form of taxation introduced by act of parliament in 1695.[13] It is a happy coincidence that this list has survived. William Sclater appears as a self-important man. He placed himself first, with Dorothy his wife and Hanna his daughter, before Thomas Hebblethwaite, a gentleman and bachelor who could afford to keep four servants to care for him, or Joseph Ward, gentleman and widower, who had two daughters and three servants. The list reveals Thomas Hebblethwaite as the probable occupier of Killington Hall, hence his certainty that the Hall did not contribute to the curate's salary, and Joseph Ward had headed the list of those who gave evidence on the curate's behalf. The five Quakers who refused to contribute are also on the list; one was variously described as yeoman or blacksmith, one was a skinner, one a husbandman; two, James and Joseph Baines, were yeomen, and in 1706 the house of Joseph Baines of Stangerthwaite was licensed for Quaker religious worship.

The curate looked after about 86 households in 1695. Altogether there were ten yeomen in the township; the same family names had been recorded as freeholders early in the century. Holdings commonly were between ten and twenty acres, though Killington Park had 160 acres of good land and a large tract of fell, or 'moss, furze and heath'. There were also seventeen husbandmen or tenant farmers, and nine day labourers and as many as a third of the households were supported through the system of parish poor relief, mainly those of widows. It is difficult to imagine such a small hamlet so bustling with activity, with two blacksmiths, a skinner, miller, tanner, cooper, cordwainer - who was a maker of good quality shoes - millwright, and two weavers. The curate had married one couple in 1695 and one in 1696; he baptised or registered the births of five children and four burials the first year but only one baptism and no burial the second. His main clerical work was clearly his weekly service and sermon.

Firbank was some four miles to the north, adding 31 households to the curate's care, seventeen headed by yeomen and six by husbandmen. Firbank chapel and school were high up on the fellside. George Fox, the founder of the Quaker movement, had come to the Sedbergh area in 1652, and preached from a rock near the chapel subsequently known as Fox's Pulpit to over a thousand people, as he was informed. Quaker influence was strong in the area. In 1842 a new Anglican chapel was built in a more hospitable position on the lower road which winds round Firbank fell. Firbank parishioners return to the site of their first chapel, which is still consecrated ground, in mid June for a service of worship 'whatever the weather', showing how strong are the roots of a township chapel.

FROM CHAPEL MINISTER TO PERPETUAL CURATE

The failure to find a comprehensive church settlement after the restoration of monarchy in 1660 resulted in over a thousand ministers leaving their livings; they would not subscribe, as required of every dignitary, fellow, incumbent and teacher by the 1662 Act of Uniformity, to the newly revised Prayer Book. Some members of their congregations, or 'hearers', stayed with them and held small nonconformist meetings known as 'conventicles'.[14] For example, in the small hamlet of Clapton in Gloucestershire, a chapelry in Bourton on the Water, the Civil War curate retained a congregation after being ejected in 1662, and there was no resident curate thereafter to win the dissenters back; in 1676 there were fifty-one conformists and eleven dissenters here. Once the difficult initial step had been taken and dissent had been established, the tradition in particular places was often long-lasting. The returns collected by Bishop Compton of London in 1676 indicated that on average there was one nonconformist or dissenter to every twenty-two conforming members of the Church of England, or perhaps up to a quarter of a million in a population of less than five million. The Compton Census certainly understated the extent of nonconformity and there are no surviving returns from the dioceses of Durham or Chester to show the position in Lancashire or Cheshire, where considerable dissent would probably have been revealed. The two dioceses with the highest rates were surprisingly Canterbury with one dissenter to every nine conformists and less surprisingly London with one to fourteen. The suspiciously simple returns of 14,000 persons in Halifax and 150 dissenters, and 12,000 in Leeds, also with 150 dissenters, made no specific references to the chapelries; but earlier returns showed that conventicles existed in six chapelries in Halifax, including Ripponden, and in two in Leeds, as well as in the main church townships. Similarly in Bakewell, conformists numbered 4235 and dissenters 200; here there were conventicles in three chapelries as well as Bakewell itself.

A second significant loss of comprehensiveness for the Church of England followed the ejection of the Roman Catholic James II from the throne in 1688 and his replacement by the Protestant Willliam and Mary. A toleration act of 1689 allowed nonconformists to meet, subject to obtaining a licence, and to have teachers and preachers, with some safeguards against extreme or subversive principles. After this, the practice of self-help in the chapelries had as much scope outside the Church of England as inside and could have resulted in a significant falling-off in voluntary offerings to Church of England chapel ministers. A curate of Heptonstall in Halifax thought so. He wrote plaintively in 1705 that his only ecclesiatical rights were 'surplice dues, so called, viz.: marriages, burials, and baptisms, not amounting to above £5 per annum, and £20 per annum lately given by one John Greenwood of this parish'. The vicar of Halifax was not paying him the £4 a year that used to be his,

> so that what remains is only the charity of the people, and grows worse by much, by reason of so many conventicles set up in nooks and corners within the said parish, so that it is too well known to what a low ebb the minister and parish is brought unto ... The election of the minister is in the people ... If timely provision be not some ways made, the present minister (whom we have enjoyed forty years) must come to great want and poverty and this great parish become a wilderness, and not one so much as to bury our dead'.[15]

The wording shows that the minister, however straitened his circumstances, was employing a curate who wrote so supportively about him.

Discussion of the needs of poor livings in the early eighteenth century, motivated by the need to counter dissent, prompted the act setting up Queen Anne's Bounty. Replies to the Board's first survey in 1705 did not report more than a handful of chapels, although the Bounty asked for details of every 'Parson, Vicar, Curate and Minister, officiating in any Church or Chapel'. Bishops and officials were used to working in terms of livings, which were under their supervision and occupied by beneficed clergy with cure of souls. But people were clearly aware of the wider possibilities. Two chapel wardens and six inhabitants of Luddenden in Halifax parish reported that same year that the endowment of their chapel was only £4. 'The place convenient and in good repair, yet no clergyman is willing to serve us for so small wages. We have been without a minister six months and never like to have any without the Queen's Bounty'. They blamed decay of the woollen trade and 'Dissenters taking advantage, building Chapels very nigh us'. Their comments, and those of the curate of Heptonstall, were both made in reply to an enterprising cleric who had sent out a questionnaire, intending to publish his own survey of the Church of England's organisation, a *Notitia Parochialis*, which is preserved in Lambeth Palace archives. Chapel ministers were not relevant to the Bounty's second survey in 1707 to discharge livings from First Fruits and Tenths, which they did not pay. But after an act in 1715 reiterated that the Bounty extended to stipendiary preachers and curates, and authorised bishops to enquire into the values of any benefices they thought fit, information and requests for augmentations began to flow. Seven chapels in Leeds, for example, received allotments of £200 between 1717 and 1731, and Headingley two; six of the seven were matched to private benefactions of an equal amount. In Halifax, eight chapels were augmented by 1732, and apart from Luddenden, again all were in response to private benefactions. In the first two decades of practical operation - no grants were made before 1714 - the Bounty had provided two northern parishes with £1600 and benefactors £1400.[16]

An important condition for an augmentation was imposed in the 1715 act: chapels had to be 'perpetual Cures and Benefices'. The intention was to safeguard them from patrons who otherwise might fail to appoint a curate and take the augmented income for themselves. Until this time, there were relatively few perpetual curacies. An alteration in the status of a chapelry could only take place with the patron's consent.[17] Furthermore, a perpetual curate came under episcopal supervision and had to be in orders, at least a deacon if not a priest. An amazing anomaly was now introduced into the parochial system: a perpetual curate could serve a chapel which was not parochial, had no defined district, and where, despite his title, he did not have cure of souls; the act specifically protected mother churches' rights in this respect. This was the situation in Leeds which Walter Farquhar Hook so deplored in the 1840s. In practice, many curates were able to baptise in their chapels with the incumbent's agreement. The mother church was still responsible for registration and normally collected fees, but baptisms performed in the chapel might also be recorded in its own register. The Revd Canon Simpson in 1884 wrote about the inhabitants of the chapelries of Kirkby Stephen 'within my own recollection' paying double fees, and an examination of the registers of one of the chapels, Mallerstang, has shown that the two sets of registers partially overlapped. The baptism register was started in 1713, probably in preparation for an endowment of the chapelry from Queen Anne's Bounty, received in 1719.[18] There was no burial ground until 1813.

A consequence of the 1715 act was the disappearance of the order of readers. As chapelries prepared for and received Queen Anne's Bounty, there were many instances of existing readers being ordained deacon. Bishop Nicolson of Carlisle made an interesting observation on their situation about this time, and on the employment which helped them to subsist; reviewing the five chapels in the large parish of Crosthwaite, where the chaplains had incomes of between £3 and £5 he wrote:

> As mean as these Salaries look, the Readers in these Dales are commonly more rich than the curates . . . in other parts of the Diocese; having the advantage of drawing bills, bonds, conveyances, wills etc. which the attorneys elsewhere claim as their property. But, since the duty of stamped paper came in fashion, their revenues are much abated on this article.

Readers were also schoolmasters; the chapel at Mallerstang had received an endowment in the seventeenth century for the 'maintenance of a person qualified to read prayers and homilies and to teach the children of Mallerstang to read and write English in the chapel there', though this stipend was not included in the valuation for the Bounty Board. Mallerstang was one of only four chapelries in Carlisle diocese before 1737 which, through private benefactions, received the Bounty. Between 1737 and 1753 nearly all did, some more than once. The bishop of Carlisle appointed in 1734 was a local man and had been archdeacon for many years previously. In 1739 he prepared a comprehensive list of forty-eight chapelries, all 'entirely distinct' from their mother churches, in need of more sufficient salaries, and he ordained the readers.[19]

No general survey of church livings was made after 1707 until the Royal Commission of 1832, though a record was kept of values returned by the bishop when augmentation was under consideration. Most chapelries had been reported by 1736 and the Bounty's published *Return* included 1678. They constituted nearly a third of the total of poor livings, and about one seventh of the clergy served chapels not parish churches. The *Return* emphasised how chapelries clustered in the north and in particular in three dioceses:

Livings of £50 a year or less in 1736

Diocese	Chapelries	Rectories and Vicarages
Chester	276	90
York	253	329
Coventry & Lichfield	208	159

Chester diocese reached from Cheshire, through Lancashire to the southern Lake District, and to Richmond in Yorkshire; there were three times as many chapelries as parishes here amongst the poorer livings. Coventry and Lichfield diocese was similar. York, despite its numerous chapelries, had even more poor rectories and vicarages.[20] The distribution of chapelries by county is very striking, showing the geographical concentration. Six counties each had more than fifty chapels:

Livings of £50 a year or less in 1736

County	Chapelries
Cheshire	51
Norfolk	60
Derbyshire	66
Lancashire	73
Staffordshire	86
Yorkshire	271

Part of Yorkshire was in Chester diocese, so that the county was more extensive than the diocese. Even allowing for its size - the three Ridings were equivalent to three counties - the situation was remarkable. The number of chapelries in Norfolk is surprising because there were numerous small parishes in this county, many of which also qualified for Queen Anne's Bounty. The guaranteed income of many chapelries in fact fell far short of £50 and in many

instances there was none at all, though this did not mean that the curates relied on their private incomes or on charity; as at Mallerstang, many were schoolmasters, too, but these stipends and the voluntary offerings of congregations were not relevant to the Bounty. Twelve of the fifteen chapels in Prestbury in Cheshire had incomes of £12 or less, nine of the fifteen in Whalley, seven of the eight in Manchester, eight of the nine in Bakewell in Derbyshire, and thirteen out of fourteen in Kendal in Cumbria: the fourteenth had £13.

Gradually chapel minsters joined the ranks of the beneficed clergy, but in relation to the standards of the period the curacies were still considered too poor to be held singly, and it was quite usual for two or more to be held by one man, or in combination with rectories and vicarages. The rules about holding several livings together were not held to apply to perpetual curacies. As a result, unbeneficed substitute curates often did the actual pastoral work for a minimum stipend of about £20. There were some 4405 curates in 1814.[21] 'Curate' began to change its generally understood meaning as the number of curates assisting rectors or vicars increased markedly, hiding the older sense of curate as applied to chapel ministers. The new curates were like the chapel curates of one hundred years earlier, before the changes brought about by Queen Anne's Bounty. Perhaps the bishops were partly to blame; from their wealthier positions they were too sympathetic to the claims of clergymen requiring higher incomes. Contemporary opinion was inclined to blame the curates themselves for being willing to serve for so little. Adam Smith, in *The*

Leafield, Oxfordshire - the former vicarage house was built in 1860 under the direction of the immensely busy Sir George Gilbert Scott and designed to be in sympathy with Cotswold vernacular style and materials, next to the church which he also designed. There was no parsonage house before 1831, when Leafield became a separate parish and the curate a perpetual curate; his stipend in 1835 was £69. The house was sold in 1989.

Middleton, Cumbria - a date stone records the rebuilding in 1893 of this former chapelry parsonage house in the parish of Kirkby Lonsdale. During the eighteenth century the chapelry stipend was augmented several times by Queen Anne's Bounty and the first parsonage house was built about 1800.

Wealth of Nations, published in 1776, offered the classic explanation: the 'long, tedious and expensive education' of churchmen 'will not always procure them a suitable reward, the church being crowded with people who, in order to get employment, are willing to accept of a much smaller recompense than what such an education would otherwise have entitled them to'.

When the Ecclesiastical Revenues Commissioners enquired into the incomes of benefices on average between 1829 and 1831, there were more than a thousand under £80 a year, which had been the criterion for a poor living in the 1705 Bounty survey, mainly perpetual curacies. In the north-west, the majority of chapelries in Greystoke, Kendal and Kirkby Lonsdale, for example, came into this category. The income of three out of four chapel curates in Greystoke only just exceeded £50. Four out of six perpetual curates in Kirkby Lonsdale received under £80 and the best paid was the curate of Middleton, with £100. In Kendal's fourteen chapelries, five curates were paid less than £80 and the best-paid received £125. Similarly the curates of the old chapelries in

Bakewell in Derbyshire had incomes which ranged from £74 to £150. Each of these chapelries had a population of much less than 1000. But where populations had increased substantially, the incomes of the perpetual curates were generally rather higher, as a result of the system of pew rents, though it could be argued that they needed to pay assistant curates to help them meet the demands of their parishes.

Population growth in Lancashire by 1831 was already overwhelming the parish churches and their chapels. There were 100,000 people in the ancient parish of Whalley, and nineteen chapel curates; Colne had a population of nearly 17,000 and Burnley nearly 16,000. The perpetual curate of Church Kirk received £220 and of Burnley most exceptionally £776; this far exceeded the stipend of the vicar, which was £140, and probably explains why he also held the chapelry of Church Kirk and paid a curate to live there. The curates of Burnley and Colne employed assistant curates, and so did the curate of Clitheroe. The church at Prestbury was similarly overshadowed by one of its chapelries, Macclesfield, which had a population of 23,129. The curate was paid £214. Three other chapelries were under £80, and six under £100. Some of Halifax's chapelries, too, had expanded tremendously: Coley's population was 13,656 and Heptonstall's 11,816; the perpetual curates of newly-founded churches mainly had incomes over £100. Manchester was exceptional. The population was 142,000 by 1831, and there were twelve churches and thirteen chapels. The older chapel curates were often not as well-paid as the new; six received between £107 and £150, while the perpetual curate of the new church of St Philip's, Salford, had £441.

Queen Anne's Bounty had been successful in narrowing the gap between the old-beneficed rectors and vicars and the perpetual curates. Kirkby Lonsdale and Kendal vicars each received £327; the vicar of Prestbury received £450 and of Bakewell £404; the rector of Greystoke failed to make a return, but later in the century his income was about £700. Only in Halifax was the gap between vicar and perpetual curates outstanding; he received £1804.

A RETIRED NORTHERN CURACY: DENT

The small town with cobbled streets, where the dale of the River Dee widens out, is along a narrow road some five miles from Sedbergh. Communication with Sedbergh probably governed ancient manorial and parish links, and Dentdale, together with Garsdale, was in Sedbergh parish in the West Riding of Yorkshire, but is now in Cumbria. As well as the closely-built Dent's Town, there were many scattered fell-side farms along the length of the dale. Most of Dent's farmers became freeholders or 'statesmen' in 1670, when they were able to buy the manorial rights over their lands. One unlooked-for effect of having many owners was that small plots of land could be purchased in this valley using a £200 grant from Queen Anne's Bounty. The first such purchase of land in the dale was 1719; in 1743 Dent itself received a grant and a second in 1812, allowing the purchase of about thirty acres. By that date, as much as a tenth of the dale was owned by twenty-six different perpetual curates, all but four of them of chapelries. St Bees on the west coast of Cumberland was the most

Dent, Cumbria - the Old Parsonage is where the perpetual curate formerly lived in the town. It has the date 1673 over the entrance, and was probably built by a newly-created Cumbrian 'statesman' rather than a cleric. Adam Sedgwick the geologist was born here. His brother in 1835 regarded the house as 'fit' for his residence, but by 1904, despite having seven bedrooms, it was 'most unsatisfactory' and sold for £225.

distant, fifty miles away across the mountains of the Lake District; most were closer at hand, including four of the chapels in Kirkby Lonsdale. One result was the large clerical vote in local parliamentary elections. Many of these plots of land were sold in the mid-nineteenth century, and the money invested differently for the benefit of the perpetual curates.[22]

Three generations of the Sedgwick family were perpetual curates of Dent between 1768 and 1885 - a span of 117 years. The family was prosperous - in 1875 two Sedgwicks owned more land in the dale than anyone - and long-established - a Sedgwick was a witness to the boundary between Dent and Barbon in 1278, no less than four of this name paid poll tax in Dent in 1379, at the end of the sixteenth century a Sedgwick is recorded owning land there, and one was a churchwarden in 1595. Adam Sedgwick, the early, eminent geologist, was one of the seven sons of the parsonage, born in 1785. Towards the end of his life, he printed his recollections of Dent in his father's time, and his reflections on the 'retired Curacies of the North of England'. His father had been to Cambridge; Sedgwick recounts that he bought a horse and rode there and then sold the horse, and he suggested that Dent folk had been proud of having a Cambridge graduate as their minister. Later he was the master of Dent Grammar School, and so supplemented his salary.[23] Adam Sedgwick went to

school there before going to Sedbergh. He considered Dent fortunate to have a Grammar School, which helped the church fill its northern curacies.

Certainly for more than two centuries the Grammar School has had a very healthy influence upon the education and manners of the valley. The leading Statesmen's sons attended the Grammar School, and acquired a smattering of classical learning: and if a Statesman's younger son, or the son of a cottager, were a lad of good promise, his education was pushed forward into a higher course, and he was trained for the Church. And many so trained, and without any other collegiate education, did enter the Church, and filled the retired Curacies in the North of England.

The vicarage house which replaced the Old Parsonage in 1904 was built for £2500. The vicar arranged the house to catch the sun all day and to enjoy the view. It was sold in 1984 and another built beside it.

There were disadvantages:

> a Curate or country Vicar with a narrow income, who had been trained among men of like habits with those of his flock, might sometimes fall into their habits and perhaps their vices, and thereby forfeit all the strength of his moral influence.

In an afterthought, Sedgwick added 'the supply of candidates for Holy Orders from the Country Schools of the North of England has been very greatly modified by the rules of admission established by the Bishops during this century'. His comment referred to the drive to a graduate profession, which he supported. Adam Sedgwick was ordained, becoming a fellow of Trinity College, Cambridge; as a result he was 'mired in celibacy', as he said, for the rest of his life, a condition of an Oxford or Cambridge fellowship.

Sedgwick wrote in perhaps unduly favourable terms of the life of Dentdale while his father was parson; he described tea at the parsonage on Sunday for those who lived at a distance from the church, and he suggested that 'in manners, habits and information, there was no difference' between the cottager and the 'statesman'. 'Even in the houses of the Clergymen and of the wealthier Statesmen, there was kept alive a feeling of fraternal equality'. The word 'even' is revealing and shows that there was a distance between the Perpetual Curate and most of the farmers who were not statesmen. The curacy of Dent was not one of the poorest. In 1736 the living was worth £34, and Sedgwick's father was himself able to maintain a curate when he became blind. In 1835, the living was worth £101; Sedgwick's own stipend as a fellow of Trinity at the same date was £400, and a prebend at Norwich, which he accepted in 1834, was worth approximately £600 a year. The population of Dentdale, nearly 2000 in 1831, was then at its highest. As mechanised stocking-knitting increased the population fell, as many had relied on spinning and hand-knitting for subsistence; Harry Speight noted at the end of the nineteenth century

> Dent has changed greatly of late years, although there is still a rather antiquated look about its one winding thoroughfare, and little cobble-laid byways. But the main street ... has lost the peculiar features that were so striking a characteristic of the place a generation or two ago. These were the projecting galleries and pent-roofs, which were approached by flights of steps from the outside, and these upper rooms obtruded so far into the street that two persons on opposite sides might almost have shaken hands.

In fact Speight exaggerated the recentness of the change. According to Sedgwick, the spinning galleries had largely gone by the end of the previous century.

Sedgwick's essays on Dent, of 1868 and 1870, were stimulated by a dispute over the chapelry district of Cowgill, three miles higher up the valley. It had been built using the materials and on the site of a mid-eighteenth century Presbyterian chapel and Sedgwick had laid the foundation stone in 1837. He used an argument based on place-names to try to prevent the curate of Cowgill enlarging his chapelry district, so removing some parishioners from Dent and from the third generation of the Sedgwick family who was parson there. Cowgill's curate was really in more need of parishioners to supplement his stipend, though neither was paid enough to be unmindful of the offerings of his congregation. There was a compromise over the district, and in 1870 Cowgill became an independent parish; but since 1932, one vicar has served both Cowgill and Dent, and the two parishes were united in 1974, after not much more than a century of separation. This is a story typical of many chapelries.

Final recognition of the reform which had slowly been engineered since the founding of Queen Anne's Bounty was the legal status of 'parish' bestowed on a large number of old as well as new chapelries in the later nineteenth century. In 1868 it was decided that perpetual curates should be called 'vicar'. The old distinctions based on tithe income had gone - commutation in 1836 and abolition of church rates in 1868 finally ended the collection of all small tithes, which had usually been the vicar's perquisite. Apart from this rational change of name, the Church of England has held on to the titles of rector, vicar and curate and has guarded the concept of the benefice which had separated perpetual curates, rectors and vicars from the chapel curates in the centuries before Queen Anne's Bounty was founded.

Mellor, Greater Manchester - the former vicarage house was an inn near the church, converted to a vicarage in the early twentieth century; previously the perpetual curate of the chapelry lived in his own house which had also been an inn, on the north side of the church. This vicarage house has now been sold so that the vicar can live near the villagers rather than the church.

CHAPTER EIGHT

A 'COMPETENT MANSE'

The dark red sandstone pele tower of Lanercost vicarage stands close to the west end of the priory church of St Mary, just outside the monastery precincts. It was built in the thirteenth century. The priory was founded about a hundred years before, on a site close to the River Irthing where the valley widens. The road from Brampton is narrow and wooded and crosses the Irthing by a modern road bridge, beside the elegant but bent early eighteenth-century bridge; beyond Lanercost, it winds steeply up the hill past Banks Turret, one of the mileposts on Hadrian's Wall, and follows the wall for three miles to Birdoswald fort. The priory setting seems one of great peacefulness, but defensive tower houses were common in this border area where Scottish attacks across the marsh and bog of the Solway plain were frequent. Lanercost was strategically placed and was several times plundered by the Scots; King Edward I stayed there for a whole winter in 1306-7, during a Scottish campaign. The priory was also a parish church, and the lands and revenues of several churches in the area were part of its foundation endowment; as Augustinian canons, the members of the community could serve these parish churches in person, but in practice they provided deputies, sometimes called vicars, sometimes curates. The Priory was dissolved in 1537 and the conventual buildings were sold, but specifically reserved for the dwelling of the vicar or curate of Lanercost was 'the mansion called the utter gate house', with the stable, granary and little garden attached.[1] Here his successors still live. This vicar's pele tower may have a claim to be the oldest continuously occupied vicarage in the country.

'Pele' or 'peel' originally meant an enclosure surrounded by a wooden stockade, often also moated, but it came to describe a simple defensive tower house. A number remain in the disputed border lands between Scotland and England. Church incumbents were probably targets of raids, as they had chalices, copes and other valuables in their care. The Vicar's pele at Corbridge in Northumberland, on the edge of the churchyard and facing the market place, was built about 1300, during the period of Edward I's wars. Roman masonry was used in its construction as in the church. The ground floor is stone-vaulted to prevent fire spreading to the rooms above; a staircase in the thickness of the wall admitted only one person at a time to the first floor living room, where there was a fireplace and other facilities, and a further staircase led to a chamber above which served as a bedroom and perhaps as an oratory. This is a typical plan, like a small Norman castle keep. Corbridge rectory was owned by Carlisle priory, which absorbed the revenues of the extensive parish and could call upon considerable resources to build well. Monasteries had to protect their possessions in compliance with a royal order of the early fourteenth century; they also had to provide a 'competent manse' for their vicars. A pele was by no means a poor house in the fourteenth century, when most were built, and the vicar of Corbridge lived in his until the seventeenth century.[2]

How often in the early medieval period was a defensive tower both church and accommodation for the priest? An excavation at Sulgrave in Northamptonshire has revealed a fortification which was 'possibly tower and church combined', near to an eleventh-century hall. Earls Barton in the same county has one of the most remarkable surviving Saxon towers which was also probably free-standing, and is on a large defensive mound.[3] The tower at Saintbury in Gloucestershire has an altar-like stone in the middle of the ground floor; the church is on the edge of a hill-fort on the Cotswold scarp. Other possible church peles in the Cotswolds are Longborough, Wyck Rissington, the old church at Oddington, and Withington; all belonged to distant religious establishments: Hayles and Eynsham abbeys, the bishopric of Worcester and the archbishopric of York. Although considered characteristic of the Borders, pele towers were perhaps more common further south than now appears.

The church itself was perhaps quite often the priest's house, or his lodging for one or more nights a week when he visited it. Bede told a story that when Cuthbert was visiting 'his sheepfolds' like the good shepherd he was, 'in the mountains no church could be found, nor any place fit to receive the bishop and his retinue. So they pitched tents for him by the wayside'. Two stories from the middle of the twelfth century show the priest lodging in the church. In John of Ford's life of Wulfric, an anchorite of Haselbury in Somerset, he mentions that the parish priest usually slept in the church. In the life of Gilbert of Sempringham it seems that he and his chaplain, who probably carried out the priestly duties, lived in the village inn until too much tempted by the host's daughter, when they moved to a room over the church porch, or perhaps over the church, and then to a house which they built on the edge of the churchyard. Gilbert later turned this parsonage into an almshouse, and himself lived in the household of the bishop of Lincoln. The priest apparently slept in Samlesbury chapel in Blackburn, Lancashire; when the Scots raided here in 1322 they carried off 'one coverlet for a bed', three blankets and two towels, as well as two sets of vestments, a missal, a chalice and other vessels.[4]

Bishop Nicolson of Carlisle in the early eighteenth century thought the choir of Salkeld church had been built as a 'secure hold or habitation for the Rector himself' as there was an iron door below, a good cellar, and several chimneys. Similarly, the church at Burgh by Sands had an old tower at the east end, 'half

*East Bergholt, Suffolk -
St Mary's church porch.
In the medieval period a
priest lodged in the room
over the porch; although
a large church and a
royal manor at the
centre of a 'soke' in
1086, East Bergholt had
the status of a chapel to
Brantham church. The
rector moved to East
Bergholt and, although
considered an inferior
match, his daughter
married John Constable,
who lived here and
painted the porch in
1811.*

broken', and a new one at the west end. The east end tower 'seems to have been intended for a Mansion house for the vicar; such fastnesses being necessary (so very near Scotland) before the Kingdoms were united'. The Union was enacted by the parliaments of England and Scotland in 1707, but Nicolson had in mind the union of the two crowns under James I in 1603.

SOME MEDIEVAL PARSONAGE HOUSES

A parsonage house separate from the church itself was generally accepted practice by the twelfth century, though very few buildings survive from either the twelfth or the thirteenth centuries. A few more survive from the early fourteenth century, including the northern vicars' peles, and the more frequent lowland timber-framed houses like the priests' houses at Kentisbeare in Devon and Muchelney in Somerset, to suggest something of the provision thought suitable at the time.[5]

The old St Alphege's rectory in Canterbury is amongst the rare surviving thirteenth-century parsonage houses, and it is probable that it already existed in the later eleventh century.[6] The house is situated on a plot of land next to the church in Palace Street. Domesday Book recorded that twenty-seven houses had been destroyed to make room for Archbishop Lanfranc's new palace. Consequently, Palace Street turns through several right-angles as it skirts round those twenty-seven plots. On the north side of the new Palace Street, twenty-eight plots were laid out: one was for the church dedicated to St Alphege, an archbishop of Canterbury who died in 1012, and next to it was the rectory, Number 8 Palace Street. The existing house was built about 1250 of two storeys; an upstairs 'hall' or living room has a stone-flagged floor laid on massive joists, supported on a central pillar and two arches. The stone floor enabled the rector to build his fire upstairs, in the middle of his hall. So strong was the method of construction, that in the sixteenth century a chimney and two fireplaces, replacing the open hearth, could be built on top of the one stone pillar which holds the whole weight. The entrance to the house was not on the street side but on the side facing the church. In the late fifteenth century a fashionable timber front was added; later still a third storey was added. The house was not sold by the church until after the Second World War.

Sometimes descriptions of parsonage houses can be found in 'ordinations', which were agreements about the institution of a vicarage made by the bishop, usually when a monastery took over the rectory revenues of a church; they often included provision of a 'competent' house or 'manse' for the vicar. A few ordinations exist from the early twelfth century, and they gradually become

Muchelney, Somerset - the Priest's House was built about 1308 when Muchelney abbey established a vicarage. As it was nearby, the abbey kitchen supplied the vicar's food, including two gallons of best conventual ale daily. The hall reached to the roof, with two-storied bays on either side. Later, a chimney was built and a floor inserted, interrupting the long hall windows. The house is now owned by the National Trust.

more numerous. They show that in some cases only the site was provided, and the vicar built the house himself; for example, in 1253 the vicar of Conisborough in Yorkshire was given two small tofts 'for a manse', suggesting he would pay for its construction, while in 1287 at Hadlow, near Tonbridge in Kent, an acre of land was allocated to the vicar specifically so that he could build a house. But at Halifax in 1273, Lewes priory agreed 'A vicarage house shall be built, in which the vicar for the time being shall reside'.[7]

A typical plan for a timber-framed house like those surviving at Kentisbeare and Muchelney was clearly described in a vicarage ordinance for Histon in Cambridgeshire in 1268: Eynsham abbey agreed to build a house of oak with a hall twenty-six feet by twenty, with on one side a 'competent chamber' or private room and on the other a *dispensa* - a storehouse or pantry; a separate kitchen, bakehouse and brewhouse were to be built. At Muchelney, no cooking facilities were needed because the vicar was supplied from the nearby abbey kitchen. The side rooms appear to have been single-storey, with no more than attics above. These houses had a cross-passage at one end of the hall, with a doorway front and back, and the dimensions of both were very similar. Halls were open to the roof so that the smoke from a central hearth could find its way out through the roof; windows without glass and doors on both sides of the house created the draught to direct the smoke upwards. Houses continued to be built on this plan until the widespread adoption of brick chimneys about 1550.

An upstairs chamber was usually known as a 'solar', a name derived from french sol, floor, and solive, beam. A house consisting of hall, two solars, and two cellars was given to the vicar of West Harptree in Somerset in 1344; in addition, a kitchen, barn, stable for three horses and dovecot were to be built.

Otham, Kent - The Rectory probably dates from the late fifteenth century; the distinctive 'Wealden' shape can be seen, and in the centre the insertion of an upper floor in the hall. On the south-east edge of Maidstone, urban development is creeping along the valley; the parish is small, but a growing population should justify keeping this oldest Kentish rectory house.

This became a more common plan in the fifteenth century. Many houses with solars above the ground floor service rooms, particularly in Kent and Sussex, had projecting first-floor joists or 'jetties'. Characteristically, the central hall, rising the full height of the two-storey building, had a wide overhanging eave. This is known as the 'Wealden' house, and is particularly associated with the Kentish yeoman. The distinctive style is recognisable at once from the large, steep roof, even when the timber frame is hidden under tiles or plaster, as it is in Otham rectory house near Maidstone in Kent. The earliest Wealden house is possibly Wardes in Otham parish, dated about 1370, but most date from the period 1450-1530. So well built were these houses, that they have withstood centuries of modernisation, starting with the insertion of chimneys. The Weald was heavily wooded, and the independent farmers who owned their land, the yeomen, built with good Wealden oak. The comparison of a parson with a yeoman is by no means a denigration of the parson's standing; Wealdens were high status houses. Of the one-time Wealden parsonages in Canterbury diocese, only Otham remained a rectory in 1999.

Wealden parsonage houses seem frequently to have been built by a religious institution which could command more resources than an individual rector or vicar: for example, St Augustine's monastery for their vicar at Stone in Oxney, Kent, after 1347, or St John's college, Cambridge, for their steward at Headcorn, Kent, about 1516, one of the finest and latest of the Wealden houses; the vicar here was allocated rooms in what was actually the rectory house, and no vicarage house was provided. In 1716 a vicar of Headcorn willed his own house in the village for the benefit of future incumbents. The Clergy House at Alfriston, Sussex, the first building purchased by the National Trust in 1896, is another example, built by Michelham priory probably at the time the tithes were appropriated in 1398; the date is confirmed by some features of the house. After being abandoned by the vicar about 1800, it was divided into five cottages and when at the end of the century the Ecclesiastical Commissioners wished to demolish it, the County Archaeological Society, the vicar and the National Trust

Easton on the Hill, Northamptonshire - the Priest's House may be earlier than 1500, but stone is more difficult to date than a timber-frame. It probably contained an open hall with windows facing the courtyard to the rear. Later the roof was raised, and rooms inserted above the hall, reached by an outside staircase. At the beginning of the twentieth century the upper floor was a hayloft and the lower floor housed cattle and pigs. The National Trust saved it from demolition in 1963. The present rectory beside it was built in the 1950s.

combined to save it. It is now thatched, but was not originally so. One unusual feature at Alfriston is that the eastern bay had a separate outside entrance and no door connecting with the hall. It has been suggested that this was to accommodate the housekeeper discreetly apart from the celibate vicar.[8] This same suggestion could explain the outside staircase to an upper room at the Priest's House at Easton on the Hill.

Responsibility for care of his house usually rested with the rector or the vicar. It was sometimes spelled out in vicarage ordinances, as it was for the vicar of Stone in Oxney. From the time that records of bishops' visitations begin in the late thirteenth century, there are complaints of dilapidations. In 1264 the vicar of Locking in Somerset refused to reside on his benefice, or even to become a priest, and the fact that his house was in disrepair may have been both cause and effect. In the visitation of Totnes archdeaconry in Devon in 1342, nearly all vicarage houses needed repairs and the condition of eight was very bad, in one case 'vile, insufficient and ruinous'; a larger proportion of rectory houses was regarded as satisfactory. The vicar at Birling in Kent in 1448 said his house was decayed because of the negligence of Bermondsey abbey, so denying his own responsibility. The bishop of Hereford asked the dean of Stottesden, Shropshire, to enquire into the 'notable and enormous defects' of the rectory of Bolde, later a chapel in Aston Botterell, 'which, as John de Colyn, the present rector claims, should be made good by the executors of John Jenynes, his predecessor'.[9] It was not easy to recover costs from a dead parson's executors. The problem of dilapidations had a very long history before the legislation of 1871, and even after responsibility was transferred to the dioceses a hundred years later, it has not necessarily been solved.

The ending of celibacy must often have encouraged the enlarging or rebuilding of parsonage houses to accommodate parsons' families. Thornham and Holme next the Sea were some two miles apart along the north Norfolk coast. In 1597 the churchwardens complained that the vicar of Holme was 'not resident uppon his vicaredge howse, by reason wherof it decayeth'. His defence was 'that it is not sufficient for him and his familie, and he is resident uppon his other benefice of Thornham'. At Thornham, the churchwardens said that 'the vicaredge barne is decayed in the tymber. He is allso vicar of Holme. It is sometymes xi of the clocke in the forenone before he begyn service. He biddeth not the fasting dayes and holidayes'. Here his defence was 'that there is noe vicaredge howse or barne ther, nor have been within the memorie of man'.[10] Possibly he lived in his own house. By the middle of Elizabeth I's reign, about half the clergy were married. William Harrison, rector of Radwinter in Essex from 1559 until his death in 1593, considered that a wife brought the parson a better standard of housekeeping:

> ... by reason that marriage is permitted to him that will choose that kind of life, their meat and drink is more orderly and frugally dressed, their furniture of household more convenient and better looked unto, and the poor oftener fed generally than heretofore they have been.

He was one who had chosen 'that kind of life', and obviously paid tribute to Mistress Harrison's skills.

Rising living standards also led to a rebuilding of houses, naturally including parsonage houses. Inventories of possessions show that by the end of the sixteenth century houses had more rooms, more soft furnishings and plate, and more furniture than at the beginning. Harrison commented on this and also on what seemed to him a dramatic change which had taken place during the lifetime of older men living in his village, the 'multitude of chimneys lately erected' in place of open hearths. Inserting a chimney into open halls permitted also the insertion of a floor and the creation of a room or chamber over the hall. This alteration was made in nearly every surviving medieval house including parsonage houses. Alternatively, a new house was built. The old one, possibly on the edge of the churchyard as at Kentisbeare, was sometimes used for the parish hall, as an almshouse, as a clerk's house, or it was let to bring the parson income; he was not allowed to sell it until the nineteenth century.[11]

At all periods, poorer houses will have been replaced, so that only the better ones survive; if not replaced, then they were added to so that the original is almost unrecognisable. The large and impressive timber-framed rectory house at Gawsworth, Cheshire, dated 1470, may have been an addition to the small timber-framed house with a first floor hall which still stands next to it. An impression of high standards in the medieval period may be misleading in relation to the majority of parsonage houses at that time.

YEARS OF NEGLECT

'The eighteenth century may be called pre-eminently the age of ecclesiastical dilapidation', the Revd. John Conybeare wrote in the Edinburgh Review in April 1853. He was referring to the repair or rebuilding of parsonage houses which he saw underway in the diocese of Llandaff, and also of churches: Llandaff cathedral was so neglected in 1722, he said, that it blew down. No doubt there were many parish clergy as conscientious as Parson Sampson at Clayworth who entered in his yearly accounts, published in the *Rector's Book* , the amount spent on 'support of the benefice', and regularly itemised repairs to house and outbuildings, but during the eighteenth century there was increasing concern at the neglect of parsonage houses, and particularly where it was the result of pluralism.

Bishop William Nicolson's notes of his visitations of Carlisle diocese suggest that neglect was already clearly noticeable at the beginning of the century. He knew the diocese well; he was born at Orton rectory and spent twenty years as a parish priest and archdeacon of Carlisle. As bishop, he made three triennial visitations between 1704 and 1713, and visited each parish. 'Ill', 'slovenly', 'ruinous', 'woeful' were among the adjectives used about eighteen parsonage houses out of fifty-one on which he commented. Neglect was not confined to the parsonage house; a certain number of churches were also in a sad state, with leaking, propped up or even fallen roofs, as at Aikton, and he repeatedly lamented that a school was taught in the church and particularly in the chancel, where the altar might be used as a writing table. At Stapleton, he reflected, there ought to be a resident rector; the chancel of the church was 'scandalous' with no glass in the windows, the rest of the church was 'a pickle', and the parsonage 'sorry'. At Kirkbride, the parson was abroad, the key to the church could not even be found, and the roof was coming down. The rector was rich and also lord of the manor.

Nicolson's comment on Castle Carrock was an epitome of the problem: 'The Parsonage House is in that neglected state, as is usual where the parson is either too rich or too poor'. When too rich, the parson lived elsewhere, like the 'somewhat too worldly' vicar of Brampton who held three other livings, typically none the poorest; his church was in a 'slovenly pickle' and his house was 'ruinous'. The rector of Crosby Garret lived with his patron in Durham, but passed the income of the living to his curate; the poor condition of the parsonage house did not affect him. At Kirk Bampton, the rector lived in his own house in town, which was described caustically as 'in better repair than his Parsonage'. The parsonage house of Melmerby was 'wholly neglected' by a previous incumbent, 'who (being as well Lord as parson) always resided at the Hall'. A more conscientious attitude had been shown by an earlier vicar of Barton, Lancelot Dawes; he lived at Barton Kirk Hall, his 'paternal estate', which was 'chiefly of his own building', but he also built a vicarage house, over the door of which he inscribed 'LD 1637' and *Non mihi sed successoribus*', 'not for me but for my successors'.

Poverty was the other reason for neglect of the parsonage house. The curate at Bolton looked 'as tattered as ever' but the rector and rectory house were in an equally sad state; so keen had the rector been to secure the living that he had contracted to pay the patron an annual 'rent', and was consequently never 'well-able to keep himself and his Family (any more than that of his Curate) out of a starving condition'. The line between simony and accepted practice was a very fine one. The vicar of Irthington was 'the wretched and beggarly father of ten poor children', and had been unable to prevent the vicarage house falling into 'scandalous ruins', and an incumbent at Dearham was also unlikely to be able to improve his 'very mean and cottage like parsonage' because of a growing number of children.

On the other hand, eight parsonage houses were described as 'new'. Two were being provided by the dean and chapter of Carlisle, the others by incumbents. At Kirkby Stephen the vicarage house had been put into as decent a state as it could be brought 'without being wholly pulled down and rebuilt' by the vicar's father (who was rich) and wished to settle his eldest son 'in such a dwelling as might incline him to love residence and keeping at home'. When Nicolson used the term 'rebuilt', it usually meant substantial renovation. Twelve parsonages came into this category. He also recorded nine other incumbents carrying out repair work. The parsonage at Sowerby had been enlarged by inserting thick, oaken planks above the hall, but the room above was 'so low as to be useless' and he could not help observing that despite improvements, the vicarage at Brough was still 'low, moist and smoaky'. He used the word 'modish' to describe modernisation. The incumbent of Plumland, for example, was putting the parsonage house 'into a more modish frame, in his apartments, windows, stair-cases etc'. Most of the houses he saw were probably thatched, but towards the end of the eighteenth century, John Waugh, chancellor of the diocese, commented that 'in the best circles' tiles were replacing thatch. Even the new houses of Nicolson's time would be old-fashioned fifty or an hundred years later and there would always be some houses reaching the end of a period of usefulness.

During the eighteenth century the problem of pluralism, and so inevitably the clergyman's absence from at least one of his parishes, increased markedly. Pluralism was permitted in certain circumstances by sixteenth-century acts of parliament and by the 1604 church canons but by the eighteenth century there had been much legal interpretation.[12] A living valued at under £8 in the *King's Book*, that is in 1535, could be held in plurality with another provided the two were not more than thirty miles apart. Bishops could give a dispensation from these requirements if a clergyman were an MA or of higher educational qualification, and did so frequently; an increase in the number of university graduates therefore facilitated an increase in pluralism. Certain privileged groups like peers were permitted to hold more than one living and most collegiate church and cathedral appointments could be held together with a parochial living. Pluralists were supposed to live in their parishes for 'some reasonable time in every year' and to appoint substitute preachers or curates. The rules had the effect of restricting poor clergy more than the well-to-do and, if the living was a good one, there was a stronger likelihood of an absentee incumbent because he probably had influential friends. The efforts of Queen Anne's Bounty to improve the incomes of small livings added to the problem: it was generally accepted that 'discharged' livings, exempt from the payment of First Fruits and Tenths, and new benefices instituted by Queen Anne's Bounty could be held in plurality.

In Hereford diocese, twice as many clergy were absentees in 1760 as in 1680; in Oxford diocese in the same period non-residence had more than doubled, and in Sussex rather more than doubled. To some extent it was a southern problem reflecting the more numerous small parishes which were combined. A fifth of parishes in Norwich diocese had resident incumbents in 1784, two fifths of parishes in Derbyshire in 1772, in Oxford in 1778, and in Wiltshire in 1783, but three-fifths in Devon in 1779 and four fifths in Chester diocese in 1778. Residence in the parish but not in the parsonage house was technically non-residence, but made only a small contribution to the situation.

Archdeacon Plymley's notebooks on his visitations of the southern part of Shropshire, in Hereford diocese, provide numerous illustrations of non-residence at the end of the eighteenth century and of the neglect resulting from it. Joseph Plymley was a landowner, a gentleman and a magistrate, as well as archdeacon of Shropshire, and wrote the *General Survey of the Agriculture of Shropshire* for the Board of Agriculture, published in 1803. In the preface he apologised for his authorship; 'I should be very sorry to see persons, whose time is more particularly dedicated to the service of Religion, engage in the pursuits of ordinary farmers'. But he excused himself on the grounds of his interest in moral improvement, natural history and the duty of a 'Country

Clergyman' to care for glebeland, 'but this should not involve him in the business of buying and selling, or in attendance on fairs or markets'. Plymley's archdeaconry reached to the Welsh border, to the suburbs of Shrewsbury and to the edge of Bridgnorth; the Severn formed much of the eastern boundary. It is generally a hilly countryside, containing Wenlock Edge, Clee hills, Long Mynd and Stiperstones, divided by valleys like Corvedale; Plymley wrote a propos Clee St Margaret that the roads were 'almost impassable for Horses even in the summer thro' parts of this and the neighbouring parishes'. It was and remains a very rural area, with no large towns; Ludlow, on the southern edge of Shropshire, was the most significant, and had a population of 3565 in 1798. Much Wenlock on the north-eastern edge of the archdeaconry was not prosperous: 'the town is poorly built and many of the Houses sadly in decay; as many tumble down as are built up, and the Inhabitants have not increased within memory'. But new industrial development was evident in the population figures of Madeley, Broseley and Bewdley (in Worcestershire), all with more than three thousand inhabitants.

In the deanery of Ludlow there were nineteen parishes and five chapelries in 1793, when Plymley's visits began; five were very small, with less than twenty families. Six of the nineteen parishes had no parsonage house, in five it was out of repair or 'unfit', and in seven, just less than a third, the houses in the archdeacon's view were suitable for the clergyman's occupation. At least thirteen incumbents and two curates were university graduates, which was superficially a big contrast with the sixteenth century situation - but only two lived in their parishes. Ludlow was far from typical. The rector, an MA, lived at the north end of College Street in an 'old and infirm building' near the church; his income was made up largely of Easter dues, worth £100, but 'nearer double to a popular man'. Three other clergymen in the parish were all MAs: a Reader, who read six o'clock prayers, a Lecturer and a curate who was also a schoolmaster. The Reader was paid by the Corporation and the timber-framed Reader's House on the east side of the churchyard shows the importance of that position. Despite four clergymen, the archdeacon observed that there were no more than seventy communicants, two thirds of whom were women. The rector of Richards Castle was the only other beneficed clergyman living in his parish, and he was also vicar of Caynham four miles away; the parsonage house there was occupied by the previous vicar's son, who rented the glebe. The curate, an Oxford BA and the present vicar's nephew, lived with his uncle in Richards Castle. The efforts of Queen Anne's Bounty to raise the stipends of chapelries had done nothing to increase the number of clergymen in the Shropshire countryside; furthermore, over half of the curates taking the place of absentee incumbents were not resident in their parishes, either.

The effect of non-residence was wryly observed at Onybury, where a farmer occupied the parsonage house: it was 'sufficient' and 'cheerfully situated in the village and near the turnpike road', but 'parlours without fires and bed chambers full of Grain take off from the dryness and comfort of a house very much'. Stanton Lacy's house, described as 'poor', was also occupied by the farmer of the glebeland. There had been no resident vicar for forty years; the

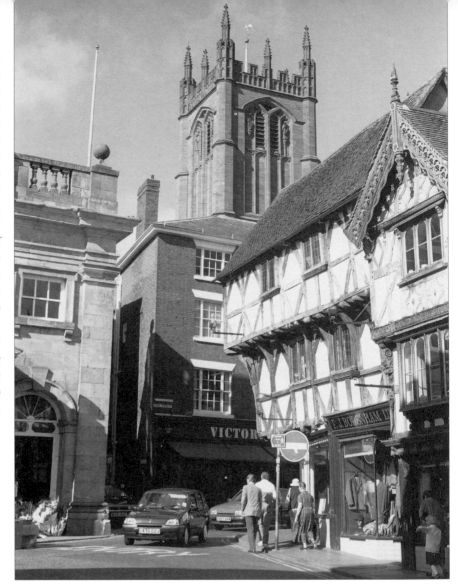

Ludlow, Shropshire - a view of the town and the tower of St Laurence's church which would have been familiar to eighteenth-century parsons who chose to live here rather than in their rural parishes. The market in front of the castle prospered because it was the centre of administration for the Marches. The church tower was built between 1467 and 1471 by the town's seven guilds. Ludlow has remained a centre for the surrounding rural area and a desirable place to live.

present one lived at Wycombe in Hampshire, and was also absent from his third living in the Peak District of Derbyshire. Wistanstow was one of the best livings in the deanery. The incumbent was in Kenilworth in Warwickshire. His predecessor had lived in the parsonage house, had filled in the moat and added two parlours and bedrooms, but the new work was 'now absolutely in want of repairs as well as the old'. The curate, who had lost a leg in an accident, lived at Church Stretton. Nonetheless the congregation was quite good and by 1804 the church had been refitted. Bitterley, about four miles north-east of Ludlow, on the western slopes of Clee Hill, had a population of over 1000. Mr Telford had reported that the church was 'extremely dangerous'. When Plymley visited it, no clergyman had been resident for sixteen years. This rectory was worth £500 a year, and had recently been sold for £3000 to the Revd James Hastings, who was both patron and incumbent. He had spent £2000 on the parsonage house, and told the archdeacon that he intended to reside. Subsequently he bought a living in Worcestershire and sold Bitterley, reputedly for £6000, a good example of advowsons being treated simply as property.

Parish clergy in the neighbourhood of Ludlow chose to live in the town rather than in their parsonage houses, like the curate of Bromfield, who was the vicar's nephew. His house, lived in by a labourer, 'suffers much from damp and want of residence'; subsequently, Plymley noted with satisfaction that the curate was married and living in the house which he had made very comfortable. When Plymley took the service in the church on 20 January 1793, eleven of the congregation of fifty-one in the morning came from Lord Clive's house and in the evening six of the seventeen were from Oakley Park. The vicar of Diddlebury in Corvedale also lived in Ludlow although he had a 'very sufficient' parsonage house two miles from his church, built by a benefactor about a hundred years before near the ruined chapel in Corfton. Similarly the rector of Culmington had become patron of his own living and had much improved the parsonage house at Seifton in the parish, 'but I fear the rector means chiefly to reside at Ludlow and keep this for the purpose of his accommodation on Sunday'. The tendency of rural parish clergymen to congregate in market towns was 'very common'. Bishop Bagot of Norwich said in 1784 'Of late years a practice hath been growing in many parts of the Kingdom (and no where doth it prevail more than in this Diocese) of a very hurtful tendency. I mean the resort of the clergy to the most considerable neighbouring Town'. Bishop Kaye of Lincoln echoed this forty years later, referring to the 'nest of rooks' at Louth; no less than nine incumbents and eleven curates of churches in the vicinity lived there in 1832.[13]

Non-residence was the major scandal of the late Georgian church, a serious abuse of the landed income of the church, even if a curate was maintained in the parish. It stimulated the reform movement of the early nineteenth century; residence in the official parsonage house could not be required until a big building programme had provided an acceptable house in a large majority of parishes.

A GREAT REBUILDING

The onus of providing a good parsonage house was fairly and squarely on the incumbent. In 1777 Gilbert's Act allowed clergy to borrow money on mortgage for parsonage house improvements up to the amount of two years income from their living, and Queen Anne's Bounty to lend money at low rates of interest.[14] A Norwich register detailed twenty-four mortgages taken out between 1779 and 1807; by 1826 the Bounty Board had made more than five hundred loans amounting to £250,000. In 1803, two acts made it possible for the Bounty to give grants and to match benefactions for the purchase of houses, and this became quite common. In 1815 an act allowed clergymen to arrange exchanges of property.

An important stimulus to parsonage house building was another act of 1803, requiring bishops to make a yearly return of non-resident clergy, which was presented to parliament. The first returns showed that something like half of all parishes in the country did not enjoy the ideal situation of a resident parson serving the church in person. As non-residence was an ambiguous term, the numbers returned varied substantially from year to year; by 1810 non-residents doing duty were distinguished from non-residents not doing duty. The 1803 act also gave bishops some more control because they had to issue a licence to permit non-residence where it was not legally permitted. An analysis of 255 licences issued between 1804 and 1827 in the archdeaconry of Derbyshire in Coventry and Lichfield diocese, shows that the lack or unfitness of the parsonage house was stated as the reason in a good majority of cases. Leaving aside those who served their churches although not living in the parsonage house, illness was the most common reason for absence. Rather over half of Derbyshire incumbents were absentees about this time.

The 1803 Residence Act and the bishops' enquiries which followed put pressure on non-resident clergy. In 1809, for example, the archbishop started to urge Sidney Smith to move from London to Foston-le-Clay in Yorkshire, where no parson had been resident throughout the eighteenth century. There were only 220 inhabitants in the parish but it was a good living, worth perhaps £1000; the parsonage house was occupied by the farmer of the extensive glebe and was not at all suited to entertaining Lady Holland or other aristocrats who visited Smith occasionally. He moved to Heslington, twelve miles away, travelling on Sundays to his parish church by phaeton. In 1812 he agreed to build a new parsonage house and borrowed £1600 from Queen Anne's Bounty, though his spacious new house, which he called 'snug', cost more than £4000.[15]

An *Abstract of benefices in which there is no Clerical Residence on account of the want or unfitness of the Parsonage House* was presented to parliament in 1817. In the clergy's own estimation, over 2000 houses were unfit for their residence, and 2600 parishes had no house at all, together totalling about two fifths of the parishes in the country. Some earlier parsons would have been surprised to find that their houses were considered unfit for their nineteenth century successors. The following year the first Church Building Act was passed; though the Commissioners could accept a house or a site up to ten acres for one, the

Kirkoswald, Cumbria - a vicarage house was built in 1867 and sold in 1984. The suppression of the college in this small market town left a poorly-paid vicar with no house. In 1725 parishioners and a benefactor endowed the vicarage with £400, matched by an equal amount from Queen Anne's Bounty; as a result the vicar's stipend was £95 in 1835, but he still had no house.

provision of houses lagged behind the surge of new church building and parish division from this time. As a result there were 250 more livings without parsonage houses in 1835 than there had been in 1818, but the number of unfit houses had fallen.[16] Carlisle and Chester diocese still had the lowest rates of non-residence, at around a quarter.

The problem of pluralism was enmeshed with every aspect of parochial organisation and parliamentary authority was needed to end it. In 1838 the Pluralities Act was drafted by the new Ecclesiastical Commission. It permitted no more than two livings to be combined except in a few exceptional circumstances (434 men had three or more), provided the population of either parish did not exceed 3000 nor the joint income exceed £1000, and the distance between the two livings was not more than ten miles, later reduced to three. The bishops' power to grant licences was severely limited. Following the act, non-residence fell sharply in the 1840s, and steadily thereafter. In Oxfordshire, the proportion of non-residents fell from forty-seven per cent in 1834 to twenty per cent in 1866.[17] No one was compulsorily displaced, but many felt a moral obligation to resign a living, and as clergy died or moved, the restrictions came into force. A Parsonages Act also passed in 1838 gave bishops the authority to demand that a house be built or an existing one repaired if a living were worth more than £100 a year; this bore hardly on men without private means and from this time dilapidations became a pressing problem. Incumbents could borrow four times the net value of the benefice, or sell a parsonage house with the bishop's and archbishop's approval.

Surviving Victorian parsonage houses are evidence of the intense activity which followed the passing of the Pluralities Act. 'Glebe houses are rising in every direction', one clerical commentator said in 1853. Fifty-six wholly new and eighteen very substantially enlarged nineteenth-century parsonage houses in Oxfordshire are mentioned in the county volume of the *Buildings of England*; sixty were built after the Act. Building work and repairs had been carried out in 112 parishes out of 178 by 1855. During the twenty-six years that Kaye was bishop of Lincoln, from 1827 to 1853, 214 parsonage houses were built, rebuilt or made fit, and the proportion lived in by their incumbents rose from sixty to eighty per cent; the one quarter of parishes without houses remained almost unchanged.[18]

A statement to parliament in 1847 showed that over £1 million had been lent by the Board of Queen Anne's Bounty, and details were given of some fifteen hundred loans, an average of £666 per parsonage house. Typically, the perpetual curate of the chapelry of Mungrisdale in Greystoke parish, Cumbria, had borrowed the very modest sum of £117, which was all his stipend would justify, to improve a modest house, but the rector of the good living of Kirkby Thore, the only one in Carlisle diocese valued at over £1000, had borrowed £1435.[19] The majority of loans were made after 1838; for example in Norfolk, of ninety-nine loans, four fifths were made after 1838. They were more often taken by southern than northern parsons. The Kent returns show that institutional rather than private patrons most often took advantage of the loans: the archbishop of Canterbury, the bishop of Rochester, the two deans and

Monk Soham, Suffolk - a rectory house designed by S.S.Teulon, and buil t with a loan in 1846 of £1000 from Queen Anne's Bounty. Both Monk Soham and Earls Soham churches, which are about two miles apart, had the same incumbent in 1835, who was also the patron of the livings; together they were worth over £1000 , which contravened the Pluralities Act .

Steeple Barton, Oxfordshire - the vicarage house was designed in 1855 also by S.S.Teulon. The vicarage was poor, £86 in 1835, and vicars tended not to live in the parish. After the house was sold in 1963, W.G.Hoskins lived here and wrote The making of the English landscape; *looking out of the window, he reflected on more than a thousand years of the parish's history*

chapters and other ecclesiastics together with Oxford and Cambridge colleges were patrons in three quarters of the cases.

Rather surprisingly, three quarters of the mortgages seem to have been for houses classed as fit in the Ecclesiastical Returns of 1835. Good houses were being improved rather than the church facing up to the need to modernise the parochial structure and use resources where population was increasing, although the Ecclesiastical Commissioners responded to the creation of 3760 new parishes or 'ecclesiastical districts' during the nineteenth century by special allocations for parsonage houses between 1866 and 1882 totalling £1.7 million.[20]

Loans by Queen Anne's Bounty for parsonage houses 1839-1847

County	Returned in 1835 as:				Total of loans post-1838	Total of loans in 1847 return
	Fit	Unfit	None	N/K		
Cumbria *	7				7	10
Derbyshire	7				7	10
Kent	21	9	3		33	72
Oxfordshire	7	4			11	17
Somerset	18	1	2		21	33
Warwickshire	2	3	1	3	9	19
Totals	62	17	6	3	88	161

* Cumberland and Westmorland

A small group of East Kent parishes provides a typical illustration. Elmstone, Stourmouth and Preston, near Wingham, together had less than 1000 inhabitants. Hasted, writing in the late eighteenth century, described Elmstone and Stourmouth as lonely, retired, unfrequented places, a description which is still appropriate at the end of the twentieth century.[21] In 1835 the dean and chapter of Canterbury was the patron of Preston, the bishop of Rochester of Stourmouth, and Elmstone had a private patron; all three were served by curates not by resident parsons. The two ecclesiastical patrons could have combined their parishes, especially as the vicar of Preston had been given a good house in 1711. Instead, Queen Anne's Bounty lent £656 to the incumbent of Elmstone to improve a fit house, and £1660 to the incumbent of Stourmouth, where the house was classed as unfit. By the end of the century, Elmstone and Preston were combined but Stourmouth survived as a separate parish until the Second World War; all three are now combined under the vicar of Wingham.

The Dilapidations Act in 1871 was another important milestone in the supervision of parsons. It removed the initiative from incumbents, requiring archdeacons to inspect all benefice buildings each time there was a vacancy; the estimated cost of repairs or dilapidations was then paid to Queen Anne's Bounty Board, who superintended necessary work. Five years later a select committee investigated how this act was working.[22] The secretary and treasurer to the Bounty said that there were 13,426 parochial benefices and he estimated there were 11,500 parsonage houses but thought that no return would give the number precisely. Before the act, archdeacons had virtually given up inspecting houses; since the act, 2500 cases of dilapidations had already been dealt with, though a proportion involved fairly small sums of money. He pointed out a major problem: that a poor living provided no security for loans, so that it could be difficult for an incumbent who moved into a dilapidated house and could not recover anything from his predecessor.

The select committee was given much personal testimony of the difficulties experienced. Most incumbents did not retire and their widows could be left with a bill for repairs judged necessary by an incoming incumbent. Typical stories of bureaucratic intervention were told, the truth of which can hardly be checked, like the parson who rebuilt his pigstye but was forced to reinstate the old one when he left. There were cases of dilapidation charges for repairing fences and hedges round the small plots of land purchased with Queen Anne's Bounty money to augment the income of the living. The rector of Saintbury in Gloucestershire was trenchant: 'I see that there are many surveyors present, and no wonder, as the Act is to them, judging from the fees charged, as good as a small bishopric, and very much better than a small deanery'. He thought the surveyors appointed by the bishop tyrannical and despotic. A solicitor from Newport in Shropshire referred to Childs Ercall - 'the house and grounds are such as a man of £2000 or £3000 would live in, and the income of the living is between £70 and £80 a year'. Nonetheless the incumbent was responsible for the dilapidations on this very large house. A London solicitor described the position of his deceased brother's house at Cassington in Oxfordshire: it was a 'very small' eight-roomed house surrounded by a farmyard and farm buildings and it had not been the custom for the incumbent to live in it as 'It was unfit indeed for any gentleman to live in'. Yet there was a bill for dilapidations.

Incumbents were probably the main benefactors to their livings, but throughout the nineteenth century, there were some private benefactors as at Kirkby Malham in 1866, where the former manor house next to the church was given for a vicarage, and parishioners occasionally subscribed for the purchase of a parsonage house as at Tewkesbury in 1886, where the abbot's house was bought. Diocesan Societies also raised money to build houses as well as churches. The first such society was in Exeter in 1841, under the auspices of the recently instituted Cambridge Camden Society, which was to influence much ecclesiastical architecture by advocating a religious or 'gothic' style of building. Oxford's society was founded in 1847. Cumbria's was not founded until 1862. As a result of its efforts and those of the energetic bishop Goodwin of Carlisle, between 1860 and 1890, 157 parsonage houses in the diocese were built, rebuilt or improved. Goodwin realised that the clergy were over-extending their standards of living;

> I confess that if I have any anxious feeling concerning parsonages, it is rather with respect to their excellence and their beauty, and the expense of living in them implied by these qualities, than to the cases in which they are wanting. Much as one delights in the thought of the clergy being housed in a manner befitting their habits and their recognised social position, I cannot but feel that in some cases a large house, built in an ornamental style, may become a heavy burden upon a slender income. I would wish that in not a few instances the purse of the incumbent, rather than the glory of the architect, had been manifestly the first consideration.[23]

By the time he wrote this, towards the end of the nineteenth century, the great parsonage house rebuilding was over. Within thirty years the problem of the overlarge parsonage house would begin to dominate discussion.

The nineteenth century rebuilding of parsonage houses was a declaration of the nature of the parsonage - it was both a professional situation and represented authority; the preamble to Gilbert's Act in 1777 had said 'many of the parochial clergy, for want of proper habitations, are induced to reside at a distance from their benefices, by which means the parishioners lose the advantage of their instruction and hospitality'. Increasing episcopal and parliamentary supervision during the nineteenth century provided more information and efficiency but less flexibility or independence for the parochial clergy. It led eventually to the late twentieth-century standardisation of the Green Guide on parsonage houses, and another great rebuilding on a quite different scale.

THE 'UNSUITABLE' PARSONAGE HOUSE

A sharp change in attitude to large houses is evident from the end of the First World War. In 1923 Diocesan Dilapidations Boards were set up to assess necessary repairs and Queen Anne's Bounty was made responsible for all dilapidations business, while financial responsibility remained with the parson.[24] It was estimated that £1.75 million was needed to put parsonages into a good state of repair and the Ecclesiastical Commissioners made an immediate

Piddletrenthide, Dorset - the former vicarage house was built with substantial assistance from Queen Anne's Bounty in 1844. It was a moderate living, £217 in 1835. The patron was the Dean and Chapter of Winchester. The house was considered 'fit' for a clergyman's residence but was occupied by the curate.

The Vicar moved from the old vicarage in 1992. The new Vicarage is now the centre for a group of livings in the Piddle valley.

grant to the Bounty Board of £500,000. Thereafter, Church Assembly spent much time discussing 'the unsuitable house issue'. The problem was the expense of modernising and maintaining very large houses for parsons without commensurately large incomes; in 1925, at least a fifth of parsonage houses were considered 'oversize' and impractical. By 1930, nearly 600 had been sold. A joint committee of the Governors of Queen Anne's Bounty and the Ecclesiastical Commissioners considered and reported in 1934 on 'Over-large Parsonage Houses'. The number was said to be 'very great', and sales of many were considered difficult if not impossible. General economic depression meant that there were few purchasers, and prices were low. Nonetheless, 700 more houses were sold before 1939. Some 600 replacement parsonages were built, and 500 purchased; these houses had approximately 2500 square feet or more of floor space, large houses by post-Second World War standards, so that there was again a problem of unsuitable, if less grandiose, parsonage houses.

The Second World War compounded the problems; 1000 or more houses had been seriously damaged, 250 beyond repair and some had been requisitioned and had to be returned to civilian use. The policy of selling and replacing was by then well-entrenched. At first, size was limited by post-war building controls and shortage of materials, but gradually these difficulties eased. The oversight of parsonage house passed to the Church Commissioners in 1948, when they were merged with Queen Anne's Bounty. In 1953 the Church Commissioners issued a Parsonage Design Guide or 'Green Guide' which had great influence, because the Commissioners had to agree any proposals for sale or purchase of a house. A survey in 1959 categorised 3769 parsonage houses out of 10,796 as unsuitable, and 2627 more were sold between 1948 and 1963. Still the problem did not go away, while redundant houses became more frequent. In 1972 Dilapidations Boards were less offensively named Parsonages Boards, and all responsibility for maintenance was transferred to them. The standards for new houses in the Green Guide have several times been redefined; the sixth edition in 1998 proposed that about 2000 square feet should be aimed at.

Between 1948 and 1994 about 8000 parsonage houses have been sold, a very large proportion of the housing stock which had been inherited in 1900 and many of the twentieth-century replacements, too. Replacement houses are purchased more often than purpose-built. In the diocese of Canterbury, ninety-nine houses were sold between 1974 and 1991, and sixty-six houses acquired; in 1994, there were 266 parishes but 153 benefices, so effectively half the incumbents were rehoused in those eighteen years. *Country Life* carried a feature on 'Ecclesiastical Houses for sale' on 22 September 1994. It suggested that old parsonages 'dominate the market for good-sized family houses', and a collection of advertisements in the magazine between 1984 and 1994 had 836 examples.[25] The commentator, Andrew Yates, said that 'Old Rectory' was among the twenty most popular house names. Such popularity became embarrassing; some dioceses started to prohibit purchasers using 'church' names and the houses' historic role is disguised by other names such as 'Manor'. A position next to the church may be the only practical historical clue.

Canon Higgins, in The Vicar's House, described this as ' a misguided decision. Not only will such houses have passed out of parish use, but posterity will no longer even be able to identify them. Such a move seems a determined attempt to stamp on history'.

Intractable problems in modernising their parsonage houses have been faced by urban dioceses like Manchester, which did not have such a valuable inheritance of gentlemen's country houses as rural dioceses. The huge effort to provide parsonage houses in the previous century had also been made with little help from ancient endowments, because of the pattern of relatively few but large parishes and numerous poorly-endowed chapelries: parishes of this type in Manchester diocese include Manchester itself, Bolton, Bury, Eccles, Middleton, and Rochdale. As central areas have gradually become wholly commercial, population has flowed outwards or been moved, but provision of

Claybrooke, Leicestershire - the former vicarage house was added to several times and there is a date '1871' on one part. In 1835 the income was over £500 a year. Manor house, church and vicarage are at Claybrooke Parva, centrally sited in an irregularly-shaped parish.

The new Vicarage was built in 1996 at the side of the old one.

Oldham, Lancashire - the recent brick St James's Vicarage is a good example of an 'executive-style' parsonage house surrounded by earlier terraced rows; it is one of the new houses in an Urban Priority Area in Manchester diocese built in the last decade, with some assistance from the Church Commissioners.

new parsonages and churches is difficult because of limited resources. A special national Parsonages Renewal Fund between 1986 and 1990 recognised these difficulties, and helped to build fifty new houses in Manchester diocese, while ninety were either purchased or had major restoration or some improvement; but three quarters of the parsonage houses are still pre-1939 buildings, and there are at least forty houses which the Diocesan Parsonages Board would like to replace. This is a great contrast with the largely new stock in the countryside. In the rural area of Oxford diocese under the bishop of Dorchester, less than a quarter of the ninety-one parsonages houses are pre-1939 and three quarters are either purpose-built or purchased since that date. In Exeter and Norwich dioceses the proportion of pre-1939 houses is less than one fifth.[26]

It made sense to create a stock of modern houses out of ecclesiastical capital, to meet the two main needs: the reduction of maintenance and running costs, and the increase of modern amenitites. The capital realised from house sales is relatively insignificant; in 1986, surplus moneys in diocesan funds from parsonage sales amounted to £39 million, which does not go far to meet the more than £600 million costs of running the Church. There remain about 9000 houses in the Church's ownership and the capital realised if they were all sold would be considerable; but a large rise in stipends would then be necessary, and calculations suggest that this would not in the long run bring any economic advantage.[27] In effect new houses have been provided through the piety and generosity of people in the past. But this is now an urban not an agricultural society, and the donations of the last two hundred years have not kept up with the rise in the population of England from 8.4 million in 1801 to 48 million in 1991.

The parson was the initiator of the sale of a parsonage house in the nineteenth century; he had a lifetime tenancy or 'freehold' in his house, and since 1838 had been permitted to sell it with the consent of the bishop and archbishop and the patron. A hundred years later, an important Measure gave bishops the right to sell a house when there was a vacancy, and this power has been used a great deal, though the bishop usually acts at the prompting of the Diocesan Parsonages Board. Incumbent, bishop, Church Commissioners and Parsonages Board still have to agree to a sale; patrons and the Parochial Church Council are 'statutory interested parties', which means that they may give their opinions. The PCC has 'almost no legal powers of any kind in the house'; the patron, whose predecessors, or even ancestors, may have provided it, cannot veto a sale, though until 1986, when this option was removed, a patron was able to buy the house at valuation before it was advertised. The erosion of private patronage, and of the parson's freehold through the practice of appointing priests-in-charge and team vicars, have made it less likely that either a parson or a patron will endow his parish with a new house. But bequests are still made for the benefit of a particular parish. One such was conditional on the vicar remaining in the Victorian parsonage opposite the church; consequently the house, at Morland in Cumbria, was reduced from a three-storey one to an attractive chalet bungalow.

It now appears that the rush to sell parsonage houses after 1945 was not always well-judged. The new stock of houses is not generally so valuable, and includes some which were poorly built and planned. There are many arguments put forward in support of older parsonage houses. They may have been pretentious, but their spaciousness gave opportunity; the obligation to be hospitable enjoined by the medieval church, and the needs of administration, press hard on the modern parson's house. The older house may be less obtrusive than the solitary 'executive-style' house, which can create an unfortunate image in an urban priority area, as John Tiller observed in his report in 1983, *A strategy for the Church's ministry*. Occasionally a traditional, larger old parsonage may be more acceptable. Experiments with dividing and subletting parts of a large parsonage house seem to require great determination by the parson against the general weight of policy and practice, and the whole legal framework within which the Church Commissioners and the dioceses work appears inflexible and hard to change.

Late twentieth-century parsonage houses are not exuberant. There seem to have been few unusual or adventurous designs, and some houses built by the church simply echo the style and materials of the old parsonage house. Houses which could have been used in new ways have been sold, while dark and little-used churches, perhaps smelling of decay and unattractive to a large proportion of the population, have been retained, sometimes through the pressure of special interest groups and heritage authorities. Parsonage house policy underlines the centralising and standardising tendency in the Church of England in the twentieth century. Will the new houses meet the needs of the twenty-first century? Or can the provision of a traditional benefice house be continued at all?

CHAPTER NINE

FIT FOR A GENTLEMAN

St Mary's church was the first meeting place of the congregation of teachers at Oxford, and behind it there is a collection of university buildings described by Pevsner as 'unique in the world', some late medieval like the Divinity School and the first part of the Bodleian Library, and others seventeenth and early eighteenth century, like the Sheldonian Theatre, the Clarendon Building which housed the University Press, and the Bodleian extension in the Radcliffe Camera. But before the university existed, St Mary's was a parish church and was one of three churches in the city of Oxford named specifically in Domesday Book. Next to St Mary's is All Souls college, founded in 1438 by the archbishop of Canterbury supported by Henry VI; 'Front Quad' on High Street dates from this time. The college paid Oriel, endowed with the rectory of St Mary's, £200 to be freed from offerings to the church.

LEFT: Oxford, St Mary's church and All Souls college

Until the nineteenth century, teaching was largely a clerical concern.[1] The medieval colleges of Oxford and Cambridge were founded to give opportunities for clergymen to study, and bishops and archbishops were prominent amongst their founders, although not all students went into the church. The colleges were staffed almost entirely by clergymen; being in orders was a condition for appointment to most fellowships and after the Reformation the requirement of celibacy was not removed as it was for other clergy. It was entirely appropriate for colleges to own advowsons of parish livings, to which fellows were presented and which later provided opportunities for those wishing to marry.

After Elizabeth I's accession, religious tests excluded those who could not accept the tenets of the new Protestantism formulated in the Thirty Nine Articles. The intention was to exclude Roman Catholics but after the religious upheavals of the Civil War period in mid-seventeenth century, they also excluded Protestant Dissenters. Dissenting academies attempted to fill this gap. Student numbers had fallen sharply as a result of the Reformation; monasteries had often maintained halls of residence for their members and nearly all these, and some colleges, were closed by their dissolution. Once Protestantism was

firmly established, the universities more than recovered their popularity. By the early seventeenth century Oxford's student population had doubled or even trebled, and Cambridge's similarly; there was no great increase in student numbers thereafter until the early nineteenth century. New college buildings accommodated the commoners pressing for admission because this was almost the only means of gaining university teaching; colleges were founded or refounded. The first Protestant college at Oxford, Jesus, given a charter in 1571, had the needs of Welsh parishes particularly in mind.

Grammar schools provided the necessary preliminary education, and also enabled many to enter the church without going to a university. William Harrison's impression in 1577 recorded in the *Description of England* was that

> There are a great number of grammar schools throughout the realm, and those very liberally endowed, for the better relief of poor scholars, so that there are not many corporate towns now under the Queen's dominion that have not one grammar school at the least, with a sufficient living for a master and usher appointed to the same.

Grammar schools taught Latin grammar; Latin remained the essential tool for university study and the international language of the Christian church, although the first translation of the Bible into the vernacular English language had been introduced into English churches in 1539 and the first English Prayer Book in 1549. The grammar schools were often closely tied with particular Oxford and Cambridge colleges. For example, Edmund Grindal, Archbishop of Canterbury, who was probably born in St Bees in Cumbria and referred to the area as 'my lawless country', obtained a royal charter for the Free Grammar School there in 1587, and provided scholarships to Pembroke and Magdelene colleges, Cambridge and Queen's college, Oxford. Local attachments continued strongly until the later nineteenth century; Jesus college, Oxford, had a big majority of its students from Wales, at Exeter well over half the students came from Devon and Cornwall, and other colleges had similar if less predominant regional ties. Scholars often did go back to their native counties, as seen in the 2420 graduates of Oxford and Cambridge 'harassed' or ejected from their livings between 1640 and 1660, of whom two thirds were serving in the counties from which they had entered university.[2]

The close connection between the two universities of Oxford and Cambridge and the church was broken in the later nineteenth century and an Oxford or Cambridge degree ceased to be chiefly a preparation for the ministry. An act in 1854 removed religious tests for undergraduates and for the BA degree, and in 1871 tests were abolished for higher degrees and for fellowships. After 1877 most fellows were not required to be in Holy Orders, nor to be celibate. These changes have been described as expropriation of the church's property, repeating Henry VIII's more dramatic example, but the colleges as secular institutions have so far retained the endowments accumulated over many centuries; *The Times* reported on 5 May 1997 that the four richest Oxford colleges, St John's, Christ Church, New and Merton, together had capital assets totalling £336.8 million, £27 million more than the single richest Cambridge college which is Trinity.[3]

GENTLEMEN AND PLEBEIANS

Students registering at Oxford paid a fee related to the status of their fathers. 'Plebeian' indicated a man without social rank or title; the term derived from the Latin word for 'people' and an alternative was 'commoner'. 'Gentleman' was an indication, though rather imprecise, of a social rank higher than a

St Bees, Cumbria - Edmund Grindal's grammar school building on the left is dated 1587. A Puritan, he left property to found the school and provide scholarships to Oxford and Cambridge, so that students might return as clergymen, and it has made an important contribution to the church in Cumbria. He was probably born in St Bees and went to school in the priory.

commoner but lacking a formal title. William Harrison discussed what made a gentleman. He suggested an education at one of the universities or Inns of Court, the profession of medicine or one of the liberal sciences (worthy of a gentleman and not servile, mechanical or narrowly technical) and the ability to live without manual labour; but most important of all, a gentleman looked and behaved like a gentleman. In 1695 a similar definition was used by the act imposing a tax on the burial 'of every Gentleman or reputed Gentleman, or owning or writing himself such'. The distinction was of considerable significance until the nineeenth century: it marked 'the exact point at which the traditional social system divided up the population into two extremely unequal sections'; the very small upper section comprised the 'political nation' whose voice counted in the affairs of the country.[4]

The courtesy title of Master or 'Mr' was society's recognition of a gentleman. It was used very sparingly indeed in a list of Gloucestershire clergy in 1551 prepared for Bishop Hooper's visitation. Mr John Chamberlayne was vicar of Beckford and Ashton under Hill; he was a notably learned man, *insigniter doctus*, and was likely to have been related to the gentry family at Churchdown and at Maugersbury near Stow on the Wold. Mr Chamberlayne lived in his parish; the other gentlemen clerics did not because they held positions elsewhere: Mr Nicholas Wotton of Dursley was archdeacon of Gloucester; Mr Gilbert Bourne was a prebendary of Worcester, and he later became bishop of Bath and Wells; Mr Geoffrey Downes was a prebendary of both Hereford and of Southwell. The scatter of gentlemen clerics is probably a good indication of the very small number in any county serving the church at this period. A sermon published in 1607 lamented that the nobility and gentry would rather their sons became anything - 'wordy lawyers, fraudulent merchants, killing physicians' - as long as they did not take Holy Orders.[5] Harrison's opinion was that the attacks on the church had created a 'general contempt for the ministry'; Archbishop Whitgift thought that it was because 'the far greatest part of learned Ministers' could not have 'sufficient maintenance'.

Gentlemen were a very small proportion of society at large at this time and in the following century. In the late seventeeth century, one in every twenty in the population at most was a gentleman. When Parson Sampson recorded the inhabitants of his parish of Clayworth in 1676, he did it in alphabetical order, 'to avoid envy', and noted four gentlemen amongst ninety-nine households. The households in the parish of Kirkby Lonsdale in Cumbria in 1695 were divided into status groups: the first group in the market town itself was headed 'Clergy and Yeomen', a straightforward declaration of social standing; farmers, labourers and poor followed. In several of the ten small communities or townships in the parish there was a resident clerk or curate of a chapel, but altogether there were only two gentlemen. The vicar was plain John Brigges, though he was a Cambridge BA. At the other end of the country in the East Kent parish of Ash next Sandwich in 1705, Mr John Shocklidge, clerk, headed one of six gentry households out of about 250; the other gentlemen were an officer of excise, a doctor ('cururgion'), Mrs May, William Wylde Esq, and the Lady Wylde in whose household there was a chaplain of suitable gentility, Mr

Maddeson, noted with the six servants. Mr Maddeson was a non-juror, one of about 400 clergymen refusing to swear allegiance to William and Mary in 1689 after James II fled. Non-jurors were sheltered by Stuart sympathisers like Lady Wylde.[6]

Macaulay was probably close to the truth, in *The History of England* published in 1848, when he wrote that at the end of the seventeenth century 'The clergy were regarded as, on the whole, a plebeian class'. 'On the whole' should be emphasised. Macaulay divided the clergy into two sections, learned men in London, the universities and cathedral establishments, and the poor, 'not much more refined, than small farmers or upper servants'; indeed, 'for one who made the figure of a gentleman, ten were mere menial servants'. He wrote about a young chaplain in a wealthy household, perhaps like Mr Maddeson in Ash next Sandwich, who might not only say grace before meals,

> might not only be the most patient of butts and of listeners, might not only be always ready in fine weather for bowls, and in rainy weather for shovelboard, but might also save the expense of a gardener or of a groom ... He was permited to dine with the family; but he was expected to content himself with the plainest fare. He might fill himself with the corned beef and the carrots: but as soon as the tarts and the cheesecakes made their appearance, he quitted his seat, and stood aloof till he was summoned to return thanks for the repast, from a great part of which he had been excluded.

This echoes Jane Austen's picture of Mr Collins' useful service to Lady Catherine de Bourgh in *Pride and Prejudice*. The chaplain might escape to a poor benefice, Macaulay continued, and marriage with a serving maid:

> As children multiplied and grew, the household of the priest became more and more beggarly. Holes appeared more and more plainly in the thatch of his parsonage and in his single cassock ... His boys followed the plough; and his girls went out to service. Study he found impossible: for the advowson of his living would hardly have sold for a sum sufficient to purchase a good theological library; and he might be considered as unusually lucky if he had ten or twelve dog-eared volumes among the pots and pans on his shelves. Even a keen and strong intellect might be expected to rust in so unfavourable a situation.

Had Trollope read this before he drew his portait of Josiah Crawley? Macaulay's influence on opinion must have been enormous: 13,000 copies of the first two volumes of his *History* were sold in four months.

Macaulay implied that the clergy's status had risen since 1700, and the time when he was writing was a high point socially. Clergy and yeomen were no longer classed together; instead, nineteenth-century Kelly's Directories placed 'Gentlemen and Clergy' before longer lists of 'commercial' inhabitants. It was not simply that the word 'yeoman' had almost dropped out of use, and 'gentleman' become more general. The numbers of gentlemen's sons entering Oxford and then going into the church had reached a high point. In the later

Kingham, Oxfordshire - a rectory house described in The Buildings of England *as 'one of the finest small houses of this date in the county'. It was built in the garden of an earlier parsonage, by William Dowdeswell M.A., rector from 1680 to 1711; the date 1688 is over a fireplace. His father, also a rector, had bought the advowson in 1664 and the Dowdeswell connection lasted until the early twentieth century. The house was sold in 1974.*

sixteenth century, when Harrison was writing, just over half of Oxford students were the sons of plebeians; by 1810 registrations of plebeians had almost disappeared. A possibly generous estimate is that two fifths of 532 clergy in Worcester diocese between 1782 and 1808 were sons of peers or gentry; one-fifth of a similar number of Cambridge graduates in Norfolk, Sussex, and Kent in 1833 were gentlemen's sons. Still a small minority of clergy, gentlemen set the tone. The early nineteenth century was similarly a high point for the proportion of graduate clergy. Comprehensive figures collected by Sir R.F.S.Scott in *The Chronicle of Congress* for the decade 1834 to 1843, showed that eight in every ten ordinations were of Oxford and Cambridge graduates and one in ten were graduates of other universities.

Three factors particularly had contributed to the changed social status of the clergy. One was that clerical family dynasties started to be established with the Protestant church's permission to marry; before 1640 sons of clergymen entering Oxford had become a significant group. Of six sons born in mid-sixteenth century to a yeoman of Marnhull in Dorset, Kelway *alias* Clarke, five entered the church, and five in turn had sons who became clergymen. Nearly all were educated at Oxford. William Kelway became both patron and rector of Ashmore about 1588, and his son followed him in 1622. Nicholas became vicar of Fifehead Magdalen and John became rector of Nether Compton and both had sons who succeeded them in those livings. Roger, rector of Todbere, was followed by three more generations of clerics, the last dying in 1719. Sons of clergymen formed a sizeable group of incumbents, for example nearly a fifth of incumbents in Oxfordshire and a quarter in Hereford diocese in 1680 and in

1760, and a similar proportion of students at Oxford and Cambridge, of which about half entered the church.[7]

A second factor was the gentry's increased involvement because so many had bought the advowson of their local church after the dissolution of the monasteries, and this in turn was probably responsible for the third factor, the increasing number of university graduates entering the church. At that time only a fifth or a sixth of the clergy were graduates in the south, and even fewer in the west and north-west, the 'dark corners of the land' as described by Puritan reformers. Even in Oxford diocese, despite the influence of the university, no more than a third of clergy were graduates in 1560. In the East Riding of Yorkshire there were just nine graduates out of 148 men presented to livings between 1545 and 1560. In the southern half of Shropshire in Hereford diocese there were seven graduates in 1567 amongst ninety-four incumbents, and one was a student at Merton college, Oxford; parishes sometimes supported their minister through a long course of study to achieve a degree. Twenty-eight of these clergymen had witnessed all the alterations of religion since Henry VIII's reign and one had taken up his position while Henry VII was still alive. In the northern half of Shropshire, in Lichfield diocese, the position was still the same in 1603; there were eleven graduates amongst eighty-seven clergy and William Baxter was reflecting accurately on the situation in his youth in Shropshire in the 1620s when he said it 'had but little preaching at all'.[8]

In dioceses near Oxford and Cambridge a change was apparent by the early seventeenth century: two thirds of Oxfordshire clergy in 1620 were graduates and by 1640 nearly all were, and so were most of the more than 4000 men ordained in Norwich between 1637 and 1800, and in Devon between 1702 and 1745. In the eighteenth century the great majority of clergymen were

Mottram, Greater Manchester - the grammar school is on the edge of the churchyard, on the hill which may have given Mottram its name , with an extensive view of Glossop and Longdendale. A stone records the foundation in 1620. It was to teach pupils 'reading, writing and the Greek, Latin and English tongue'. It was still in use in the 1960s.

graduates, though there were still exceptions like Chester diocese where over the last fifty years of the eighteenth century less than half the clergy had degrees, and the south Wales diocese of St David's in the same period, where only six in every hundred men ordained were graduates.[9] But the general perception of a graduate profession added considerably to its status, and fuelled the nineteenth-century movement to provide higher education for all clergy.

THE GENTLEMAN HERESY

Trollope in *The Last Chronicle of Barset* created the compelling image for the gentleman heresy; Josiah Crawley, the poor perpetual curate of Hogglestock, was a man with a university education but without influential connections. He reported to his wife a conversation he had with the wealthy Dean of Barchester:

> "I would we stood on more equal grounds", I said. Then as he answered me, he rose from his chair. "We stand", said he, "on the only perfect level on which such men can meet each other. We are both gentlemen". "Sir", I said, rising also, "from the bottom of my heart I agree with you. I could not have spoken such words; but coming from you who are rich to me who am poor, they are honourable to the one and comfortable to the other."

Hurrell Froude characterised the idea that clergy were and must be gentlemen as the 'gentleman heresy'; he used the phrase about Bishop Coleridge, who had 'the gentleman heresy in an intense degree' and would not open the doors of Codrington College in Barbados, where Froude was teaching temporarily, to those without Latin and Greek. A bishop might well have a keen sense of gentility; between 1860 and 1960, most of the bishops came from ten leading public schools.[10] Froude died aged thirty-three in 1836 but he had been one of the key men in the Oxford Movement, attending the meeting at Hadleigh in Suffolk to discuss ways of publishing their new 'Catholic' thinking. He disputed that social and intellectual position gave superior insight into Christianity; 'the Church will eventually depend for its support, as it always did in its most influential time, on the very poorest classes of the country'. He observed acutely that 'The kind of evangelism necessary for an urban, industrialised society could not be encompassed by a Church which was based on privilege and class'. In practice, the gentleman heresy permeated nineteenth century attitudes, for example in attitudes to the foundation of theological colleges.[11]

George Henry Law, bishop of Chester and son of a bishop of Carlisle, founded the first theological college at St. Bees in 1816, 'for the better instruction of those candidates for Holy Orders who were unable to obtain a University education'; not until after the First World War was one year's training in a theological college required of graduates before they were ordained.[12] The bishop of St. David's founded the second theological college at Lampeter in 1822, and Durham was founded in 1831 with a main aim of defusing criticism of the cathedral's wealth. By 1877, there were diocesan colleges at Chichester, Lichfield, Salisbury, Gloucester, Lincoln and Truro. At St

Bees, as might have happened in the sixteenth century, college and vicarage were combined, and the choir of the ruined priory church was rebuilt as a lecture room and library. The college drew recruits from a wider social spectrum than the universities: a few were trying again after failing elsewhere, a larger number were mature students. St Bees made a useful local contribution; in 1868, six per cent of clergy in Carlisle diocese had been to theological college, just over half were university graduates and over a third had no stated qualifications. But only a small number of St Bees' students stayed more than a few years in the diocese; then they went south in search of better pay. Some had opposed the introduction of theological colleges for this reason. A principal of Lichfield college, founded in 1857, suggested how wrong it was to say to these men 'that the Church of England has no room in her ministry for other than graduate and gentlemen clergy - in other words, that she is dying (or is dead) of dignity'.

But the gentleman heresy was deeply entrenched. An article on 'The Church in the Mountains' in the *Edinburgh Review* in April 1853 talked of one thousand 'ill-educated peasants' who were clergymen, some in Cumbria, most in Wales. The writer was W.J.Conybeare, son of the dean of Llandaff but eventually patron and rector of the family living of Axminster in Devon. Bishop Wilberforce in his address to the Oxford Diocesan Society in 1866 said

I maintain this, that the ministry of the Church of England has been hitherto and is at this time, filled by gentlemen of the nation of England, by men who have had a gentle education, who have come often - yea, and in most numerous cases of gentle, and even of the highest blood of this land and who have entered the Church with all that distinctive formation of character which comes from such an education and such an inheritance.[13]

And Trollope was imbued with the same attitude. In his semi-fictional descriptions of the *Clergymen of the Church of England* (1866), which were informed by his experience of numerous villages and towns gained in his travels for the Post Office, he held the new theological colleges responsible for training a clergyman who was 'less urbane, less genial,- in a word, less of a gentleman'. The bishop of Winchester in 1887 reluctantly considered that once ordained a training college man had to be called a 'gentleman' and shortly after St Bees college closed in 1895, the writer of *Highways and Byways in the Lake District* commented that it would be remembered as a 'prolific nursery of north country parsons, and as the best known perhaps of all those gateways to the Anglican ministry, which are somewhat invidiously known as 'back doors'.

If almost true at the beginning of the nineteenth century, after mid-century the gentleman heresy was suffering erosion. The number of graduates seeking ordination had begun to decline, and this became obvious from about 1860. Non-graduate clergy were termed 'literate'. Three times as many 'literate' clergy were ordained in 1862 as had been twenty years earlier, and they were a third of the year's total, though Oxford and Cambridge still provided the majority. There were other factors also at work. The restrictions placed on pluralism may have deterred a few from a clerical career; after 1838 it was no longer possible to accumulate a big income by holding several livings together. Most important, while the number of students expanded rapidly after 1860 at Oxford and after 1870 at Cambridge, more graduates were finding careers outside the church. One reaction was seen in an Archbishop's Report in 1908 recommending that the theological colleges grant degrees; it envisaged an all-graduate clergy by 1917.

After the First World War, the decline in graduate clergy continued more steeply and between 1954 and 1962 less than one fifth of those accepted for ordination were Oxford and Cambridge graduates and more than two thirds were non-graduates. The clergy's numerical significance had also changed amongst professional men; at the end of the nineteenth century there had been roughly equal numbers in the three main professions: Church of England clergymen, judges, barristers and solicitors, and physicians and surgeons.[14] In the twentieth century numbers in other professions greatly increased, but Church of England clergymen's numbers diminished. Their status was inevitably affected, too, by the fall in the committed membership of the church, while a simultaneous change in relative incomes put the clergy very much behind practitioners of the other two traditional professions.

The clergy had never been a homogeneous class. It was probably unfortunate for the Church of England that in the nineteenth century, when an immense effort was made to modernise and to increase provision of parish clergymen, the gentleman heresy was widely and strongly held, particularly by the upper clergy; the result was that much work was directed to providing incomes and houses to attract gentlemen, as well as to building over-grandiose churches. As the *Guardian* wrote on 10 December 1856: 'Is it not extravagent to hamper ourselves with the idea of supplying all England with adequate spiritual ministrations through none but "resident gentlemen"?'

'RICHES MAKETH GENTLEMEN'

A writer on the County Palatine of Chester in 1656 noted simply 'Riches maketh Gentlemen in all countries of England' - countries for seventeenth century people being counties. In terms of income, a clergyman could not match a gentleman, but he was not poor in comparison with the humblest in society; statements about poverty were coloured by the superior position of a small number of upper clergy. In the sixteenth and seventeenth centuries most parish clergy were not strongly differentiated from the majority of their parishioners, but by the nineteenth century the gap had widened.

In 1535 acording to the *Valor* more than half of English and Welsh livings were below £10, while a craftsman or labourer in full employment might have received between £5 and £8. This supports the statement of Richard Hooker, the eminent theologian and apologist for the church of Elizabeth I, that 'ordinary pastors of the church' were comparable with 'a common artisan or tradesman of the City'.[15] Protestant reformers lamented the poverty of parish clergy; they considered that a parson needed a good education in order to teach the newly-reformed doctrines; but a man who had been to university would not be content with a parish priest's income. Archbishop Whitgift thought £30 needful for a preaching minister; William Harrison complained of being a poor man himself on £40 a year: his household made three hogshead of beer, 'as is meet for poor men as I am to live withal ... (for what great thing is forty pounds a year, *computatis computandis*, able to perform?)'.

A different impression is gained from inventories or lists of possessions made in connection with proving a will. Some inventories from Lincoln diocese for the last decade of the sixteenth century suggest that those parsons who made wills had larger, better-furnished houses than farmers or husbandmen, and were in this respect comparable with yeomen. Servants' chambers were frequently mentioned, and there was almost always a study; one or two parlours downstairs and bed chambers upstairs had replaced the all-purpose living room or hall, and there were several specialist rooms for food preparation: dairy, cheese house, buttery (for beer butts), bolting house (for flour) and kitchen. Their estates were also on average more valuable than the layman's, and they had more plate, and also more clothes. Most had agricultural equipment and produce in or around their houses but at Skendleby the parson kept his beans in the belfry. They had riding horses and they were unusual in having books. But most clergy did not reach the standard of affluence requiring a will to be made. There are 163 surviving wills or inventories for Oxfordshire clerics in the seventeenth century, excluding Oxford itself, with its population of canons and college fellows, an average of less than one per parish; numerous parsons or curates had come and gone leaving no record of their possessions.

Interesting pointers to the size of clerics' houses at the end of the seventeenth century can be found in the Hearth Tax. The tax of one shilling for each hearth or chimney was introduced in 1662 and collected for twenty-seven years, one of several money-raising ideas of post-Restoration governments. The

Great Snoring, Norfolk - the old rectory. The Shelton family was patron at least from 1358; one member of the family was rector in 1517 and again in 1539; the house was built about that time. The advowson was later given to St John's College, Cambridge. Seven hearths were taxed in 1666, and there are seven 'moulded, autumn-coloured brick' chimneys.

Sible Hedingham, Essex - Moses Cooke, 'the late worthy Rector here, built a very good Parsonage-house of brick; laid out a handsome garden; and in all respects greatly adorned and improved this Parish'. He was a Cambridge MA and rector from 1690 to 1733. His father, a gentleman of Little Hadham, presented him and then gave him the advowson; he built his house soon after.

richer the household, the more the number of rooms likely to have a fire. The precints of Canterbury cathedral, where a number of canons lived, are included in the surviving 1664 return for Kent. William Somner, auditor and chapter clerk, listed sixty houses there, together with the Glaziers' Office, the Plumbery and the Audit House, each with its one hearth. Not surprisingly Dr Thomas Turner, the Dean, headed the list with twenty-seven hearths, a large house in any context; just under half of the houses in the precincts had five or more hearths; two had fourteen; William Somner the chapter clerk had seven; Dr Casaubon had eleven, his name reminding one of George Eliot's vainly scholarly clergyman of that name in Middlemarch. The cathedral close was full of large houses. In contrast, the great majority of English citizens had one or two hearths, while at the bottom of the economic scale, numerous poor householders were exempt or excused from the tax, possibly a third or even more of the households in each parish or township.[16]

Occupations were not generally stated in the Hearth Tax lists, but some Norfolk constables noted 'clerk' as they did other descriptions of status like 'Lord' or 'Sir' or 'Mr'.[17] Leaving aside a few ancient parishes like Pudding Norton where the church was in ruins, or Pattesley where the church had disappeared at least a century before, and which were in practice amalgamated with other parishes, there were sixty parishes in the three deaneries of Brisley, Heacham and Toftrees; clerks were specifically recorded in thirty-three, and a 'Dr' in two more, probably at this date a Doctor of Divinity. It appears that the clergy occupied rather larger houses than most inhabitants. The average was two hearths per household, but the clerical average was four hearths, and nearly half the clerks had five hearths or more; the rectory at Gressenhall had eight. Above them were a few oustanding gentry: Horatio, Lord Townsend at East Raynham with 56 hearths and Sir Nicholas le Strange at Hunstanton with

37, and not far away, John Coke Esq. at Holkham with 34 and Sir John Hobart at Blickling with 58. Although parsons' houses were not comparable with those of the gentry, the Hearth Tax shows a good proportion of rectors and vicars well above the level of the cottager.

Gregory King's 'Table of the income and expense of the several families of England calculated for the year 1688' confirmed the relative position of the clergy in society. He was a pioneer in calculating average family size, income and expenditure for households categorised by 'Ranks, Degrees, Titles and Qualifications' and his calculations have been supported by later work. He divided the population into twenty-six classes, reaching from 160 lords at the top of the social pyramid to vagrants at the bottom. Two archbishops and twenty-four bishops were 'spiritual lords', as reflected in their seats in the House of Lords. Lower in Gregory King's list were 2000 'eminent' and 8000 'lesser' clergymen. Neither came anywhere near the gentleman's average income.

Gregory King's analysis of English Society in 1688

Social class	Number of families	Number in household	Average income
Temporal lords	160	40	£3200
Spiritual lords	26	20	£1300
Gentlemen	12,000	8	£280
Persons in the law	10,000	7	£154
Eminent clergymen	2000	6	£72
Lesser clergymen	8000	5	£50
Farmers	150,000	5	£42.10s.
Artizans and Handicrafts	60,000	4	£38
Labouring People	364,000	3 1/2	£15

Gregory King's unpublished notebook shows that by 'eminent clergymen', he had in mind archdeacons, deans and cathedral dignitaries, clergy who were gentlemen's sons, those having a living of £50 or £60 a year, and the 'Double Beneficed clergymen of £120 p.a.'.[18] The 'lesser clergymen' were the poorest of

Ripple, Worcestershire - the bishop of Worcester was the patron of the rectory, and in 1729 he gave permission to Dr John Holte to rebuild the parsonage house, to be 51 feet by 41. Dr Holte was the son of a baronet, studied at Oxford, and became rector in 1727. Ripple was worth over £1000 in 1835, but a curate did the duty of the church for £84 a year; the rector probably lived in Hereford where he held a cathedral prebend.

those who could be termed 'professional' but their average income was nearly four times the labouring man's. Gregory King's poverty line for a family of four was £20 a year; below this, heads of households had more expenses in caring for their families than they could meet. Labouring men were below this line, and so were cottagers and paupers, no less than 700,000 'poor Housekeeping Men and Women not paying to Church and Poor'. Excusal from paying parish rates was the accepted test of poverty.

By the end of the eighteenth century, the position of the lesser clergy had improved, in part due to the efforts of Queen Anne's Bounty, and the gap between clergymen and artisans had widened.[19] A survey in 1809 placed the great majority of clergy in the fifteen per cent or so of households paying income tax, which since 1806 had been charged on incomes over £50; under a tenth of livings, 860, were below £50. This number had been substantially reduced by 1835 to 297; about the time of the royal commission report, a good urban artisan's wage was 'round about a pound a week', and this was rather more than the mass of town and country labourers received. Incomes of between £60 and £180 were comparable with teachers, clerks and shopkeepers, and only four per cent of parsons received less than £60. William Farr, Head of the Statistical Branch in the General Register Office, estimated for 1847-8 that just over 1.3 million people in Great Britain had incomes of £50 or above, but only 341,000 of £150 and above, and two thirds of clergy had been in this group a decade earlier.[20] To suggest that all clergymen should receive £400, as Lord Henley, a well-known lawyer, did in his *Plan of Church Reform* published in 1832, was to raise them very much above the great majority of their parishioners and contributed to the sense that the clergy belonged to a superior social class. £200 was the minimum clerical stipend aimed at by the Ecclesiastical Commission for most of the nineteenth century.

Perceptions are vividly coloured by the literary portrayals of Jane Austen and Anthony Trollope rather than by the statistics of the 1835 parliamentary returns. The average clergyman was by no means rich, but he was rather better-off than nearly all his parishioners, and family background allowed many to live like gentlemen. It was authoritatively suggested in 1854 that the private income of the clergy doubled their official income.[21] But livings began to decline in value with the acute fall in wheat prices after 1879, an experience repeated again after 1918. In 1891, 4173 livings were under £200; 1586 had fallen into this class since 1879, and in 1903 they, too, were exempted from First Fruits and Tenths. In 1911 the Report of the Archbishops' Committee on Church Finance said that the clergy were not paid a 'living wage'. 'It is scarcely necessary to point out how seriously the income from the endowments of benefices has been affected by the fall in the value of land'. An original £100 of tithe rent charge had fallen in value to £71. Mrs Pember Reeves' book *Round about a pound a week* was published in 1913; by that time it was a very poor wage, although a good artisan's income was less than £100 a year. Clerical incomes dropped even more after tithe rent charges were abolished in 1936, which was estimated to have reduced them overall by nearly £1/2 million. The relative financial decline in the position of the clergy became sharper again after the Second World War. Barristers, solicitors, dentists, and general practitioners all on average had incomes approximately twice a clergyman's before the First World War, but three times as much after the Second World War.[22]

FAMILY LIVINGS

> The house stands among fine meadows facing the south-east, with an excellent kitchen-garden in the same aspect; the walls surrounding which I built and stocked myself about ten years ago, for the benefit of my son. It is a family living, Miss Morland; and the property in the place being chiefly my own, you may believe I take care that it shall not be a bad one. Did Henry's income depend solely on this living, he would not be ill provided for.

Jane Austen knew the world of the family living, which was her own, and in *Northanger Abbey* gave this clear fictional description. Henry Tilney's father thought it 'expedient to give every young man some employment', though little of the young rector's time was 'necessarily spent there' as he kept a curate. 'We are not calling it a good house', he said later, 'We are considering it as a mere Parsonage, small and confined, we allow, but decent perhaps, and habitable'. It stood 'at the further end of the village, and tolerably disengaged from the rest of it ... a new-built substantial stone house, with its semi-circular sweep and green gates.' When Jane Austen was writing, rather more than half the livings of the Church of England were 'family' livings. Private patronage gave a living an hereditary aspect encouraging to a potential builder of a new parsonage house. But there was a limitation to the patron's position; once instituted, a rector or vicar had the benefice for the rest of his life if he so wished, and there were few circumstances in which he could be displaced.

Redmarley D'Abitot, Gloucestershire - the front of the handsome red-brick Queen Anne rectory house was once plastered. It is on a moated site a little away from the church; the rector perhaps moved from the timber-framed house on the edge of the churchyard. From 1662, incumbents were themselves patrons, and it was a good living, in 1835 just under £1000. A new house was built nearer the church in 1964-65.

The family living became significant as a consequence of the Reformation. By the 1530s, monasteries were the patrons of about 4000 churches, so the patronage of something close to half of all English livings changed hands after they were closed. The majority were sold by the Crown to laymen, in this way entrenching the dissolution firmly amongst influential men in all counties. A survey of Gloucestershire diocese made for Bishop Hooper in 1551 shows that within a decade of the dissolution well over a third of livings, 117, were in the hands of lay patrons. Out of 288 livings, including eleven in Gloucester, the king was patron of ninety, the new bishop and dean and chapter of Gloucester cathedral of twenty-three, and other clerical bodies, including the bishops, deans and chapters of new cathedrals at Oxford and Bristol, of forty. In a few places a member of the family apparently held a family living; Lady Baskerville was the patron of the rectory of Westcote, also known as Combe Baskerville, held by Dr Baskerville though he did not reside there, and Thomas Wye was patron of the rectory of Rodmarton held by William Wye. John Somerfield Esq was patron of Aston Somerfield and John Slaughter of Upper Slaughter. The owner of the large estate at Great Badminton in the southern part of Gloucestershire had purchased the advowson of the rectory there; similarly the owner of Sudeley Castle near Winchcombe had bought the advowson of

Sudeley rectory. By 1603, the laymen's share of advowsons in Gloucester diocese had increased to rather over half, and three rectors were patrons of their own livings, a practice which later became much more common.

Some purchasers bought advowson and rectory estate together and so became 'lay rectors' and patrons of the vicarage. Particularly attractive to gentlemen building up estates were the opportunities to purchase a manor and rectory in the same place. Typical examples are the Cotswold estates of Sherborne and Stanway. Sherborne was one of the most important manors of Winchcombe Abbey, where the monastery had collected its sheep together from all over the Cotswolds for washing in the stream before shearing; in 1551 Thomas Dutton Esq. purchased both manor and rectory with the advowson of the vicarage. The abbot of Winchcombe's house was enlarged to become one of the finest mansions in the county. Dutton also bought the adjacent manor of Windrush, which had been in the hands of Llanthony Priory, but the rectory was sold to another. Early in the next century, William Dutton was able to purchase the advowson of Windrush vicarage, and after 1758 one vicar served both Sherborne and Windrush churches. But the rectory land in Windrush eluded the Dutton family's control and remained in different hands until 1852. The owner was then persuaded to exchange his 330 acres in Windrush for 455 acres in Upper Slaughter, including the beautiful gabled manor house of the Slaughter family. Through this transaction virtually all of Sherborne and Windrush parishes was consolidated in Lord Sherborne's estate.[23] At Stanway, on the western scarp of the Cotswolds, the Tracy family similarly purchased both manor and rectory. This estate had belonged to the abbot of Tewkesbury who had a grand house and tithe barn there; the Tracy family added to it a gabled building in more characteristic vernacular style than at Sherborne. In cases like these, the new lay patron did not necessarily present a member of his family to the living, which was usually not well-endowed unless he made it so, and did not have a good parsonage house; a vicar or curate sometimes lodged in the big house and acted as domestic chaplain.

The bishops claimed that over the whole country five sixths of advowsons were in lay hands, and complained that lay patrons were abusing their power; Archbishop Parker lamented as early as 1567 that in Norwich diocese 'some one knight had four or five, some seven or eight benefices clouted together, fleecing them all'.[24] But in this part of the country many were likely to be small parishes and poor livings which were being combined. Their figure was an exaggeration for Gloucestershire, and for Worcestershire, where lay patronage was nearer half, despite a doubling, and for Lancashire, where local families had increased their patronage from a third in 1530 to half in 1560. But in the new diocese of Oxford more than two thirds of advowsons were in lay hands in 1586, and in Lincoln in 1603 lay patrons had 1031 out of 1271 livings. Even in Kent presentations by lay patrons more than doubled in the years immediately following the dissolution.[25] The local rootedness of the Church of England had been much increased.

Advowsons were bought and sold like other property and the price naturally varied according to the value of the living and the condition of the parsonage house. Not until 1898 was their sale prevented unless accompanied by 100 acres of land, and in 1923 the practice was finally ended. Patronage on a single occasion could also be sold, known as the 'next presentation', and this, too, was abolished in 1898. The value of lead tithes at Eyam, a penny on every dish of ore, rose so much in the mid-eighteenth century that a speculative cleric bought the next presentation for a large sum; when output dropped dramatically, 'he tried, but in vain, to back out of the bargain and revenged himself on the parish by never residing'.[26] The sale of a next presentation was useful for a patron who had no member of family or other protégé to present, or who was in financial difficulties; the fictional owner of Jane Austen's Mansfield Park was in this position when he sold the next presentation to Mansfield rectory, and the son of the big house had to wait for the rector to resign before he could have the family living. Also a well-to-do man might buy a next presentation for a son or relative; the Austen family provided real examples of this.

George Austen, the father of the novelist, became perpetual curate of Shipbourne in Kent when his cousin moved to the rectory of Steventon in Hampshire; he succeeded him again at Steventon, where Jane Austen was born. The patron was a relation, Thomas Knight, who owned most of the land

Manningford Bruce, Wiltshire - the rectory house until 1964 appears to be eighteenth century, but there is a timber-framed core. Between 1722 and 1842 members of the Wells family were rectors. Several were Oxford graduates. John Wells, purchased the advowson in 1762. His son, an Oxford doctor of civil laws, became rector in 1763 and probably cased the house in brick.

in the parish. George Austen stayed in Oxford for three years after his appointment to Steventon in 1761; then he married and moved to Deane rectory house, not far from Steventon. His own parsonage was said to be dilapidated and Deane was vacant because the rector lived in his family home at Ashe Park. George Austen and his growing family did not move to Steventon for several more years. Shortly afterwards, an uncle bought the next presentations to both Deane and Ashe, intending to make his nephew rector of whichever first fell vacant; this proved to be Deane, and the next presentation to Ashe was again sold. George Austen let Deane parsonage house while serving the church himself. His oldest son, James, lived in Deane in turn after his marriage, though he already had two livings by courtesy of his mother's family, and later George Austen vacated Steventon rectory house for him while he remained rector until his death.

Thomas Knight had adopted Jane Austen's brother Edward as his heir, and he took the Knight surname when he inherited Godmersham Park in Kent in 1812. After James Austen died, his younger brother was temporarily rector of Steventon but had to resign as soon as Edward Knight's son reached the age to be ordained. In the 1835 returns Edward Knight was recorded as patron and his son as rector; the income of the living was £500, a valuable rectory compared with most, the population was 197. Hicks Beach was patron of Deane and Ashe, and these were valued at £350 and £487; the parishes contained respectively 163 and 146 inhabitants. Jane Austen's fictional clerical portraits had as background her family's experience.

After the later sixteenth century, the number of family livings did not alter dramatically until the twentieth century; in 1700, a little over half were controlled by lay patrons, and in 1835 a little under half. In 1835 one in ten patrons in Norfolk and in Somerset were also incumbents, a striking aspect of family livings; this practice declined during the century, to an estimated one in eighteen in 1878.[27] Most lay patrons held only one or two advowsons, though there were exceptions. Norfolk in 1835 provided the example of eleven men who controlled eighty livings, amongst whom were the Townshend and Coke families with nine each, and Baron Suffield with eleven, though none rivalled the Lowther family in Cumberland and Westmorland which had thirty-one. By this date, lay patronage was coming under attack because it was thought to encourage pluralism; nearly half of all benefices in 1835 were not served by the incumbent. But bishops were just as likely to create pluralists. For example, the bishop of Bath and Wells had the disposal of forty-four livings in his diocese; in five cases he had presented a man to two, which brought their incomes well above the average, and in the case of the vicar of East Brent and of Western Zoyland, to over £1000. The Archbishop of Canterbury had presented G.Moore to the valuable living of Wrotham and J.Croft to Cliffe at Hoo: the first was his son and the second his son-in-law; both men held a second living only a little less valuable. If a bishop presented a member of his family to a living in his gift, he was castigated as a nepotist, though it was normal practice for a layman.

The 254 richest livings in the country in 1835, valued at £1000 or more, display the typical pattern of patronage:

Piddlehinton, Dorset - the rectory house was built in 1753, as recorded on a date stone, by Philip Montague, rector from 1751 to 1782. It has been in the patronage of Eton College since 1442, and the rector was a scholar of Eton and of King's College, Cambridge, like his father and brother who also entered the church. This living was not notably wealthy, £326 in 1835. Piddlehinton was combined with Piddletrenthide in 1972 and the house sold.

Patronage of the 254 richest livings in 1835

Oxford and Cambridge colleges	22	Archbishop and bishops:	
Crown	19	Canterbury	11
Deans and chapters	13	Ely and Winchester	7 each
Eton and Charterhouse	1 each	Durham and London	10 each
Laymen	136	other bishops	15

Leeds church was controlled by trustees; St Olave's Hart Street, London, by the parishioners

At least fifty patrons were either incumbents or had presented one of their family, as indicated by their shared surnames; the true number of family livings, though, was larger because sons-in-law and other relatives cannot be identified through a common surname. One Norfolk incumbent was the patron of his two benefices, both over £1000. Only in Hampton Lucy, Worcestershire, did patron and rector bear the name which also distinguished the parish: George Lucy the patron, John Lucy the rector.

During the nineteenth century, the bishops began to increase their patronage, which rose from a total of 1248 to about 3000, mainly because when new benefices were created, the relevant bishop often became the patron; about 3510 benefices were created between 1835 and 1900. During the century, a number of trusts were set up to purchase advowsons, with the aim of putting parsons into livings whose ideas were in accordance with the trustees' principles; they came to control a small but widespread number of churches. But although a report in 1902 on *The Position of the Laity in the Church* noted the loss of lay advowsons, laymen in fact still controlled half the country's livings.[28] In the twentieth century, the campaign against lay patronage gathered momentum; patrons appeared to stand in the way of a business-like and cost-effective reorganisation of parishes and clergy. Leslie Paul in 1964 in his report on *The Deployment and Payment of Clergy* recommended ending the patronage system and substituting a staffing and appointments system. Canon Fenton Morley's less radical review of the same problems, *Partners in Ministry*, repeated this call. Neither was accepted. Despite this, a quiet revolution has occurred, if Gloucester diocese is still typical of the country as it was in mid-sixteenth century and in 1835.

Patronage of benefices in Gloucester diocese separately listed in:

	1551	1835	1987
Bishop of Gloucester	9	23	45
Crown	90	29	8
Oxford & Cambridge colleges & clerics	54	70	19
Single layman	114	142	16
Shared	3	3	61
Trustees and Miscellaneous		14	16
Not known	18		
Totals	288	281	165

Most strikingly, a lay patron now controls only a tenth of the much reduced number of separate benefices. The drive to unite benefices is the important factor in the change. Reorganisation has often resulted in there being several patrons of one living: sometimes patronage is exercised jointly by all former patrons, sometimes by each in rotation; the bishop may be one of the group. The official Board of Patronage in Gloucester diocese, controlling six benefices in 1987, contained one more layman than cleric, but lay involvement is mainly achieved through consultation with the Parochial Church Council, which is advisory only. The family living is almost gone, though a few owners of the big country houses keep their local advowson. In 1987 The Duke of Beaufort was still patron of Badminton, with its three associated churches of Little Badminton, Acton Turville and Hawkesbury, the Earl of Berkeley of Berkeley with Wick, Breadstone and Newport, Lord Dulverton of Moreton in Marsh with Batsford, Todenham and Lower Lemington, Lord Neidpath of Didbrook with Stanway and Hailes, and Mr Dent-Brocklehurst of Winchcombe with Gretton, Sudeley and Stanley Pontlarge. They were survivors of the old order. 'Ownership' of the parsonage house has gone with the family living and the parson's attitude to the parsonage house has changed radically.

CHAPTER TEN

FICTIONAL SCENES OF CLERICAL LIFE

Was Adlestrop House the inspiration for Jane Austen's portrait, in *Mansfield Park*, of Thornton Lacey parsonage with its 'air of a gentleman's residence'? Jane Austen stayed here three times with the rector, Revd Thomas Leigh, who was her mother's cousin. He 'turned' the house, as Henry Crawford in the novel suggested should be done, placing the entrance on the side with the view where the garden slopes down to an artificial lake; the entrance was restored to the south-east in the early nineteenth century, and the prominent bays were added. The approach to the house also used to be as Jane Austen described, along a lane now disused, though a lodge and gates at one end are still standing. Is it chance, too, that the living was worth £700 in 1814, the value of Thornton Laccy? Fiction draws on experience, but it is reworked in the imagination; nonetheless details of an author's life help to establish the authenticity of tone and setting of a novel.

LEFT: *Adlestrop, Gloucestershire - the former rectory house*

The gabled house which is the core of Adlestrop House was built in 1672, and then had eight hearths. Adlestrop Park on the other side of the church had thirteen hearths; Humphrey Repton's 'unnatural' landscaping of the park, together with a small park for the rector which took in the village green, is considered to have prompted unfavourable comment on such schemes in *Mansfield Park*.[1] Adlestrop was a 'family' living, such as Jane Austen described several times. Technically the rectory was in Broadwell parish, and Adlestrop was a chapelry; the medieval rector of Broadwell paid a small stipend to Adlestrop's chaplain. The arrangement reflected the fact that, probably since the early eighth century, both were Evesham abbey estates. Most of the rector's income was drawn from glebe land and tithes in Broadwell township, on the other side of the Evenlode River. The Leigh family bought Adlestrop in 1553 and purchased the advowson in 1627. Even before the dissolution of the abbey, Broadwell's rector was living at Adlestrop, and after the Leigh's purchase of the advowson, that became the usual arrangement; until 1960 Broadwell had the resident curate. A member of the Leigh family was frequently presented to the rectory, but in 1937 Adlestrop was linked with Oddington and Lord Leigh became the owner of the former rectory house.

The fictional parsons described by Jane Austen and by Anthony Trollope are influential in shaping impressions of a rural clergyman's life in the past. Mr Collins and Lady Catherine de Bourgh, Barchester and Mrs Proudie are well-known in dramatised adaptations, but these examples do not do justice to the variety of scenes and situations which were portrayed. George Eliot's first book, *Scenes of Clerical Life*, is not so well-known; she wrote of a very different urban and Midland setting.

THE PARSON AND THE COUNTRY GENTLEMAN: JANE AUSTEN (1775-1817)

Jane Austen's novels were placed in a narrow world of leisured country gentlemen, with a scattering of richer and occasionally titled characters. With the exception of the unfinished *Sanditon*, all have a clergyman amongst their characters, often being portrayed as a man of private means occupying an attractive parsonage house. She explored the nuances of social status within this limited section of society, and there is particular reason to trust her judgement in her portraits of clergymen because of her personal experience.

Jane Austen was the daughter of George Austen, rector of Steventon in Hampshire and a member of a landed Kentish family which contained several parsons.[2] George Austen married the well connected Cassandra Leigh; the Leighs were related to a number of aristocratic and gentry families, also containing several clergymen. The suggestion that Jane Austen was 'not quite a member of the gentry class' is based on a rather snobbish comment by Fanny Knight, the daughter of Jane Austen's brother, Edward, who inherited Godmersham Park in Kent. He had married Elizabeth Brook Bridges, a member of an undeniably Kentish gentry family. Fanny wrote some time after Jane Austen's death that her social circle 'was not at all high bred, or in short anything more than <u>mediocre</u>'. She accused Jane Austen of signs of 'common-ness', and somewhat arrogantly assumed that her knowledge of 'country house life' was owed to visits to Edward and his kindly mother-in-law at Godmersham. Godmersham Park was important in Jane Austen's experience, but by no means the only 'great house' which she visited. Fanny's viewpoint was from the wealthier background of her home, but if Jane Austen was not properly 'gentry', nor were most of the country clergy. Perceptions of status were rather different for those of superior social standing than for humbler members of the same class, as Jane Austen well understood.

Steventon parsonage house as Jane Austen knew it had a symmetrical Georgian facade, with two square sashed windows on each side of the front door, and three above. There were also two dormer windows lighting three bedrooms in the attics, where either servants or pupils slept. Behind were probably two projecting wings of an older house. There were three living rooms downstairs, and seven bedrooms on the first floor. Jane Austen's nephew wrote of Steventon rectory house:

the rooms were furnished with less elegance than would now be found in the most ordinary dwellings. No cornice marked the junction of wall and ceiling; while the beams which supported the upper floors projected into the rooms below in all their naked simplicity, covered only by a coat of paint or whitewash.

Here, Revd George Austen brought up eight children and Jane Austen lived until she was 25. The rector kept a carriage and two horses and had five Alderney cows; at some periods there were also three servants, and he was able to pay a curate to assist in the work of the parish. His income was about £600 a year, placing him very well up the clerical ladder - it was an affluent if not a wealthy household. George Austen's death in 1805 left his family not well provided for, although his son James, who then became rector of Steventon, had an income of over £1000 a year; Edward Knight helpfully made Chawton Cottage available for his mother and two sisters. Jane Austen's niece, Caroline, wrote: 'The house was quite as good as the generality of Parsonage houses then – and much in the same style – the ceilings low and roughly finished – some bedrooms very small – none very large but in a number sufficient to accommodate inmates, and several guests'. Steventon rectory house was demolished in 1826 by William, son of Edward Knight, who built a larger house on higher ground.

Jane Austen's imagination was stocked with impressions of parsonage houses. She stayed several times with her brother Edward at Godmersham Park and explored Kent. Edward's grandson described Godmersham:

Soon after you pass the Wye station ... you see Godmersham Church on your left hand, and just beyond it, comes into view the wall which shuts off the shrubberies and pleasure grounds of the great house from the road; close to the church nestles the home farm, and beyond it the Rectory, with lawns sloping down to the River Stour.

She had several friends who were married to clergymen, for example at Ashe near Steventon, where a long-standing friend was married to the rector. She was friendly with the rector of Farringdon, near Chawton, and of course knew Chawton rectory house, occupied by a relation and newly built just before she went to live at Chawton Cottage. Her portraits of parsonage houses drew on these and other examples.

Pride and Prejudice was probably the first of her novels to be written, though not published until 1813. The portrait of Hunsford rectory house and the big house, Rosings, is thought to have been based on Chevening in Kent, where a Lady Stanhope lived who was reputedly like the domineering Lady Catherine de Bourgh; Hunsford was said to be near Westerham. The fictional clergyman was Mr Collins, a young man of 25. He is the antithesis of Jane Austen's ideal. Mr Collins said he had been

so fortunate as to be distinguished by the patronage of the Right Honourable Lady Catherine de Bourgh, widow of Sir Lewis de Bourgh, whose bounty and beneficence has preferred me to the valuable rectory of this parish, where it shall be my earnest endeavour to demean myself with grateful respect towards her Ladyship.

The tone is quickly established. Hunsford parsonage largely existed for the well-being of the aristocratic owner of 'Rosings'; the rector was compliant in making an agreement for tithes 'beneficial to himself and not offensive to his patron'; the parsonage house was at the entrance to the drive, and the rector was required to provide the widow with company twice a week.

The parsonage house had a short gravel walk to the front door, green pales and a laurel hedge to the roadside, and a garden neat and well-laid out. Mr Collins spent much time working in his garden. There was a dining parlour and a book room, as well as a drawing room in which the ladies often sat. The standard of living implied was comparable with that of Jane Austen's father, comfortable but needing good management. Despite Mr Collins' pretensions, the daughters of the better-off Bennett family did not wish to marry him 'for Mr Collins was only a clergyman'. Mr Collins himself asked 'leave to observe that I consider the clerical office as equal in point of dignity with the highest rank in the kingdom – provided that a proper humility of behaviour is at the same time maintained.

In *Mansfield Park* the clergyman is central to the story; it was the fullest and most important of her fictional portraits of clergymen and was written between 1811 and 1813, during Jane Austen's second burst of creative energy. Edmund Bertram, the younger son of Mansfield Park, was preparing to be a parson. The family living of Mansfield was worth nearly £1000 a year, but his father was unable to give it to him because the next presentation had been sold to pay the debts of the elder brother. Instead, he was to go to Thornton Lacey. Later he was able to become rector of Mansfield when the incumbent was given a prebend at Westminster, 'which, as affording an occasion for leaving Mansfield, an excuse for residence in London, and an increase of income to answer the expenses of the change, was highly acceptable to those who went, and those who staid'. Jane Austen accepted without criticism the 'family' living.

She made clear the proper duty of the clergyman to live in his parish. Edmund could have lived at Mansfield Park, which was eight miles from his church, but his father stated forcefully

> ... a parish has wants and claims which can be known only by a clergyman constantly resident, and which no proxy can be capable of satisfying to the same extent. Edmund might, in the common phrase, do the duty of Thornton, that is, he might read prayers and preach, without giving up Mansfield Park; he might ride over, every Sunday, to a house nominally inhabited, and go through divine service; he might be the clergyman to Thornton Lacey every seventh day, for three or four hours, if that would content him. But it will not.

Henry Crawford's sister regarded the 'profession' of clergyman, which was Edmund's term, as beneath her. 'His curate does all the work, and the business of his own life is to dine'. She looked at a late seventeenth-century chapel in a

Farnborough, Berkshire - the former rectory is said to have been designed by Inigo Jones in mid-seventeenth century; the bell probably called pupils to lessons. It is a good example of a 'family' living. The house originally belonged to the Price family who also owned the advowson from about 1720 to 1883 and served as rectors. When John Betjeman came in 1945, he said the house was '1730-ish. Red brick seven hundred feet up on the downs. No water, no light, no heat. Beech trees all round'. There was still no electricity when he left six years later.

country house and observed 'in those days, I fancy parsons were very inferior even to what they are now'. That 'even' may have echoed accidental remarks in conversations heard by Jane Austen herself in her visits to big houses such as Godmersham Park. On a second occasion, Miss Crawford says woundingly 'A clergyman is nothing'.

As Miss Crawford enjoyed living in London, Jane Austen took the opportunity to discuss the problems of the urban church compared with the ideal of the rural parish.

> We do not look in great cities for our best morality ... A fine preacher is followed and admired; but it is not in fine preaching only that a good clergyman will be useful in his parish and his neighbourhood, where the parish and neighbourhood are of a size capable of knowing his private character, and observing his general conduct, which in London can rarely be the case. The clergy are lost there in the crowds of their parishioners.

Between Mr Collins of *Pride and Prejudice*, written when Jane Austen was young and high-spirited, and Edmund Bertram in *Mansfield Park*, when she had settled to writing as her main occupation, there were two early novels, *Sense and Sensibility* and *Northanger Abbey*. The clergymen were important to the plots but peripheral to the story-telling. Status and income were as always of interest to Jane Austen, whether of rural society or of clergymen, and the parsonage houses illuminated them. In *Sense and Sensibility* his mother's pretensions had prevented Edward entering the church:

> 'I always preferred the church, as I still do. But that was not smart enough for my family. They recommended the army. That was a great deal too smart for me. The law was allowed to be genteel enough ... But I had no inclination for the law ... As for the navy, it had fashion on its side, but I was too old when the subject was first started to enter it ... I was therefore entered at Oxford and have been properly idle ever since'.

Cut off from his inheritance because of his proposed marriage, Edward decided to enter the church, but

> He could get nothing but a curacy, and how was they to live upon that? ... They will wait a twelvemonth, and finding no good comes of it, will set down upon a curacy of £50 a year, with the interest of his £2000 - Then they will have a child every year! and Lord help 'em! how poor they will be.

A modest rectory proves to be the answer, given by the patron who, having no suitable relative, could well have sold the next presentation for £1400. 'Delaford is a nice place, I can tell you ... Oh! 'tis a nice place! A butcher hard by in the village, and the parsonage-house within a stone's throw'. The living was worth £200 a year, Edward's patron mused; a bachelor, perhaps, would be comfortable on that. Moreover, the house was 'small and indifferent', or so it seemed to him; another observer thought he should not apologise for 'a house that to my knowledge has five sitting rooms on the ground floor, and I think the housekeeper told me, could make up fifteen beds!' It was also out of repair. 'Well, and whose fault is that? why don't he repair it?- who should do it but himself?' An outgoing incumbent should have made good any dilapidations but in practice it was often the patron who paid for repairs and improvements. At Mansfield it was a cause of unpleasantness: a new rector and the widow of the previous rector 'were seldom good friends; their acquaintance had begun in dilapidations'.

The least well-endowed and stylish of Jane Austen's clerical characters was Mr Elton in *Emma*. He was considered 'quite the gentleman himself', but it could only be said of his family that they were 'without low connections'. Significantly, he was a vicar. His house was to be found 1/4 mile down Vicarage Lane, past 'a few inferior dwellings'; it was 'an old and not very good house almost as close to the road as it could be. It had no advantage of situation'. Much lower on the social scale was the curate who was a peripheral figure in *Persuasion*. He was easily dismissed by the baronet:

I remember no gentleman resident at Monkford ... Wentworth? Oh! ay,- Mr Wentworth, the curate of Monkford. You misled me by the term *gentleman*. I thought you were speaking of some man of property: Mr Wentworth was nobody, I remember; quite unconnected; nothing to do with the Strafford family.

The baronet, who could not afford to live in his family home, exemplified the most unpleasant and ultimately unrewarded snobbishness. Jane Austen's brother, Henry, became a clergyman at the age of 45 and assistant curate of Chawton, just before her death; his stipend was a mere £55. He never achieved a rectory nor a vicarage, and his experience might have provided her with a story centred round a curate if she had lived longer.

Her village of Uppercross in *Persuasion* might have been Jane Austen's ideal:

... a moderate-sized village, which a few years back had been completely in the old English style; containing only two houses superior in appearance to those of the yeoman and labourers,- the mansion of the 'squire, with its high walls, great gates and old trees, substantial and unmodernised - and the compact, tight parsonage, enclosed in its own neat garden, with a vine and a pear tree trained round its casements.

Squire and parson relied on each other for companionship; there was no other company for an educated man. For Jane Austen, a clergyman was on the edge of the gentlemanly class, and the social circle of the gentry in the countryside was small.

OBSERVING CLERICAL NUANCES:
ANTHONY TROLLOPE (1815-1882)

Anthony Trollope, in his portraits of the bishop and prebendaries of the cathedral of Barchester, of the life of the cathedral close and of neighbouring parsons, followed Jane Austen in writing about gentlemanly clergymen. Like her he thought that the essence of English character was not in great cities but 'in the mansions of noblemen, in country-houses, in parsonages, in farms and small meaningless towns'. He was similarly interested in questions of money, but was influenced by reforming ideas current after the royal commission published the 1835 Returns. Anthony Trollope, too, could regard himself as a gentleman by virtue of his family background, though his father was not wealthy enough to continue to support that life style; both his mother's and his father's families had baronets in the family tree. His family was also clerical; both his grandfathers were clergymen: Revd Anthony Trollope died before he was born, but Revd William Milton, his mother's father, died in 1824, when Trollope was nine, so he could have visited the Tudor vicarage at Heckfield in Hampshire. Anthony Trollope's brother described Revd Milton as

after the fashion of his day – kindly, liberal to the poor, liked by his neighbours, a charming old man, gentlemanlike, suave, and unquestionably clever in a queer, crotchety sort of way ... But he would have had no more idea of attempting anything

of the nature of active parochial work ... than he would have had of scheming to pay the national debt. Indeed, the latter would have been the more likely to occupy his mind.

Two of Trollope's aunts married clergymen and also important, perhaps, his mother's first book was about clergymen. Trollope's novels drew on these family situations, and also on his clerical schoolmasters; one, Charles Longley, became Archbishop of Canterbury and was the inspiration for the character of Bishop Yeld in *The Way We Live Now*. Several friends were clergymen. He stayed a number of times with Revd Lucas Collins at Lowick rectory in Northamptonshire, a convenient base from which to hunt; this friendship dated from 1870, after his Barsetshire novels had been completed. In 1879 he stayed a month and wrote to Collins, 'That I, who have belittled so many clergymen, should ever come to live in a parsonage! There will be a heaping of hot coals! ... Ought I to affect dark garments?'[3]

Four of the six novels which made up The *Chronicles of Barsetshire* explored the characters and positions of Church of England clergymen, incidentally drawing out current notions about reform. *The Warden*, published in 1855, was the first. The central character was a cathedral precentor with a useful income from an ancient charitable foundation caring for twelve old men; he was brought to resign by a campaign against his apparent appropriation of too much of the charity's income to his own well-being. *Barchester Towers*, which appeared two years later, displayed the arguments of high church and low church, modernism and traditionalism, through the conflicts between a new bishop of Barchester and his diocesan clergy. *Framley Parsonage* (1861) examined a 'hunting' parson who was too young, too affluent and too weak in character to behave in accordance with current notions of propriety in a churchman. *The Last Chronicle of Barset* (1867) was the most passionate of the series, placing the personal tragedy of a proud but poor perpetual curate at the centre. The four were linked with two others in a common setting which Trollope himself said in his *Autobiography* he knew 'as though I had lived and wandered there', and were collected together in 1878 as *The Chronicles of Barsetshire*.

The church provided a gentle context for the conflicts between religious ideals, human nature and practical situations which interested Trollope. He was once asked where he gained his knowledge of the politics and personalities of a cathedral close; he replied that he had none, but 'My archdeacon, who has been said to be life-like, and for whom I confess that I have all a parent's fond affection, was, I think, the simple result of an effort of my moral consciousness'.

The Bishop's Palace in Salisbury, now the Choir School, occupied seven and a half acres. On the left, parts are early thirteenth century, with eighteenth-century windows, as also in the central, seventeenth-century part; the principal rooms were all on the first floor to avoid the damp. On the right, the Great Hall was rebuilt soon after the Restoration. Constable's well-known painting was a view a little to westward.

Salisbury, Wiltshire - the Close contains eighty-three acres and many fine houses. The three houses in the north-west corner were all rebuilt by early eighteenth-century leaseholders: the grandest, by Sir Charles Mompesson, MP, in 1701. The bishop occupied this house from 1946 to 1951.

It has been suggested that his career in the Post Office showed Trollope how the 'establishment' worked. After some unhappy years in the General Office in London, Trollope went as clerk to a post office surveyor in Ireland, which involved checking Post Masters' accounts and dealing with complaints; later he surveyed and organised the rural delivery of letters, which allowed him to travel extensively on horseback. He did the same for a large western part of England and also negotiated some international postal agreements. His travels introduced him to many characters whom he used in his novels, while rarely interfering with his writing which was accomplished before he started his daily work.

The idea for the first of the Barset stories was conceived one day when carrying out his Post Office duties in Salisbury. In his *Autobiography* Trollope wrote that 'whilst wandering there on a midsummer evening round the purlieus of the cathedral I conceived the story of *The Warden,*- from whence came that series of novels of which Barchester, with its bishops, deans, and archdeacon, was the central site'. When he started to write the book, it was over a year since he had 'stood on the little bridge in Salisbury, and had made out to my own satsfaction the spot on which Hiram's hospital should stand'. At the end of his life, he stayed near Wells with the Oxford historian Edward Freeman. In answer to Freeman's questions he agreed that Barsetshire was Somerset, but was emphatic that Barchester was not Wells. St. Cross Hospital in Winchester, he said, was the origin of the story of a Warden accused of misappropriating charitable funds; the case had been in the news about the time of the visit to Salisbury. He told Escott that he had tried to imagine the characters of the writers of letters to *The Times*. Trollope had also used his memory of Winchester; he had been sent to the school aged 12, but had stayed only two and a half years because his father could not afford it. Fictional places were the product of these experiences.

The landscape of Barsetshire, with its small cathedral city and surrounding rural villages, contained several parsonages. The largest was probably the Archdeacon's rectory at Plumstead Episcopi, sustained by Dr Grantly's private fortune, which he had inherited from his father, the last bishop of Barchester. Framley Parsonage may have been nearly as large as Plumstead Episcopi; Framley was a typical 'family' living, in the patronage of the owner of the big house, and was worth more than £900 a year, 'an income sufficient for a gentleman's wants'. The incumbent and his wife were on intimate terms with the aristocrats of Framley Court. There was a more modest parsonage for the rector of St. Ewold's, where according to Archdeacon Grantly the dining room was too small and the cellars needed attention before wine could safely be stored in them; the new rector, having given up his college fellowship, was going to accept a less affluent style of life here than he had been accustomed to. The vicar of Puddingdale held one of the poorer livings in the neighbourhood of the cathedral city, and was extremely glad to move his fourteen children into a better house when he added the wardenship of Hiram's Hospital to his vicarage. At the bottom of the scale, there was the perpetual curate of Hogglestock, who was too poor even to furnish the room on the right of the passage in his obviously double-fronted house.

Trollope was never inclined to describe his fictional houses in much detail, but in *Framley Parsonage* he indicated many of the characteristics of a village dominated by its manor house, even to the diversion of the road away from it.

> Village there was none, properly speaking. The high road went winding about through the Framley paddocks, shrubberies and wood-skirted home fields, for a mile and a half ... Framley church ... stood immediately opposite to the chief entrance to Framley Court ... Beyond the church, but close to it, were the boys' school and girls' school ... then came a neat little grocer's shop ... And here the road took a sudden turn to the left, turning, as it were, away from Framley Court; and just beyond the turn was the vicarage, so that there was a little garden path running from the back of the vicarage grounds into the churchyard.

He noted that the aristocratic lady of Framley Court, like Lady Catherine de Bourgh, regarded the vicar as one of her servants, and thought his sister an unsuitable match for her son. As to the vicarage house, 'It had all the details requisite for the house of a moderate gentleman with moderate means, and none of those expensive superfluities which immoderate gentlemen demand, or which themselves demand immoderate means'. However, four servants were kept: a footman and cook, a groom and gardener; there was a library as well as a dining room and a drawing room; the former dairy had been converted to accommodate the groom and his wife; there were stables and a farmyard. Trollope should surely have made the lucky young Mark Robarts a rector rather than a vicar.

Not far away was the unattractive parish of Hogglestock, which contained two populous villages, and no gentleman's house beside that of the clergyman;

> and this, though it is certainly the house of a gentleman, can hardly be said to be fit to be so. It is ugly and straight, and small. There is a garden attached to the house, half in front of it and half behind; but this garden, like the rest of the parish, is by no means ornamental, though sufficiently useful. It produces cabbages but no trees: potatoes of, I believe, an excellent description, but hardly any flowers, and nothing worthy of the name of a shrub.

Here lived Josiah Crawley, the perpetual curate of the parish. Even here, there was a single maid servant of sixteen, although the stipend was only £130; indeed, the same man had a servant girl when he lived on £70 a year in Cornwall and had a rented cottage. Hogglestock parsonage was later described in negative terms; it was

> not placed on a green slopy bank of land, retired from the road, with its windows opening on to a lawn, surrounded by shrubs, with a view of the small church tower seen through them; it had none of that beauty which is so common to the cosy houses of our spiritual pastors in the agricultural parts of England. Hogglestock parsonage stood bleak beside the road, with no pretty paling lined inside by hollies and laburnam, Portugal laurels and rose-trees.

There is a small inconsistency here, as the house was previously said to have a garden in front.

Josiah Crawley's tragic character and situation was explored in *The Last Chronicle of Barset*, which was effectively a sustained appeal for improvement of the position of perpetual curates. The man was diligent, learned, sympathetic to his lowly parishioners who were brickmakers, but forced to accept charity from the local gentry, unable to pay his day-to-day bills and nearly destroyed by his wounded pride. The inspiration for this exceptionally strongly-drawn character was Trollope's own father, though he was a lawyer, not a clergyman. The ability to live simply was impossible for Crawley and his wife and had also been impossible in Trollope's own home. 'None but they who have themselves been poor gentry,- gentry so poor as not to know how to raise a shilling,- can understand the peculiar bitterness of the trials which such poverty produces'. Trollope also understood Josiah Crawley's position from his own experience; as a young Post Office clerk, he had experienced the ease with which debts could accumulate and the difficulty of paying them off, on a salary of £90 a year.

In *Barchester Towers*, the clergymen were all placed exactly by reference to their income. The bishop was paid £5000, as a result of the Ecclesiastical Commission's reforms, whereas his predecessor had drawn about £9000 from the bishopric; the Deanery was worth £1200; Puddingdale brought Revd. Quiverful only £400, but happily for him and his large family he was able to add £450 from the Wardenship of Hiram's Hospital, and to live in the beautiful Warden's House; the living of St Ewold's was worth £300 to £400, 'not a rich piece of preferment', while the tiny city parish of St Cuthbert's, to which the saintly Septimus Harding retired when he felt obliged to surrender the Wardenship of the Hospital, was worth less than £200. At the bottom of the scale was the perpetual curacy of Hogglestock, worth £130. The figures were available to all in the 1835 Returns. It is not accidental that the holder of one of the cathedral prebends, who spent his time in Italy, was named Dr Stanhope; Stanhope was notable as the second wealthiest parsonage in England in 1835 and Doddington as the wealthiest, and in *Framley Parsonage* both were made the subject of an extended reflection on the inequalities of clergymen's remuneration.

Higham, Kent - Gad's Hill Place, now a school, was occupied for a number of years by the vicar of Higham before it was bought in 1856 by Charles Dickens, who had long wished to live here. His book-lined study is on the right. Here he wrote Great Expectations*; opposite is Forge Lane, perhaps stimulating the choice of a lonely blacksmith's for Pip's home.*

In both their plots and their incidental comments, the *Chronicles of Barsetshire* reflect the discussion on the Church of England in the decades following the Royal Commission. Any reader of the current periodicals, like *the Pall Mall Gazette* or the *Cornhill Magazine*, for which Trollope wrote, or the *Edinburgh Review*, could hardly fail to have read some of the debates of the period. Trollope was also concerned to stimulate reform in the Church of England. 'I have ever thought of myself as a preacher of sermons, and my pulpit as one which I could make both salutary and agreeable to my audience'. 'The novelist, if he have a conscience, must preach his sermons with the same purpose as the clergyman, and must have his own system of ethics', he wrote in his *Autobiography*.

Trollope wrote a more obvious call for reform in *Clergymen of the Church of England*, ten essays or characterisations of churchmen: Archbishop, Bishop, Dean, Archdeacon, Parson, Town Incumbent, College Fellow, Curate, Irish Beneficed Clergyman and the Clergyman who adopts broad church, reformed theology; they were published anonymously in the *Pall Mall Gazette* in 1865 and 1866 and then collected into a book. The essays show that he had absorbed the Liberal views of the period about the upper hierarchy of the church. He gently ridiculed the restoration of a cathedral chapter house by ladies of the diocese, suggesting 'There is something charming to the English ear in the name of the Dean and Chapter. None of us quite know what it means, and yet we love it'.

Trollope saw the need to modernise the anomalous and ancient methods by which a clergyman was paid.

> One clergyman, with little or nothing to do in his parish, has fifteen hundred a year and a beautiful house for doing that little,- which after all is done by a curate; while his neighbour in the next parish with four times the area and eight times the population, receives one hundred and fifty pounds a year in lieu of the little tithes!

He observed that 'The very irregularity of the payments still made to parish parsons, and formerly made to bishops, half justifies a latent idea that clergymen, though they work and receive payment, are not labourers working for hire'. Another criticism was the fact that rectors in wealthy livings employed a curate, giving him 'one-fourteenth of the wages while he does three-fourths of the work'. How galling it was to the curate to know that the rector was 'not only idle but has bought a new carriage'. Trollope noted that nothing was known about the number of services taken by assistant curates, how many sermons they preached, the number of baptisms, burials and marriages they conducted, 'and, above all, how many cottages visited', nor about their remuneration, because the bishops had not been required to furnish such statistics.

When the essays appeared, he was taken sharply to task for exaggerating his case: Dean Alford of Canterbury said that curates were paid a minimum of £80, rising to £150 according to the population of the parish. The Dean may have been stung by criticism of his own position. A curate went into print confirming that Trollope was correct as far as 'assistant' curates were concerned, that is,

Higham, Kent - The flint and ragstone church of St Mary's, Higham is on the edge of the Thames marshes, beside a track once leading to a river crossing. The convict hulk was nearby from which Magwitch in Great Expectations *escaped to shelter in the churchyard. The village developed near the London turnpike road and a new church was built there. The old church has been cared for by The Churches Conservation Trust since 1987.*

The 'Clerks House' close to the old church was perhaps abandoned by earlier vicars for a more fashionable house on the London Road. In 1835 a glebe house was said to be unfit for the vicar to live in, although the living was nearly £600 a year. John Clare observed about this time 'The cottage now, with neither lawn nor park Instead of vicar, keeps the vicar's clerk'.

those working under the rector or vicar of the parish; the Dean's figures related to 'perpetual curates', who were in sole charge of a parish or new district. The two were easily confused. He replied to the Dean that he did not care about the rough handling he was given if 'it may be the means of drawing continued attention to that special subject which has brought down upon me the worst of the flagellation,- namely the salaries now paid to curates for their work'.

> Is there any profession in which such salaries will obtain the services of efficient men in the prime of life? Is there any other profession in which efficient men in the prime of life cannot obtain a much more adequate payment for their work? Both these questions must be answered in the negative.[4]

Trollope saw clergymen as 'gentlemen' and as men with a 'profession'. He assumed that in the past, a clergyman had automatically been a gentleman; 'Alas! that the day should have gone by when the same might have been said of every clergyman bearing orders in the Church of England'. He thought the status of the profession was changing and held the new Theological Colleges responsible. He defined a profession as 'a calling by which a gentleman, not born to the inheritance of a gentleman's allowance of good things, might ingeniously obtain the same by some exercise of his abilities'. For himself, he regarded writing as both a profession and a trade; at the time *Framley Parsonage* was being published in instalments, he was being paid £1000 for the novel, and could afford to spend an equal amount on improvements to his house in Waltham. When he died he was comfortably off, leaving £26,000. This no doubt coloured his approach to the proper level of remuneration of clergymen.

The historic endowments of the church were disguising the real problem;

> the members of the Church of England, however, are as willing to pay their clergymen as they are to pay their doctors or their lawyers. But the present nature of the Church Establishment, as an endowed Church,- as a Church in possession of a fixed property supposed to be sufficient to support itself,- is altogether antagonistic to that increase in the total amount of remuneration required which the increase in population demands. The country can afford to pay him better for his work, and would do so if things were placed on a better footing.

This hints at an attitude which by 1866 was no longer tenable: that the country's taxpayers should support a national church. The possibility of such an established position had in fact passed with the Whig government's reforms in the 1830s. But Trollope was accurate in his prediction: 'That there will come an adjustment between work and wages in the Church, as in all other professions, is certain'.

Unfashionable Midland scenes:
George Eliot (1819-1880)

Marian or Mary Ann Lewes (alias George Eliot) would not have called herself the daughter of a gentleman, although her father, a carpenter by upbringing, became the supervisor of the 7000 acre Arbury Hall estate in Warwickshire, and lived in an imposing house. Going with him about his work, George Eliot came in contact with 'all sorts and conditions of men', the working men and the occupants of the Hall. When young, she had a period of intense religious fervour, which she later dated to the years from 1834, when she was fifteen, to 1841, when she rejected her faith and refused to go to church at the age of twenty-two. The major influence on her seems to have been a Baptist minister in Coventry, the father of the Misses Franklin whose school she attended between 1832 and 1835. A deep interest in religion and in the tasks of the clergyman remained with her and was the theme of her first three short novels, which were published in *Blackwood's Magazine* in 1857, and collected together in 1858 under the title *Scenes of Clerical Life*. George Eliot even seems to have wished she could have been a clergyman, and when George Lewes offered the stories to John Blackwood, he said that they were by his 'clerical friend'. In London, George Eliot mixed in the same literary circle as Trollope; she said that Trollope was 'a Church of England man, clinging to whatever is, on the whole, and without fine distinctions, honest, lovely and of good report'.[5] Her experience was different from his, and as portrayals of clerical life, the 'scenes', too, were in contrast with both Trollope and Jane Austen; they were placed in the Midlands, each clergyman was presented in a tragic situation, and only one of the three mixed in local gentry society.

The second story of the three, 'Mr Gilfil's Love Story', had least to say about the Church of England. It was mainly set in a large country house where the clergyman, Mr Gilfil, was chaplain to the landowner and was also curate of the local church. One ideal parsonage house was described, though George Eliot rarely spent much time on such particularities. Mr Gilfil's sister had married a parson:

> Nowhere was there a lawn more smooth-shaven, walks better swept, or a porch more prettily festooned with creepers, than at Foxholm Parsonage, standing snugly sheltered by beeches and chestnuts half-way down the pretty green hill which was surmounted by the church, and overlooking a village that straggled at its ease among pastures and meadows, surrounded by wild hedgerows and broad shadowing trees, as yet unthreatened by improved methods of farming ... Brightly the fire shone in the great parlour, and brightly in the little pink bedroom, which was to be Caterina's, because it looked away from the churchyard, and on to a farm homestead, with its little cluster of beehive ricks, and placid groups of cows, and cheerful matin sounds of healthy labour.

Later, Gilfil became vicar of Shepperton, the scene of another of the stories. It was glancingly indicated that Mr Gilfil was a 'pluralist' holding two livings, and 'now his hunting days were over' his chief relaxation was supervising the buying and selling of horses and cows to stock his grazing land. Gilfil was a gentleman, and 'the farmers themselves were perfectly aware of the distinction between them and the parson, and had not at all the less belief in him as a gentleman and a clergyman for his easy speech and familiar manners'.

The other two stories were more clearly directed to the current state of the Church of England. They were set some twenty-five years before the time of writing, that is, just before the reforms of the 1830s began to change the church. George Eliot later remarked that 'there are ideas presented in these stories about which I care a good deal, and am not sure that I can ever embody again'.[6] 'The Sad Fortunes of the Reverend Amos Barton', was placed in the village of Shepperton; some parishioners were miners, some were visited in the Workhouse, ironically called 'the College', but it was generally a rural scene. Mr Gilfil had been vicar here in the past but now Amos Barton was a curate, paid £80 while the absentee vicar retained £35 from the living for himself.

> Those were the days when a man could hold three small livings, starve a curate a-piece on two of them, and live badly himself on the third. It was so with the Vicar of Shepperton; a vicar given to bricks and mortar, and thereby running into debt far away in a northern county.

There are many references to the relative poverty of the curate, with his steadily growing family, and a requirement to dress himself more respectably than could properly be afforded in a 'suit of black broadcloth'. Like Trollope's Josiah Crawley, the curate accepted kindly gifts from parishioners. Even so, he had a servant, Nanny, who was 'nurse, cook, and housemaid, all at once'. His wife died, and Amos Barton was forced to leave Shepperton because the vicar returned to serve the church in person, though the curate knew that this was only a ruse to remove him so that the vicar could put his brother-in-law in his place. Sadly he moved his motherless family to a large manufacturing town, 'where his walks would lie among noisy streets and dingy alleys, and where the children would have no garden to play in, no pleasant farmhouses to visit'.

A wide variety of clerical situations were sketched in the seven clergymen who attended the Clerical Meetings and Book Society at Milby Vicarage on the first Thursday of the month. They met in the dining room 'where the closely-drawn red curtains glow with the double light of fire and candle, where glass and silver are glittering on the pure damask'. Mr Ely, the vicar, was a good host, and a good listener; 'by his brother clergy he was regarded as a discreet and agreeable fellow. Mr Ely never got into a warm discussion; he suggested what might be thought, but rarely said what he thought himself'. Mr Fellowes, a rector and JP, had a 'mellifluous voice and the readiest of tongues' and a 'very pleasing perception of his own wisdom' but 'he is always at fierce feud with a farmer or two, a colliery proprietor, a grocer who was once a churchwarden and a tailor who formerly officiated as clerk'. In other words, he was in dispute about tithes. Revd Archibald Duke 'takes the gloomiest view of mankind and their prospects'. Though not burdened with a family, 'his yearly expenditure was apt considerably to exceed his income; and the unpleasant circumstances resulting from this, together with heavy meat breakfasts, may probably have contributed to his desponding views of the world generally'. Mr Furness was young, had failed his examinations at Cambridge because he spent his time writing poetry, and also wrote his own sermons, which bore a strong

Tunstall, Lancashire - St John the Baptist is mainly fifteenth-century, though a church is recorded in 1086. It is disguised as 'Brocklewood', attended by the pupils of 'Lowood' school in Charlotte Brontë's Jane Eyre. 'We set out cold, we arrived at church colder: during the morning service we became almost paralysed'. Dinner was eaten in the room over the porch, before afternoon service.

Haworth, West Yorkshire - church and parsonage are near the top of the hill; the moor behind and black headstones in the churchyard, 'no handsbreadth untenanted' as Virginia Woolf said, are a fit setting for the Brontë's lives. Haworth was a chapelry in Bradford parish, and had no parsonage until the trustees built one in 1779. It was like Trollope's Hogglestock, one room on each side of the passage.

resemblance to the earlier poetry. Mr Pugh was another young curate, who 'read prayers and a sermon twice every Sunday, and might be seen any day sallying forth on his parochial duties in a white tie, a perfect suit of black, and well-polished boots – an equipment which he probably supposed hieroglyphically to represent the spirit of Christianity to the parishioners of Whittlecombe'. Mr Baird was a good Greek scholar, who preached above the heads of his small congregation but became a writer and a noted lecturer in London.

A good parson is represented by Martin Cleves, not concentrating on appearances but on sympathy with his parishioners. He had a

> negligently tied cravat ... is the plainest and least clerical-looking of the party; yet, strange to say, there is the true parish priest, the pastor beloved, consulted, relied on by his flock ... he can call a spade a spade ... there is a great deal of humour and feeling playing in his grey eyes, and about the corners of his roughly cut mouth:- a man, you observe, who has most likely sprung from the harder-working section of the middle class, and has hereditary sympathies with the chequered life of the people.

Amos Barton was not at this meeting, giving Fellowes an opportunity to say that he never liked him, 'He's not a gentleman', but Cleves predictably showed proper appreciation of a fundamentally right-minded man who was much misunderstood. Cleves is an early example of what George Eliot later wrote about a clergyman: 'A clergyman ... should feel in himself a bit of every class'.

The third scene, 'Janet's Repentance', was set in the market town of Milby, 'a dingy-looking town, with a strong smell of tanning up one street, and a great shaking of handlooms up another'. George Eliot hints at one of the changes occurring in the first half of the nineteenth century; at the time of the story, Milby was served by a curate, but was said to be much improved by the date of writing - when there was a resident rector, who kept a carriage. Within the parish were manufacturing villages and hamlets, particularly Paddiford Common, which 'by the by, was hardly recognizable as a common at all, but was a dismal district where you heard the rattle of the handloom, and breathed the smoke of coal-pits'. Here a fervent evangelical clergyman, Edgar Tryan, perpetual curate of the chapel of ease, worked hard amongst the poor; he was persecuted by some of the better-off inhabitants of the parish but also earned the respect of others who helped him in his ministry. He chose to live in lodgings among the people.

> I've no face to go and preach resignation to those poor things in their smoky air and comfortless homes, when I come straight from every luxury myself. There are many things quite lawful for other men, which a clergyman must forego if he would do any good in a manufacturing population like this'.

His story is not about his parishioners' poverty but of how, before his early death, he reached the desperate mental suffering of Janet, whose rejection of alchohol and acceptance of religion is implied in the story's title..

The character of Edgar Tryan was based on an Evangelical preacher in Nuneaton who died in 1831, when George Eliot was only twelve; his story must have been known to her largely by hearsay, and was not the source of her own earlier fervent religious feeling. Mr Gilfil and Amos Barton were both based on vicars of Chilvers Coton near Nuneaton, the parish in which George Eliot's father lived, and where she was herself baptised by Revd Bernard Gilpin Ebdell.[7] When the stories were published, people in Nuneaton were convinced they recognised themselves, and a key to the characters was in circulation. An inquirer into George Eliot country within a few years of her death reported a local informant saying 'Oh, yes, all the people in *Scenes of Clerical Life* are real - Dead and gone now, but with relatives still in the town'. A 'real' curate justified Trollope's portrait of the curate's lot in *Clergymen of the Church of England*, but one of George Eliot's fictional clerymen actually identified himself as a real parson in a letter to the Editor of *Blackwood's*; Revd Gwyther expressed his astonishment at reading his own story - he was Amos Barton - and at the next two *Scenes* which were 'historical reminiscences of the Former vicar- where I was Curate and of a Clergyman and the persecutions to which he was subject, all in the immediate Neighbourhood where I resided, during the events recorded in the Story of Amos Barton'. George Eliot did not deny that the groundwork of the story was true, but suggested that her imperfect knowledge and the large amount of 'arbitrary, imaginative addition' must have made it vary from the actual facts.

There are a number of allusions to current concerns in the stories, for example, the references to sermons: Mr Furness wrote his own, not the usual situation; more typical was Mr Gilfil, with his

> large heap of short sermons, rather yellow and worn at the edges, from which he took two every Sunday, securing perfect impartiality in the selection by taking them as they came without reference to topics; and having preached one of these sermons at Shepperton in the morning, he mounted his horse and rode hastily with the other in his pocket to Knebley, where he officiated in a wonderful little church, with a chequered pavement which had once rung to the iron tread of military monks ...

and which the local gentry family regarded as a sort of family temple. At the opposite extreme was Amos Barton, who tried *extempore* preaching in cottages, a mark of the Evangelical, though he wrote his sermons for Shepperton church. By the time she wrote *Middlemarch*, George Eliot's referential style was even more developed. 'Few readers realise they are reading a historical novel full of documented, accurate historical information; none feels history obtrudes inorganically upon the fiction'.[8] George Eliot portrayed a variety of clerical situations, as well as the infinite variety of human nature. The *Scenes of Clerical Life* already showed her range. They provide a balance to any over-idealised impression of the clergy which may be gained from nineteenth-century fiction.

CHAPTER ELEVEN

THE TRIUMPH OF
THE PARISH

The collegiate parish church of St Mary, Manchester, became a cathedral in 1847. The medieval church was already being overshadowed by the mills, warehouses and banks which were displacing residential houses, and around them were the amazingly overcrowded courts and alleys of poor Manchester workmen and their families. The stone of the parish church and of all the buildings in the town was grimed and eroded by the coal smoke from the rapidly expanding mechanised cotton spinning mills, by the railway engines - the Manchester to Liverpool railway had opened in 1830 and by 1846 seven lines came through the town - and by pollution from thousands of domestic hearths. At first, a new cathedral was planned at Cheetwood, but the project was abandoned because of the expense. Instead, the external faces of the collegiate church were rebuilt, and the bishop's *cathedra* or throne was installed in 1855. More of civic pride went into the building of a town hall between 1868 and 1877, to a monumental Gothic design by Alfred Waterhouse. A second new cathedral scheme in 1876 was also abandoned. Piecemeal rebuilding, extension and renovation continued, including a higher tower in 1864; altogether it has resulted in the effective reproduction of a grand late medieval church. Some of this work had to be undertaken again after air raid damage in December 1940.[1]

In 1847, Manchester became the capital of a diocese which contained nearly all Lancashire, including the large area placed in the diocese of Blackburn in 1926; it contained 284 churches and a million people lived beyond Manchester parish's boundaries. To become the seat of a bishop may have seemed a fitting acknowledgement of Manchester's economic importance and the size of its population. The royal commission estimated the population at 271,000 in 1831, half of which was concentrated in the town, and the other half scattered over the sixty square miles of the historic parish; the fastest growth ever experienced nationally was in the previous decade and in Manchester the population had nearly doubled. The few years prior to the creation of the diocese had been of great significance. In 1838, the medieval manorial court had been displaced by a Borough Council created by Royal Charter; in 1844 and 1845, the framework of modern public health administration had been pioneered in advance of national legislation. In 1846 John Owens had died leaving a large bequest for the founding of a secular university in Manchester which would not apply religious tests. But in social terms, the new diocese may have seemed unimportant or even inappropriate. Richard Cobden, who was a notable political figure, and with John Bright was instrumental in forming the national Anti-Corn Law League in Manchester in 1839, had refused to contribute in 1842 to building ten new churches, saying 'The feeding of the hungry should have priority over all other 'public undertakings''. The Chartists met in Manchester that year and during large-scale riots had attacked factories powered by steam which were putting handloom weavers out of work, by pulling the plugs out of the boilers. *The Report on the Sanitary Condition of the Labouring Population of Great Britain,* which was published by Edwin Chadwick in 1842, pointed out the depressingly high death rate and infant mortality of Manchester compared with a rural area such as Rutland. In 1844, Engels published his account of *The Condition of the Working Class in England,* drawing on his knowledge of Manchester, and making a thorough condemnation of the economic system.

The new diocese brought church administration closer to Manchester than the Bishop of Chester had been, and it transferred responsibility for the extremely large parish to a bishop; the warden or rector of Manchester collegiate church became dean of the cathedral and the four fellows became canons. The bishop was to be the spearhead of a campaign to reclaim Manchester for the Church of England, just as an early missionary bishop was the key figure in the conversion of an Anglo-Saxon kingdom. The first bishop was also to support the division of the parish of Manchester by act of parliament against the interests of the collegiate church. His successor was told by Gladstone that he could not exaggerate 'the importance of the area, or the weight and force of the demands it will make of the energies of a Bishop, and his spirit of self-sacrifice'.[2]

THE REGULATION OF VICTORIAN ENTERPRISE

The legal difficulties in the way of altering parish structure were formidable. Starting in 1818, general acts of parliament were passed which attempted to facilitate church building and parish re-organisation, but as act succeeded act, they created yet more tangled complexities in trying to avoid legal obstacles to effective action.[3] By 1856, there had been twenty-one acts 'so complex and conflicting in their nature as to have defied all endeavours to arrange or classify them, or render them at all intelligible to the general reader'.

The ending of the Napoleonic Wars had released both funds and energies. The Church Building Society was founded in 1817 to raise money, an example quickly followed by diocesan societies. The Church Building Commissioners started in 1818 with £1 million of parliamentary funds at their disposal, and were given another half a million in 1824. The first Church Building Act in 1818 set out the main principles followed in subsequent acts. The

Commissioners could make grants towards building churches in 'populous parishes' where the population was 4000 or more and there was church accommodation for a quarter or less, or where at least 1000 people lived more than four miles from the parish church. £1 million was not thought enough to solve the urban problem but could be used to supplement private or community enterprise. The aim was to accommodate one third of the country's population in church. The proposers of the legislation could not have foreseen how rapidly population would continue to grow throughout the century.

Churches built by the Commissioners were popularly named 'Waterloo churches' on the supposition that the grant by parliament was a thanksgiving for victory at the battle of Waterloo in 1815. Many were built without thought as to their power of attraction, in expectation that if conveniently situated, the people would come. The terms of the first Church Building Act were condescending and utilitarian, providing for 'proper accommodation for the largest number of persons at the least expense' and the Commissioners' initial policy was to accommodate at least 1000 people in each church at a cost of not more than £20,000. This encouraged the construction of large, unfriendly buildings like St Matthew's, Campfield in Manchester (1824), with seats for nearly 2000 (only 600 were free), designed by Sir Charles Barry, the architect of the Houses of Parliament.[4]

The bishop had a key role in agreeing to proposed changes in parishes. Three principal methods were authorised by the 1818 act but in all cases full implementation was delayed until an existing incumbent vacated the benefice. The most obvious but least used was a straighforward division of the resources of a living in tithes, glebeland, and other parishioners' payments and then the new parish church had the same status as the old one, either rectory, vicarage or perpetual curacy as appropriate. In this case the commissioners had to obtain the consent of the patron. Other methods resulted in the institution of a perpetual curate who could discharge a full range of 'ecclesiastical duties' but had no share in the tithes of the old parish. One was to create a 'parochial district'. This was inherently more flexible, especially as the bounds of a district could be varied by Order in Council; it did not require the patron's consent, but he nominated the new incumbent. The other and most usual method was to create district chapelries, effectively chapels of ease, where the incumbent of the parish church nominated the perpetual curate and some fees might still be paid to the parish church. The 1818 act took for granted that perpetual curates would be funded out of pew rents and there were provisions for fixing the amounts and allocating pews; not less than one fifth of the pews were to be free. The minister was to have a convenient pew seating six persons for his family, and another, less well-placed and seating four, for his servants. Financing a minister through pew rents had been accepted for many centuries, though the logical next step of popular nomination was regarded with dismay.

During the period of their existence, 1818-1856, the Church Building Commissioners built 615 churches, and obtained 1200 church sites, but only a quarter as many sites for parsonage houses. They helped in setting up 1077 new church districts of which only forty were wholly separate parishes, a mere four

Salford, Greater Manchester - St Philip's Rectory, on the right, illustrates Trollope's comment on the incumbent of a new town district; 'he is too often simply recognised as the professional gentleman who has taken his family into the last built new house in Albert Terrace'. This late Georgian row has survived because of the rectory; only the end house, drawn by Lowry, has been demolished.

per cent. The new districts were purely ecclesiastical and did not replace existing poor law areas. The Building Commissioners did not always act where need was greatest but responded to private initiative. Where a good number of ratepayers were Dissenters, the creation of new districts was sometimes blocked because churchwardens of the new churches could raise a rate for its repair while the inhabitants still had to contribute for twenty years to repair of the older parish church. The ratepayers of Stockton in 1835 were 'apprehensive that any division would occasion unnecessary expense with regard to church rates' and they 'wished that the new church should only be considered a chapel of ease'. The bishop of Durham achieved the division of this parish after two years of agitation.[5]

These reforms accepted the basic parochial structure at the same time that it was being superseded in its civil functions. Most significant, in 1834 the Poor Law Amendment Act authorised the grouping of parishes into larger units or Unions, each comprising perhaps a dozen or more parishes. At first, each parish in the Union still paid for its own poor, though the workhouse was run economically as a joint enterprise; but by 1865 it was realised that contributions should be based on ability to pay, so that wealthy rate-payers could subsidise poorer ones. The Poor Law provided one pattern which could have been studied by the Church, if it had been more radical in its thinking. But a view of reform even on this scale was obstructed by the Church's medieval inheritance of property rights - the patron's property of the advowson, the clergyman's property of the benefice, and episcopal control within each diocese. Effort was concentrated on creating more benefices, ensuring that clergy carried out their obligations by living in their parishes, and raising the incomes of the least well-off.

The failings of the Church of England in manufacturing districts were apparently underlined in 1838-9 and 1841-2 by the demonstrations of the

St Philip's church, built in 1825, was a 'Waterloo' church designed by Sir Philip Smirke, architect to the Church Building Commissioners, and better known for the British Museum in London. The neo-classical south facade and the clock tower show to good advantage along the approach road, although originally designed for a more usual position at the west end.

Chartists, who wanted all men to be able to vote for members of parliament as a means of securing social policies more sympathetic to their needs than the New Poor Law. Peel, who had returned to office as Prime Minister by 1841, recognised the overwhelming importance of economic factors in social unrest, but was also willing to help the Church of England in the towns. In 1843 the Ecclesiastical Commissioners were given power to create new parochial districts before a church was built; services could be held in a building licensed by the bishop.[6] Perpetual curates of 'Peel districts' were to have not less than £100 a year funded by endowment and £150 a year once a church was built and the district became a full parish; the curate would then collect Easter offerings. The

commissioners could augment incomes as necessary. Substantial private benefactors were offered the encouragement of becoming patron of a new church. So there was added another layer to the hierarchy of parishes each with its peculiar legal limitations.

The Ecclesiastical Commissioners started work briskly. Between 1844 and 1846 they demarcated 194 new parishes and districts, but their funds were quickly exhausted. In 1856, the Church Building Commissioners were dissolved and the Ecclesiastical Commissioners were given their powers to divide parishes and, more important, to create unendowed district chapelries whose perpetual curates depended on pew rents; this act specified that half the pews or seats should be free. The commissioners were also given powers to define districts for existing chapels and upgrade them into parishes. The intention was eventually to convert all the new ecclesiastical areas into full parishes whose minister could perform all the offices of the Church and collect the fees. The Ecclesiastical Commissioners could also build churches. In 1868, perpetual curates with full parochial positions were renamed 'vicars'.

The years of the triumph of the parish were between 1857 and 1890. The Ecclesiastical Commissioners created 1829 chapelry districts in this period, and 416 new districts and parishes. By 1938, the commissioners had created 2651 chapelries and 1037 districts and parishes since Peel's Act. Apart from a short experiment between 1867 and 1880, the commissioners did not endow new livings but paid contributions to stipends, although they did make grants to match private benefactions in order to encourage a flow of private capital into the church; in the first forty years of their existence, about a quarter of the capital employed came from private sources. Their new parishes were consequently often guided by the availability of endowments; they could not conduct more radical reappraisals because of the continuing position of the bishops.

Incumbents of Peel district churches were more fortunate than many. Parish boundaries were often drawn so that the old church retained prosperous areas and the new church was allotted poorer areas where church attendance was in any case low, and the ability of parishioners to contribute to parish work limited. Such clergymen were hard pressed to carry out the work expected of them: build schools, pay curates' wages, help the poor directly. Especially, support to schools was considered important; where there was difficulty raising money for a new district, at least one influential bishop, Blomfield of London, said that the school should come before the church. Some spent their own money; some, like Trollope's Josiah Crawley or George Eliot's Edgar Tryan, worked at the cost of personal misery.

DIVIDING THE TOWN PARISH

Manchester, Leeds, Stoke on Trent and Liverpool are four important examples of the Church's responses to the urban problem in the nineteenth century. As Canon Hume of Liverpool suggested, success in meeting the problem tended to be measured in terms of numbers of seats in churches rather than of people going to church. The 1851 Religious Census, the only one yet taken, displayed

Stockport, Greater Manchester - the tower and spire of St George's church can be seen from many viewpoints. Stockport grew from 18,000 in 1794 to 70,000 in 1891, when the new parish was approved, but it was as much a response to High Church practices at St Thomas's in Stockport as to population growth. One benefactor financed church, vicarage and schools, all grouped in a leafy enclave between two main roads. The church seats over 1000, and pew rents were collected for 488 seats, not ended until 1977.

in convincing detail the terrible weakness of the Church of England.[7] The census asked for information on the numbers attending morning, afternoon and evening services on census Sunday, 30 March 1851; people going to church more than once were counted more than once and some probably went to both church and chapel. Adding together attendances at all three services and relating the figures to population gives an index of attendance which must considerably over-estimate actual churchgoers. Horace Mann, who studied the results and wrote the report, suggested that fifty-eight per cent of the population could go to church, allowing for children, the infirm and sick, those working, for example in public transport, and those left at home to look after the house. Mann's conclusion was that, at the most optimistic, half of those who could did go to church, and of that number only half went to the Church of England. His report made clear that the Church of England faced a crisis of attendance, especially in the sixty-six large towns, including London, for which he provided individual statistics. He concluded that there was a choice of responses:

> either a much minuter sub-division of existing districts - with the erection of much
> smaller churches - or (if large churches are to be retained) the employment, in each
> district, of a number of additional agents as auxiliaries to the regular incumbent.

He recorded 1255 sub-divisions of parishes made under acts of parliament by 1851, and noted that a number of 'conventional' districts existed through informal understandings. Where there were four or five thousand people in a parish, he thought that a single clergyman could not effectively visit and supervise more than a third of his parishioners. His emphatic view was that the church needed more agents. There was 'No scheme for giving to a clergyman the cure of souls, within a small and definite locality, apart from the very onerous duties which attach to the possession of a church'. He put forward suggestions about a lay ministry.

Manchester and the collegiate church

While the creation of Manchester diocese was being discussed, the first step was taken by the Church Building Commissioners to sub-divide the ancient parish. In 1839 a scheme was given the royal assent which drew boundaries round districts for twenty-three existing churches. Although there had been eight chapels within the parish for several centuries, some certainly, and probably all, of medieval foundation, none had a parochial district.[8] Since the beginning of the eighteenth century, a further twenty-one churches had been built, but only three, built with the assistance of the Church Building Commissioners in Salford, Hulme and Ancoats, had districts assigned to them. Congregations were drawn to the chapels by choice or convenience, but not by 'belonging'. The ministers of three eighteenth-century chapels were misleadingly styled 'rector': Manchester's first new town church, St Anne's, (1712), nearby St Mary's (1756, built by the collegiate church to rival St Anne's) and St John's

(1768), but these chapels did not enjoy full parochial rights before or after 1839. Two chapels were owned by their incumbents, in missionary ventures reminiscent of ancient practice. All ministers relied on freewill offerings and pew rents and none had the sole right to collect parochial fees.

This was a typical problem, partly tackled by the commissioners in Manchester in 1839, although they were not able to persuade the collegiate church to give up all its rights. Baptisms and burials took place in Manchester's chapels, and after 1837 marriages, but the collegiate church had been ruthless in demanding their historic fees, which added up to a significant sum. Out of the twenty-three new districts created in 1839, only ten were allowed sole rights to collect fees for baptisms, churchings and burials; in the other thirteen, a fixed fee had also to be paid to the collegiate church. Full rights went to the eight ancient chapels, together with Trinity Church, Salford, now Sacred Trinity established in 1635, and the church in the wealthy district of Ardwick, established in 1741. The town centre churches, geographically close to the collegiate church, remained effectively chapels of ease, and so did four outlying churches.

Criticism of the wealth and monopoly of the collegiate church came to a head in 1846, when one of the canons became president of St Bees in Cumbria; the churchwardens entered a protest in the parish journal: 'the large parish of Manchester requires an increase rather than a diminution of clerical superintendance'. At the same time, attention was focused by the act to create

Salford, Greater Manchester - Sacred Trinity church, rebuilt in 1752, might have been demolished in 1904, but it is on the site of the first Salford chapel and the railway lines were made to curve round it. Salford was a borough and head of an extensive Domesday manor which included Manchester, but until the mid-nineteenth century was a chapelry . Lowry drew the church in the 'Flat Iron Market'. It is an Ecumenical centre.

the bishopric of Manchester. Should the collegiate church's resources be divided? The college denied that it had responsibility for care of the parish but after its charter was published, could not maintain this defence. Public agitation for the division of large parishes was widespread. A Reform Association in Manchester, led by Evangelicals in the town, secured the election of its nominees as churchwardens, and they introduced a bill into parliament in 1850.[9] The first Bishop of Manchester supported the reformers.

The Manchester Rectory Division Act of 1850, which is still operative, created rectories in parochial districts then existing and in any to be defined in the future, so removing all rights of the cathedral church over them, except in a very small parochial area round it. The preamble to the act noted that some districts were 'endowed to a small extent, but wholly insufficient for properly providing for the cure of souls in such Districts'. The act provided that, after fixing the income of the cathedral dean and four canons, the surplus be divided between Manchester's new parishes. No new pew rents were to be introduced, and no fee asked for baptising on a Sunday. The new dean and chapter, some of whom were the former warden and fellows, did not forgive the bishop; relations were distant for the rest of his episcopate, which was no doubt one reason for their slowness in installing the bishop's throne. Conflicts over the style and theology of the Church of England also underlay the coldness, as the bishop had little time for the ritualism of the former collegiate church.

The 1850 act specifically prevented new parishes raising church rates. There had been strong opposition to the Church Building Commissioners in Manchester since 1820 on the issue of rates. Dissenters fought further vigorous campaigns between 1831 and 1835, particularly because they hoped to persuade the Whig government to abolish church rates throughout the country, and after this, rates to support the collegiate church in Manchester could not be collected but continued on a voluntary basis. For the next half century, churchwardens continued to be chosen for each of Manchester's original townships at the cathedral's Easter Vestry meeting, the meeting of the parish ratepayers, but their duties were nominal apart from some charity disbursements.[10]

The centuries old stranglehold of the collegiate church on the parish may have been responsible for some lack of enthusiasm for Anglicanism in Manchester. Habits of independence had been fostered by the need to build their own chapels in settlements at a distance from the parish church, and to maintain their own ministers, which no doubt also fostered secession to Nonconformist churches. It was claimed in 1820 that the twenty-seven churches then existing were never more than one quarter full. It is perhaps still surprising to find that, on the most optimistic assumptions, a mere thirteen percent of the population in the boroughs of Manchester and Salford had attended an Anglican church on Census Sunday 1851, rather less than the national average; perhaps about a quarter of those able to go had gone to a church of whatever denomination. Returns were made by forty Anglican churches, ninety-seven Dissenting chapels and eight Roman Catholic churches within the areas of the two boroughs of Manchester and Salford, which was a

less extensive area than the old Manchester parish but covered the most populated core. The Nonconformist churches were marginally stronger than the Church of England, and the Roman Catholic church had some significance, particularly in Manchester though less so in Salford. Morning service attracted much the largest congregation of the day, twenty-one percent of the inhabitants, but only one third of these were Anglicans.

There were many empty pews in Manchester on census Sunday, which did not prompt the conclusion that more churches should be built. It was true that the Anglican churches could accommodate only twenty per cent of the population at one sitting, but in practice they were less than half full. The Dissenters' chapels were fuller, but they, too, could have seated half as many people again. Exactly the same proportion of Dissenting congregations paid pew rents as in the Church of England. Manchester and Salford were not the least religious towns in the area: Oldham, Preston and Sheffield had slightly lower proportions attending a church of any sort, and Bradford and Rochdale had lower proportions going to Anglican churches, though compensated for by the Nonconformist chapels. Amongst sixty-five towns analysed by Horace Mann, only Carlisle had figures similar to these seven industrial towns.

Despite these facts, church building in Manchester continued. An average of sixteen churches in each decade between 1841 and 1890 were built in the former parish. Bishop Fraser said in 1880 that in the central district there was still only accommodation for ten per cent of the population but the churches were normally nearly empty. Between 1901 and 1914, through the efforts of

St Anne's, Haughton, Manchester - the unusual Rectory House has recently been restored. Church and house were built in 1882 by a wealthy local man, to a design inspired by an early Norwegian church. The small District on the edge of the former parish of Manchester was then largely rural, although it included two collieries owned by the benefactor, and a cotton mill; in the twentieth century, housing joins it to Manchester, and the M67 rushes past.

the Bishop's Special Commission, money was raised to build another twenty-eight churches. There is no doubting the enormous effort made, much of it funded from outside Manchester, to meet the phenomenal increase of population, which had trebled since 1831. In the area of the modern diocese, which is more extensive than Manchester's ancient parish, Richard Murphy has recorded 415 Anglican churches built between 1800 and 1914; two thirds were financed by private subscription or by contributions from church building funds, one fifth by private individuals and one eighth wholly or in part by the Church Building Commissioners.[11] New districts were created on nine occasions between 1839 and 1914; by the end of the century, 122 parishes had been formed within the ancient parish, and 136 by 1914. But the parochial system was ill-suited to the pastoral problem of Manchester. 'The possibility of any concerted effort to tackle its problems was deferred indefinitely by the triumph of Anglican parish mythology in the Manchester Rectory Division Act'.

Leeds and W.F.Hook

W.F.Hook was chosen to become their vicar in 1837 by sixteen out of the the twenty-three trustees for St Peter's parish church, Leeds.[12] Townsfolk had bought the advowson about 1589, and trustees presented the vicar thereafter.[13] While vicar of Christ Church, Coventry, Hook's reputation was established as a preacher and for his generosity and pastoral care for all his parishioners; nonetheless some trustees opposed his election to Leeds because of his High Church sympathies. Hook was not a Tractarian, and did not attend the meeting in the library in the Deanery Tower at Hadleigh which led to the publication of Tracts setting out High Church religious views, but he was in touch with those who went. When he moved to Leeds, he was faced with seven Dissenting churchwardens who opposed any and every expense on the rates; the vicar chose one warden, for Kirkgate Ward. Typically, at his own expense he introduced a choir dressed in robes, a High Church innovation, and he held on to his patronage of other Leeds' churches because it enabled him to provide 'some place for persecuted High Churchmen to flee into'. Hook was soon personally very successful, drawing congregations which filled the church to overflowing; numbers of communicants rose tenfold. An attempt to restore the church and make it easier to hear the preacher met with so many technical problems that eventually the church was demolished, and a new one was consecrated in 1841. In 1851 the evening congregation in the church was 2800, and it was usual for 'more people to attend than there were sittings and for people to have either to stand or even to be turned away'.

There were other challenges in Leeds. The parish church served most of the 123,400 people counted in the Census in 1831, and there were nearly 30,000 more by 1841, while the staff of the parish church consisted of the vicar, a curate, and a clerk who was in orders. 'Nearly the whole of their time was occupied in discharging the mere mechanical functions of the clerical office'. Every morning between 8 and 11.30 they were at the parish church for marriages; twice a day they baptised children and churched their mothers; every day there were at least two burials. In 1843 there were well over four

15. Grantchester, Cambridgeshire - already The Old Vicarage when Rupert Brooke came here in 1911. In 1685 it was a 'good, new built Vicaridge House', but another was built about 1853. Brooke's host was a bee-keeper so there was honey for tea. There has been a vicarage since 1380 when the first master of Corpus Christi College, Cambridge, transferred his rectory to the college.

16. Rye, Sussex - the parsonage house similarly became the Old Vicarage in mid-nineteenth century. It was built soon after 1701. The earlier house was in the north-west corner of the churchyard and was demolished. Within the walled town of Rye the streets are narrow and steep, but the church stands in a secluded close at the top of the hill and the steeple was a famous 'seamark'. Henry James stayed here before he was able to move into Lamb House.

17. Threlkeld, Cumbria - the chaplain's house and the church of St Mary immediately behind it are 'at Blencathra's rugged feet', Wordsworth's description of the mountain, in English called Saddleback. The chapelry was in Greystoke parish and has a claim to be the oldest in the diocese of Carlisle; a priest was recorded in 1220. The chaplain first had a house in 1602, and later received several augmentations from Queen Anne's Bounty; a new house was built in 1857. The bell tower and two bells were in an earlier thatched church, replaced in 1776.

18. Eyam, Derbyshire - the Rectory house was rebuilt in 1960, but preserves on the right a small part of the house in which William Mompesson lived at the time of the great plague in 1665-6. The rector told the inhabitants to cut themselves off from the outside world. He recorded 259 plague deaths, his wife among them; his two children had been sent away, and more villagers, had they fled, might have been spared.

thousand entries in the registers. As at Manchester, fees were significant; Hook said they were worth £600. Leeds parish covered 34 square miles; Leeds township consisted of nine 'Divisons' and contained in 1841 rather over half the population of the parish. There were ten more townships in the parish, each maintaining its own poor. All but the small township of Potter Newton had its chapel, eight of seventeenth-century date or earlier.

Before Hook arrived in Leeds eight churches had been built beside the parish church; three were 'Commissioners' churches'. Hook's opinion was that these were large, ugly and 'total failures'. Apart from the unattractiveness of some of the new churches, Hook considered that they suffered from a lack of parochial authority within a defined district as they were chapels of ease to St Peter's. The older township chapels were the same; they had been made 'perpetual curacies' in order to qualify for augmentations from Queen Anne's Bounty but despite their titles the curates did not have 'cure of souls'; a double fee had to be paid for a baptism, while all marriages and burials took place in the parish church. Hook summarised the situation in 1844: twenty churches apart from the parish church, eighteen without cure of souls; thirteen had no parsonage house; three had no free seats for poor families, and in the ten churches in Leeds township less than half the seats were free. The vicar held the patronage of fourteen of the churches, partly because in the mid-eighteenth century the rights of inhabitants of some chapelries to choose their minister had been defeated by a determined vicar.

By 1843, Hook had made up his mind to make all existing churches into parish churches 'and sink from Vicar of Leeds to Incumbent of St Peter's'. Each new vicar would be given the offerings and fees appropriate to his district, which he estimated was worth '£400 out of my £1200, on condition that the Ecclesiastical Commission will purchase the pews of all the churches and make them free ... we can do this if we go to a smaller house, so this Vicarage must be sold'. He attached great importance to making the floor of each church 'free', though there could still be galleries where seats could be rented. This part of the scheme ran into difficulties with the Ecclesiastical Commissioners.

> So convinced am I that unless the church of England can be made in the manufacturing districts the church of the poor, which she certainly is not now, her days are numbered, and that her very existence would be scarcely desirable, that I am willing to make any sacrifice to accomplish my object, even to the resignation of my living.

Apparently he did not find it necessary to leave his vicarage house. An act of parliament was introduced and passed in 1844, five years after the first districts were defined in Manchester but six years before that parish was divided; it made provision for future districts to become parishes once a church and parsonage house were built.

In 1851 Hook reviewed his progress with satisfaction: ten new churches, seventeen new parsonage houses 'thereby securing to as many districts the advantage and blessing of a resident minister', seventeen endowed parishes in the ancient parish of Leeds, sixty clergy and twenty-one schoolrooms, many with schoolmasters' houses. At the same time the Religious Census could not have given him complete satisfaction, although it perhaps demonstrated the difference one man of energy, enthusiasm and charisma could make when compared with the lack of imaginative leadership shown by Manchester's collegiate church. Total attendances at all churches in the municipal borough of Leeds amounted to nearly half the population, but only one third of those were in the Church of England, three per cent more than in Manchester, and Methodism was stronger than Anglicanism.

Hook left Leeds in 1859 for a Chichester prebend and what he hoped would be a quieter life. It is sad but significant for the story of the parish that in retrospect Hook did not think all had been for the best.

> I brought in a Bill (worse luck!) for the division of this parish, but why? The old system, if it could have been sustained, would have been the best. Here was a vicar, de facto the *episcopos*, with his twenty or thirty clergy. The best reform would have been to have consecrated him to perform episcopal acts. Thirty years ago at the great festivals the whole parish met at the parish church. There were two thousand communicants, and twenty clergymen officiating. Old people speak of it as a glorious sight.

He was perhaps also reflecting a little ruefully on the unpopularity of St Saviour's church, which had been a High Church project in Leeds. Staffed by a small, semi-monastic group of clergy, and situated in a difficult part of the town, the church was never very full, and several of the clergy became Roman Catholics. But the Leeds Parish Act had made district churches autonomous, and there was little Hook could do about it.

Stoke on Trent and the 'Five Towns'

> Beneath them ... stretched a maze of roofs, dominated by the gold angel of the Town Hall spire. Bursley, the ancient home of the potter, has an antiquity of a thousand years. It lies towards the north end of an extensive valley, which must have been one of the fairest spots in Alfred's England, but which is now defaced by the activities of a quarter of a million people. Five contiguous towns - Turnhill, Bursley, Hanbridge, Knype, and Longshaw - united by a single winding thoroughfare some eight miles in length, have inundated the valley like a succession of great lakes. Of these five Bursley is the mother, but Hanbridge is the largest ... Nothing could be more prosaic than the huddled, red-brown streets ... On the one side is a wrestling from nature's own bowels of the means to waste her; on the other, an undismayed, enduring fortitude.

The small, rounded hills on either side of the Trent valley had governed the layout of roads and buildings as well as the location of resources of coal, water and clay for the potteries, giving an impression of extensive yet strangely patchy development which Bennett captures at the beginning of *Anna of the Five Towns*. 'Five Towns' can be dismissed as no more than euphony. There were then six: Tunstall is the most northerly, followed by Burslem, Hanley, Stoke, Fenton and Longton. Bennett called them Turnhill, Bursley, Hanbridge, which as Bennett said was the largest of the five towns, Longshaw, and Knype for Stoke, derived from Knypersley at the head of the River Trent. He omitted Fenton. A modern biographer has suggested, implausibly, that he 'stuck so close to the original that he forgot which was which'.[14] Bennett had lived in Burslem and in Hanley until he was twenty-one. He later said that he omitted Fenton intentionally. 'It is to be remembered that Fenton had not then the same status as it has now'. Hanley, Longton, Stoke and Burslem had all become municipal boroughs with town councils, a proper recognition of a nineteenth-century town. Burslem's second town hall, with the golden angel on top, was built in 1854 but neither Fenton nor Tunstall became boroughs. Perhaps to soothe Fenton's offended pride, he suggested that he liked the sound of 'Five Towns' better than 'Six Towns' or even 'Four Towns'. 'Stoke' was the name of the parish to which four of the 'five' belonged, and became the name of the whole conurbation, illustrating how a parish gave identity to a group of places.

Stoke on Trent, Staffordshire - the parish church of St Peter Ad Vincula (St Peter in chains, one of nine known dedications in the country) was rebuilt in 1830 and the churchyard enlarged. At the end of the nineteenth century, some stonework from the old church was rescued and placed on the old foundations; Josiah Wedgwood is commemorated close to this arch. The Norman font was later restored to the church from the Rector's garden. Now main roads separate the church from its parishioners, but with its spacious green site, a variety of uses are being sought.

The parish of Stoke had an unusually complicated history. Stoke itself was not a township, in the way that Manchester and Leeds were; the church was in Penkhull township, and Penkhull village, about a mile from the church, was the nearest centre of population for many centuries. In the late eighteenth century

> there were five or six houses only, near the Church, which constituted what was then properly the Village of Stoke, including the Hall, or Rectory House, and the Curate's House, now recently taken down for improving the Church yard.[15]

'Stoke' is a very common place-name; the *English Place-Names Dictionary* has more than two columns of examples from all parts of the country. The Anglo-Saxon word indicated an administrative centre and Stoke parish, which included land on both sides of the upper part of the River Trent, had possibly been organised just before 1086, as a church was recorded in Domesday Book. It contained numerous small and scattered settlements, grouped in 1334 into twelve vills, but fifteen tithe districts in 1535. It did not match medieval manors, in fact positively ignored them. Newcastle under Lyme was a manorial centre, an early market borough with the right to send representatives to Westminster, but a chapelry in Stoke parish. Tunstall was the centre of a manor covering parts of Stoke parish, but a chapelry in the neighbouring parish of Wolstanton.

There were six medieval chapels in Stoke parish and from the mid-sixteenth century at least, unlike Leeds, they were parochial. Norton, as its name suggests, was the most northerly and the chapelry's inhabitants, with those of Burslem, Newcastle, and Whitmore chapelries, seem 'to have borne a very long exemption from the repairs of the Mother church'; Bucknall and Bagnall did not. Burslem was the most important. Bennett referred to Bursley as the 'mother' of the five towns, echoing Simeon Shaw in 1829 in the *History of the Staffordshire Potteries*, and the earliest potteries seem to have been there. The chapel was at a little distance from the main settlement until later eighteenth-century development.

Five of the ancient chapels became parish churches in 1807 through the first Stoke Rectory Act; Bagnall remained a curacy attached to Bucknall. For Newcastle under Lyme, parish status emphasised the separation of this ancient borough from the developing 'Potteries'. The rector of Stoke owned the advowson of his rectory and he promoted the act, which was described as 'quite the noblest bit of self-surrender that I have ever come across'.[16] It endowed the new rectories with the tithes of their areas but in fact, the sacrifice was not as great as might appear because the five new advowsons were sold, reputedly for £10,000, which was invested for the benefit of Stoke rectory, leaving its income unimpaired.

John Tomlinson, a former lawyer of Hanley, bought the advowson of Stoke rectory in 1817 and he also leased the tithes from the rector. He set about reviving tithe payments which had been allowed to lapse. Despite protests, his income rose considerably. In 1827 he promoted the second Stoke Rectory Act,

LEFT: *Burslem, Staffordshire - the tower of St John the Baptist church was being restored in 1536, so was already old, and it was preserved when the church was rebuilt in 1717. Burslem was an ancient parochial chapelry in Stoke parish, and the tower was an important symbol of that status. Burslem was described as the mother of the potteries, and bottle ovens close to the church are a reminder that pottery-making seems to have started here; the Wedgwood family business was next to the churchyard.*

which allowed tithes to be sold to the landowners, a form of commutation they were probably now pleased to accept. It also allowed glebeland to be sold, and where it could be developed, as for example for a railway station, this was profitable to the rector. The second act made provision for the enlargement and thorough repair of the ancient moated parsonage house, Stoke Hall. Later in the century, the Rector moved to a more modern house, leaving a farmer to occupy the old parsonage and it was demolished in 1891.[17] The rectory remained a wealthy one because of the size of the parish and of its population. The parliamentary returns of 1835 show it was one of the best in the country; the income was £3000, one of only eight reaching or exceeding this amount. The average income of the five new rectors ranged from £300 for Bucknall to £530 for Burslem; four of the five rectors left their new parishes in charge of a curate, but drew rather more than two thirds of the income for themselves.

A new Stoke church was built about the time of the second Rectory Act. The rector himself contributed £3300, and a parish rate was collected which matched that contribution. Grants were made by the Church Building Commissioners, and Josiah Spode, John Tomlinson and George IV each contributed about £1000. The poorer members of the parish, the 'working classes of Stoke' who did not pay rates, provided the equivalent of another £1000 either in money or by giving their services free. The new church was consecrated in 1830 and the old one demolished. Soon after this there was a 'violent spirit of opposition' to church rates; a 'poll was taken in the several quarters of the parish in January 1834, when the object of laying a rate was defeated by a considerable majority, and at a vestry meeting, held the 29th September, 1837, a rate of one penny in the pound, proposed by the Churchwardens, was negatived by loud acclamation'.[18]

The 1827 act had provided for two more 'District Rectories' to be endowed by amounts of not less than £10,000 each, provided the Church Building Commissioners contributed to the erection of the churches. As a result, St James the Less was built in Longton and consecrated in 1833, and St Mark's in Shelton, consecrated in 1834; St Mark's seated over 2000. Parish districts were defined a few years later (1839 and 1843) and they became rectories. The popular opinion of these new arrangements was critical and the grand style of Longton's new rectory house provoked particular hostility. The 'handsome square building in the Italian style ... agreeably situated in a newly-planted curtilege' was attacked and burnt during a demonstration in 1842 by the Chartists. The Building Commissioners also contributed to building St Paul's, Burslem, and Christ Church, Tunstall.

There were two private chapels in Stoke, in Hanley and Lane End. It was envisaged in the 1827 Stoke Rectory Act that the two chapels could become parish churches. The inhabitants of the chapelry districts were to 'buy' Easter offerings and dues paid to Stoke's rector for £500; this money would be returned as endowments for the new parishes and Stoke rector would have the patronage of the new parish churches. This did not happen until 1866 for St John the Baptist, Lane End, and 1890 for St John the Baptist, Hanley. Both received additional endowments under the third Stoke Rectory Act of 1889, and became rectories. By the end of the century, the ancient parish had been broken up into twenty-six parishes with rectors and in addition numerous Mission Centres were opened in each parish.[19]

The Pottery towns became a parliamentary borough in 1832, which included Tunstall and much of the original Stoke parish but not Newcastle. For a population of 84,000 in 1851, there were eighteen Anglican churches: five built in the 1830s and ten in the 1840s, a ratio of one church to 4700 people, which shows a considerable effort to keep pace with growing numbers. But there were thirty-five Methodist churches. Bennett portrayed Anna as a Methodist Sunday School teacher and Bennett himself had been brought up as a Methodist. Many more Methodists than Anglicans went to church on Census Sunday. Their church attendances together equalled a third of Stoke's people, or nearly half of the adult and able - not as good as Leeds, but better than Manchester.

Liverpool and the town council

In Liverpool, whether 'deliberately or otherwise, the town council subverted the traditional parochial system'.[20] Until 1699, the port and ancient borough of Liverpool was a chapelry of Walton parish; then an act of parliament made the town council patron of a rectory with two rectors, for a parish which was to comprise 'all the said borough town, township, and Liberties of Liverpoole, as the same is butted and bounded by Neer (Meer) Stones, which are constantly repaired every year by the said town and Corporation and as the same hath been usually perambulated'. The parish was centred on the ancient church of St Nicholas on the waterfront, and a second new church, St Peter's, which was consecrated in 1704. The Council paid the rectors good stipends. During the eighteenth century, while the population of the borough and parish grew from about 10,000 in 1700 to 77,000 in 1801, nine more churches were built, eight by the council, each with two perpetual curates. They were paid by the parish Vestry and the council through a mixture of land rents, pew rents, rates and council grants, which was an effective combination of centrally collected funds and congregational contributions. Between 1801 and 1831 the population more than doubled, and nine more churches were built, three by the council, making a total of twenty.

The parish was not divided, and the new churches were technically chapels of ease. Lack of district bounds might not be considered important when the population was always shifting, and popular preachers attracted congregations from far and wide. However, by the early nineteenth century the ideal of the parish system was running strongly, and the bishop of Chester gained powers by act of parliament in 1829 to define districts in Liverpool with the consent of the patron and incumbent. The Corporation and the incumbents agreed but the private patrons did not. Districts were organised, but had to be conventional rather than legal. It is understandable that some patrons did not want their church's congregation effectively limited to people drawn from areas which might be poor and very over-crowded parts of the town. In the 1840s Liverpool was the most densely populated town in the country, with some terrible living conditions described by public health enquiries. The average life expectancy

was a mere seventeen years, lower than anywhere else in the United Kingdom.

In 1835, with perpetual curates and assistant curates, there were thirty-six clergy in Liverpool parish for a population of 165,000. Typically, none of the incumbents had a parsonage house. The two rectors each received £615 and each paid two curates. Under the Municipal Corporations Act that year the borough was enlarged to match the parliamentary borough defined three years previously, and from this time the borough no longer corresponded with Liverpool parish but included parts of surrounding parishes as they were absorbed in the expansion of Liverpool. The changes in boundaries make comparisons difficult.[21] The council built no more churches after 1835, and it had to sell the advowsons; rectors were no longer appointed in accordance with the political opinions of the council. As happened in other boroughs, when elections were held on the wider franchise required by the act, the old Tory monopoly was swept away and the Whigs gained a majority. They were much less inclined to support the Church of England, but in Liverpool, in a compromise with Tory councillors, they agreed that the council should continue to pay generous stipends and to maintain the Corporation churches, an arrangement accepted until 1897. In 1838, it was agreed that there should be one rector not two, evidence of the strength of conventional opinion. Payment of church rates, which had effectively been a council tax, became voluntary in 1854, rather later than in most towns.[22]

There were fifty-nine Anglican churches in the municipal borough of Liverpool in 1851, and a population of 376,000. Total attendances at church were equivalent to forty-five per cent of the population, much higher than at Manchester and only a little lower than at Leeds. Anglicans accounted for a small proportion of the total. It is suggested that the council's actions in building churches meant that Liverpool was less influenced by Methodism than many large northern towns; Methodist and other Dissenting churches were both insignificant. But fifteen per cent were Roman Catholic. Of sixty-six large towns, only Wigan had as high a proportion of the population in Roman Catholic churches on census Sunday. Roman Catholics formed under a quarter of the population in 1831, before the great influx of Irish fleeing from the Famine after 1845. There was a Roman Catholic bishop of Liverpool in 1850, thirty years before the Anglican diocese was defined. In 1881, according to an Anglican census of religious affiliation, a quarter of the population were Roman Catholic, but at that date a minority attended mass. Dissent and Anglicanism were both losing ground in proportion to the growing population. The decision to build a new Anglican cathedral in Liverpool was not made until 1901.

Canon Abraham Hume, for thirty years until his death in 1884 vicar of the poor parish of All Souls, Vauxhall, wrote many articles and pamphlets about the church in Liverpool. His paper, *State and Prospects of the Church in Liverpool*, published for the Church Congress in 1869, was a critical review of the history of the Church of England in the borough. He was convinced that the lack of a conventional parochial framework was crucial. Although there were forty-eight districts in the borough in 1841, neither the census registrars nor the people were aware of them. 'If the people ignore parochial limits, they are keenly alive

Liverpool Cathedral - stands on a hill-top, a statement of the presence of the Church of England amongst Liverpool's great civic buildings, warehouses and offices, where separate parishes struggle for identity. Inside, too, it is awesome. In 1901 the decision was taken to build a new cathedral, and it was finished in 1978. From chapelry to cathedral city is a dramatic transformation.

to changes in weather, or the state of the streets', and they chose the church they would attend accordingly. Many incumbents confessed to having 'only the vaguest notion of their district'. Canon Hume said that 'The most extraordinary guesses at the numbers in various Districts had been made for years, 10,000 being currently named almost as a matter of course'. In 1861 there were seventy-four districts; only four Peel districts were legal parishes with vicars; the perpetual curates of other churches in the old parish of Liverpool could only perform marriages by special permission of the bishop, not by right. The legal structure of the parish hindered the triumph of the parochial ideal in Liverpool.

Like other reforming thinkers, Hume considered that pew rents were one of the ways in which the church failed the people. At the beginning of the century hardly any poor could have a free seat: 'Thus our fathers sowed the wind, and we are left to reap the whirlwind'. The Religious Census disclosed that one third of the seats in the Anglican churches in the borough were free. Hume suggested that two thirds of the population could not afford to pay for their seats in church. As people moved away, their pew rents were not paid, but the pews could not be freed. The Corporation churches, as they were the oldest in Liverpool, were particularly affected by the sifting of poor people into previously fashionable neighbourhoods and the consequent removal of the fashionable to new suburbs. Hume showed how Dissenting chapels moved out and deserted the poor but the Church of England stayed tied to its church sites; even so, it 'was not free from the charge of clinging to the skirts of the rich', and building more churches in fashionable areas than in poor areas.

Like Hook, Hume criticised the nature of the church building in Liverpool. 'We had relied too much upon mere bricks and mortar'. He thought that the churches were too large, 'mere preaching houses' built on the assumption that, like a theatre, a large church 'will hold more money'. Christ Church, built in 1797 and consecrated in 1800, was 'literally an ecclesiastical theatre, with pit, boxes, and gallery' and seated 2800. If churches had been designed to seat about 800, he thought they would have been better attended. They were also built too expensively; 'in other places as well as Liverpool, thousands which ought to be expended in endowment are wasted upon the fabric'. Some churches were demolished after only a few years to give place to railway lines: he quoted three examples. Others were left nearly deserted by rapid commercial development. He foresaw that the movement would continue: 'Immense stacks of office buildings will radiate further and further from the centre; and private residences of all classes will retire steadily before them'.

By the time of the Church Congress in 1869, Liverpool displayed in sharp focus the problems faced by the Church of England in the rapidly growing urban centres. The moral could be drawn here that lack of parish boundaries left ministers without clear responsibilities and people without strong local church affiliations. Small urban parishes, manageable in terms of population, seemed to duplicate rural experience, and were a natural response to urban expansion. One church to 1000 inhabitants was the ideal; in London Bishop

Blomfield in 1836 took 3000 as a possible target, and the Ecclesiastical Commissioners aimed at 4000.[23] The Bishop of Manchester's Special Commission in 1914 still recommended a target of one clergyman for every 3000 people, with no parish greater than 10,000 as a general rule; it also suggested the modest aim of church accommodation for one tenth of the population, and proposed including Protestant Dissenting churches in the calculation.

Whether the parochial pattern was the appropriate response to the urban situation is not so certain. Boundaries were difficult to draw through densely populated streets, and urban parishes did not have the cement of other local administrative functions to help to create a community, as had been the case in the countryside for many centuries. More seriously, urban parishes were not self-supporting. Even as the Ecclesiastical Commissioners were stepping up the pace of parish formation, contrary viewpoints were being argued. An 'anti-parochial' viewpoint was quite often expressed at Church Congresses, at which lay people as well as clerics were present.

The problems of new urban parishes might have been anticipated from the experience of York, where the city's parishes were ancient and small, but only a quarter of church attendances in 1851 were in the Church of England. Canon Robert Fausset, rector of St Cuthbert's, in 1865 recommended an anti-parochial approach, because the problems of parishes like his were too great to be solved without help from outside and the rector of All Saints, Pavement, told the archbishop in 1868 that it was 'the excessive number of Parishes which fritters away the parochial principle'; the better-off would not go to churches situated in poor areas and the Minster attracted churchgoers. The architect Gilbert Scott the younger explained to the Church Congress in Leeds in 1872

> I cannot but think ... although it is almost heresy to say so in Leeds, that the sub-division of parishes has been carried a great deal too far. We have pushed the parochial system to an extreme. Everywhere one sees little churches, little parsonages, little schools, where, to meet the real wants of the day, everything should be large.

He went on to suggest that large churches gave space for all social classes, and could be 'serviced by a numerous clergy'.[24] Experience of the Building Commissioners' churches earlier in the century seems to suggest the opposite conclusion.

The urban problem for the Church of England was not easily solved, and still is not. Money was poured into church building; but because of the parochial ideal money which might have been used for the urban ministry was spent on churches, parsonage houses and stipends in tiny rural parishes. The Church of England's ability to draw all the country into an appreciation of its position was limited by its organisation in dioceses and parishes, and only the centralisation of the twentieth century has brought a national strategy closer. Eventually, the need has become not only to share burdens across a group of parishes, but across regions of the country.

CHAPTER TWELVE

NEW PATTERNS OR OLD FOR THE FUTURE?

LEFT: *Thaxted, Essex*

'This little town is seated very pleasantly on a Hill, by the River Chelmer'.[1] Thaxted church is at the highest point, and tower and spire are the backdrop for the market and early fifteenth century Guildhall. Thaxted in the late twentieth century is a little town still, and a good example of a successful parish. The town is small enough to have a sense of community, of clear bounds, of identity, while it is just large enough, about 2500 people, to provide a congregation, though the upkeep of this very large church is a considerable financial burden.

Before the Norman Conquest, Thaxted church became the property of the collegiate church of Clare, which later made provision for a vicar for the parish; the impressive fourteenth-century church was a demonstration of the standing of the de Clares, patrons of Clare college and lords of Thaxted manor, who were amongst the wealthiest and most powerful families in the land. There were about 500 medieval inhabitants of the town, and they contributed to the building. Now the church is light and airy, with whitewashed walls, no heavy pews or woodwork and many clear windows, but the stained glass was destroyed by the Puritans in mid-seventeenth century, and some decades later the church was filled with box pews, which were removed in 1877 and replaced with chairs. Thaxted has been served by some remarkable parish priests. John Ball, one of the leaders of the peasants' revolt in 1381, may have been vicar here, and Thaxted men marched with the rebels. In the early twentieth century Conrad Noel was vicar (1910-1942), a distant descendant of the de Clares; he dressed in medieval priest's costume, and with Gustav Holst, who lived in the town, created a notable musical tradition. Noel was a Christian Socialist, and owed his benefice to a wealthy patron who had been converted to socialist principles.[2]

Thaxted church receives many visitors. The countryside can be destroyed by too many feet, the church could thrive on them. It is estimated that thirty million people visit the country's historic churches each year; two million visit

Canterbury cathedral.[3] What are people looking for when they visit a church? It is partly contact with the ancient, with what is rooted in an age of apparently greater certainties and simplicities. Visitors are looking for an experience beyond their normal frame of reference. Some are looking for silence and peace in a building where many generations have prayed. Churches witness to the faith of Christians. They are also powerful signs that the Church of England throughout the country is available to all. But congregations, whether urban or rural, are too small to maintain their buildings, yet are reluctant to sacrifice them. There are difficult decisions to be made about which to keep, which to support.

The possibility of government aid to maintain church buildings was mooted in 1964, but the conditions for grants were too stringent, leaving the Church with no freedom to alter interiors. *Developing the partnership between Church and State over the ecclesiastical heritage* (1996) continued consideration of this possibility; the report suggested that 'Only the government can convert the nation's love of church buildings into material support'. Nearly 13,000

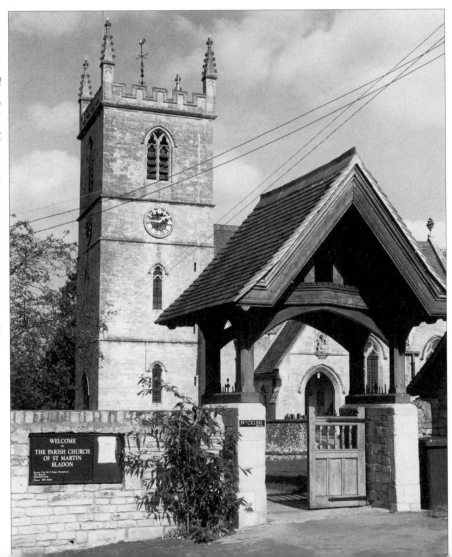

Bladon, Oxfordshire - St Martin's church welcomes modern pilgrims who have come since 1965 in search of Winston Churchill. The family connection dates from 1705 when Queen Anne gave Woodstock Park to John Churchill, Duke of Marlborough, for Blenheim Palace; it was not in a parish, but Bladon was the nearest parish church. St Martin's is on rising ground above the confluence of the rivers Evenlode and Glyme; it was rebuilt in 1804 and remodelled in 1891 and a rector gave the lych gate in 1893.

churches were listed as being of architectural or historical interest, nine-tenths of the inheritance received at the beginning of the century, and the annual repair bill was £100 million. Archbishop Carey has said that public funding was essential 'if they are to continue to speak strongly of spiritual values to the nation in the next millennium'. Yet maintenance without use is hardly justifiable, and is particularly difficult to justify if the church is usually locked.

A survey of the fifty-two churches in the largely rural deanery of Ripon in Yorkshire, including Holy Trinity, Ripon but not the cathedral, showed eighteen churches were only open when in use for a service. Four churches were cared for by The Churches Conservation Trust and one by the National Trust; the remaining forty-seven churches were staffed by fifteen incumbents and two assistants. This is not untypical. In Manchester diocese, 'Step Inside' - an open church weekend in September 1997 - celebrated 150 years of the diocese by encouraging every church to be open; during the weekend the four bishops and three archdeacons visited each parish which asked them to. Exhibitions, demonstrations, activities and a welcoming steward provided an exciting meeting between parishioners' outside lives and interests and the church. But only one third of the 310 churches in the diocese took part.[4]

Flexibility and variety are the keys to the future of church buildings. The transformation imaginatively wrought at Charlbury in Oxfordshire between 1990 and 1995 shows how a church can be made light, airy, warm and welcoming. Taking advantage of the unusually wide arches of the aisles at the west end of the church, the normal focus has been reversed, and light oak chairs are arranged in a semicircle across the whole width to face a sanctuary under the tower. Apart from a stained glass window in the west wall of the tower, this end of the church is naturally well-lit with clear windows. Essential structural work gave the opportunity, and two-thirds of the cost of £385,000 was given by parishioners of this small town. The simple but helpful church guide ends: 'Thank you for coming. We hope you have enjoyed your visit. May God bless you as you go'.

THE AGE OF BUREAUCRACY

An observer of the Church of England at the end of the twentieth century must be astonished at the evident central bureaucracy, and yet the Church has no real central authority. The established Church of England resulted from the Acts of Supremacy and Uniformity agreed by Elizabeth I, together with subsequent Acts, Injunctions, Articles and Canons, all having royal agreement; it was unified through doctrine and allegiance to the Crown. The two archbishops and the bishops are circumscribed by the constitutional position in which the Crown is the 'Supreme Governor' of the Church, by whom, if nominally, they are appointed. Convocation, the clerical assembly, met when summoned by the Crown, and canons or Church laws which were drafted and approved by Convocation were not legal without royal assent; the same is still true for canons drafted by the General Synod. Convocation was originally called to agree how much tax would be paid by the clergy, not to discuss theology, so that when clergy were included with other citizens in parliamentary grants of taxation, its meeting became unnecessary. It was discontinued after 1717 because there was a danger that it might express views hostile to the Protestant monarchy: the Roman Catholic James II was forced to leave the country in 1688, and the Protestant William and Mary were offered the throne by parliament, but some clergy continued to support the displaced Stuart kings. So this one mechanism for consultation between clergy was lost. The Governors of Queen Anne's Bounty became the only coordinating body for the church. Although there were several hundred lay governors of the Bounty, the bishops naturally came to dominate, and met each other in its London offices.[5] As parliament established control of policy, the Crown's powers have passed to the Prime Minister, leaving the monarch as titular Supreme Governor. Parliament in turn has delegated powers to Synod, but retains ultimate authority.

A muddled situation of several parallel authorities answerable to parliament appears to have been stumbled into without plan or even intention. The first important step was made in 1836 when the Ecclesiastical Commission was set up. During the nineteenth century, the Commission gradually took on a wide range of administrative and financial work particularly relevant to the parochial system. Its limitations as a central financial body were sharply exposed in a report by the Archbishops' Committee on Church Finance in 1911, a criticism precisely repeated in the report published in 1995 by the Archbishop's Special Commission on the Church's Organisation. The 1911 committee commented that there was no 'organised system', which the committee recognised was 'a deep-seated defect in the history of the church in this island'. An introduction to a reprint of the report in 1918 said more baldly that the church had been near financial bankruptcy at the beginning of the century, and that 'strangling restictions of political convention, of an outworn system of finance, and of administrative anomalies dating back to an almost forgotten epoch ... were choking its life in the nineteenth century'. Each parish was 'a self-sufficient entity, possessing its own endowments and managing its own affairs', leading to an 'exaggerated parochialism which could not see beyond the needs and rights of the parish, and was wholly incapable of dealing with changed conditions'. There were no funds for training to help entrants to the ministry, and the clergy were not paid 'a living wage'. People had the idea that with 'an established and endowed church everything must be provided for them'. This viewpoint is still prevalent at the very end of the twentieth century.

The 1911 Report recommended that the Diocese should be the essential unit of church life, and that Diocesan Boards should be set up to deal with Finance, Maintenance and Church Buildings. These were established before 1914, together with a Central Board of Finance; this had limited resources but cooperated with the Ecclesiastical Commission, which still controlled the only large central fund of money. Also recommended in 1911 was the general adoption of schemes of voluntary offerings on a regular basis on the pattern of the 'Envelope' scheme, and a parochial quota for diocesan expenses, first introduced in Manchester in 1912.[6] Voluntary offerings were significant - £5.5million in 1909-10; by 1994 the dioceses were contributing £13.2 million

to the Church's Central Board of Finance, in addition to the monies used in their own administrations.

A second parallel strand of government was introduced in 1919 by the Church of England Assembly (Powers) Act. Known as the Enabling Act, it may have done more to 'marginalise' the church than any other single measure. It removed debate from parliament, transferring it to a church assembly which was elected by a select group of churchmen.[7] Preliminary moves towards an assembly had been made before the First World War. Clerical Convocations, one for Canterbury Province and one for York, had been revived in the mid-nineteenth century, with Houses of Laity added to them about thirty years later, in 1886, when Parochial Church Councils also began to be set up; in 1904 the two Convocations were combined to form a Representative Church Council. After the war, there was a strong desire to strengthen lay participation in the government of the Church, especially by working men following the vivid and tragic experiences of all in the fighting services, but it failed; amongst other reasons, working men could not afford the requisite three weeks without wages to attend meetings.

In parliament, different political considerations were important. Until 1918, most members were concerned with the maintenance of the Church of England; they were largely gentlemen of property and there were some vivid parliamentary battles on religious issues. Such issues included the possible use by the Roman Catholic church of titles identical to those in the Church of England (1851); the abolition of Church Rates and reform of the Anglican Church in Ireland, both first put forward in the 1830s but not passed by parliament until 1868; and the two major Education Acts of 1870 and 1902. The number of adult men who could vote in parliamentary elections was enlarged in 1867 and 1884, though one third were still not qualified to vote; from this time the concerns of the Church often failed to gain parliamentary time.[8] Further extensions to the franchise were held up by the First World War; universal adult male suffrage and limited female suffrage were introduced in 1918, and inevitably made a big difference to the attitudes and interests of members of parliament. Social and economic issues were central; the Church's debates were sidelined to a Church Assembly.

The Church Assembly started to meet in 1920. Its structure was drawn up by the two Provincial Convocations. It consisted of a House of Laity and an Upper and a Lower House of Convocation representing both Provincial Convocations. The Assembly could debate and make changes in the practical running of the Church, but questions of doctrine and worship were the responsibility of Convocation. The House of Laity rested on a very small foundation of Parochial Church Councils, also given statutory backing in 1919. The PCCs were elected by those committed enough to be on church electoral rolls. 'At no time since 1930 have the electoral rolls included more than forty-one per cent of the confirmed or sixteen per cent of the baptised members of the Church', according to the Church and State report of 1970; in 1968 they equalled about a quarter of those confirmed or a tenth of those baptised, yet about two thirds of the population claimed an allegiance to the Church of England. By 1995, the numbers on the church's electoral rolls had fallen to 1.5 million, but the 'Anglican penumbra - the distinguishing feature of the Church of England in this country', still included two thirds of the population. The members of the PCCs chose the delegates to ruri-decanal and diocesan conferences, who elected members to the House of Laity, an exclusive electorate which numbered some 17,832 people in the whole country in 1955, spread over forty-three dioceses, of which only a little over half bothered to vote.[9]

The Church Assembly was not given real authority, which remained with parliament. This was seen when the Assembly tried to introduce a new Prayer Book and was defeated in parliament in 1927 and again in 1928. Measures passed by the Church Assembly that were regarded as substantive had to be submitted by its Legislative Committee to the Ecclesiastical Committee of both Houses of Parliament, which reported on the measure at the same time as laying it before Parliament. If approved, it had the force of a statute. In presenting measures to parliament, the Church Assembly was equivalent to a government minister, or perhaps to a private member of parliament submitting a bill. The Church of England has commissioned no less than ten reports in the twentieth century on its relationship with the state, but short of disestablishment there is no way round the authority of parliament.

In 1969, the Church Assembly voted to alter its constitution, without changing its relation to parliament. The new General Synod combines meetings of members of the three Houses: Bishops, Clergy and Laity, and is a smaller body of 543 members instead of the Assembly's 746. The House of Laity has a slightly larger share in the church's deliberations as a result, but the two Provincial Convocations retain their ultimate control over doctrine and worship, and the three Houses of General Synod can meet separately if they wish. The members of the House of Clergy are elected in the two Convocations, and of the House of Laity in the Deanery Synods. Deanery and diocesan conferences are recast as synods, and every parish sends one or more representatives to a Deanery Synod. General Synod's base in the Parochial Church Councils, elected by those on the church electoral rolls, is unchanged; 'Only a dramatic increase in the number of those signing the rolls can give the Synod an electorate comparable with the wider membership of the Church'. Communication does not easily reach the ordinary parishioner.

One unforeseen result of the establishment of the Church Assembly was to foster a centralised bureaucracy. Until the early twentieth century, the offices of the Ecclesiastical Commission and of Queen Anne's Bounty were small and the parson remained largely independent. After 1921, the Church Assembly introduced measures and rules dealing with all parishes, notably on the care of parsonage houses and on pensions. The Church Assembly, and since 1970 General Synod, meets for such a short period each year, that numerous boards, standing committees and permanent commissions have been set up to provide continuous leadership. The only way a new measure or procedure can be prepared is for Synod, or an archbishop, to set up a special commission; hence the enormous number of reports that have been published in the twentieth century. Central offices at Church House have been enlarged in step with the proliferation of committees. In addition, there were thirty-one dioceses in 1921 and now there are forty-three, each with its own ration of synods, boards and committees echoing the central machinery.

Thirty-seven pages of the Year Book in 1994 were taken up with the names of members and secretaries, and with the constitutions of the Church's central committees, boards and commissions, each with its own structure of committees and sub-committees. The Church Commissioners divided their work between five main committees, the Central Board of Finance had seven and the Pensions Board had three. The important Standing Committee of Synod had four sub-committees; there were two other 'principal' committees and five advisory boards, ten permanent commissions and four other committees. The Synod's boards had between them set up thirty-three committees, groups, departments and 'reference panels'. In addition there were some other Funds and committees, and a Corporation of Church House. Some of the work of all these bodies related to the Church of England's continuing interest in 4900 schools, fourteen theological colleges and ten colleges of higher education. Some related to the Church of England's perceived role in national affairs through the Board of Social Responsibility, which had committees for Industrial and Economic Affairs, International and Development Affairs, Social Policy, Race and Community Relations, and 'reference panels' for legal and criminal justice, environmental issues and medical issues. Some work related to hopes for ecumenical collaboration, though it should be noted that reunion with the Methodist Church in 1972 failed to achieve the agreement of three-quarters of General Synod which had been set as requisite, and a decade later the proposal for a covenant to form the basis of union of Christian churches also failed to reach the required two thirds majority.[10] Surrounded by all these large concerns, the committees for the selection, training and support of clergymen appear relatively unimportant. The whole organisation cost £26 million in 1994, equivalent to the stipends of 1733 clergymen, or the total costs, including houses and pensions, of over a thousand. Perhaps the attempt to control parochial work from the centre is mistaken since it seeks to regulate what is essentially personal, the individual clergyman's way to carry out his ministry, which is the practical presence of the Church for most of the country.

The financial implications of clerical pensions provided the shock in the 1990s which has led to fresh discussion of the divided leadership of the Church of England. A pension scheme which depended on contributions had been started by the Ecclesiastical Commission in 1907; poor clergy were given help. After 1919, the Commission provided finance for schemes drafted by the new Church Assembly. In 1926 a comprehensive scheme was introduced requiring a three per cent contribution, and a Clergy Pensions Board instituted, but money still came from the Commission, and similarly for a non-contributory pension scheme introduced in 1954, which was actuarially unsound. It was overtaken both by demographic change - the lengthening lifetimes of clergy and the increasing numbers of pensioners - and by the rising level of pensions related to stipends. Retirement at seventy became compulsory in 1975, but did not apply to those reaching that age and holding the same benefice as when the

Amersham, Buckinghamshire - unusually for a new parsonage house, an engraved tablet records that the foundation stone was laid by the Bishop of Buckingham, 16 June 1985; architect, Patrick Ettwein of Basil Spence Partnership. The old rectory, further from the church, was sold some three decades earlier, and had been the house for a very wealthy living.

Heacham, Norfolk - A modern and attractive Vicarage House, purpose-built in 1985, has been placed in a small development close to the church, and fits closely with vernacular styles. Heacham is a growing sea-side town, and the centre of a deanery; the patronage has passed from the L'Estrange family to the bishop and dean and chapter of Norwich cathedral.

measure was introduced, so that the church still has some long-lived clerics determined not to retire from what was before 1975 a lifelong position. In 1954, only seven per cent of the Church Commissioners' income was spent on pensions; by 1994 it had risen to half and is projected to rise to ninety per cent by 2010. An Archbishop's Committee quickly decided that a special commission was needed to investigate how such lack of foresight could have occurred.

The Archbishop's Special Commission on the Organisation of the Church was set up in 1994 under Bishop Turnbull, and the Report, *Working as One Body*, was published in 1995 and has been accepted and implemented. The report suggested that divided leadership was one of the main reasons for financial mistakes. It was one more attempt to square the circle, or more accurately, perhaps, should be described as trying to bring into a triangular relationship three independent points: the Church Commissioners, the Bishops and General Synod. Parochial organisation was specifically excluded from the remit of the report. The balancing power is placed with the bishops and the House of Bishops will play a more active part. Turnbull suggested that General Synod should be the Church's 'deliberative body', but not its executive or legislative, an example of the principle of the separation of powers. In an effort to compensate for a definite loss of function, General Synod was to be allocated power to approve departmental budgets, but this gives only broad brush control. Turnbull glossed the arrangement as 'the Bishop-in-Synod', a phrase reminiscent of 'the Crown-in-Parliament' but quite different in practical application; the bishops do not have titular positions like the Crown, but executive positions more like cabinet ministers, without being answerable to Synod as ministers are to parliament.

Turnbull proposed a new National Council to control central executive departments. It is not subordinate to General Synod. In a Council of up to seventeen members, two members are elected by the Laity in General Synod and one by the Laity and Clergy together, two by the bishops and two by provincial Convocations, arrangements which keep the constitituent parts of Synod firmly apart. No less than seven members of the National Council were to be the Archbishop of Canterbury's nominees, and he would need the support of only one other member to have a majority. It is a thoroughly 'clerical' solution to the Church's problems. Central failures have led to the suggestion of stronger centralisation. Reform of the Church Commissioners was also considered, but apart from a reduction in their numbers from ninety-five to fifteen, the report suggested that they remain like charity trustees of assets which had been acquired largely through the State's actions. One Estates Commissioner would continue to be a member of parliament. The Commissioners would act as independent investment bankers, making income available annually to the National Council.

'The Church of England does not need a large centralised bureaucracy', the Turnbull report suggested; the 'fundamental responsibility for the maintenance of the ministry rests with the bishop and his diocese', but this has been obscured by the Church Commissioners' work, for instance in sanctioning though not initiating pastoral reorganisation. 'No strategic view can be taken at a national level on matters of diocesan or pastoral reorganisation'. A reduction in General Synod's functions might lead to reduced central bureaucracy, but diocesan administrations will expand, though for many purposes the forty-three dioceses could be grouped into regions, perhaps six or nine. The Church

of England still cannot resolve the inherent conflicts between central organisation and diocesan and parochial autonomy. These conflicts are about the nature of the Church of England. Is the Church's role as 'public conscience' most important, for example through the bishops' comments on political issues and the Synod's Board of Social Responsibility, or should it concentrate on parish ministry? There can only be one anwer: without the contributions of parishioners to the support of the Church, it cannot have a central presence.

FACING REALITIES

'The mission of the Church of England is most clearly and gloriously seen in the parishes', the Turnbull report proclaimed. 'The parish church is the main focus of the spiritual lives of most Anglicans'. The report also commented 'The Church must recognise the realities of how the parochial system can work today. It should not romanticise.'

Apart from the very significant problem of finance, there have been three other aspects of the experience of the Church of England in the twentieth century which prompt talk about a 'crisis'. The first was appreciation of the mismatch between the parish structure and the population. Ironically, the rural parochial structure which provided the ideal was considerably modified in an attempt to reduce the contrast with the urban. Leslie Paul, in a report on *The Deployment and Payment of the Clergy* in 1964, pointed to dramatic disparities: more than a third of clergymen served one tenth of the population of England and Wales in small livings of under 2000 people; at the other extreme, less than

Tunstall, Lancashire - the village school has been very successfully converted into The Vicarage. It is immediately next to the church, but a little distance from the village, which avoids the vicar being too closely identified with one place in an ancient and large parish of several townships, now enlarged with an adjacent parish.

one fifth of clergymen in livings of over and sometimes very much over 10,000 people served more than a third of the population. About half the parishes in the country, with between 2000 and 10,000 people, were served by about half the clergy. Paul commented that 'elements of luck seem to govern the distribution of clergy'; the luck was whether a benefactor had come forward in the past, or whether vested interests had been sufficiently powerful to resist division of an ancient parish. The largest population of any parish in the country was 50,000 in Kirkby St Chad in Liverpool, which seemed to perpetuate the situation on which so much Victorian energy had been expended. If a parish clergyman was to have a personal relationship with a significant proportion of his parishioners, it semed obvious that a transfer of resources should take place from rural to urban parishes.

The Bishop of Sheffield headed a committee which proposed in 1974 that dioceses should gradually bring their numbers of clergy into conformity with a diocesan ratio based on population, numbers of churches, geographical size of area and numbers on the electoral roll. As clergy retired or left, their places were not filled in order to approach closer to the Sheffield Quota. This brought change without a very clear overall plan for the rural parishes, and it is doubtful whether reducing the numbers of rural livings has resulted in an increase in clergy entering urban ones - there are many vacancies, for example, in Manchester diocese - though it may have helped a fairer distribution of financial resources.

A second aspect of the crisis is the considerable fall in the number of clergy and in those coming forward for ordination. In relation to population there are probably half as many clergy in 1994 as there were at the beginning of the century. In 1911, there were nearly 14,500 parishes in England and Wales, approximately 14,000 incumbents and 8000 curates for a population of thirty-three million, a ratio of one clergyman to 1500 people. Wales accounted for two million people and a little under a thousand incumbents and 550 curates. This was a high point for the Church of England; growth in numbers of priests throughout the nineteenth century had kept pace with growing population, if not with its distribution, but decline started soon after. The Welsh church was disestablished in 1920. In 1994 there were 13,000 English parishes and just over 10,000 'diocesan' clergy, with perhaps 2000 or so in positions outside the parochial system, for example chaplains in hospitals, prisons and schools. The population of England in 1991 was 48 million. On the other hand, in 1911 a parish clergyman had his benefice for life, and only retired by employing a curate, and gentlemen clergy paid a curate to do parochial work for them, so that the number of effective parish priests at that date is exaggerated. It might be more appropriate to compare the total of 17,600 active and retired clergy in England in 1994 with 1911; retired clergy often continue to minister at church services if not more widely and this gives a ratio of one clergyman to 2720 people. All religious denominations experienced a similar contraction. It was expected that numbers of Church of England priests would continue to fall. In 1993 the decision was taken to ordain women and the first women priests were ordained in March 1994. Three years later, a survey by the National Association of Diocesan Advisers in Women's Ministry found that 1604 or sixteen per cent of the total of 10,449 stipendiary clergy were women. The dioceses of Oxford (101) and Southwark (91) had most women priests, followed by St Albans (80); only eight dioceses had fifty or more. The ordination of women has prevented a further fall in numbers, and has added some strength to the parish clergy. So too have schemes of shared ministry in Local Ecumenical Partnerships.

There are many possible explanations of the drop in numbers of clergy. Openings have increased for professional careers (though the Church is not strictly a 'career' but a 'calling'). Incomes have declined in comparison with industrial and commercial incomes. Loss of lay patronage also played some part, as lay patrons were gradually persuaded to hand over advowsons to the bishops, so ending the traditions of 'family livings' which had encouraged men to enter the church. Less tangible disincentives to entering the Anglican ministry might be suggested in the loss of important areas of work to the parish parson, and to the loss of confidence in the rural parochial ideal. Reference to the first was made in a 1902 report on *The Position of the Laity in the Church,* which detailed tasks once carried out by the clergy but now secularised: responsibility for education, for example, and for the registration of births, marriages and deaths. The report also mentioned the removal of compulsory support for the church by abolition of church rates in 1868 and the creation of urban and rural district and parish councils (1888 and 1894) - not to be confused with the ecclesiastically sponsored Parochial Church Councils - so taking civil duties away from churchwardens. In effect, legislation was separating the laity from the Church. The word 'marginalised' is used to describe the Church's position; it was vividly demonstrated in the decision of the BBC in 1996 that the archbishop of Canterbury's New Year message should be displaced from its midnight slot in favour of another hour's coverage of Hogmanay, or in the statement that the Presidents of Churches Together in England, the archbishop of Canterbury, the archbishop of Westminster and the leaders of the Free Churches, would be 'welcome guests' at the Millennium celebration at midnight in the Dome.[11]

The decline in church attendance is the third factor in the perceived crisis. The position was already worrying by the beginning of the twentieth century, as attendances were substantially lower than in 1851. *Facts and figures* in 1911, summarising statistics for 1908 diocese by diocese, showed ratios of Easter communicants to population varying from four per cent in Durham, the lowest, to fourteen per cent in Hereford, the highest. Half the dioceses had proportions of under seven per cent, including all the northern dioceses, four in the London area, two in the south-west and surprisingly, Canterbury. For the whole country there were 1.8 million communicants. Bishop Davidson of Winchester suggested in 1899 that the bicycle was seriously affecting Sunday church attendance; it enabled them to travel in a way which had never been possible before. So did pleasure trips by train. The *Liverpool Daily Post* in 1902 carried Bishop Chavasse's reflection that weekend outings were carrying away 'the very men who were once the flower of the Sunday School teachers'; as early as 1825 it was said that 10,000 people from Liverpool crossed the Mersey on

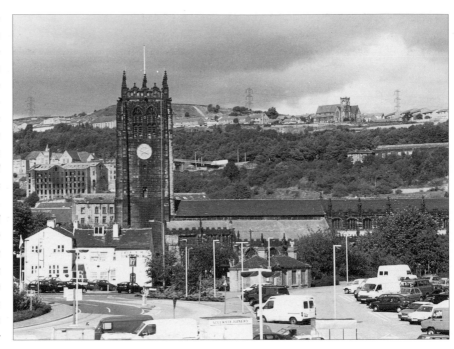

Sundays for a day out in the Wirral.[12] It was particularly an urban problem. Being indoors on Sundays was less objectionable to an agricultural population whose weekday work had been mainly outdoors. For the industrial and commercial workers Sunday was the only day for outdoor activity; most worked at least Saturday morning if not all day. The Sunday outings were also for many their only holidays.

After the First World War the number of communicants increased to 2.4 million in 1930 and stayed close to this level until about 1960, but thereafter declined to 1.6 million people, three per cent of the population; those taking communion at Christmas now equal or exceed Easter communicants. Sunday attendances are generally a little lower. The distribution amongst the dioceses has not altered significantly.[13] Rural Hereford has the highest proportion of communicants and the most parish clergy. The social structure of rural areas may favour church attendance, but it is not accidental that congregations keep up best where there are parish priests able to relate personally to their parishioners. When the one rector of a group of Oxfordshire churches is not taking the service in a particular church, he finds the inhabitants consider that they 'have that Sunday off'.

Churches have faced serious crises before and survived. But more than on any previous occasion, the situation at the end of the twentieth century deserves that description. About one million people were estimated in 1996 to be regular Sunday churchgoers, the same number attended mass and a slightly smaller number were Free Church members. One and a half million were on the churches' electoral rolls. About a quarter of the babies born were baptised in the Church of England.[14] It has become imperative to rethink the parish.

Reforming the Parish by Stealth

Many faithful congregations have been disappointed to find that when their parson left there was to be no replacement. Strategies to cope with the shortfall of priests and the shortage of money for stipends must group parishes together. By 1994, for example, 175 parishes in Manchester diocese had been amalgamated with others, reducing by two-thirds the number of benefices. Townships or chapelries made independent parishes by the Victorians once again share a minister in the late twentieth century. The schemes are bishop-led, in collaboration with archdeacon and rural dean.

There are three principal approaches. The simplest is to unite two or more parishes into one new benefice. The Ecclesiastical Commissioners acquired powers to unite benefices in 1919, but amalgamations gathered pace after the 1968 Pastoral Measure.[15] Shipton under Wychwood in Oxfordshire is a 'united benefice'. It includes Milton under Wychwood with Lyneham, two ancient townships in Shipton parish which in 1895 became a separate parish. It also includes two former chapelries, Fifield and Idbury; they were anciently attached to Swinbrook church because of an arrangment made about 1220 for a prebend at Salisbury cathedral, but in 1750 became perpetual curacies and in 1864 Fifield was annexed to Idbury to form one parish. All four churches remain in use, though there are no marriages in the 'district' church of Fifield, and in 1999 there were 336 on the three electoral rolls. Of the other townships in the ancient parish of Shipton, Leafield and Ramsden became parishes in the mid-nineteenth century, but are now grouped with other churches in the area, and Langley remains with Shipton.

It is suggested that 'the single-handed, multi-charge incumbent is a recipe for long-term disaster'.[16] This might particularly apply where a large number of former parishes are united into one benefice, like Shill Valley and Broadshire in Oxfordshire. It contains twelve churches and eleven very small parishes each with its parochial church council and covers some sixty-four square miles. The total number on the church electoral rolls is 267. The rector lives at Shilton vicarage, an associate priest at Filkins vicarage, and there are two non-stipendiary priests. Eight of these parishes are ancient ones, and three were chapelries: Holwell and Filkins became parishes in 1850 and Little Faringdon in 1864; Kelmscott has always been a chapelry. The Bishop of Dorchester, in his first eight years in office, largely restructured the parochial ministry in the large part of Oxfordshire in his episcopal area by creating united benefices. Much thought has gone into the arrangements, with a conference in January 1993 on 'Rethinking Pastoral Strategy' which led to a paper, 'The Future of Our Past'. It suggested there would not be wholesale abandonment of the countryside by the Church of England, nor a dismantling of the parochial system, but the development of 'major benefices' centred on a ministerial team. In 1997, eighty-six stipendiary clergy and thirty non-stipendiary ministers looked after 197 parishes, including nine 'major benefices', and 229 churches were maintained in use. Despite Oxfordshire having many small rural parishes, very few churches have been closed. Active participation by the laity is stimulated, leading to growing numbers of people training for ordination, often for part-

time non-stipendiary ministry, or 'ordained local ministry', in order that they may take part in a 'collaborative ministry as part of a local ministry team'.[17] With a few exceptions, the 'ministry team' is informally constituted.

Alternative approaches are through 'pastoral schemes' which set up 'groups' and 'teams'. The first informal experiments with groups started in 1947 in South Ormsby in the Lincolnshire Wolds, in an area notable for its many small parishes. At that time twelve small parishes with a combined population of 1100 and an area of seventy-five square miles had six elderly clergymen, but by 1952 there was one rector, two assistants and a deaconess. In 1961 ten parishes in the Breckland of Norfolk formed the Hilborough group. The 1968 Pastoral Measure provided a legal basis for further group and team developments. In 1983, the Church of England had ninety-one groups and 333 teams at work.[18] Groups appear to be more difficult to organise than teams. In the Dorchester episcopal area there were no groups but seven teams in 1998, three centred on the old market towns of Banbury, Bicester, and Thame. Typically they consist of a team rector and two team vicars, with other associated priests and lay workers. Even though the circumstances are so different, there are no groups in Manchester diocese, either. In this densely populated diocese of nearly two million people in 1991, there are 310 churches; sixteen teams are in existence, and another three or four are in process of being organised, some very large.

The differences between groups and teams are practically and legally important and the regulations in the *Code of Recommended Practice* in 1996 illustrate well Leslie Paul's statement that

> It is doubtful if any institution in the land is so bound round with legal complications: they determine just about everything from the words of its (authorized) prayers to the ornaments and memorials on the walls of its churches, from the rights of patrons to the coronation oath of the Queen. Perhaps it is best to say that the Church is (institutionally) primarily a legal body watched over by lawyers.[19]

Each pastoral scheme requires an Order in Council prepared by the Church Commissioners. A group ministry consists of two or more parsons who cooperate but are incumbents and beneficed. 'They have all the rights and authority which that involves'. For example, one member of the group working in a benefice 'other than his or her own' is subject to the direction of that incumbent. Judging from the small number of groups compared with teams, it seems that cooperation between equals is less easy than the more clearly defined hierarchy of a team. In a team ministry, only one priest is beneficed for a period of years, often seven, and given the designation 'Rector'; he is the holder of the property of the former separate parishes. He shares the responsibility of cure of souls with other full-time and stipendiary clergy, called 'team vicars', who are of 'incumbent status', which means they have security of tenure for the agreed period of the pastoral scheme. Non-stipendiary and lay members may also form part of a team, with the bishop's licence though not of incumbent status, and it might also include ecumenical officers. The scheme specifies if members are to have special responsibility for a particular church or

Northleach, Gloucestershire - the former vicarage house and the church of St Peter and St Paul. The house was built in 1863, the church mainly by John Fortey, a woolman of the town who died in 1458. Revd Francis Witts in 1839 found the previous house 'capable of being made comfortable, though not a good house' which 'stands in a cheerful garden and pleasure ground'. The River Leach runs through the garden, in which the new vicarage house has been built.

Canon Philip Brown moved into The Vicarage in January 1982. It is the centre for seven parishes, shortly to become a united benefice. Northleach is a small market town which owed its medieval development to Gloucester abbey, and it is a typical example of the natural and historic focus for the church in a rural area.

area, but relationships 'should be based on parity'. Teams tend to have a life cycle reflecting the initial strengths and talents of those involved. 'Clarity about the task', it is suggested, aids collaboration, but the tightness of regulation could obstruct individual vision, enthusiasm and initiative. In practice, regulations may be more honoured in the breach than the observance. The successful operation of a team ministry depends very much on the Rector at its head.

The parish of Kirkby Lonsdale in Cumbria now consists of the church in the market town and six former chapelries which have been returned to the mother parish after about a hundred years of independent existence; one former chapelry, Killington, in the Lune valley, has been attached to the nearer parish church of Sedbergh. Where there were once seven ministers, in 1996 there were the Rector and Team Vicar, with six part-time assistants: a school chaplain who was an assistant priest in the parish, three non-stipendiary ministers and two readers. Most of the former Vicarage house is renamed The Rectory, but the team vicar lives in part of the house, still The Vicarage, and the oldest part in 1996 housed a retired clergyman. There is one Parochial Church Council for the seven churches but 'District Councils' for each consitituent parish. So here, too, Victorian parish making has been undone. The distance of the former chapels from the mother church encourages each to maintain church services, which can be done with volunteers. 'But the situation is that the ever increasing cost of running the churches means more time trying to raise more money just to stand still'.[20] Reviewing the necessity of this burden seems imperative.

Redundant churches reveal the retreat from the parish; about 2000 churches have gone since 1949. In 1924 a Union of Benefices Measure had made the disposal of redundant churches easier. In 1949, a Church Assembly committee found 412 disused churches; 128 were said to be worthy 'ancient monuments'. By 1956, 120 nineteenth-century churches had been demolished, together with a very small number from different periods. An archbishop's committee under Lord Bridges in 1958 reported that 790 churches were then redundant or likely to become so soon; more than half were considered of historical interest or architectural merit. Between 1969 and 1997, 337 redundant churches have been demolished and 842 were found alternative uses; 317 are cared for by The Churches Conservation Trust formerly the Redundant Churches Fund, which was set up in 1968 with funds from central government as well as from the Church. In the last decade of the century, forty to forty-five churches a year become disused. Against this should be set 470 new churches built in the last twenty-five years. The Methodist church has sold no less than 7000 chapels since 1932, though many were tiny and remote.[21] Arrangements for sharing between two or more denominations has made a small contribution to the 'buildings problem', facilitated by the Sharing of Church Buildings Measure, 1969, by Local Ecumenical Partnerships, and by a new canon in 1989.

'Parish' and 'benefice' have therefore undergone subtle changes of meaning. The words were once largely coincident: the benefice was a 'living' or means of

Kirkby Lonsdale, Cumbria - The Rectory, formerly the vicarage was built about 1783 by a Joseph Sharpe, MA, who had married a local heiress. The top storey was added later to accommodate resident pupils. Vicars were customarily fellows of Trinity College, Cambridge, the patron of the living. The old house is adjoining, and is lived in by an assistant, and the coach house and stable block has been converted for the Team Vicar. As head of a team ministry, Kirkby Lonsdale's incumbent is now styled 'rector'.

maintenance for a lifetime, and allowed for individuality and enterprise in an uniquely independent position; the parish was the area of the clergyman's parochial responsibility. Now 'benefice' describes the area within which cure of souls is exercised by one or more clergy; 'parish' is an area with a separate parochial church council and one or more churches. The Pluralities Acts are still in force, and it is not legal to hold more than one living except within a 'pastoral scheme', but 'livings' in the old sense have almost disappeared since 1972 with the Central Stipends Authority, and the intention of the Victorian legislation to secure a parish priest in every parish is clearly no longer viable.

RETHINKING

The Times reported on 18 October 1994:

> After three months in a caravan touring all 452 parishes across his 2000 square mile diocese, Bishop Stancliffe has decided that the only solution to a serious clergy shortage is to ordain dozens more. He has asked each parish without a vicar to nominate a man or woman to be ordained.

The diocese is Salisbury. The Bishop was consecrated in 1993 and found 600 churches and only 270 full-time paid clergy. His peripatic lifestyle was an echo of the first Christian bishops in England; his response to the current situation was radical, strongly parish-based and clerical.

In Manchester diocese, too, the Bishop made a radical endeavour in 1994. 'The Way Forward' was a valiant campaign to bring parishes closer together with the bishop and his three suffragan bishops. The diocese in 1994 had 309 parishes, 340 clergy and 373 churches. Volunteers, some clergy, some lay, agreed to be 'Bishop's Visitors', and every parish had a discussion with two Visitors on a clear agenda. There was hopefulness pervading the subsequent report, but it was made clear that people in the parishes felt out of touch with the diocesan organisation, a little disquieted about their financial contributions to what seemed an invisible and irrelevant organisation, and desperate about the costs of maintaining their church buildings. People wanted sometimes to see the bishops outside the framework of church services and to talk to them. They were keen and enthusiastic about playing a larger part in the running of their churches. It was concluded that the diocese needed to 'develop a strategy for more appropriate patterns of ministry', and that the laity should 'take a fuller share in decision-making at all levels in the diocese'. This way forward could lead to wider lay participation, but there are deeply-embedded assumptions in the Church of England about clerical and lay roles.

The Church of England's central structures hardly reflect the fact that churchgoers in the parishes in 1994 provided nearly two thirds of the £615 million spent in maintaining the Church.[22] Democracy is only given scope when a church is about to be closed; then fund-raising may demonstrate what can be done. The costs of the church of England's administration are less willingly shouldered. Mr Richard Freeman wrote to *The Times* on 2 May 1995:

19. Stow on the Wold, Gloucestershire - an informal market in the Square, as might have been seen many times on Thursdays, market day in the past. Some buildings have encroached on the Square since the market charter was granted about 1108; they include the row seen in front of St Edward's church tower.

20. Canterbury cathedral - a view of the full range of the south side only temporarily available when a new Marks and Spencer's store was being constructed in the 1970s. The cathedral is a continuing focus for pilgrims and of the Church of England.

21. Ashton under Lyne, Greater Manchester - the parish church of St Michael and All Angels. Manchester, Stockport and Oldham, left; Huddersfield right: the road was driven through the churchyard between 1974 and 1976, a vivid statement of late twentieth-century priorities. Outside it appears nineteenth century, inside a joyously colourful and light remodelling in 1844 of a fifteenth-century building; it is arranged like a meeting house with box pews and galleries and a three-decker pulpit. Can new ways be found of drawing people into the church?

The parish of Brundish is a farming community in mid-Suffolk of about 60 houses and 150 inhabitants. It has an ancient church of simplicity and tranquillity. I have been in charge of its restoration for ten years, during which time much money, time, effort and care has been given by very many people and organisations.

The congregation at our two hour-long services a month, averages about ten people. Our principal expense is a quota payable to the diocesan board of finance. We are expected to contribute £3800 this year through the quota, and next year £5000. This we cannot do.

Elementary arithmetic shows that for each hour our rector spends with us in church we are expected to pay to the diocese £158, and next year £208.

We are told that the Church is suffering a crisis of giving. May I repectfully suggest that the crisis is not a crisis of giving, but one of taking?

The church is inhibited from going to the community as it would for an appeal for restoration of a church building, explaining clearly the enormous financial problem. The supposed misjudgements of the Church Commissioners have even served to disguise the financial position rather than reveal it. Improved communication was recommended in the Turnbull report: each parish should have a clear statement of costs of ministry in that particular parish and of its contributions to it. A similar mismatch between reality and popular perception prevented parliament in the 1840s making national funds available for ministry in the expanding towns.[23]

Without communication, it will become increasingly difficult to hold in balance the financial willingness of some areas with the overall needs of the Church. An active church community perhaps cannot be denied its own parish priest because of the needs of other areas; Bishop Turnbull noted the power of congregations in this respect. How then can the church respond to the urban problem, especially in the 'priority areas' where its support is so small in proportion to the population? In the nineteenth and twentieth centuries, ministry has been financed largely through individual generosity, and in the twentieth century by a tax on churchgoers through diocesan quotas. The 1995 report by the Bishops' Advisory Group on Urban Priority Areas, *Staying in the City*, made a case for government assistance. Does parliament know or care that the national framework of the Church of England's parishes can no longer be maintained?

There is a climate of change and experiment in face of late twentieth-century problems, of which the movements to share buildings or, more far-reaching in its implications, to share ministry, are examples. In parallel with the attempt to re-unite the Methodist Church with the Church of England, and to draft a form of words or covenant for unity, other ways of bringing churches together have continued to be discussed and implemented. The Consultative Committee for Local Ecumenical Projects, since renamed 'Partnerships', was set up in 1971, and increasing numbers of these Partnerships effectively alter the parish structure. The example of Milton Keynes, which has a Christian Council, a new Foundation Training and Community Centre and twenty-four Local Ecumenical Partnerships in its area, shows that through rethinking the church

Dethick and Lea, Derbyshire - the former vicarage is now where the suffragan bishop of Repton lives. The unusual Arts and Crafts style house was designed by a local architect, P.H.Currey, probably about 1901-3, at the same time as the church. Dethick, Holloway and Lea, near Matlock, were constituted a parish in 1899. Lea chapel became disused after the Reformation. Dethick chapel, in Ashover parish, has survived.

in a new town, large-scale cooperative structures can be created. In 1990 Churches Together in England was formed, and an examination of issues which distinguish the thinking of the different churches, *Called to be One*, was published.[24] But the Church of England is peculiarly constrained by state-imposed requirements: an episcopal church, and elements of Catholic and of Calvinist doctrine in the Prayer Book and the Thirty-Nine Articles.

The Church of England need not be, as its title implies, centralised and uniform. Parochial arrangements should be alterable without the permission of Church Commissioners or an Order in Council.[25] Parallels with schools may be helpful. A teacher is comparable with a clergyman in the basic solitariness of the work. A head teacher of a large secondary school manages perhaps a hundred teachers; there are heads of subjects who coordinate, encourage, and lead a smaller number of teachers. The state sets limits on the activities but detailed arrangements are made locally. Bishops could be seen like heads of large schools, each with about a hundred ordained ministers in his diocese; enough bishops and suffragan bishops already exist if all were equal and some ten thousand clergy are equivalent to the staffs of perhaps one hundred large schools. Rural or district deans could be comparable with subject heads in schools, with scope for initiative.

Rethinking the diocese has also been proposed. The dean of Worcester in his Introduction to the 1994 Year Book asked for 'a total re-examination of provinces and dioceses ... the church needs to strip off its trappings of grandeur'. There are forty-three diocesan administrations in England and Wales, but their bishops cannot function effectively as pastoral leaders because the dioceses are too populous and their time is too much occupied with adminstration. Diocesan administration would be more economical if it were handled in a few regions - six or nine were suggested by Turnbull - each with a group of bishops. Probably most of General Synod's functions, too, could be dispersed amongst regions. It has proved easier to reform cathedrals than the whole diocesan and parish framework, as the Royal Commission found in 1835. Rethinking the constitution of the cathedrals offers an opportunity for experiment with democracy: each could be the responsibility of the whole diocese, managed by the people who finance and use it. The cathedral centre would become more purposeful.

A powerful case for a fundamental partnership between clergy and laity, or 'shared ministry', was made by Canon John Tiller in his report *A Strategy for the Church's Ministry*, published in 1983. It openly recognised the increasing difficulty of placing a parson in every parish, which was radical because 'At the moment, it is directly against agreed policy to suggest abandoning the attempt to staff the parishes with stipendiary clergy'. Tiller proposed that those who were full-time paid priests should be used as 'consultants', helping Christians to accept responsibility for their community's church. Clergy should also do more in other contexts, particularly workplaces - working people are missing from the parish on weekdays, while Sunday is taken up with formal services which could be taken by 'a local ordained ministry'. He did not suggest the abolition of the parish but instead 'The parish must have freedom to make its own plans within the fellowship of the diocese and the national Church through which it finds much of its identity'. Lay ministry, he suggested, is not a poor substitute for clerical but essentially is the church and its vitality. The implications were that a considerable shift in clerical attitudes was needed and in the clergyman's training and preparation for the priesthood.

Anthony Russell has concluded that lay involvement usually follows from clerical leadership.[26] It can also arise spontaneously. A letter to *The Times* on 17 April 1996 from Rusland, near Ulverston, reported how 'untrained' parishioners of the parish of St Paul's take their own family services once a month. 'We aim to ensure that the children of this tiny parish enjoy the service and that it contains some Christian message usually more to do with conduct than with catechism'. The children ring the bell and take the collection. 'We will attract children only if we involve them in our worship'. A retired canon takes a monthly communion service. Self-help in Cumbria seems to be as alive as it was in earlier centuries; here is a model for Brundish in Suffolk. There are remarkable experiments with 'congregationalism', for example by Revd Roy Barker in the Lancashire parish of Upton in the Wirral, between 1962 and 1979. He introduced house groups and lay ministers, amongst a host of initiatives which revivified this church.[27] Ecumenical projects also encourage lay activites. But from a clericalist standpoint these initiatives can be categorised as 'make do and mend'. For this reason an ecclesiastical historian has seen the various forms of part-time ministry as unconstructive; non-stipendiary ministers have allowed the bishops to close their minds to the 'general priesthood'.[28]

There are three modern interpretations of 'parish'. Firstly, parishes are the framework for fulfilling the established Church's obligation to offer baptism, marriage and burial services to every person resident in each parochial area. This right could be fulfilled in larger units, say a deanery or a diocese, or even quite simply by abolishing the residence qualification and making these services in any church the right of every English citizen. A second interpretation is that the people attending a church are its parish. Turnbull noted that 'Particularly in suburban areas some parishes have attracted large congregations from a wide area and it is probable that significant numbers of worshippers in many parish churches no longer live within that parish's boundaries. Just as people travel to work or to reach other facilities, so some travel to other churches'. These are termed 'associational' or 'eclectic' churches. But in the countryside there is strong attachment to often ancient boundaries and a strong sense of belonging to a particular 'community' church. People are reluctant to go, even occasionally, to another church within a united benefice. As Russell noted, the local community church has deep roots.

A third interpretation relates parish to a wider community than those who go to services, the community which accepts the burden of physical care for a church building. Churches once served as community centre, schoolroom and meeting place. The Puritan campaign against 'church ales', the Oxford movement's removal of non-religious activity from the church, and the secular assumption of responsibility for education have left churches 'high and dry'. Responsibility for the buildings could be returned to the community, for example to parish councils (not parochial church councils). In the past the church adopted civil boundaries; modern civil parishes are adjusted to population and have a stronger territorial rationale than many ancient parishes. Bringing church parishes into line with civil parishes would help to strengthen both; people are confused by the existence of a parochial church council and a parish council. Further, parish councils are elected through electoral rolls which contain all enfranchised adults. The loyalty and enthusiasm for a locality could be harnessed further.

When so many inside the Church of England's organisation are thinking about the ministry, and there is so much conscientious endeavour, are there any useful insights gained from an historical enquiry? The most important may be that it does not provide a simple stereotype of an ideal by which the present can be judged a failure. One parish: one parson was never universal, nor was churchgoing, though the 'village myth' has been and remains powerful. Nor should history be used to justify present problems. More hopefully, the history of the parish shows the variety, experiment and change there has been within and between communities and townships. Many possible ways forward can be inspired by the past. What is needed is flexibility, scope for initiative, and a 'strategy of vision'. The inevitable fear is that change will lead to total dissolution, while no change represents hanging on to a system with much natural power of survival, like a medieval church roof even while it is almost imperceptibly crumbling away.

NOTES AND BIBLIOGRAPHY

Introduction

[1]J.P.Cooper 'The social distribution of land and men in England, 1436-1700' in *Essays in Quantitative Economic History* ed. R.Floud (1974), 121.

[2]*PP 1835* (22).

[3]P.Hughes, *The Reformation* (1963), 32-34.

[4]W.E.Tate, *The Parish Chest* (1969), 28.

[5]C.Taylor, *Village and Farmstead* (1983), 44, 62, 104-5; P.O'Hare, 'Yorkshire boundaries and their development' in M.H.Long & M.F.Pickles eds., *Yorkshire Boundaries* (Yorkshire Archaeological Society, 1993), 17; D.J.H.Michelmore, 'The reconstruction of the early tenurial and territorial divisons of the landscape of northern England', *Landscape History*, 1 (1979), 3-4; M.L.Faull & S.A.Moorhouse, *West Yorkshire: an archaeological survey to AD1500* (1981), 18-20, 138, 215, 235, 272; D.Hall, 'The open fields of Northamptonshire', Northampton Record Society, 38 (1995), 107-113.

[6]A.J.L.Winchester, *Landscape & Society* (1987), 29.

[7]R.Lennard, *Rural England 1086-1135* (1959), 269-70; J.Campbell, 'Some agents and agencies of the late Anglo-Saxon state' and Glanville R.J.Jones 'The portrayal of land settlement in Domesday Book' in *Domesday Studies* ed. J.C.Holt (1987), 184-5, 206; H.Cam, 'The community of the vill' in *Medieval Studies* presented to Rose Graham eds. V.Ruffer & A.J.Taylor (1950), 1-3; A.J.L.Winchester, 'The medieval vill in the western Lake District: some problems of definition', CW2, 78 (1978).

1 Foundations of the Parish

Bishops and kingdoms

[1]P.Wormald, 'Bede, *Bretwaldas* and the origins of the *Gens Anglorum*' in ed. *Ideal and Reality in Frankish and Anglo-Saxon Society* (1983), 124-9; relevant references to Bede: Book 1, c26, c27, c.29, c33; Book 2, c1, 3; Book 3, c7; Book 4, c.27.

[2]N.Brooks, 'The creation and early structure of the kingdom of Kent' in *The origins of Anglo-Saxon kingdoms* ed. S.Bassett (1989), 57-8, 68.

[3]Early bishoprics: J.Campbell ed., *The Anglo-Saxons* (1982), chapters 3 & 4; J.Blair & R.Sharpe eds., and H Pryce, 'Pastoral care in early medieval Wales' in *Pastoral care before the Parish* (1992), 5, 47.

[4]N.J.Higham, The Convert Kings (1997); Wormald, 'Bede, Bretwaldas...', 111-12; J.Blair, *Anglo-Saxon*

Oxfordshire (Stroud, 1994), 45.

[5]H.M.Jewell, *The North-South Divide* (1994), 11, 15, 22, 32.

[6]P.H.Sawyer, *Anglo-Saxon Lincolnshire* (Lincoln, 1998), 61, 235-38.

[7]Campbell, *Anglo-Saxons*, 152, 172; M.Gelling, *The West Midlands in the early Middle Ages* (1992), 127-28, 130, 139-41, 156.

[8]Jewell, *The North-South Divide*, 156-57; Sawyer *Anglo-Saxon Lincolnshire*, 151-52.

[9]Eleventh century dioceses, archdeacons and deans: F.Barlow, *The English Church 1000-1066* (1979), 162-67, 208-31, 247-8, 302; F.Barlow, *The English Church 1066-1154* (1979), 48-50.

Arrangement or chance?

[10]Bede: Book 2, c.14; Book 3, c.7, c.19, c.24; Book 4, c.13; J.Campbell, *Essays in Anglo-Saxon History* (1986), 52.

[11]M.Deanesly, 'Early English and Gallic Minsters', *Transactions of the Royal Historical Society*, 23 (1941).

[12]P.H.Sawyer, 'The royal *Tun* in Pre-Conquest England' in *Ideal and Reality in Frankish and Anglo-Saxon Society*, ed. P. Wormald (1983), 277-78; Barlow, English church 1000-1066, 183; ECWM, 163-64.

[13]Campbell, *Anglo-Saxons*, 74-75; Bede: Book 5, c.12.

[14]Campbell, Essays, 15; Finberg, *ECWM*, 217-18; P.Sims-Williams, *Religion and Literature in Western England, 600-800* (1990), 169-70.

[15]E.Cambridge & D.Rollason,'Debate: The pastoral organisation of the Anglo-Saxon Church: a review of the 'Minster Hypothesis' and J.Blair, 'Debate: Ecclesiastical organisation and pastoral care in Anglo-Saxon England', *Early Medieval Europe* 4, 1 & 2 (1995); C.Cubitt, 'Pastoral care and conciliar canons: the provisions of the 747 council of *Clofesho*' in *Pastoral care before the parish*; A.Everitt, *Continuity and colonisation* (1986), 195.

[16]D.Hooke, The Anglo-Saxon Landscape (1985), 37, 137; S.Bassett, 'In search of the origins of Anglo-Saxon kingdoms' in ed. *The origins of Anglo-Saxon kingdoms* (1989), 18-19, 21.

[17]Sawyer, 'The royal Tun', 277, 285; J.Blair, 'Secular minster churches in Domesday Book' in *Domesday Book A reassessment* ed. P.H.Sawyer (1985), 118-19.

[18]A.Thacker, 'Monks, preaching and pastoral care in early Anglo-Saxon England' in *Pastoral care before the parish*, 140; Campbell Essays, 86-7, 111-13.

[19]F.M.Stenton, *Anglo-Saxon England* (1950), 157, 149.

Patterns of pastoral care

[20]Bede Book 1, c.22.

[21]S.Bassett, 'Church and diocese in the West Midlands: the transition from British to Anglo-Saxon control', in *Pastoral care before the parish*, 13-26; *Councils and Synods* 1, 635; I.Atkins, 'The church of Worcester from the eighth to the twelfth century', *The Antiquaries Journal*, 20 (1940), 204-7; M.O.H.Carver, *Medieval Worcester* (Worcester Archaeological Society Transactions 3 (7, 1980), 30-37, 115-124.

[22]*Worcester Priory Cartulary* ed. R.R.Darlington, Pipe Roll Society 76 (1968), 32-33; *VCH Worcestershire* (3), 509.

[23]Campbell, *Essays* 53-56.

[24]T.Williamson, 'Parish boundaries and early fields: continuity and discontinuity', *Journal of Historical Geography* 12 (1986), 245; B.Cox, 'The significance of the distribution of English Place-Names in -HAM in the Midlands and East Anglia' in *Place-Name evidence for the Anglo-Saxon invasions and Scandinavian settlements* ed. K Cameron (EPNS, 1987), 56; N.Scarfe, *The Suffolk Landscape* (1972), 121.

[25]Campbell, Essays, 60-61, 71; R.Sharpe, 'Churches and communities in early medieval Ireland: towards a pastoral model' in *Pastoral care before the parish*, 81-109; D.N.Dumville, *The churches of North Britain in the first Viking-age* (Whithorn Trust, 1997), 18, 29-34.

[26]C.Phythian-Adams, Land of the Cumbrians (1996), 55, 65, 72-3, 80, 83, 109-10, 136, 155-56, 171; R.Newman, 'The problems of rural settlement in Northern Cumbria in the Pre-Conquest period' in *Studies in late Anglo-Saxon settlement* ed. M.L.Faull (1984) 158, 162, 164, 166-8.

[27]Bede Book 3, c.4; Book 4, c.27.

[28]'A breviate of the cartulary of ... Lanercost', 445.

Fixing parish boundaries

[29]Canon law and tithe: C.E.Boyd, *Tithes and parishes in Medieval Italy* (Cornell University Press, 1952), 5, 26-28, 32-3, 42-5, 138-40, 142, 156; G.Constable, *Monastic tithes* (1964), 3-4, 38; C.R.Cheney, *From Becket to Langton* (1965), 123.

[30]Campbell Essays, 49-50; Stenton, *Anglo-Saxon England*, 152-5; Barlow, *English church 1000-1066*, 145, 160-62, 184-5, 187, 195.

[31]Blair, 'Secular minster churches', 106, 119.

[32]C.N.L.Brooke 'The missionary at home: the church in the towns, 1000-1250', SCH, 6 (1970), 68, 72; P.H.Hase, 'The mother churches of Hampshire' in *Minsters and Parish churches* ed. J.Blair (1988), 64 note 41.

2 The pattern in the South

[1]R.Gem, 'The English Parish Church in the 11th and early 12th centuries: a great rebuilding?' in *Minsters and Parish churches* ed. J.Blair (1988), 21; F.Barlow, *The English Church* (1979), 221.

[2]T.Williamson, *The origins of Norfolk* (1993), 108-9; N.Batcock,'The parish church in Norfolk in the 11th and 12th centuries' and S.Heywood, 'The round towers of East Anglia' in *Minsters and Parish churches*, 169-71, 179.

Distinctive parish names

[3]Based on index to the *Compton Census of 1676*.

[4]F.W.Maitland, 'The surnames of English villages', *The Archaeological Review* 4 (1889), 233-240; D.Dymond, *The Norfolk Landscape* (1990), 81-2.

[5]*VCH Wiltshire* (10) 106-119, 204-214.

[6]A.Everitt, *Continuity and colonisation* (1986), 7-10; C.Taylor, *Dorset* (1970), 51-54; P.H.Sawyer ed. *Medieval Settlement* (1976), 6; ECWM 174.

[7]Puddletown assessed at 1/2 hide but 15 ploughs; Little Puddle and Waterston reduced from 20 1/2 hides to 12 ploughs and other townships reduced by smaller amounts.

[8]C.Taylor, 'Dorset and Beyond' in *Making English Landscapes* eds. K.Barker & T.Darvill (1997), 12 and *Dorset* 56-59, 114.

Celtic saints and parish names

[9]B.L.Olson & O.J.Padel, 'A tenth-century list of Cornish parochial saints', *Cambridge Medieval Celtic Studies* 12 (1986), 34, 42-62; O.J.Padel, *Cornish Place-Names* (1988); O.J.Padel, 'Cornish names of Parish churches', *Cornish Studies* 4/5 (1976-77).

[10]A.Preston-Jones, 'Decoding Cornish churchyards' in *The Early Church in Wales and the West* eds. N.Edwards & A.Lane (1992), 106, 109, 117-18, 120-24; N.Orme, ed. *Unity and Variety A history of the Church in Devon and Cornwall (1991)*, 4-7, 16-17, 20.

[11]A.Preston-Jones & P.Rose, 'Medieval Cornwall', *Cornish Archaeology*, 25 (1986), 112, 135, 155, 158, 160; H.Miles Brown, *The church in Cornwall* (1964), 27.

[12]Orme, *Unity and Variety*, 14; P.Hughes, *The Reformation* (1963), 35.

[13]M.W.Beresford, 'Dispersed and grouped settlement in medieval Cornwall', *Agricultural History Review* 12 (1964), 14-15; Preston-Jones & Rose, 'Medieval Cornwall', 142-45, 151, 158, 164.

[14]B.I.Coleman, 'The nineteenth century: Nonconformity' in *Unity and Variety*.

Patterns on the map

[15]Everitt, *Continuity and colonisation*, 65, 97, 181, 184, 190-94, 223.

[16]Everitt, *Continuity and colonisation*, 109-13, 192;

G.Ward, 'The topography of some Saxon charters relating to the Faversham district', AC, 46 (1934).

[17] 1831 census.

[18] Edward Hasted, *The History and Topographical Survey of the County of Kent* (12 vols, 1797-1801), (6) 532-34.

[19] P.H.Reaney, 'Place-Names and early settlement in Kent', AC, 76 (1962), 68-9.

[20] Early Wealden history: K.P.Witney, *The Jutish Forest* (1976), 31-2, 37, 39, 50, 52, 68, 97-8, 112, 121, 123-24, 126, 131-32, 145; Everitt, *Continuity and colonisation*, 37, 56.

[21] G.Ward, 'The lost dens of Little Chart', AC, 58 (1945), 4-5.

[22] Hasted, *History of Kent*, (3) 276; Everitt, *Continuity and colonisation*, 228, 235, 239; P.Sawyer, 'The royal *tun* in Pre-Conquest England' in *Ideal and reality in Frankish and Anglo-Saxon Society* (1983), 283.

[23] J.C.Ward, 'The Lowy of Tonbridge and the Lands of the Clare family in Kent, 1066-1217', AC, 96 (1981), 120, 129.

[24] (Reaney says dens named 48 times); G.Ward, 'The list of Saxon churches in the Textus Roffensis', AC, 44 (1932), 57, 81 (no. 355) - Egerton in Charing identified with *Eddintone* in Domesday and *Eardingtun in Domesday Monachorum*; T.Tatton-Brown, 'The Churches of Canterbury Diocese in the 11th Century' in *Minsters and Parish churches* ed. J.Blair (1988).

[25] R.Furley, *History of the Weald* (1871 & 1874), (2), ii, 499; Everitt, *Continuity and colonisation*, 295.

[26] Everitt, *Continuity and colonisation*, 150.

Monastic reform or parish formation?

[27] J.Campbell, *The Anglo-Saxons* (1982), 195.

[28] W.Stubbs, *Memorials of St Dunstan* (Rolls Series, 1874), civ.

[29] For Hampshire: P.H.Hase, 'The church in the Wessex Heartlands' in *The Medieval Landscape of Wessex*, eds. M.Aston & C.Lewis (1994), 68-69; R.Lennard, *Rural England 1086-1135* (1959), 302.

[30] P.Stafford, *The East Midlands in the Early Middle Ages* (1985), 35-6, 125-30; Lennard, *Rural England*, 288.

[31] Stubbs, *Memorials*, 64; N.Scarfe, The Suffolk *Landscape* (1972), 93.

A landscape full of churches

[32] *VCH Suffolk* (2) 13-14; *VCH Norfolk* (2) 235, 267.

[33] Williamson, *Norfolk*, 110, 154, 158; Dymond, *Norfolk*, 81, 97; Lennard, *Rural England*, 288; J.Campbell, *Essays in Anglo-Saxon History* (1986), 146-7.

[34] P.Warner, 'Shared churchyards, freemen church builders and the development of parishes in eleventh-century East Anglia', *Landscape History*, 8 (1986), 50.

[35] B.M.S.Campbell, 'The complexity of manorial structure in medieval Norfolk: a case study', *Norfolk Archaeology*, 39 (1986), 225-27; Williamson, *Norfolk*, 163-7; Batcock, 'The parish church in Norfolk', 179-83.

[36] A.Whiteman, *The Compton Census of 1676* (1986), 210.

[37] Warner, 'Shared churchyards'; F.Blomefield & C.Parkin, *An essay towards a topograpical history of the county of Norfolk*, (8) (1808), 225, 244.

[38] Scarfe, *Suffolk*, 140.

[39] Williamson, *Norfolk*, 117-21, 157-61; Warner, *Suffolk*, 196-8; R.W.Finn, *Domesday Studies. The Eastern Counties* (1967), 199; Lennard, *Rural England*, 218-19, 225.

[40] B.Cox, 'The significance of the distribution of English Place-Names in -HAM in the Midlands and East Anglia', in *Place-Name evidence for the Anglo-Saxon invasions and Scandinavian settlements* ed. K Cameron (EPNS, 1987), 66; Scarfe, *Suffolk*, 107; Williamson, *Norfolk*, 85-88, 107-10.

[41] P.Stafford, *The East Midlands in the Early Middle Ages* (1985), 156-58, 161.

[42] Campbell, 'The complexity of manorial structure', 251; Williamson, *Norfolk*, 8-10, 110, 114-122, 181-2; Scarfe, *Suffolk*, 32; Finn, *The Eastern Counties*, 56; K.J.Allison, 'The Lost Villages of Norfolk', *Norfolk Archaeology*, 31 (1955), 139; A.R.H.Baker & R.A.Butlin eds., *Studies of Field Systems in the British Isles* (1973), 306.

3 The pattern in the North

[1] C.Hole, *English custom and usage* (1950), 57.

[2] 'A breviate of the cartulary of ... Lanercost', 437; R.J.Glanville Jones, 'The portrayal of land settlement in Domesday Book' in *Domesday Studies* ed. J.C.Holt (1987), 189; A.Alexander, 'Perambulations and boundary descriptions' in *Yorkshire Boundaries* eds. M.H.Long & M.F.Pickles, (Yorkshire Archaeological Society, 1993), 44, 49; C.Phythian-Adams, *Land of the Cumbrians* (1996), 8-9, 78.

[3] J.Barnatt & K.Smith, *The Peak District* (1997), 56-7; J.C.Cox, *Notes on the churches of Derbyshire*, 2 (1877), 189; W.B.Bunting, *Chapel en le Frith: its history and its people* (1940), 17; P.H.Sawyer, 'The charters of Burton abbey', *Northern History*, 10 (1975), 32; P.Stafford, *The East Midlands in the Early Middle Ages* (1985), 129.

Conquest and lordship

[4] *VCH Derbyshire* (1) 397; N.J.Higham, *The origins of Cheshire* (1993), 171-77.

[5] R.Somerville, 'Commons and wastes in North-

West Derbyshire - The High Peak "New Lands"',
DAS, 97 (1977), 17, 27.

6M.Gelling, *The West Midlands in the early middle ages*(1992), 189.

7J.C.Cox, 'Plans of the Peak Forest', *Memorials of Old Derbyshire* (1907), 2, 16, 21.

8D.Roffe, 'The Origins of Derbyshire', *DAS*, 106 (1987), 104, 113; Sawyer, 'The charters of Burton abbey', 32.

9For individual Derbyshire parishes: Cox, *Derbyshire Churches* (2), particularly 5-6, 142, 209, 214, 363, 499.

10J.C.Cox, 'Ancient Documents relating to tithes in the Peak', *DAS*, 5 (1883), 133.

11Stafford, *The East Midlands*, 141; Higham, *Cheshire*, 95-6; D. & S.Lysons, *Magna Britannia: 2 Cheshire* ii (1810), 696; J.P.Earwaker, *East Cheshire: past and present*, 2 (1877), 112-14.

12H.Lawrance, 'The Registers of Glossop Parish Church', DAS, 38 (1916), 160; A.Jones, 'Basingwerk Abbey' in *Historical essays in honour of James Tait* eds. J.G.Edwards, V.H.Galbraith & E.F.Jacobs (1933), 172 (the abbey was founded 1123x1148).

13W.E.Wightman, 'The significance of "waste" in the Yorkshire Domesday', *Northern History*, 10 (1975), 55-71.

14N.Brooks, M.Gelling & D.Johnson, 'A new charter of King Edgar', *Anglo-Saxon England*, 13 (1984), 137-155.

15J.Hanmer & D.Winterbottom, *The Book of Glossop* (1991), 66; Lysons, *Derbyshire* (2), 165-8.

16A.M.Ashworth & T.F.Oldham, *Mellor Heritage* (1985), 12.

17Feudal Aids, 1 (1895), 283.

18Bunting, *Chapel en le Frith*, 26-29.

Parishes and shires

19Stafford, *The East Midlands*, 141; Higham, *Cheshire*, 115; D.Kenyon, *The origins of Lancashire* (1991), 151; J.Campbell, *Essays in Anglo-Saxon History* (1986), 168.

20P.O'Hare, 'Yorkshire boundaries and their development' and K.M.Hall, 'Pre-Conquest estates in Yorkshire' in *Yorkshire Boundaries* eds. H.E.J.Le Patourel, M.H.Long & M.F.Pickles (Yorkshire Archaeological Society, 1993), 13-15, 35-6; R.J.Glanville Jones, 'Multiple estates and early settlement' in P.Sawyer ed., *Medieval Settlement* (1976), 35-38.

21M.L.Faull & S.A.Moorhouse, *West Yorkshire: an archaeological survey to AD1500* (1981), 218, 365-65, 385, 519.

22J.Crabtree, *A concise history of the parish and vicarage of Halifax* (1836), 546.

23I.N.Wood, 'Anglo-Saxon Otley: an archiepiscopal estate and its crosses in a Northumbrian context', *Northern History*, 23 (1987), 35.

24D.J.H.Michelmore, 'The reconstruction of the early tenurial and territorial divisions of the landscape of Northern England', *Landscape History* (1979), I 7; D.Hey, *The making of South Yorkshire* (1979), 21, 27-29.

25R.Lomas, *North-east England in the Middle Ages* (1992), 23, 84, 175; P.A.G.Clack & B.H.Gill, 'The land divisions of County Durham in the early medieval period', *Annual Report of the Medieval Village Research Group* (1980); Hall, 'Pre-Conquest estates', 26-8, 35; Glanville Jones 'Multiple estates', 24, 35; D.M.Hadley, 'Multiple estates and the origins of the manorial structure of the northern Danelaw', *Journal of Historical Geography*, 22, 1 (1996).

26Kenyon, *Lancashire*, 48, 56, 90, 94-95, 99, 115, 123, 141-42, 150.

27R.B.Smith, *Blackburnshire* (Leicester Department of Local History Occasional Paper 15, 1961), 3, 37, 43-4.

28W.E.Kapelle, *The Norman Conquest of the North* (1979), 78-81.

29J.E.W.Wallis, *A History of the Church in Blackburnshire* (1932), 84, 92; T.Woodcock, *Haslingden: a topographical history* (1952), 19-20.

The significance of 'Kirkby'

30M.Gelling, *Signposts to the Past* (1988), 216, 234.

31D.N.Dumville, *The churches of North Britain in the first Viking age* (Fifth Whithorn lecture, 1997), 7-15; D.P.Kirby, 'Strathclyde and Cumbria; a survey of historical development to 1092', *CW2*, 62 (1962), 85; D.M.O'Sullivan, 'Pre-conquest settlement patterns in Cumbria' and R.Newman, 'The problems of rural settlement in Northern Cumbria in the Pre-Conquest period' in *Studies in late Anglo-Saxon settlement* ed. M.L.Faull (1984), 144, 149, 151, 162; A.J.Winchester, *Landscape and Society in Medieval Cumbria* (1987), 3-14.

32H.C.Darby & I.S.Maxwell, *The Domesday geography of Northern England* (1962), 74.

33For Cartmel and Kirkby Ireleth: C.Phythian-Adams, *Land of the Cumbrians* (1996), 63-66; *VCH Lancashire* (8) 254-83, 389, 392; Kenyon, *Lancashire*, 157-8; J.C.Dickinson, 'The architectural development of Cartmel priory church', *CW2*, 45 (1946), 50.

34Winchester, *Landscape & Society*, 13-14; Kenyon, *Lancashire*, 159.

35Rose 127; Winchester, *Landscape & Society*, 24, 26-7; Phythian-Adams, *Land of the Cumbrians*, 125-6; Kenyon, *Lancashire*, 147-8; C.N.L.Bouch, *Prelates* and People of the Lake Counties. A history of the diocese of Carlisle 1133-1933 (Kendal, 1948), 163.

[36]Winchester, Landscape & Society, 24.

[37]O'Sullivan, 'Pre-Conquest settlement patterns', 149.

[38]O'Sullivan, 'Pre-Conquest settlement patterns', 148.

4 A variety of structures

[1]J.Blair, 'Secular minster churches in Domesday Book' in P.H.Sawyer, Domesday Book A reassessmented (1985), 108-10.

[2]H.Owen & J.B.Blakeway, A History of Shrewsbury (1825), (1) 583; (2) 99, 209, 268-9, 271, 341, 415-16, 420; VCH Shropshire (2) 105, 114-15, 119; J.B.Blakeway, 'History of Shrewsbury Hundred or Liberties', TSAS2 1-6, 8, 9 (1889-1897).

[3]P.H.Hase, 'The mother churches of Hampshire' in Minsters and Parish churches ed. J.Blair (1988), 59.

[4]C.H.Drinkwater, 'The inner wall of Shrewsbury' TSAS1, 6 (1883), 256-61; J.Haslam, 'Parishes, Churches, Wards and Gates' in Minsters, 39.

[5]M.Gelling, The West Midlands in the early middle ages (1992), 164-6 and 'The early history of western Mercia' in The origins of Anglo-Saxon kingdoms ed. S.Bassett (1989), 191.

[6]S.Bassett, 'Anglo-Saxon Shrewsbury and its churches', Midland History 16 (1991), 5, 12, 21.

[7]S.Reynolds, 'Towns in Domesday Book' in Domesday Studies ed. J.C.Holt (1987), 300; Plans of the Cities & Boroughs of England & Wales 1832; J.Morris 'The Provosts and Bailiffs of Shrewsbury', SAS3, 1 (1901), 163-180.

Canons and prebendaries

[8]Blair, 'Secular minster churches', 115-17, 123-24, 132; K.Edwards, The English Secular Cathedrals in the Middle Ages (1949), 1-8, 33.

[9]A.Hamilton Thompson, 'Notes on Colleges of Secular Canons in England', Archaeological Journal, 74 (1917), 142.

[10]F.E.Harmer, Anglo-Saxon Writs (1989), 415-9, 531.

Portionary churches

[11]C.E.Boyd, Tithes and parishes in Medieval Italy (Cornell University Press, 1952), 59.

[12]VCH Shropshire (2) 117, 120 and (8) 213-15; 283-86, 326-27.

[13]J.W.Evans, 'The survival of the clas as an institution in medieval Wales', T.Roberts, 'Welsh Ecclesiastical Place-Names and Archaeology', and T.James, 'Air photography of ecclesiastical sites in south Wales' in The Early Church in Wales and the West eds. N.Edwards & A.Lane (1992), 36 & 40, 43-4, 66-7.

[14]Based on records of commutation: PP 1847-8 (49); 1856 (46).

[15]H.Munro Cautley, Suffolk Churches (1982), 337.

[16]Thompson, 'Notes on Colleges', 168-173; D.M.Loades, 'The Collegiate churches of County Durham at the time of the Dissolution', SCH, 4 (1967), 65-75; R.Surtees, The history and antiquities of the county palatine of Durham (1816), (2) 309-10.

[17]N.Brooks, The early history of the church of Canterbury (1984), 106, 256; A.M.Coleman & C.T.Lukehurst, East Kent (1967), 16; A.Everitt, Continuity and colonisation (1986), 83; T.Tatton-Brown, 'The Churches of Canterbury Diocese in the 11th Century' in Minsters and parish churches ed. J.Blair (1988), 115.

[18]Thompson, 'Notes on Colleges', 158-161; A.Hussey, Chronicles of Wingham (1896), 37, 114-33, 143-51; L.Parkin, 'Wingham, a medieval town', AC, 93 (1977), 61-71.

[19]J.R.Planché, A corner of Kent (1864), 52-3, 252; Everitt, Continuity, 107, 230, 255; Edward Hasted,The History and Topographical Survey of the County of Kent (1797-1801), (9) 216-17; Brooks, 'The early history', 339 note 46; Fleota which pertained to Folkestone in Domesday Monachorum seems wrongly identified with Fleet in Ash.

[20]D.Knowles & R.N.Hadcock, Medieval Religious Houses, England and Wales (1953), 364; C.R.Cheney, From Becket to Langton (1965), 99.

[21]In the Valor , the abbey collected 'Peter's sheves and Pons sheves', which looks like a bridge tax; Owen & Blakeway, Shrewsbury (2), 11, 142-3.

[22]Gloucester City Library, Hockaday Abstracts 368; A.Jones & J.Grenville, 'Some new suggestions about the Pre-Conquest History of Tewkesbury and Tewkesbury Church', Southern History, 9 (1987); VCH Gloucestershire (8) 110; A.Jones, Tewkesbury (1987), 53.

[23]K.J.Beecham, History of Cirencester (1887/1978), 84-6; Harmer, Anglo-Saxon Writs, 211-13.

[24]R.A.A.Hartridge, A history of vicarages in the middle ages (1930), 25, 32.

[25]F.Barlow, The English Church 1066-1154 (1979), 51-2, 132; Cheney, From Becket to Langton, 14-15, 104, 126-29, 136-37.

[26]Hartridge, A history of vicarages, 19-21, 79; D.M.Owen, Church and Society in Medieval Lincolnshire (1971), 12.

Chapels in the parochial system

[27]C.J.Bond, 'Church and parish in Norman Worcestershire' in Minsters.

[28]G.Ward, 'The list of Saxon churches in the Textus Roffensis', AC, 44 (1932), 40.

[29]VCH Shropshire (2) 29-30, 123-28; J.Croom, 'The

fragmentation of the minster parochiae of South-East Shropshire' in *Minsters*, 77-79.

[30]J.E.W.Wallis, *A History of the Church in Blackburnshire* (1932), 89, 94, 163; J.C.Cox, 'Ancient Documents relating to tithes in the Peak', *DAS*, 5 (1883), 154-55.

[31]Hase, 'The mother churches of Hampshire', 57-8; C.N.L.Brooke, 'The missionary at home: the church in the towns, 1000-1250', *SCH*, 6 (1970), 72-3.

[32]Blair, *Early medieval Surrey* (1991), 95, 133, 154-57; Owen, *Church and Society*, 5, 8-12.

[33]Hartridge, *A history of Vicarages*, 28, 134; J.C.Cox, *Notes on the churches of Derbyshire* (1877), (2) 5-6; G.H.Tupling, 'The Pre-Reformation Parishes and chapelries of Lancashire', *Lancashire and Cheshire Antiquarian Society Transactions*, 67 (1958), 10.
 E.Duffy, *The Stripping of the Altars* (1992), 42.

5 Private enterprises, public duties

[1]E.Mason, 'The role of the English Parishioner', *JEH* 27,1 (1976), 24-5; B.Kümin, 'The English parish in a European perspective' and K.French, 'Parochial fund-raising in late medieval Somerset' in *The Parish in English Life 1400-1600* eds. K.French, G.G.Gibbs & B.A.Kumin (1997), 24-5, 120-21, 123-24; *Councils & Synods* (2) 1003; S. & B.Webb, *The Parish and the County* (1963), 20, 22, 24.

Extending the parish's services: chantries

[2]E.Duffy, *The Stripping of the Altars* (1992), 112, 124 139, 149, 328, 369; D.M.Owen, *Church and Society in medieval Lincolnshire* (1971), 92-101.

[3]Glos.City Library, Hockaday Abstracts 300.

[4]C.Kitching, 'Church and chapelry in sixteenth century England', *SCH*, 16 (1979), 284; J.C.Cox, *Notes on the churches of Derbyshire* (1877) (2) 5-6, 105; C.N.L.Bouch, *Prelates and People of the Lake Counties A history of the diocese of Carlisle* 1133-1933 (Kendal, 1948), 165; J.Nicolson & R.Burn, *History and antiquities of the counties of Westmorland and Cumberland* (1777/1976), 128.

[5]J.P.Earwaker, *East Cheshire: past and present* (1877), (2); D. & S.Lysons, *Magna Britannia: 2 Cheshire* (1810) (2) 723-745; Gastrell, *Notitia Cestriensis* (8).

[6]N.Orme, 'The dissolution of the chantries in Devon, 1546-8', *Devonshire Association Transactions*, 77; P.Tyler, 'The status of the Elizabethan parochial clergy', *SCH*, 4 (1967), 80; P.Marshall, *The face of the Pastoral Ministry in the East Riding*, 1525-1595 (University of York Borthwick Paper 8, 1995), 3.

Chantry college and guild chapel in Stratford upon Avon

[7]D.Hooke, *The Anglo-Saxon landscape* (1985), 45, 157, 165, 173, 208 (Bushwood next Lapworth); *VCH Warwickshire* (3) 223, 247-8.

[8]Details of family from *Dictionary of National Biography.*

[9]W.Dugdale, *The antiquities of Warwickshire* ed. W.Thomas (1730), (2) 692-3; *VCH Warwickshire* (3) 271.

[10]J.Blair, 'Secular minster churches in Domesday Book' in *Domesday Book A reassessment* ed. P.H.Sawyer (1985), 137.

The suppressison of chantries, guilds and colleges

[11]Orme, 'The dissolution of the chantries'; C.Kitching 'The disposal of monastic and chantry lands' in *Church and Society in England* ed. F.Heal & R.O'Day (1977) 128-136; M.Clark, 'Northern light? Parochial life in a 'dark corner' of Tudor England' in *The Parish in English Life*, 63.

[12]Duffy, *The Stripping of the Altars*, 450, 455-6, 476; C.Haigh, *Reformation and Resistance in Tudor Lancashire* (1975), 148; *VCH Suffolk* (2) 29-30.

[13]P.H.Hase 'The church in the Wessex heartlands' in *The Medieval Landscape of Wessex* eds. M.Aston & C.Lewis, 72-3; J.Blair ed. and C.J.Bond 'Church and parish in Norman Worcestershire' in *Minsters and Parish churches* (1988), 15, 138, and J.Blair *Early medieval Surrey* (1991), 157; T.F.Dukes, *Antiquities of Shropshire* (1844), xi-xiv; Kitching, 'Church and chapelry', 280, 286, 289-90.

[14]*VCH Kent* (2) 71.

[15]Mrs Fetherstonhaugh & F.Haswell, 'The college of Kirkoswald and the family of Fetherstonhaugh, CW1, 14 (1914), 204-5; Clark, 'Northern light?', 56-73; Bouch, *Prelates and People,* 104.

[16]A.J.Dobb, *Like a mighty tortoise* (1978), 66; *Lancashire Chantries* 19, 55 (1,056 communicants); *VCH Lancashire* (4), 192-3; G.H.Tupling, 'Medieval and early modern Manchester' in *Manchester and its Region* (1962), 121, 123.

[17]*VCH Warwickshire* (3) 247 (gives the date as 1539), 248, 259, 278.

[18]H.Owen & J.B.Blakeway, *A History of Shrewsbury* (1825), (1) 31, 322; (2) 330.

The duties of the parish

[19]Duffy, *The Stripping of the Altars*, chap. 13, 566-7; C.Litzenberger, 'St Michael's, Gloucester, 1540-80: the cost of conformity in sixteenth-century England', W.Coster, 'Popular religion and the parish register 1538-1603' and Clark, 'Northern light?', in *The Parish in English Life*, 65, 107, 230-249.

[20]E.Carlson, 'The origins, function, and status of the office of churchwarden, with particular reference to the diocese of Ely' in *The World of Rural Dissenters*, 1520-1725 ed. M.Spufford (1995), 170-75; Bishop Redman's Visitation 21.

Puritanism and parochial reform

[21]Bouch, Prelates and People, 154-5, 222-23; Bishop of Barrow-in-Furness (Henry Ware), 'On the Readers in the Chapelries of the Lake District', CW2, 5 (1905), 89.
[22]Kitching, 'Church and chapelry, 289; G.H.Tupling, 'The Pre-Reformation parishes and chapelries of Lancashire', Lancashire & Cheshire Antiquarian Society Transactions, 67 (1951) 9; Haigh, Reformation and Resistance, 239.
[23]Bouch, Prelates and People, 161, 165, 245; D. & S.Lysons, Magna Britannia 4 Cumberland (1816), 108; Kelly's Directory; Nicolson & Burn, Westmorland and Cumberland, 140; Records of Kendale (3) 107, 157.
[24]Revds Ware & Simpson, 'Killington, Kirkby Lonsdale, its Chapel Salary', CW1, 8 (1886), 114, 116.

6 Parishes and Livings

[1]A.Jones, J. Howard-Drake, S.Jourdan & T.McQuay, 'Eggs for the Vicar', Wychwoods History, 11 (1996), 4-23.

The parson's due

[2]S.Wright, 'Easter Books and Parish Rate Books: a new source for the urban historian', Urban History Yearbook, (1985); S.Wright, 'A Guide to Easter Books and related parish listings', Local Population Studies, 42 & 43 (1989); A.G.Little, 'Personal Tithes', EHR, (1945).
[3]C.Hill, Economic Problems of the Church (1963), 78-88.
[4]Rector's Book, 60-63.
[5]J.C.Cox, 'Derbyshire Easter Dues', DAS, 11 (1889), 53.
[6]Diary 10-11, 135-7; Life and Letters 151.
[7]Rector's Book, 28, 33, 48, 72.

Ordained inequality

[8]D.M. Barratt, 'The condition of the Parish Clergy between the Reformation and 1660', (D.Phil. Oxford,1949) 190-2: Collier calculated 4,543 livings under £10 a year out of 8,803 benefices.
[9]M.Zell,'Economic problems of the parochial clergy in the sixteenth century' in Princes and Paupers in the English Church 1500-1800 eds. R.O'Day & F.Heal (1981), 33; P.Tyler, 'The status of the Elizabethan Parochial Clergy', SCH, 4 (1967), 77-9: Yorks 392 out of 622; Lincs 876 out of 1225; Hill, Economic problems, 144-5.
[10]W.G.Hoskins, The Age of Plunder (1976), 121-139.
[11]Tyler 'The status of the Elizabethan clergy', 91: Elizabeth I sold 2216 lots of parish tithes, James I sold 1453.

Narrowing the gap: Queen Anne's Bounty

[12]Best especially 28-34, 80, 86-93, 108-9, 130-32, 202, 205, 210-21, 230-31, 450-51, 451, and appendix IV; Ian Green, 'The first years of Queen Anne's Bounty' in Princes and Paupers.
[13]M.R. Austin, 'Queen Anne's Bounty and the poor livings of Derbyshire - 1772-1832', DAS, 92 (1972), 79-83.
[14]£652,000 from its funds, benefactions of over £250,000, and £1.1 million of the parliamentary grants; Virgin 17.

Abolishing tithes - bit by bit

[15]E.J.Evans, 'Some reasons for the growth of English rural anti-clericalism c.1750-c.1830', Past and Present, 66 (1975); W.R.Ward, 'The tithe question in England in the early nineteenth century', JEH, 16 (1965).
[16]Derbyshire examples: M.R. Austin, 'Enclosure and benefice incomes in Derbyshire, 1772-1832', DAS, 100 (1980); 'Tithe and benefice incomes in Derbyshire 1772-1832', DAS, 102 (1982).
[17]PP 1867 (54).
[18]A.Jones The Cotswolds (1994), 148-9; D.Cannadine, The decline and fall of the British Aristocracy (1990), 9.
[19]Ward 'The tithe question', '73-4.
[20]H.G.Hunt, 'Landownership and enclosure 1750-1830', Economic History Review, 11 (1958-9), 500.
[21]E.J.Evans, 'A nineteenth century tithe dispute and its significance: the case of Kendal', CW2, 74 (1974), 162, 168.
[22]E.J.Evans, Tithes (British Association for Local History, 1993).
[23]GRO/P224a/SD1/1 and AP31.
[24]PP 1847-8 (49); 1856 (46); 1887 (64).

Towards equality: the Ecclesiastical Commission

[25]Best 272, 277, 298, 307.
[26]PP 1835 (22) Abstract 1053-1056.
[27]W.B.Maynard, 'The Response of the Church of England to Economic and Demographic Change: the Archdeaconry of Durham, 1800-1851', JEH, 42 (1991).
[28]For account of Ecclesiastical Commission: Best especially 332, 351-52, 438, 464, 509; Virgin 102.
[29]M.Turnbull (chairman), Working as One Body (Report of the Archbishop's Commission on the Organisation of the Church of England, 1995), 82.

7 Poor as chapel mice

[1]J.H.Priestley, 'The history of Ripponden church', Transactions of Halifax Antiquarian Society (1958), 6, 9.
[2]G.Lawton, Collections relative to churches and chapels within the dioceses of York and Ripon (1842), 134.
[3]Archbishop Herring (3), 19.

Short-lived reform: 1642-1660

[4]R.O'Day & A.Hughes, 'Augmentation and amalgamation: was there a systematic approach to the reform of parochial finance, 1640-60?' in *Princes and Paupers in the English Church 1500-1800* eds. R.O'Day & F.Heal (1981).

[5]K.Clark, '"A good and sufficient maintenance': the augmentation of parish livings in Derbyshire, 1645-1660', *DAS*, 100 (1980); J.C.Cox, *Notes on the churches of Derbyshire* (1877), (2) 5-14, 199-219; (4) 492-3, 495.

[6]C.Hill, *Economic Problems of the Church* (1963), 113.

7The Chantries commissioners in 1548 returned 1,056 communicants, implying a population of under 2,000; Bishop Gastrell c.1714 noted 2,763 families, about 12,500 population.

[8]A.J.Dobb, *Like a mighty tortoise* (1978), 66; G.H.Tupling, 'The Pre-Reformation Parishes and chapelries of Lancashire', *Lancashire and Cheshire Antiquarian Society Transactions*, 67 (1958), 12-16; G.H.Tupling, 'Medieval and early modern Manchester' in *Manchester and its Region* (1962), 125.

[9]*VCH Lancashire* (6) 356; Hill, Economic Problems, 152; *Lancashire & Cheshire Church Surveys*, 161-8.

[10]*VCH Lancashire* (4) 308; (Hill, Economic Problems, 296, seems to have reversed protesters and supporters).

The breakdown of uniformity

[11]D.M.Butler, *Quaker Meeting Houses of the Lake Counties* (Friends Historical Society, 1978), 146.

[12]Revds Ware & Simpson, 'Killington, Kirkby Lonsdale, its Chapel Salary', CW1, 8 (1886), 93-119.

[13]Kendal R.O. WD/Ry/Box 32; *Records of ... Kendale*, (2) 424-39; (3) 306.

From chapel minister to perpetual curate

[14]I.M.Green, *The re-establishment of the Church of England 1660-1663* (1978), 35, 144.

[15]Lawton, *Collections*, 131, 133.

[16]Best 81-2, 210; I.Green, 'The first years of Queen Anne's Bounty' in *Princes and Paupers*, 240; Lawton, *Collections*.

[17]Best 90-91; *Bishop of Barrow-in-Furness* (Henry Ware), 'On the Readers in the Chapelries of the Lake District', CW2, 5 (1905), 92-3.

[18]Ware & Simpson, 'Killington', 114.

[19]Bishop William Nicolson, 98; *Bishop of Barrow*, 'On the readers', 92.

[20]Green, 'The first years', 243, 247.

[21]J.R.Guy, 'Perpetual curacies in eighteenth century South Wales', *SCH*, 16 (1979), 332-3; Virgin, 220.

A retired northern curacy

[22]H.Speight, *The Craven and North-West Yorkshire Highlands* (1892/1989), 427-28, 431; F.W.Stacey, 'Dentdale - the 'Bounty'-full valley', *The Sedbergh Historian*, 3 (1995), 32-37.

[23]A.Sedgwick, *Adam Sedgwick's Dent* (1868 and 1870, reprinted Sedbergh 1984), x, 8-10, 21, 26, 78-9, 85, 89; *The Life & Letters of the Revd. Adam Sedgwick* eds. J.W.Clark & T.McKenny Hughes (1890), 35.

8 A 'competent manse'

[1]J.R.H.Moorman, 'The estates of the Lanercost canons', *CW2*, 48 (1948), 79 and 'Edward I at Lanercost Priory 1306-7', *EHR*, 67 (1952), 163-7, and ex inf Vicar.

[2]Inscription; F. Graham, Hexham and Corbridge (Newcastle, 1984), 44-5; B.A.Bax, *The English Parsonage* (1964), 24.

[3]P.Stafford, *The East Midlands in the Early Middle Ages* (1985), 165.

[4]Bede's Prose Life of St Cuthbert ed. B.Colgrave (1940), 257-9; R.Lennard, *Rural England 1086-1135* (1959), 333-37; J.E.W.Wallis, *A History of the Church in Blackburnshire* (1932), 88-9.

Some medieval parsonage houses

[5]M.Wood, *The English Medieval House* (1990) 21, 67-8; W.A.Pantin, 'Medieval Priests' Houses in South West England', *Medieval Archaeology*, 1 (1957), 118-28.

[6]E.W.Parkin, 'The old rectory of St Alphege, Canterbury', *AC*, 84 (1969), 201-10.

[7]R.A.A.Hartridge, *A history of vicarages in the middle ages* (1930), 48, 150-51; J.Crabtree, *A concise history of the parish and vicarage of Halifax* (1836), 546.

[8]Edward Hasted, *The History and Topographical Survey of the County of Kent* (12 vols, 1797-1801) (5) 189; (6) 562; K.Gravett, 'The Clergy House, Alfriston: a Reappraisal', in *National Trust Studies* ed. G.Jackson-Stops (1981), 103-8.

[9]*Bishops Registers, Hereford*, 5.

[10]*Bishop Redman's Visitation*.

[11]P.Cowley, *The Church Houses* (1970), 64.

[12]W.M.Jacob, 'A practice of a very hurtful tendency', *SCH*, 16 (1979); Virgin, 2-3; M.R.Austin, 'Clerical residence and pluralism in Derbyshire 1772-1832', DAS, 103 (1983); J.Addy, 'Bishop Porteus' visitation of the diocese of Chester, 1778', *Northern History*, 13 (1977), 175, 180.

[13]Jacob, 'A practice of a very hurtful tendency', 319; F.Knight, The Nineteenth-Century Church and English Society (1995), 142.

A great rebuilding

[14]Best 200, 205-6, 217-9; Jacob, 'A practice of a very hurtful tendency', 324; Austin, 'Clerical residence', 119-122; Virgin 66, 147, 203, 209-10,

291-4.

[15]P.Virgin, *Sydney Smith* (1994), 150, 196-200.

[16]Of 10,540 returns to the Ecclesiastical Revenues Commission, 2878 had no parsonage house, and 1735 houses were unfit.

[17]Virgin 203; D.M.McClatchey, *Oxfordshire Clergy 1777-1869* (1960), 22, 24, 31.

[18](W.J.Conybeare) 'The church in the mountains', *Edinburgh Review*, 97 (April 1853), 370; Knight, *Nineteenth century church*, 120, 135-36, 141.

[19]*PP 1847/8* (49).

[20]A.Savidge, *The Parsonage in England* (1969), 116, 118.

[21]Hasted, *History of Kent* (9), 126,140.

[22]Best 449; *PP 1876* (9) 17.

[23]C.N.L.Bouch, *Prelates and People of the Lake Counties A history of the diocese of Carlisle 1133-1933* (1948), 437-8.

The 'unsuitable' parsonage house

[24]Savidge, *The Parsonage in England*, 168-9, 172-5, 203; M.Higgins, *The Vicar's House* (1988), 13, 86, 138, 153.

[25]Higgins, *Vicar's House* 184: 1978-84 - 755 purchased and 702 built new, and ex inf Julian Litten, architectural historian.

[26]Information from the archdeacon of Oxford diocese, the property secretary of Manchester diocese, and surveys carried out for Save Our Parsonages.

[27]Higgins, *Vicar's House* xi: 8887 houses in 1986.

9 Fit for a gentleman

[1]*VCH Oxfordshire* (3) 5, 8, 21, 119-21, 129-30, 173-4.

[2]C.N.L.Bouch, *Prelates and People of the Lake Counties A history of the diocese of Carlisle 1133-1933* (1948), 201; Ian Green, 'Career prospects and clerical conformity in the early Stuart church', *Past and Present*, 90 (1981), 89-91.

[3]A.J.Engel, *From Clergyman to Don* (1983), 1.

Gentlemen and plebeians

[4]P.Laslett, *The World we have lost* (1971), 27.

[5]Ian Green, ''Reformed pastors' and Bons Curés: the changing role of the parish clergy in early modern Europe', *SCH*, 26 (1989), 71.

[6]*Rector's Book*, 14-18; Cumbria Archives Service WD/Ry/Box 32; Kent Archives Office Q/CTz (not all household divisions are perfectly clear); E.Hudson, 'The tale of the square pew', *Bygone Kent*, 2 i (1990), 21-4.

[7]C.H.Mayo, 'The Social Status of the Clergy in the Seventeenth and Eighteenth Centuries', *EHR*, 37 (1922), 263; Virgin 126, 132, 281; L.Stone, 'The size and composition of the Oxford student body 1580-1910' in *The University in Society* ed. L.Stone

(Princeton 1974), 5, 37-9, 92-3, 95; A.Haig, *The Victorian Clergy* (1984), 31, 36.

[8]*Clergy returns*; C.Hill, 'Puritans and 'the dark corners of the land', *Royal Historical Society Transactions* 5, 13 (1963), 84.

[9]Gastrell, *Archdeaconry of Richmond*, 20-23 and index.

The gentleman heresy

[10]P.Brendon, *Hurrell Froude and the Oxford Movement* (1974), 22, 112, 155-6; L.Paul, *A Church by Daylight. A reappraisal of the church of England and its future* (1973), 156-57.

[11]Virgin, 132-4; Haig, *The Victorian Clergy*, 29, 38, 119, 126, 144-45, 160; B.Heeney, *A different kind of gentleman: Parish Clergy as Professional Men in Early and Mid-Victorian England* (Ohio 1976), 21, 28-32.

[12]Bouch, *Prelates and People*, 394, 422-3.

[13]A.Russell, *The clerical profession* (1980), 48.

[14]A.Armstrong, 'The use of information about occupation' in *Nineteenth-century society* ed. E.A.Wrigley (1972), 274-81.

'Riches maketh gentlemen'

[15]C.Hill, *Economic Problems of the Church* (1963), 188, 207, 240; F.W.Brooks, 'The social position of the parson in the sixteenth century', *British Archaeological Association Journal*, 188 (1945-7), 25.

[16]Kent Archives Office Q/R Th; K.Schurer & T.Arkell eds., *Surveying the People* (Local Population Studies 1992) for discussion of Hearth Tax and also of Gregory King.

[17]*Norfolk Hearth Tax Returns* 1664 & 1666 (Norfolk Genealogy, 15 (1983) & 20 (1988)).

[18]J.P.Cooper, 'The social distribution of land and men in England, 1436-1700' in *Essays in Quantitative Economic History* ed. R.Floud (1974), 124.

[19]Best 202, 205, 446-47, 508 ; Virgin 94, 274-77; S.Pollard & D.W.Crossley, *The wealth of Britain* (1968),186, 206-7, 238, 243.

[20]*PP* 1852 (9) 693-95, 958-59 (Appendix 462).

[21]Heeney, *A different kind of gentleman*, 31-2.

[22]Best 479; G.Routh, *Occupation and pay in Great Britain 1906-79* (2nd. ed. 1980), 63.

Family livings

[23]*VCH Gloucestershire* (6).

[24]*VCH Norfolk* (2) 267 (1563); Hill, *Economic Problems of the Church*, 66.

[25]D.M.Barratt, 'The condition of the Parish clergy between the Reformation and 1660' (D.Phil. thesis, Oxford, 1949), 353 & 361; C.Haigh, *Reformation and Resistance in Tudor Lancashire* (1975), 24; M.Zell, 'The personnel of the clergy in Kent, in the Reformation period', *EHR*, 89 (1974), 526; R.O'Day, 'Ecclesiastical Patronage: who controlled the

Church?' in *Church and Society in England* eds. F.Heal & R. O'Day (1977), 140.

[26]Best 510; M.J.D.Roberts, 'Private patronage and the Church of England, 1800-1900', *JEH*, 32 (1981), 203; M.R.Austin, 'Tithe and benfice income' *DAS*, 102 (1982), 122.

[27]Virgin, 181, 188-9, 288.

[28]Roberts 'Private patronage', 202; Paul, *A Church by Daylight*, 92.

10 Fictional scenes of clerical life

[1]*VCH Gloucestershire* (6) 8-15, 56.

The parson and the country gentleman

[2]I.Collins,*Jane Austen and the clergy* (1994), ix-x, 6, 18, 29, 63, 69; P.Honan, *Jane Austen. Her life.* (1987) 26; J.Halperin, *The Life of Jane Austen* (1984), 14-15, 24, 68, 183, 212.

Observing clerical nuances

[3]N.John Hall,*Trollope. A Biography* (1991) 4-6, 166, 387, 410, 461, 513; T.H.S.Escott, *Anthony Trollope: his work associates and originals* (1913), 29, 103-4.

[4]R.apRoberts, *Introduction to Clergymen of the Church of England* (Leicester, 1974), 45.

Unfashionable Midland Scenes

[5]G.Handley, *George Eliot's Midlands: Passion in Exile* (1991) 52, 131, 163; Hall, *Trollope*, 184.

[6]T.A.Noble, *Introduction to Scenes of Clerical Life* (Oxford 1985), xiii.

[7]S.Parkinson, *Scenes from the 'George Eliot' country* (1888), 10.

[8]J.Beaty, 'History by Indirection: the era of reform in Middlemarch', *Victorian Studies*, 1 (1958), 179.

11 The triumph of the parish

[1]*The Treasures of Lancashire*, 195; A.J.Dobb, *Like a mighty tortoise* (1978), 26-7, 46-7, 50.

[2]W.H.Chaloner, 'The birth of modern Manchester' in *Manchester and its region* (1962), 136; A. Briggs, *Victorian Cities* (1990), 124.

The regulation of Victorian enterprise

[3]Church Building Commissioners: J.C.Traill, *The New Parishes Acts* (1857); M.H.Port, *Six hundred new churches* (1961), 21, 28, 113, 125; Best 401-2.

[4]Dobb, *Like a mighty tortoise*, 138, 142; R.Murphy, *Vanishing Churches* (A Report and gazetteer prepared for the Dept. of Architecture and Landscape of Manchester Polytechnic, Manchester Metropolitan University,1987), 22; D.E.H.Mole, 'The Victorian town Parish: Rural vision and Urban Mission', *SCH*, 16 (1979), 364.

[5]W.B.Maynard, 'The Response of the Church of England to Economic and Demographic Change: the Archdeaconry of Durham, 1800-1851', *JEH*, 42 (1991), 452-3.

[6]Peel districts: Best 196, 356-8, 408-10, 427, 498 & Appendix vii (he comments that no history of this has been written); Traill, *The new parishes acts*, 32-33.

Dividing the town parish

[7]PP1852 (89); B.I.Coleman, *The Church of England in the mid-nineteenth century* (Historical Association 1980); K.D.M.Snell, *Church and Chapel in the North Midlands: Religious Observance in the Nineteenth Century* (1991), 9-14.

[8]*London Gazette* 29 March 1839, 698.

[9]For agitation and subsequent reforms: W.R.Ward 'The cost of establishment: Some Reflections on Church Building in Manchester', *SCH*, 3 (1966), 278-79, 285-6, and *Religion & Society* (1972), 179-83, 221-232.

[10]Dobb, *The mighty tortoise*, 157, 245-7; A.D.Gilbert, *Religion & society in industrial England* (1976), 119.

[11]Murphy *Vanishing churches*, 35; *The church in Manchester* (Report of the bishop of Manchester's special commission, 1914), 67-69; *VCH Lancashire* (4), 249.

W.F.Hook and Leeds

[12]Hook at Leeds: *Life and Letters of Walter Farquhar Hook* ed. W.R.W.Stephens (1889), 222, 362, 377-81, 383-4, 430, 463, 465-6.

[13]R.J.Wood, 'Leeds Church patronage in the eighteenth century', *Publications of the Thoresby Society* 12103 (1948), 103.

Stoke on Trent

[14]M.Drabble, *Arnold Bennett* (1985), 4, 94; E.J.D.Warrillow, *Arnold Bennett and Stoke on Trent* (1966), 51-2; *VCH Staffordshire* (8) 88, 253.

[15]*Parish and chapelries*: J.Ward, The Borough of Stoke-upon Trent (Stoke on Trent, 1843), 212-13, 456-58, 466, 498; Appendix XV.

[16]R.Talbot, *The church and ancient parish of Stoke* (Stoke, 1969), 56.

[17]*Rectory houses and church*: VCH Staffordshire (8), 154, 186-87, 190, 233-34.

[18]J.Ward, *The borough*, 495.

[19]S.W. Hutchinson, *The Archdeaconry of Stoke on Trent* (1893), 17.

Liverpool

[20]*Account based on VCH Lancashire* (4), 43-52; R.B.Walker, 'Religious Changes in Liverpool in the Nineteenth Century', JEH, 29 (1968), 195-211; A.Hume, *State and Prospects of the Church in Liverpool* (1869), particularly 4-7, 9-11, 17-22, 39, 42, 44.

[21]Population: borough 1845: 300,000; parish 1851: 258,000.

[22]Best, 192-3; W.R.Ward, *Religion & Society*, 183.

[23]Best, 447, 508.

[24]E.Royle, *The Victorian Church in York* (Borthwick

Paper 64, 1983), 11, 24, 29-31, 33, 38;
A.Symondson, 'Theology, worship and the late
Victorian church', in *The Victorian Church* eds.
C.Brooks & A.Saint (1995), 200-1.

12 New patterns or old for the future?
[1]R.Newcourt *Repertorium Ecclesiasticum* (2) (1710),
578.
[2]M.Arman, *A short history of Thaxted church* (1993);
R.Groves, *Conrad Noel and the Thaxted movement*
(1967), 10-15.
[3]*The Times* 19.11.96.
[4]ex inf. Revd Brian Abell and Revd Ian Johnson.
The age of bureaucracy
[5]Best, 237.
[6]A.J.Dobb, *Like a mighty tortoise* (1978), 270.
[7]L.Paul, *A Church by Daylight. A reappraisement of the
church of England and its future* (1973), 109, 117,
123, 125.
[8]A.Hastings, *A history of English Christianity* (1986),
51: 1880-1913 - 217 church-related bills, of which
162 were not discussed, 183 were dropped and 33
passed.
[9]*The Times* 7 Feb 1997; G.Davie, *Religion in Britain
since 1945* (1994), 50, 143.
[10]P.A.Welsby, *A History of the Church of England
1945-1980* (1984), 252, 264-8.
Facing realities
[11]*The Times* 25.2.99; 4 & 5.3.99.
[12]A.Russell, *The Country Parson* (1993), 118;
R.B.Walker, 'Religious Changes in Liverpool in the
Nineteenth Century', *JEH*, 29 (1968), 210.
[13]Paul, *A Church by Daylight*, 184.
[14]*The Times* 7.2.97.
Reforming the parish by stealth
[15]Best, 509-19.
[16]R.Gill, *The Myth of the Empty Church* (1993), 290.
[17]*Oxford Docese Year Book* 1999.
[18]Russell, *The Country Parson,* 126-27.
[19]Paul, *A church by daylight,* 113.
[20]*Parish Review* 1995-1996.
[21]D.Findlay, *The Protection of our English churches*
(1996), 52-3, 106, 110-111; Welsby, *A History of the
Church of England,* 138; *The Times* 19.11.96 on
Developing the partnership and 18.1.97.
Rethinking
[22]M.Turnbull (chairman),*Working as One Body*
(Report of the Archbishop's Commission on the
Organisation of the Church of England, 1995), 108,
114.
[23]Best, 338.
[24]J.Evans, *The Ecumenical Scene* (Hereford Diocesan
Ecumenical Committee 1994), 6-13. (I owe this
information to Lady Anne Kerr).

[25]Turnbull Report, 84.
[26]Russell, *The country parson,* 228.
[27]R.A.Pullan & K.J.Burnley, *Set upon a hill* (1993),
113-141.
[28]Davie, *Religion in Britain,* 176; W.R.Ward,
'Pastoral office and the general priesthood in the
Great Awakening', *SCH,* 26 (1989), 326-7.

Notes and Bibliographical references
Abbreviations
AC	Archaeologia Cantiana
Best:	G.F.A.Best, *Temporal Pillars Queen Anne's Bounty, the Ecclesiastical Commissioners and the Church of England* (1964)
BGAS	Bristol & Gloucester Archaeological Society
CW Rec	Cumberland and Westmorland Antiquarian & Archaeological Society Record Series
CW1 & 2	Transactions: Old Series & New Series
DAS	Derbyshire Archaeological Society Journal
ECNE	*Early charters of Northern England and the north Midlands* C.R.Hart (1975)
ECWM	*Early charters of the West Midlands* H.P.R.Finberg (1972)
EHR	English Historical Review
EPNS	English Place Name Society
JEH	Journal of Ecclesiastical History
NA	Norfolk Archaeology
PP	*Parliamentary Papers*
SAS1 & 2	Shropshire Archaeological Society Transactions 1st & 2nd series
SIA	Suffolk Institute of Archaeology and Natural History Proceedings
SCH	Studies in Church History
VCH	*Victoria County History*
Virgin:	P.Virgin, *The church in an age of negligence* (1989)

Source material referred to in the text, in
abbreviated form in the notes to chapters, or of
relevance throughout:
Anglo-Saxon Chronicle trans. G.N.Garmonsway
(1978)
'A breviate of the cartulary of the Priory Church of
St Mary Magdalene, Lanercost', ed. M. Walcott
(*Royal Society of Literature of the United Kingdom
Trans2,* 8, 1866)
'A Survey of the Diocese of Gloucester, 1603',
Religious Miscellany (BGAS Records 11, 1976)
Anglo-Saxon Charters P.Sawyer (1968)

Archbishop Herring's visitation Returns 1743 ed.
S.L.Ollard & P.C.Walker (Yorkshire Archaeological
Society 71, 72, 75, 77, 1928-30)
Archdeacon Plymley's visitation notebooks,
Shropshire Records and Research Unit MSS 6001/6860-
6865 (In 1804 he adopted the surname of Corbett)
Articles of Enquiry addressed to the clergy of the Diocese
of Oxford at the Primary Visitation of Dr Thomas Secker
1738 (Oxford Record Society 38, 1957)
Bede's Ecclesiastical History of the English People eds.
B.Colgrave & R.A.B.Mynors (1979)
Bede's Prose Life of St Cuthbert ed. B.Colgrave (1940)
'Bishop Hooper's Visitation', ed. J.Gairdner, *English*
Historical Review 9 (1904)
Bishop Redman's Visitation, 1597 ed. J.F.Williams
(Norfolk Record Society 18, 1946)
Bishop William Nicolson's Miscellany Accounts of the
Diocese of Carlisle ed. R.S.Ferguson (1877)
Bishops Registers, Hereford (Canterbury and York
Society 22, 1918)
Clergy returns for Lichfield diocese 1602-3: 'An
Elizabethan Clergy List of the diocese of Lichfield',
ed. J.C. Cox, DAS 6 (1884)
Clergy returns for Shropshire archdeaconry, Hereford
diocese, 1563, c.1567 and c.1593 ed. A.J.Knapton:
'The rural deanery of Ludlow in the 16th century'
SAS4, 43 (1925-26)
'The rural deanery of Wenlock in the 16th century'
SAS4, 44 (1927-28)
'Clergy list of the archdeaconry of Salop in
Hereford, 1563' & 'The rural deaneries of Burford,
Stottesdon, Pontesbury & Clun in the 16th
century'SAS4, 45 (1929-30)
'Another Elizabethan clergy list' SAS4, 46 (1931-
32)
Compton Census of 1676 ed. A.Whiteman (1986)
Councils & Synods of the English Church
(1) D.Whitelock, M.Brett & C.N.L.Brooke (1981)
(2) F.M.Powicke & C.R.Cheney (1964)
Derbyshire Hearth Tax Assessments 1662-1670
(Derbyshire Record Society 7, 1982)
Diary of Ralph Josselin ed. A.Macfarlane (1976)
Domesday Book (Phillimore editions of county
volumes ed. J.Morris)
Gastrell, Bishop Francis
Bishop Gastrell's Notitia The Cumbrian Parishes ed.
L.A.S.Butler (CW Rec 12, 1998)
Bishop Gastrell's Notitia The Archdeaconry of
Richmond ed. L.A.S.Butler (Yorkshire
Archaeological Society Record Series 146, 1986)
Notitia Cestriensis ed. F.R.Raines (The Chetham
Society 8, 19, 21, 22, 1845-50)
Gregory King's Scheme of the income and expense
of the several families of England calculated for the
year 1688', *Surveying the People* eds. K.Schurer &
T.Arkell, (Local Population Studies, 1992)
Illustrated journeys of Celia Fiennes, 1685-c.1712 ed.
C. Morris (Exeter, 1982)
Index to the Probate Records of Oxfordshire 1733-1857
ed. D.M.Barratt, Joan Howard-Drake & M.Priddy
(Oxfordshire Record Society 61, 1997)
Journal of George Fox ed. N Penney (1924)
Kelly's Post Office Directories
Lancashire and Cheshire Church Surveys ed.
H.Fishwick (Record Society 1879)
Lancashire Chantries ed. F.R.Raine (Chetham Society
59, 1862)
Later records relating to North Westmorland or the
Barony of Appleby J.F.Curwen (CW Rec 8,1932)
Lay Subsidy of 1334 ed. R.E. Glasscock (1975)
Leland's Itinerary in England and Wales (5 vols) ed.
L.Toulmin Smith (1964)
Life and Letters of Walter Farquhar Hook ed.
W.R.W.Stephens (1889)
Monasticon Anglicanum (W.Dugdale 1817-1830)
Oxford Dictionary of Place-Names (A.D. Mills. 1998)
Records relating to the barony of Kendale ed. W. Farrer
(CW Rec 4 & 5, 1923-4)
Rector's Book, Clayworth, Notts eds. H.Gill &
E.L.Guilford (1910)
Register and Records of Holm Cultram eds. F.Grainger
& W.G.Collingwood (CW Rec. 7, 1929)
Register of the Priory of Wetheral ed. J.E. Prescott (CW
Rec 1, 1897)
Report of the Archbishops' Committee on Church Finance
(1911)
Taxatio Ecclesiastica Angliae et Walliae aucto-26291
(Record Commission, 1802)
The Buildings of England (county guides general
editor N.Pevsner)
The Church of England Yearbook (1994)
The church in Derbyshire ed. M.R.Austin (DAS
Record Series 5, 1974)
The church in Manchester (Report of the Bishop of
Manchester's special commission, 1914)
Thomas Wilson, 'The state of England AD1600,
ed.F.J. Fisher, *Camden Society Miscellany,* 16 (1936)
11
Valor Ecclesiasticus temp. Henr.VIII auctoritate regia
institutus (Record Commission, 1810-34)
William Harrison, *Elizabethan England* ed.
L.Withington (n.d.)
Worcester Priory Cartulary ed. R.R.Darlington, Pipe
Roll Society 76 (1968)

GLOSSARY

advowson the right to present the incumbent to a living, in practice limited by the bishop's right to induct the incumbent

appropriator/impropriator one with an entitlement to collect tithes who is not the parson of the church to whom they would normally be due: a religious person or body appropriates, takes the tithes for his own use; an impropriator is a layman

benefice that which brings benefit to the holder for his lifetime, and cannot be withdrawn from him

berewick a subordinate and outlying component of a manor, in origin a 'barley farm'

burh a defended site or 'bury', for a manor house, a church or a larger settlement

canon a leading member of a collegiate church community, living according to a rule alternatively - one of the rules agreed by a council of bishops and, for the Church of England since the Reformation, by the Crown.

cartulary the collection of charters relating to a church's property

carucate Domesday term for a ploughland in the Danelaw area - about 120 acres

chantry an endowment provided for singing masses for the soul of the benefactor

chantry chapel the building within a parish church, or a separate chapel, where special masses were to be sung for ever

chapel a subsidiary building with an altar, or part of a church, but whose minister was neither rector nor vicar and did not have complete authority

chaplain one looking after a chapel, providing religious services

charter an early written deed concerning property

college a legal corporation able to buy and sell property - usually applied to an educational or religious institution

constablewick an area smaller than a parish under the supervision of a constable for purposes of law and order

curate one with 'cure of souls', charged with baptising and burying parishioners, but from the nineteenth century an assistant working with an incumbent

dean the man originally in charge of ten priests; later the head of a collegiate church's canons and other clerics

ferding a 'fourth part' of a county or other administrative area

glebe literally 'soil', gleba, but used specially to describe the land belonging to a church

hide Anglo-Saxon term for arable land (about 120 acres) together with pasture and other shares of natural resources

hundred an administrative area or group of estates in Anglo-Saxon dominated parts of the country, in use until the mid-nineteenth century (see wapentake)

incumbent one who is a 'burden' on a benefice: who holds the official position looking after a church and its parishioners

lathe early administrative division of Kent

minster the Anglo-Saxon word derived from Latin monasterium, but indicating a church in an enclosure, not a monastery as now understood

mother church the superior church to which others, called chapels, were subject

oblation offering

pannage the right to pasture a certain number of pigs in a wood not otherwise owned by the manor or estate

parson the person in full possession of a church benefice

parsonage the set of rights belonging to a parson, but in modern usage the house of either rector or vicar

patron the person or persons with the right to present to a church; the owner of the advowson

pele or peel a 'pale' or fenced enclosure for defensive purposes, in practice applied to a defensive tower house

prebend the provision made for the maintenance of an individual canon in a collegiate or cathedral church

rector the holder of a living with full authority over it - implying collection of all tithes

rectory formally: rights and lands belonging to a church's rector, but customarily the house lived in by the rector

Rogation 'asking' for blessing on land and crops; Rogationtide processions round parish boundaries were once customary

scot tax

sinecure a rectory without the practical task of cure of souls

sulung a measure of land peculiar to Kent, similar to a hide

thegn a high status Anglo-Saxon freeman

tithe a tenth - usually of produce but possibly of wages - paid to the church

tithing an area within which ten free inhabitants
were bound together to maintain law and order,
and for some purposes independent of the parish
to which it belonged

township an agricultural unit of land shared
between cultivators of the land; also an area for tax
collection

vicar substitute for either a rector or a canon

vicarage like rectory, either the legal rights of the
vicar or the house

vill Latin term for township

wapentake in the Danelaw parts of England,
equivalent to a hundred in Anglo-Saxon areas

units of money:
marks: 3 marks = £2
         1 mark = 13 shillings and four pence
           (13s.4d.) = 67p
pounds, shillings and pence:
         20 shillings = £1
         12 pence (12d.) = 1 shilling (1s.) = 5p

INDEX

diocese 261
shire 93
Blackstone Edge 171
Bladon, Oxfordshire *286*
Blickling, Norfolk 229
Blomefield, F. 73
Blomfield, C.J., bishop of London 267, 282-83
Bocking, Essex 71
Bolde, Shropshire 199
Bolton, Cumbria 201
Bolton, Gtr Manchester 213
bookland 63, 64
Booth, Humphrey 176
borough in Kent 24
Bosham, W.Sussex 38
Bosel, bishop of Worcester 43-4
boundaries *see* parishes
Bourne, Gilbert 220
Bourton on the Hill, Gloucestershire 178
Bourton on the Water, Gloucestershire (and Lower Slaughter chapel *and see* Clapton) 160-61, 181
Bowden, Derbyshire *see* Chapel en le Frith
Bradbourne, Derbyshire 118
Brampton, Cumbria 47, 48, 201
Brantham, Suffolk 195
Bray, Berkshire 118
Breedon on the Hill, Leicestershire 42
Bridgewater, Somerset 125
Brigges, John 220
Brighton, E.Sussex 126
Brisley, Norfolk, deanery 151, 228-29
Bristol cathedral/dean &chapter 232
diocese 155
Brixworth, Northamptonshire *41*
Brontë family 257
Bromfield, Shropshire 205
Broseley, Shropshire 203
Brough, Cumbria 97, 201
Brougham, Cumbria 47
Broughton, Shropshire 102
Brundish, Suffolk 305, 307
Buckinghamshire 52
Buckland next Faversham, Kent 63, 64
Bungay, Suffolk 46
Burford, Shropshire 110
Burgh by Sands, Cumbria 194-95
burh 35, 82, 88, 105
Burslem, Staffordshire 275, 276, 277,

278
Bury St Edmund's, Suffolk 36
Bury, Gtr Manchester 213
Buxton, Derbyshire *174*
Calder, River 89, 93, 171
Calixtus, St 120
Cambeck, Cumbria 47
Cambridge university 220, 222
colleges 134,143, 162, 190 198, 218, 219, 236
and see Oxford and Cambridge
Cambridgeshire 36, 73, 160
Camden Society 210
canon 107
canon/prebendary 107-110, 134, 147, 167, 190
and see portionary churches
canon law 16, 30, 41, 42, 49, 115, 118, 125
Gratian's Decretum and Pope Gregory's Decretals 49
and see Church of England
Canterbury, Kent 62, 64, 65, 101, 149
archbishop 40, 63, 109, 112-14, 167, 177, 196, 207-9, 217, 235-36, 297
cathedral/dean & chapter *26*, 27, 30, 63, 67, 112, 207-9, 228, 286, *Pl 20*
diocese 181, 212, 297
precincts 228
St Alphege's rectory 196
St Augustine's abbey 27, *28*, 67, 109, 198
Carey, George, archbishop of Canterbury 287
Carlatton, Cumbria 48
Carlisle, Cumbria 95, 160
bishop 141, 184
cathedral/dean & chapter 201
diocese 21, 37, 47, 79, 99, 109, 184, 207, 225
priory 194
Cartmel, Lancashire 94-5
cartularies 44, 120
carucate 72
Cassington, Oxfordshire 210
Castle Carrock, Cumbria 201
Castleton, Derbyshire 80
cathedra 16, 261
cathedrals, deans & chapters 69, 109, 134, 137, 152, 154, 155, 164, 166, 167, 174, 236
and see dioceses

Caynham, Shropshire 203
Celtic saints 58-61
Census 1801 onwards 18, 21-22
and see Religious Census 1851
Ceolfrith, abbot 40
ceorl 74
Chad, bishop of Lichfield and St 103, 148
Chadwick, Edwin 262
Chamberlayne, John 220
chantry 127
chantries 127-30, 172, 176, 177
relationships with parochial system 128
and see suppression
Chapel en le Frith, Derbyshire 80, 85-7, *86*, 175
chapel/chaplain 17, 19, 49, 120
chapel-of-ease 19, 123
chapels/chapelries 22, 39, 54, 59, 61, 70, 83-4, 87, 90, 91, 93, 94-6, 97, 99, 112-13, 114, 119-23, 125, 135, 142-44, 156, 171-91, 267
architecture 119
'free' chapels 39, 102, 172
and see chantries
Charing, Kent, deanery 67, 151, 153
Charlbury, Oxfordshire 287
Charles II (1660-1685) 126, 175, 176, 178
Charlesworth, Derbyshire 178-79
Charterhouse 236
charters 80, 84, 99, 104-5
Chartists 262, 265, 278
Chavasse, Francis, bishop of Liverpool 297
Chawton, Hampshire 241, 245
Chelmorton, Derbyshire 157
Cheshire 21, 80, 87, 155, 176, 181, 184
Chester 88, 226
diocese 130, 152, 155, 166, 181, 184, 202, 207, 223
St John's 35
St Michael's 149
St Werburgh's 107, 128, 129, *155*
Chester le Street, Co.Durham, 34, 93-4, 110, 112-13
Chesterfield, Derbyshire 84
Chetham's College, Gtr Manchester *138*, 139
Chevening, Kent 241
Chichester, W.Sussex diocese 35
theological college 224

Child's Ercall, Shropshire 210
Chilvers Coton, Warwickshire 259
chrism 120, 149
Christchurch, Hampshire 103, 109, 121
Church Assembly 212, 290-91; *and see* Synod
Church Building Commission (1818-1856) 158, 206, 262-64, 265, 267, 268, 272, 273, 278
creation of new parishes 263-64
response to benefactors 264
'Waterloo' churches 263
and see Ecclesiastical Commission
Church Commission (1948) 212, 215, 294
Central Stipends Authority (1972) 304
Church Congress 281, 283
Church of England
and education 267, 274-75, 292, 297
and laity 304, 307
and relationship with parliament 288, 290, 291, 294; *and see* statutes
attendance statistics 297-98
canons 126, 141, 202, 287
establishment 287-88, 291
organisation since 1919:
bureaucracy 291-92, 294-95
finances 288, 292-93, 304
National Council 294
Reports: 226, 230, 237, 286, 288, 290, 291, 294, 295, 297, 305
women priests 296-97
Yearbook (1994) 19, 292-93, 306
Church Stretton, Shropshire 204
church ales *see* churches, wardens
church scot *see* parishes, endowment
Churches Conservation Trust (The) formerly Redundant Churches Fund 252, 253, 287
Churches Together in England *see* Ecumenical movement
churches: buildings 69, 71, 75, 107, 114, 140, 141, 147, 164, 263, 273, 282
chancels 126
towers 45-6, 51, 126, 194-95
porches 147, 194-95
dedications 47, 58-60, 66, 99, 103, 114, 120, 196
numbers of visitors 285-86
preservation 286-87, 308

rates 19, 125-6, 264, 270, 272, 278, 281
abolition (1868) 164, 191, 290, 297
redundant 303
used for schools 200
wardens 38, 125-26, 139-42, 270, 272, 297
church ales 126, 141
yards 49, 73, 93, 103, 112, 147
Cirencester, Gloucestershire 116-17, 118
Civil Registration 164
Clapton on the Hill, Gloucestershire 181
Clare, Suffolk 135
Claybrooke, Leicestershire *213*
and see Wibtoft and Wigston Parva
Clayworth, Nottinghamshire, Rector's *Book* 148, 149, 200, 220
clergymen
absenteeism 163, 164-65 *and see* pluralism
celibacy 118, 190, 199, 217, 219, 222
clerical families 222
education 142, 173, 189-90, 202, 203, 204, 221-24, 232, 229, 236
and see Oxford and Cambridge
ejected from living (1640-60) 219; (1662); 1688 (non-jurors) 221
income *see* livings; pluralism
'literate' 225
numbers of clergy 296, 297
proportions of gentlemen's sons 221-22
of graduates 223-24, 225, 226
retirement 292-93, 296
social comparisons 159, 198, 220,221-22, 224-31, 297
surveys 150
Cliffe at Hoo, Kent 235
Clitheroe, Lancashire 21
Clofesho 40-41, 42
Clopton, Hugh 133
Cobden, Richard 262
Coddenham, Suffolk 75
Coke family 229, 235
college 107
collegiate churches 101, 107-110, 133, 134, 135, 136-39, 166
and see canon/prebendary; suppression
Collingwood, Ralph 133

Columba, St 46
commutation of tithes *see* tithes
Compton Census (1676) 181
Conisbrough, S.Yorkshire 197
constable/constablewick 24
conventicles 181-82
Convocation 287-88, 290, 291
Conybeare, Revd. John 200, 207, 225
Cooke, Moses 228
Copeland, Cumbria 97
Corbridge, Northumberland 193-94
Corfham/Corfton *see* Diddlebury
Cornwall 21, 35, 58-61, 219
Cornish language 59-60
Coventry, Warwickshire 149
diocese 35; *and see* Lichfield
Cox, J.C. 81, 85
Crabtree, J. 90
Cranbrook, Kent 66, 67, 68, 153
Cravenshire 89
Crediton, Devon 35, 134
Creed, Cornwall 61
Croglin, Cumbria 47
Crosby Garret, Cumbria 97, 201
crosses, stone *76*, 77-81, *92*, 93, 95
Crosthwaite, Cumbria 141, 183
Crowland abbey, Lincolnshire 70
Culmington, Shropshire 205
Cumberland 21 , 37, 78, 160, 235
and see Cumbria
Cumbria 46, 94-9, 135, 141, 143-44, 149, 179, 209, 225
Cumrew, Cumbria 47
Cumwhitton, Cumbria 47
curate 16
usage in 19th century 185-86
curates/chaplains 153, 164, 166, 171-91, 220, 221, 257, 258, 267
domestic 220-21, 233
school-masters 157, 173, 180-81, 183, 185, 188-89, 203, 253-54
and see perpetual curates
cure of souls 16, 49, 108, 115, 182, 268, 270, 273
Cuthbert, St 34, 42, 47, 95, 194
Cutsdean, Gloucestershire *Pl 1, 2*
Cynegils, king of West Saxons (611-643) 30
Dacre, Cumbria 94, 137
Danes 35, 46, 74, 80, 82, 88, 94, 99
Darley, Derbyshire 148
Dartford, Kent 64
Davidson, Randall, bishop of Winchester 297